A YEAR AND A DAY

366 DAYS OF SPIRITUAL PRACTICE IN THE CRAFT OF THE WISE

About Timothy Roderick

Timothy Roderick is the author of *The Once Unknown Familiar* and the award-winning *Dark Moon Mysteries*. He holds a master's degree in clinical psychology from Antioch University, and is a psychotherapist and educational psychologist. He is the founder of EarthDance Collective, a Wiccan community that sponsors open rituals, classes, and workshops that promote awareness of feminist spirituality. He has served as their spiritual director for over a decade. He also teaches classes that blend Western psychology and native shamanistic wisdom.

Timothy Roderick has been a practicing Witch for over twenty years. He is the author of *Apprentice to Power, The Once Unknown Familiar* and the award-winning *Dark Moon Mysteries.* He is a trained initiate in the oldest established lineage of British Traditional Wicca in the United States, and has been a longstanding student and teacher of the occult, Eastern mysticism, shamanism, and earth-centered spirituality. For more information about Timothy and his teachings, visit timothyroderick.com.

To Write to the Author

Llewellyn Worldwide cannot guarantee that every letter written to the author can be answered, but all will be forwarded. Please write to:

Timothy Roderick
c/o Llewellyn Worldwide
P.O. Box 64383, Dept. 0-7387-0621-3
St. Paul, MN 55164-0383, U.S.A.

Please enclose a self-addressed stamped envelope for reply,
or $1.00 to cover costs. If outside U.S.A., enclose
international postal reply coupon.

Many of Llewellyn's authors have websites with additional information and resources. For more information, please visit our website at http://www.llewellyn.com.

TIMOTHY RODERICK

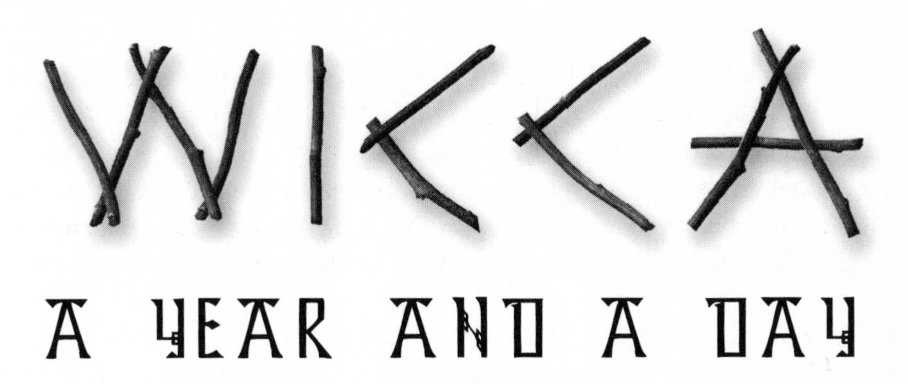

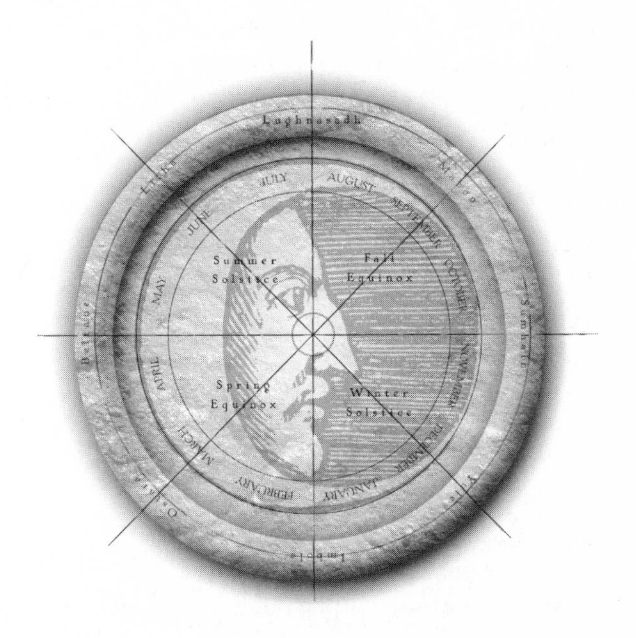

366 Days of Spiritual Practice in the Craft of the Wise

Llewellyn Publications
Saint Paul, Minnesota

First Edition
First Printing, 2005

Cover design by Kevin Brown
Interior illustrations by Kevin Brown

Library of Congress Cataloging-in-Publication Data
Roderick, Timothy.
Wicca : a year and a day : 366 days of spiritual practice in the craft of the wise / Timothy Roderick.
p. cm.
Includes bibliographical references and index.
ISBN 0-7387-0621-3
1. Witchcraft. I. Title.
BF1566.R58 2005
299'.94—dc22 2004063242

Llewellyn Publications
A Division of Llewellyn Worldwide, Ltd.
P.O. Box 64383, Dept. 0-7387-0621-3
St. Paul, MN 55164-0383, U.S.A.
www.llewellyn.com

Printed in the United States of America

Contents

Other Books by Timothy Roderick

The Once Unknown Familiar

Dark Moon Mysteries

Apprentice to Power

Acknowledgments

A work of this scope and breadth requires a contribution from many minds, hearts, and spirits. It has taken over twenty-three years to compile and distill the information you read in these pages, and during that time I have absorbed techniques and disciplines that have influenced my own spiritual practice and hence my writing. So whether their participation in the book was direct or indirect, I am grateful to an array of individuals for their various contributions.

Many thanks to Mead Hunter, the editor of this and each of my previous works. His sharp eye and even sharper red pencil have kept me making sense on paper for the past ten years. It is his advice, wisdom, and insight that you will find pervading this book. My gratitude goes to my long time friend and High Priestess, Varda Ninna, who has supported my path with humor, kindness, compassion, political awareness, and a keen shamanic sense of the Craft. Varda also reviewed portions of the manuscript before publication, and I relied upon her input while making critical adjustments to the text. May the Goddess bless members of Moontydes, a women's Wicca community in Riverside, California. These women have read my works and have unselfishly given me time to expand my practice and to explore new techniques in their community include Saga Gefjon, Kestrel Morgan, Brigit Silverbranch, Athena, and Suleima. Saga was also instrumental in shaping the runes section of this book.

I have lit a candle and a stick of incense to the members of The Rainbow Warriors, who have contributed to my knowledge and understanding of many occult matters: Jayson, Druimaelduin, and Collie Valadez. Thank you, magical men. Love and blessings go to Christopher Penczak who has listened to me kvetch and who has guided me in many matters—both magical and mundane. I would also like to thank Matthew Ellenwood, Barbara Ardinger, and Karen Cummings for their time and insights over the years. P. McGill unquestioningly offered a collection of internet links that you will find in this work and on my website.

A big, appreciative *gassho* and bow go to Roshi Wendy Egyoku Nakao, who has facilitated my ever-gradual awakening and who has inspired the wisdom of Wisdom Moon.

Finally, *un beso grande* to my partner Edu, for opening many doors, for expanding my horizons, and for offering patience, support, and love during my latter adventures in the Craft.

Cerridwen's Cauldron

An Introduction to A Year and A Day

Her cauldron was great, for it held the wisdom of all time. Cerridwen called her potion a *greal*, and fashioned it of cowslips and fluxwort, hedgeberry and vervain. Though she knew each ingredient by its rightful name—Llew's pipes, Gwion's silver, Taliesin's cresses—she dared not speak them aloud lest she conjure a fateful sign. She added the holy mistletoe for good measure, if the Old Ones were ever to bless the thing. Then she infused the pounded muck into a vast salty sea that gurgled within her vessel, darker than a thousand midnights. Fairies, dragons, or perhaps glowing embers danced 'round the vat as the universe bubbled and churned.

"Stir this, but do not taste," she warned Gwion, eyeing her apprentice with her one good, bleared eye. And then she was gone. To where, the sacred texts are unclear. Perhaps they never knew, or could not say. But this much they reveal: that she was gone for a year and a day while her wisdom, her magic, sputtered, and Gwion churned and toiled day and night with a long wooden spoon.

Where his mistress had gone, he did not ask. His business was made clear. To one task he must attend: stir. To drag the spoon through the forbidden drink in spirals, widdershins then deosil, was his labor. That was all. That was enough, for his Lady was a mistress of the old ways; she did not lack cunning or art, and these were things that one with a whit of sense should fear. Might he ever come to learn, to know her ways deeply? He did not speculate, nor was conjecture expected from one of his station. Silence was his sole enterprise.

But temptation was great—as would have known the great Goddess Cerridwen. And taking a chance, the poor lad dipped a finger and sucked it. Life, death, and the great round of existence were known to him then. The knowledge, secrets, mysteries, the arts of magic and of love filled him. But above all, he became wise.

Cerridwen's cauldron awaits you as well.

Wicca is a shamanic, magical, and spiritual tradition that can guide you to the wisdom and the promise of Cerridwen's cauldron. The word "Wicca" is of Middle-English origin and it means "craft of the wise." This wisdom to which Wicca refers is innate. It is the wisdom of nature that dwells within each of us—you and me—from birth. Or more precisely, it is each of us from birth. But most of us live our lives disconnected from nature and her precious gift of wisdom. There is no one to blame for this condition. Culture, history, gender, family, politics, and all of the limits of conventional knowledge shape our psyches, our lives, from childhood. These are the veils that conceal our wisdom and magical human potential.

Through the path of Wicca, we learn to penetrate these veils, tap into our potential, and discover innate knowledge, insight, judgment, and sense. It takes time to trust the process and to become wise like this—just as it takes time for the sap of a barren snow-covered tree to wake into motion, revitalize the tree's limbs, and produce blossom and sprout. This is the way of nature.

It is also the traditional way that masters of the Old Arts have taught their apprentices throughout the ages. The withered woodswoman leads her dutiful charge into the dark forests to school her in the roots, stems, and healing properties of trees. The village sage leads a youth to the standing stones at dawn in order to practically illustrate generations of solar myths, rites, and secrets.

One cannot learn the things that unmask wisdom at the speed to which we have become accustomed in contemporary living. There are no short cuts. There are no drive-throughs or just-add-water formulas when it comes to learning about the spiritual matters of magic and the mystical ways of the Old Ones. Slowly, slowly, at the pace of life itself, can one truly absorb the knowledge, customs, and wise practices of our ancient pagan ancestors—those things which form the basis of the Wiccan path.

A year and a day of study and spiritual practice offers students the chance to move at this natural pace in their learning. It gives them the opportunity to learn, just as the ancients did, through personal experience, trial and error—which are all guided by the experienced hand of a trained elder. In the case of this book, the elder is myself. And just as I have learned, so will I teach you. Through these pages you will discover the very same techniques (both ancient and modern) that I learned and have subsequently taught to my own dedicants and initiates over the years.

A year and a day is often a rigorous affair. That is because, traditionally, it is a preparation period that precedes an individual's initiation (or formal commitment) to the Craft. As you read this book, perhaps you are preparing for your own initiation. Or maybe you have been on the Wiccan path for some time and you are looking to deepen your spiritual practice by committing to a year and a day of focused spiritual training. Whatever it is that brought you to these pages, you should know from the outset that the course of study I propose is basic, but not simple by any means. Certainly you will learn the core content of Wiccan practice: the tides of time, the wonders of the seasons, of herbs and magic, and the inner disciplines of seers. And through the content, you will thoroughly engage with the bones and structure of Wicca.

Touching upon the spirit, the tender, enchanting flesh of Wicca, is another matter altogether. I am referring to the mystical experience of Wicca, which cannot be taught. Transcendent experiences occur to the student often without prior notification, but not without some foreshadowing and preparation. It is through the daily work of this book that readers will be led to their own mystical experiences and connection with the divine.

One method that helps to facilitate success in a reader's year and a day is the combination of traditional spiritual techniques with practical application to everyday life. From my personal understanding, the experiences of spirit and of everyday living are one and the same. Planting a garden and going to the grocery store (within the proper framework) are just as important to one's spiritual growth as is drawing pentagrams and calling the names of the gods. In this sense, the course of study I prescribe is not a retreat from the world to some mystical, mythic realm where you might encounter magic and fantastic beings. It is a facilitation of your wakeful, attentive participation in the world, where you are assured of encounters with magic and fantastic beings.

So, the lighting of a candle and the invocation of an elemental spirit can also open you up to discovery of just who and what you are in the deepest sense of these terms. This inner knowledge comes at a price. If you stand steadfast as this course progresses, you will find that it can expose both your vulnerabilities and your assets. Sometimes spiritual progress and personal growth can be uncomfortable, but the overall process can teach you how to access your strengths and how to skillfully wield (and learn from) your human frailties and failings. There is great power in this form of knowledge and practice; it is the very crucible of human transformation, magic, and natural wisdom. "Who am I?" "What am I about?" "What is life?"—these are the questions that underpin the solid spiritual training of one's year and a day of Wiccan practice. They are also the themes that lie at the heart of this book.

Dare you dip your finger into the great cauldron and taste this wisdom? No. Jump in. Bathe in the broth and drink, drink deeply.

A Word to the Wise

This book assumes that the reader is practicing a year and a day as a solitary student. One customarily practices a year and a day of spiritual training with a seasoned Wiccan elder. The elder's responsibility is to act as a guide, teacher, and practical example. He or she would take measures to assure efficient learning. For instance, your teacher might advise you long in advance of when it was time for you to collect specific items (magical tools, herbs, and the like) that would be necessary for your training. Or you might learn the "oral" traditions practically, through demonstration, trial, and error.

I have attempted to provide you with some of these same standards you might encounter if you were studying with a coven that gathers in your neighborhood. You will notice, however, that some of the conventions that I have used call for the periodic interruption of what appears to be a linear progression of teaching. I do this for several reasons. First, it is important that practitioners learn to flow with the circumstances of life—no matter what they might be. Water learns how to flow around stones. Snow learns how to balance on branches when it cannot reach the ground. You will discover that you access a steady inner strength when you learn to flow like nature. Second, I have attempted to keep readers following a specific timetable for learning, which progresses in approximately thirty-day segments. I have punctuated each segment with a three-day cycle that includes a day of devotion, a day of contemplation, and a day of silence. These three days offer the reader a chance to integrate new learning, to review what has been missed, and to assimilate the teachings in a natural way.

As part of the training, readers will need to secure specific items. The most called-for items include herbs, candles, and essential oils. Readers will be instructed on their uses and purpose, but they will also be asked to procure these items with some advance notice. Other items that readers will need to find include the athame (a black-handled, double-edged knife), a chalice (a ritual cup), and a pentacle (a 5–6-inch diameter disk upon which a pentagram has been inscribed). These last three are the most costly of the items that complete the set of four basic magical tools that Wiccans use in their regular spiritual practice.

The central portion of the book is the day-by-day training guide. Two appendixes follow this. The first appendix is a full moon ritual that you should attempt (at each full moon) after you have mastered the art of circle casting (as outlined in days 230 through 244). Although you will have daily magical workings, meditations, or spiritual explorations, I encourage you to spend time practicing the ritual in this appendix on all full-moon nights. In that ritual appendix, I have also included a lunar rite that you can practice prior to knowing how to formally cast the magic circle. The second appendix is a suggestion for resources where readers can procure their magical tools, herbs, and other items. The book also contains notes and bibliographical references that can be useful for you.

Guidelines for Readers

Here are some specific guidelines to keep in mind that can help you to complete your year and a day successfully. These are guidelines that I recommend to all who enter the practice of a year and a day of Wiccan study:

- Begin your year at any time you would like. Traditionally, Wiccans consider the period between October 31 (the feast of Samhain) and February 2 (Candlemas) to be a time of little or no magical growth. For this reason, many teachers encourage students to begin their year and a day of studies either prior to this tide or to wait until this time period has passed. This is by no means a rule, but rather a custom based on ages of sympathetic magic, which means mirroring ritually that which is occurring in the physical environment. The actual waning of the sun's light and the end of the crop-growing season can symbolize a dearth of external activity and growth. Trees do not form bud or sprout, but the trees' energies do move inward to the center of the trunk. Therefore, in some magical traditions, this fall/ winter tide can also symbolize internal movement and growth for the spiritual practitioner. I have had many successful students begin their spiritual journey during this time period—and you should feel free to begin your year and a day at any time of your choosing.

- Commit to completing the full year and a day of study and then progress through the text one day at a time. This does require some discipline on your part. If you leave your regular routine to go on a trip, or if there are life events that naturally disrupt the flow of your study, simply return to the practice when you feel things have calmed and you are ready. Then resume the book (and your year) where you left off.
- Do not skip any of the days or try to combine two days of practice into one. Simply progress at the book's pace.
- Be patient with yourself during the unfolding of your process. Through the work in this book, you may uncover insights, memories, feelings, visions, or any number of phenomena that can be disturbing or even elating. The appearance of these things is a natural process—and you should simply allow them to be as they are without either clinging to them or running from them. It is important not to squelch feelings and sensations as they arise. Simply feel them and they will subside over time. Emotional states are transient creatures. It may take years of your own internal exploration and observation to actually experience what I am saying here as your own reality. In the meantime, try to trust this point (from someone who is both an experienced clinical psychotherapist and a Witch) as an honest-to-goodness truth. Over time, as you observe the courses of your ephemeral emotional states, you will learn a great deal about what actually holds power and what lacks it in your life.
- Be proactive. Each month or so I provide a list of magical items that are necessary for you to progress in the year's cycle. When you receive this notice, act immediately and procure the items. Otherwise, you will encounter delays in completing your year and a day.
- The year and a day is work—but it is also fun. Life's too short to not approach each day in the spirit of play and adventure. Is your life play—or is it work? How you frame your experiences certainly shapes the outcome.

Important Fire Safety Considerations

This book makes frequent reference to candle use throughout your year and a day of spiritual practice. It is important, therefore, that you regularly observe standard candle and fire safety procedures whenever you light that fire. The National Fire Protection Agency states that "approximately 10,000 residential fires per year are candle-related, causing 1,000 injuries, 85 fatalities, and $120 million in property loss." They also wisely recommend that we observe the following:

- Most candle fires occur because candles were left unattended while burning. Be sure to extinguish candles whenever you leave a room or go to sleep.
- Homes have an unusually high number of flammable objects within them. Take a look around your home for a moment with an eye for fire hazards and you'll probably notice things such as clothing, books, paper, curtains, and flammable decorations. You will want to keep candles away from any of these items that can catch fire.
- The safest way to burn most candles is in a sturdy, fire-resistant candle holder. Before you select a candle holder, check it to be sure it won't tip over easily, and that it is large enough to collect dripping wax.

- Be sure that you don't place a lit candle in a window where blinds and curtains can close over them.
- Place your candle holder and lit candle on a sturdy, uncluttered surface.
- Keep lit candles away from places where they could be knocked over by children or animals.
- Keep candles and all open flames away from flammable liquids.
- Keep candle wicks trimmed to one-quarter inch. It reduces candle flickering and smoking. Also, it is best to extinguish taper and pillar candles when they burn down to within two inches of the holder or decorative material.
- Votive candles (usually cylindrical in shape and burned in a "cup"—usually made of glass—which holds the liquefied wax that results from burning) should be extinguished before the last half-inch of wax starts to melt.
- Avoid candles that have combustible items embedded in them.

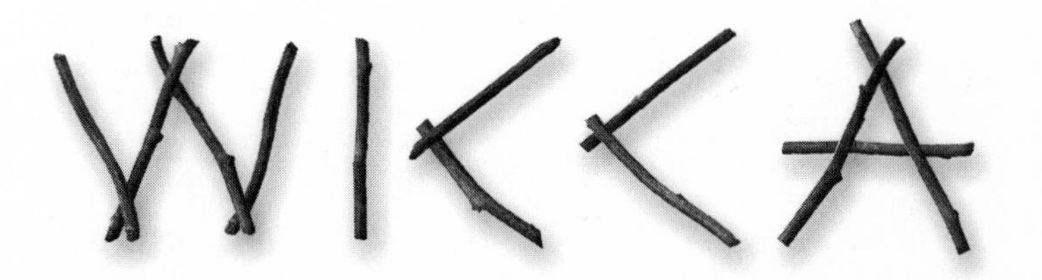
WICCA

Day 1

Earth-Centered Spirituality

In Europe's Neolithic past, long, long ago when human communities were mostly tribes, in the ancient days of our ancestors well before the introduction of any spiritual path we know—or could possibly imagine—earth-centered spiritual practices were customary. Long before religion became Religion, full of dogma, regulations, ceremonial figureheads, theme parks, and teleministries, there was simply nature. The first spiritual impulses were born of a people who lived close to the land and who relied on it for survival. They knew the ways of the seasons: the annual promise of the warming days, the long period of growth that followed, the importance of harvest, and the seasons of frost and death. Women knew the ways of the moon, of healing and childbirth. Men knew the movement of the herd animals and the secret ways of the hunter and the hunted. There were no holy books or official spiritual doctrines. The divine did not exist in some inaccessible realm. It lived among and through the people. It sang in bird songs, it formed the ocean's waves, it filled the human body, plants, and animals with life.

Spirituality had its birthplace right here—in the dirt, in the soil, in the struggles and triumphs of everyday life. It emerged from human laughter and fear. It was something that pervaded one's eating, sleeping, eliminating, and reproducing. It governed family and community life, the coming of age, marriages, births, and deaths. Spirituality had little to do with lofty philosophical notions—the things that emerge from thinking—it centered on the hard facts of life. The soft facts of life must have played their part too. Love, tenderness, and compassion are universal human emotions that have long quickened the heart and informed the spirit.

These are the ancient, indigenous roots of the spiritual system that we today call Wicca or Witchcraft. In considering Wicca's earthy spiritual roots, most likely it will come as no surprise that getting started in this path requires you to settle down into the metaphorical *dirt*—the experiences of the world itself—and get your hands and feet muddy. You'll need to taste, touch, smell, hear, see, and experience life and the spiritual energy that infuses all.

Let's get down and dirty, shall we? Go outside. Find a green patch of grass, a dark, rich, root-buckled swath of earth, a stone formation, or a tree, and touch it. Rub your hands across it. Sit down and feel the weight of your body on the land. Breathe deeply and allow the earth to hold you. This is where you belong. Welcome home.

A Word to the Wise: Are you troubled about traipsing through the chill of the night? Do you get singed in the sun or think an icy downpour is a downer? Wicca is a spiritual tradition that includes many practices that bring the practitioner into direct contact with nature. It seeks to harmonize the Witch with life as it is happening in this very moment. To be a person of magical power, one embraces the entire array of life's experiences. When Witches routinely make space in their lives for nature, for life, in the right-here-and-now, it gradually strips away accumulated layers of social, emotional, and psychological conditioning. It frees up the mind, the heart, and spirit. It places the practitioner into direct accord with life, nature, and the direct current of spiritual power. Can you face each moment of life unflinchingly—despite rain, sleet, or hail?

Not everyone can go outside no matter the weather conditions. There are always exceptions and accommodations to be made. If your health will be jeopardized by venturing out of doors into inclement weather, by all means try the following alternative exercise: Fill a tray or empty pot with potting soil and rub your hands through it. Bring a handful to your nose and inhale the earth's rich perfume.

The earth is our birthplace, yet for millions of us, it feels strangely foreign. Most of us busily scurry through our lives taking little notice of the earth. There are several reasons for this. First, many Westerners live in cities, and by and large our societies are no longer based in agrarian culture. Agriculture naturally relies on human attunement to the seasonal cycles, and this is no longer a customary way of life for many people. In contemporary life, agriculture is a job, a career choice. Because we are, for the most part, removed from an immediate and visceral connection with nature, our awareness of how the earth sustains our lives has waned. In addition to this, our contemporary, mainstream religious paths promulgate a central doctrine that characterizes the natural world as inherently flawed, sinful, and wrong. We all grow up with these teachings that infuse everyday life and that consequently shape our worldviews. As a result, many of us presume nature has no value beyond our ability to exploit it.

Our first steps on the path of Wicca require us to connect to the earth and at least wonder about its inherent value. Could the earth, its seasons, and the natural realm really have value beyond material or monetary advantage? Could it be (as indigenous people across the globe say) "sacred?" What does sacred mean?

In Wicca, the term refers to something that is holy or that has a direct relationship with deity. In pagan spiritual paths like Wicca, practitioners come to a mystical, intuitive understanding that all things are manifestations of an underlying energy or spiritual force.

Each of us must unveil these mysteries for ourselves. The path of the Witch involves this slow process of unveiling the power of the earth, particularly as it manifests in our own lives. This process moves at the pace of the seasons themselves. Like the seasonal turnings, this process does not culminate in abrupt changes. Understanding of the truth of our existence and our connections to all is gradual, like standing in a cool mist that eventually soaks you to the bone.

Exercise: Connecting to Earth

Sit somewhere in a natural setting: on a beach, in a forest, a field, or even in your own backyard. Breathe deeply and close your eyes.

A Word to the Wise: If your health will be compromised by exposure to inclement weather, by all means practice this and other outdoor exercises in an indoor environment.

As you sit, imagine that you have roots that extend from the base of your spine. These roots reach not only down into the earth, but out to everything on it. Imagine that this vast network of roots connects you to humans, animals, plants, objects. Take a moment to feel the pulse of your connection to the great *All*. Notice where your connection to things and people might be weak and where it feels strong.

Spend ten minutes (or longer, if you can) simply feeling your connection. When you are finished, open your eyes. Consider the following questions:

- In what way was my connection strong?
- What do you suspect is the reason for any strong connections?
- In what way was my connection to things weak?
- What do I suspect is the reason for any weak connections?
- What actions can I take that may strengthen any weak connections?

Spend the rest of the day acting in accord with your heightened awareness to people and things around you.

Days 1-30

Magical Items to Gather

Every 30 days, you will encounter a list of magical items I recommend that you procure for the following 30 days of spiritual practice. You will be able to find most items at your local metaphysical bookstore. See the *Resource Guide* in the back of the book to locate sources for the items listed in the "Magical Items to Gather" list.

You will need the following magical items during the next 30 days of training:

Day 3

- A 5–6 inch white taper candle
- A candle holder

Day 17

- A *Farmer's Almanac* (generally available at your local bookstore or library)

Day 20

- A 5–6 inch orange taper candle
- A compass (also needed on days 22, 25, 27, 30)

Day 22

- A 5–6 inch orange taper candle
- ¼ ounce (or less) of myrrh resin or dried, powdered orris root
- Self-igniting charcoal (such as Three-Kings®)

Day 25

- A 5–6 inch green taper candle

Day 27

- A 5–6 inch green taper candle
- ¼ ounce of an herbal blend consisting of dried meadowsweet and powdered oak bark
- A compass

Day 30

- A 5–6 inch indigo taper candle

Day 2

Those Upsetting Words

They cause discomfort and embarrassment. They're difficult to explain to your friends and family. They can be downright hard to accept. No, I'm not talking about plantar's warts. It's all of those darn Witchy words! Wicca is a practice filled with terms that can enchant, amuse, and even bewilder.

Ironically, Wicca is not ultimately about words. Wiccan practices aim to take the practitioner far beyond the limiting worlds of language and terminology. The words of the Craft are meant to transport the practitioner into the heart of life itself, where words are ultimately limitations and qualifiers. More specifically, they can guide practitioners toward a direct mystical experience of deity, nature, and the individual spirit. Words obliterate and become meaningless when the practitioner achieves this experiential state of understanding. Wiccans therefore first come to accept that words are only valuable as signposts and guides that point toward mystic experience.

To Wiccans, a word is not reality itself. For example, the word "apple" is not itself an apple. You can hear the word and understand it intellectually. However, in order to know an apple you must hold it in your hands, smell it, and take a big juicy bite. Likewise, the word "god" is not deity itself. It is only a mental abstraction, a convenient symbol that we can all use to refer to something that goes beyond the word.

As you walk the Wiccan path, you will eventually have your own experiences of direct mystical contact with the divine. But before that happens, it is understandable and natural that you might struggle with the language of Wicca, which often flies in the face of convention and social norm. As a practice today, take a look at the list of words that follow:

Wicca	**Ritual**	**Pagan**
Witchcraft	**Magic**	**Spell**
Power	**Occult**	**Earth-Religion**

Regarding each of these words, explore the following questions:

- What is my comfort level in using each word?
- How do I understand each word?
- How do I imagine that each word impacts other people who are not involved with Wicca?

Take time to commit your feelings (whatever they may be) about each word to paper. You will use today's writing in tomorrow's exercise. So when you are finished, set the paper aside. After you have explored your own understanding and reaction to each word, take a look at how Wiccans generally define them.

Wicca

Wicca is both a religion of nature and a magical practice. It is a spiritual tradition centered in the earth-based, mystic practices of the people of Old Europe. Wicca is a *shamanic* spiritual path. The word "shaman" is an anthropological one that refers to a type of indigenous, natural-magic practitioner. A shaman is a person, usually in a tribal culture, who is a healer and an interpreter of the unseen world (which shamans refer to as the *world of spirits*). She or he conducts rites of passage, divines the future, and walks the path of magic. Although Wicca is not a path that can claim an unbroken lineage to the ancient past, many of the contemporary practices of Wicca are adapted from traditional shamanic practices that link us back to our tribal ancestry. Wiccans understand the natural world, the sun, the moon, the seasons, male and female bodies and the earth itself as expressions of sacredness. Learning to live in conscious connection with all of nature (including human nature) within each moment helps Wiccans forge a deep bond with the divine.

Contemporary linguists debate the origins of the word "Wicca." Some say that it originated from the Indo-European root *weik;* it is a term that links the concepts of religion and magic. Other linguists assert that the word is of Middle-English origin, derived from the Anglo-Saxon root word *wic*, which means "to bend or to shape." An alternative meaning of the root word is *wise*. From this root, it is believed that the word "Wicca" means both "the craft of the wise" and "the craft of bending and shaping." Both meanings are applicable to contemporary Wiccans. Their simple spiritual practices such as meditation and mindfulness in daily activity help them acquire mental, emotional, and spiritual flexibility. Wiccans practice bending and shaping their consciousness so that they live in accord with each moment of life.

Wicca is not an "ancient" religion. It has practices that contemporary practitioners have derived from (and interpreted from) the ancient past, but it is a religion of recent development. The contemporary Craft traces much of its known lineage to approximately the 1950s in England. Gerald Gardner, a retired civil servant, is generally cited among Witchcraft historians and many practitioners as the founder of contemporary Wicca. Gardner claimed to have been initiated by a woman named Dorothy Clutterbuck into what he called the Old Religion in the New Forest area in 1939. He further claimed that the coven into which he was initiated was one of a cluster founded some forty years earlier by a man named George Pickingill. According to Gardner, Pickingill asserted that his "lineage" was founded on a succession of initiations that stretched back some eight centuries. Some Witchcraft history enthusiasts believe that Gardner pieced together his version of Wicca from elements of obscure occult literature and contributions from Aleister Crowley, a famous early-twentieth-century occultist, a contemporary of Gardner and founder of the Golden Dawn. Whether or not Gardner's assertions or his claims of lineage are factual, we do not know for certain. However, he was the first of a succession of individuals to step forward and publish what was then considered authentic Witchcraft material.[1]

Witchcraft

Throughout the Middle Ages and particularly during the Renaissance period, the word "Witchcraft" was liberally applied by the Christian church and its authorities to the native religious practices and customs that existed for thousands of years before Christianity. Many people with indigenous European spiritual roots met their fates on the gallows or in the fire simply because of their religious expression. Aside from practitioners of native spiritual beliefs, there were other groups of people that the church targeted, tortured, and burned for the crime of "Witchcraft." One might be accused of Witchcraft simply because of a bad dream, or because one was left-handed or had bodily imperfections (believed to be "devil's marks"). Jews, Gypsies, homosexuals, unwed women, midwives, herbal healers, social outcasts, people who were too rich or too poor, the disabled, and the infirm were also convicted for the crime of "Witchcraft." Some scholars claim that over 250,000 people were put to death for the crime of Witchcraft during the "burning times" in Europe, while others say the number reached as high as nine million. The contemporary spiritual practice of Witchcraft is based on many of the old customs and folk wisdom of old Europe. Because of this, practitioners have reclaimed the word "Witch." Contemporary practitioners view the word as one of power and they reclaim it in an effort to be mindful of the cost of religious intolerance, to release negative associations and to forge a new future.

Power

For Wiccans, power has little to do with control over people and things. Power is a natural state of being that comes from uniting with the vast flow of nature and operating from an experience of accord with that flow. In the Wiccan view, power is a shared, subtle energy that flows through all things.

Ritual

Ritual is the enactment of a myth. In this definition, the word myth refers to a system of spiritual symbols. Rituals in Wicca usually involve symbolic words, sounds, colors, and gestures. Wiccans understand that each element of a ritual speaks the language of the deep mind (the unconscious mind), and thus awakens the movement of psychological and spiritual energy. The symbols in Wiccan ritual emerge from both time-honored, shared mythological correspondences (for example, traditional associations that orient the practitioner to time, place, color, sound, and movement) and personal associations that can emerge from dreams, meditations, and personal insights.

Magic

Magic is a term that sometimes causes confusion and fear. Many people recall scenes from movies, television shows, or fairy tales when they first think of magic. In the popular imagination, magic is about getting things that you want through forbidden, dark, or dangerous forces. Wiccans understand magic as a natural process. It is the ability to change one's consciousness—one's frame of mind. It is the ability to arrive at substantial realizations and broadening insights that change one's relationship as a human being to the world. Out of one's change of consciousness comes change in the world. The processes of magic reveal our internal patterns that can help us to live in close contact with our full human power. The methods of magic are simple. Lighting candles, chanting, or focusing one's intention with drumming or dancing are all methods that Wiccans use to create magic and change.

Occult

The word "occult," derived from the Latin *occultusanum,* literally means "secret." Few Wiccans today use this term when referring to their contemporary magical or spiritual practices. However, the word refers to hidden teachings that are available to adepts of any magical or metaphysical path.

Pagan

Pagan comes from the Latin *paganus*, a peasant or country dweller. Formerly people used the word in reference to a non-Christian. The word then expanded over time to pejoratively mean anyone who was not "of The Book," namely a person who was not a Christian, Jew, or Muslim. It gained negative connotations over time and came to mean someone who was an uncivilized "idolater." In contemporary practice, a pagan is someone who follows a polytheistic/pantheistic spiritual system. Typically, a pagan is someone who believes that the universe, the earth, and all of its inhabitants contain divinity.

Spell

A symbolic act through which anyone can channel nonphysical energies to attain some particular goal.

Earth-Religion

A pagan spiritual path that reveres the earth, the seasons, and all creatures.

Day 3

Melting Beliefs

Yesterday you wrote down your initial reactions toward the following words:

Wicca	**Ritual**	**Pagan**
Witchcraft	**Magic**	**Spell**
Power	**Occult**	**Earth-Religion**

The questions I asked to prompt your exploration of these words were:

1. What is my comfort level in using each word?
2. How do I understand each word?
3. How do I imagine each word impacts other people who are not involved with Wicca?

Today you can perform your first ritual act that will make use of your answers to these questions.

Practice: Melting Beliefs

What You'll Need:

- Your answers from yesterday's exercise
- A 5–6 inch white taper candle
- A candle holder

Take out the paper on which your thoughts are written. If you haven't taken the time yet to consider your reactions to these words, look at your answers now, and pay special attention to words that are laden with emotions such as *fear, anger, anxiety, hope, hopelessness, sadness*, etc. Perhaps you've also expressed some positive associations with these words, but if you are like most readers, a common emotional reaction to these words is fear and the entire spectrum of related emotions: anger, anxiety, and sadness.

Take time to review your answers to the questions and try to identify a common emotional theme or "tone" that may thread through your written reactions. Certainly you might encounter fear as a common theme, but what about curiosity, wonder, mistrust? The deeper you plunge into your thematic exploration, the more you may uncover. Once you have identified a common theme, write the theme in a single word. Take out your white taper candle and, using a pin, etch this single word lengthwise into the candle's shaft.

In this next part of the exercise, you will explore the origins of your feelings and themes. From where do they arise? Are these feelings based in fact? Are they "inherited" beliefs?

Find a comfortable sitting position and close your eyes. Take a few breaths and allow the dominant feeling, the main theme of your emotional reactions, to emerge in your awareness right now. Whatever the emotional state you've noted, try to feel it fully within your body. Allow this feeling to transport you back in time to a scene from your life that can explain your feelings. The scene can be just about anything: a frightening bedtime story about Witches, a film, an illustration. Do not deny whatever scene emerges. Once you have an image that makes some sense, open your eyes.

Light the candle. As it burns, vow to remain aware of your feelings during your learning process over the course of this year and a day. As the candle melts your emotionally charged word away, changing its form into something else, imagine that your concepts formed from the past also melt and transform. When the candle finishes burning, take the wax and bury it someplace far from your home.

Note: A taper candle is a slender (usually slightly conical) candle, sometimes referred to as a dinner candle. I recommend 5- to 6-inch taper candles simply because you can find them almost anywhere, and they don't take nearly as long to burn as the average 10-inch taper.

Now think over, discuss, and journal about these questions:

- What was it like to take part in this small ritual?
- What emotions did the ritual bring up in me?
- Did I "let go" of anything with this ritual?

Day 4

Questioning Your Path

The greatest source of power for Wiccans is, above all else, spiritual truth. Wiccans leave blind faith to the practitioners of other spiritual paths. Wicca should help you to face life candidly. Through persistent spiritual inquiry you can maintain a heightened perspective about your path and your growth. The ability to make honest, powerful life choices comes with clear perspective.

Be honest with yourself now. Explore the following questions listed below and commit your feelings to paper. You might facilitate your writing process by first discussing your responses to these questions with a friend.

- Why am I exploring the Wiccan path?
- What were my previous spiritual practices?
- Did any of these past practices lead me to investigate Wicca? How?
- What are my hopes in engaging in this path?
- What are my fears in engaging in this path?
- How will I handle friends and family members who might not approve of my spiritual search?
- Aside from transitioning to a new spiritual path, are there other major events that impact my life at this time (for example, deaths, births, divorce, job loss, etc.)?
- If I have major life events happening right now, is this the best time to explore a new spiritual path? Why/why not?

After you have completed your responses on paper, spend time in quiet contemplation of them.

Day 5

Natural Sacred Energies

While mainstream religions look to a holy book, a central prophet, savior, or religious figure for their spiritual understanding, Witches look to life itself; they contemplate and study nature. The earth, the sea, animals, and the heavens are themselves among the many, living, ever-changing expressions of sacredness. Witches learn to pay close attention to the natural world in order to find inspiration and magical insight within each moment.

Since Wicca is a nature religion, one important goal of the path is to experience the life force of nature, the animating energy, as it flows within you. Witches believe that this force is, in essence, the divine. Through experiencing this natural energy, Witches come to know that (as author Barbara Ardinger says), "matter is clotted, lumpy spirit, and spirit is finely strained matter."[2] Once you recognize this energy within yourself, it becomes easier to notice that this same natural energy shapes the substance of other people, stones, birds, trees, water, and everything else you can see.

These are not Witch beliefs; Witchcraft is not a spiritual system of beliefs, per se. It is an experiential practice. You don't need to *believe* in the sacredness of the earth. You don't need to believe that natural energy pervades all things. The practices of Wicca facilitate your immediate and personal understanding of these principles.

No Witch worth her cauldron invests herself in beliefs. Beliefs spring forth from the limits of the critical, thinking mind. Thinking can help you understand spirituality in theoretical terms, but it stops short when it comes to the *experience* of spirituality. The thinking mind does have its purposes, its uses. It knows how to do math, how to read a book, and how to make decisions. It knows how to drive a car, make dinner, and not step in front of a bus. However, thinking comes to a halt when faced with whatever cannot be rationalized.

Critical thinking is limited because it relies on opinions and beliefs. It is locked in the head and does not know how to inhabit the entire body. Spirituality is a holistic experience. It includes not only the head but everything else as well. The full human potential, which is capable of multidirectional, simultaneous experience, comes to the fore when we literally come to our senses—our sensations and experiences of life. Opening to your full experience of the world, of your body, and of the energies that flow within you are the first stages of awakening your spiritual power. Let's begin the process.

Practice: Experiencing Life's Energy

You can try this exercise from where you are sitting right now. Close your eyes and take several deep, slow breaths. With each exhaled breath, feel your body relax and release all the tensions that it might store. Become internally quiet; try not to allow thinking to interfere with simple breathing and sensation.

◐ Breathing is not a concept. It isn't a thought or an activity that you can think your way through. If you find yourself thinking your way through this exercise, break it down into segments. Begin by just breathing and paying attention to where the breath begins and ends in your body. Then try adding on the other parts of the exercise.

If thoughts come up, simply observe them with detached curiosity. Perhaps you might notice how thoughts are creating muscle tensions or contractions in your body. Notice, too, how these tensions transform themselves into your emotions. Try not to get involved in the story line of your thoughts and subsequent tensions—that is a trap that can keep you from the experience of this exercise.

Now, refocus your attention on your solar plexus region (around the lower stomach and navel area). Focus your attention on the feeling of the life force inside of your body within this region. Most likely it will feel like a humming, buzzing, or tingling sensation. Now, widen your awareness. Allow your focus to include your chest. Feel the inner body's energies in the chest and in the solar plexus regions. Now include your hips and legs. Feel the sensation of energy buzzing within this region. Now add your feet into your focused awareness. Now add your arms and hands into the awareness. Finally, add your neck, head, and face into your awareness. You should now be fully aware of your inner life energy from head to toe.

Stay with this feeling for a few minutes. When you sense that you are ready, open your eyes. How did it feel? If you felt "cut off" in any area of experiencing your body, it is important that you continue with this basic energy practice several times a day for 5–10 minutes at a time, until you are able to sense a unification of your body's energies.

Day 6

Wicca and Shamanism

Wicca is a shamanic spiritual path. More than one religious historian has suggested that the ancient archaeological evidence found throughout the excavation sites of Old Europe points to shamanic activity. While the entirety of the religious systems of the Europeans who lived in the Paleolithic and Mesolithic periods may not have been shamanic, it is likely that the shaman played an important role in ancient tribal life. Additionally, it is likely that substrate of beliefs and religious traditions spring forth from shamanic practices. [3]

A shaman is a spiritual leader who serves many important functions, usually within a tribal society. The shaman may be a priest, a mystic (someone who has an immediate, direct connection to the divine force), a counselor, an interpreter of spirits, a healer, and a magician. A shaman presides over the rites of passage from birth to death and foretells the future.

The gods of the shaman are not generally known by the rest of the community, since the way of the shaman is a secret way. The shaman's gods are totemic; they take many forms such as stone, plant, animal, human, and spirit. The powers of the shaman are those of the earth, the wind, the waters, and the fire. Shamans also gather secret, magical knowledge from the hidden worlds of their familiar spirits.

The shaman's power comes from *ecstatic* rites and practices that transport him or her to the magical *otherworlds,* where the energies of powerful spiritual forces are encountered and harnesses. The word "ecstasy" comes from the Greek *ekstasis,* which means "to be placed outside" or "to be placed." The shamanic magical state of ecstasy is an altered frame of awareness during which a person may feel as though he or she transcends him- or herself. The core experience of the shaman in the ecstatic state is the realization, as psychoanalyst Carl Jung states, that "he is of the same essence as the universe, and his own mid-point is its center." [4]

One does not choose to become a shaman. Likewise, one does not actively choose the path of the Witch. Rather, the path chooses the individual. The consensus of anthropological literature confirms that the "call" to the magical path often emerges from an individual's deeply transformative experiences of consciousness. Typically these experiences emerge spontaneously and often follow events such as near-death experiences, high fevers, falling from great heights, life-threatening illnesses, lucid dreams, strong visions, or "near-psychotic breaks" (which are mental or perceptual deviations from shared reality).

Hallmarks of the shamanic experience include:

- A traumatic incident (such as the near-death experiences, lucid dreams, visions, or near-psychotic breaks mentioned previously), which typically occurs in childhood
- A close relationship with nature
- Demonstration of natural psychic, magical, or healing abilities
- The ability to spontaneously "move between the worlds" of physical and nonphysical reality; this usually entails extended periods of disorientation induced either by trance, drumming, dancing, or psychoactive herbs
- The ability to understand the underlying spiritual or energetic nature of all things (both animate and inanimate)
- The ability to receive intuitive messages (whether in the form of words, images, or sensations) from both seen and unseen sources
- The ability to harness spiritual power
- The ability to cause change through unseen or magical means

The Madman

There is a difference between a shaman and a madman. The shaman is someone who experiences a degree of control over his or her otherworld experiences. The shaman can move between the worlds and can function effectively within both a mundane and a spiritual context. Not only can the shaman converse with spirits, but he or she can function concretely and practically within the framework of a society.

The madman goes off into the otherworld and is never heard from again. A madman cannot maintain balance, nor can he or she perceive a difference between physical and spiritual realities. The madman cannot come back to everyday reality and function effectively within the community. When mad, an individual lacks stability in work, in relationships with other people, and in states of mind.

A Word to the Wise: In many ways, the contemporary practices of Wicca link directly to the tribal rites and beliefs of our ancient shamanic predecessors. Those who practice these mystic arts today have at the basis of their work over 30,000 years of history to support them. From the caves of Lascaux in Dordogne to the ancient civilizations of Catal Huyuk of ancient Anatolia, history supports the fact that the rites and practices of shamanism have occurred globally much longer than any other known spiritual path.

- Describe in writing your own "calling" to the Witch's path. Take note of which of the shamanic hallmarks describe your own experience.
- We all have characteristics of both the shaman and the madman. In what ways are you a shaman? In what ways are you a madman or madwoman?

Day 7

Witches and Sacred Symbols

Mythologist Joseph Campbell once stated, "anything that can be named and that can be regarded as a form . . . is also a *symbol*."[5] A symbol is a form that represents something else. In spiritual practices, a symbol typically represents an abstract principle, a philosophical point, or a religious concept. In Wicca, symbols are the distillation of spiritual insights and magical wisdom. Symbols are the essence of divine principles that are neatly summed up by images, artifacts, sounds, words, colors, movements, or even smells.

Anthropologist Adolf Bastian was first to recognize that certain basic principles reoccur as symbols through the world's mythologies and religious systems. He called these reoccurring principles "elementary ideas."[6] If we were to translate the images of the symbol world into words, some of those most repeated symbolic motifs might be, for example, "life must feed on life," or "life does not end with death." Bastian went on to point out that although the elementary ideas are the same across religious systems, the basic axioms generated various costumes, expressions, applications, and interpretations from one culture to the next. He called the specific cultural expressions of elementary ideas "folk ideas" or "ethnic ideas." Ethnic ideas can change from one setting to another, but elementary ideas always remain intact. Wicca taps into these elementary ideas through symbols and ideas common to all cultures. The sunrise, a circle, the change of season, and fire are examples of Wiccan symbols that transcend culture, time, and place. We all experience them as part of living in this world.

To understand symbols more clearly, let's look at one familiar example. A dove can be more than a bird. In some cultures and religious systems it can represent peace. In Wicca, a seasonal tide, such as the Winter Solstice, is not only a celestial (and terrestrial) event. The days become shorter and darker until the Solstice. Then the tide changes and the light of the sun begins to grow from that point on in the year. It is a tide in which the seasonal darkness releases itself to the growth of solar light. This seasonal event can also represent the release of old, unwanted life patterns; it is a symbol of hope and promise. Another example can be the earth itself. If you consider the earth symbolically, it can be a universal representation of "mother" energy. After all, the earth gives birth to forms and nurtures those forms, just as a mother gives birth and nurtures her young.

Why are symbols important? In all spiritual paths, symbols represent truths that go beyond mere words. Symbols speak a poetic language of inference. That is because the extraordinary experiences to which they refer cannot be adequately, or directly, expressed in ordinary, linear words. For example, the term "god" is an ordinary word, but it refers to something extraordinary that would be difficult to capture through the limited venue of verbal expression. Deity is something that transcends the limits of words and ideas. When you interpret them correctly, the symbols of any spiritual path should be like a road map directing you to some immediate, personal experience.

In Witchcraft, symbols are the primary means for reaching and transforming the deep mind, known in psychoanalytic terms as the unconscious mind. It is from this deep mind that the arts of magic begin. Freud, Jung, and other pioneers of psychoanalysis discovered that the unconscious can only be reached and expressed in symbols—through art, myth, dream, and fantasy. In reaching the unconscious mind through symbols, the Witch's practices result in psychological integration and spiritual empowerment.[7]

Unfortunately our Western spiritual traditions are heavily influenced by Aristotelian philosophy with its emphasis on "facts" and rational cogitation.[8] When the rational mind apprehends the fluidity and poetic eloquence of spiritual symbols, it renders them dull and lifeless. They become concrete. The critical mind erroneously interprets symbolic information as fact, as history and geography. Once we lose touch with the message behind symbols we start to cling to beliefs—sometimes irrational ones. For example, one might insist that Jesus *was* born of a virgin, or that he *did* ascend physically into heaven. From this concrete perspective, there is an insistence on unlikely historical events when all along the messages that underlie spiritual symbols always refer to processes that should be going on inside of us right now.

This deceptive Western style of handling symbols touches all of us, no matter what our spiritual path. Without diligent awareness, you can transplant this habit into the fertile soil of your new spiritual practice. Witches make use of hundreds of symbolic correspondences. It would be easy to become lost in these external forms and rob yourself of internal content. Under those circumstances, spirituality becomes a straightjacket of dogma, obsession, and compulsion. In order for symbols to transform your mind and spirit, in order for them to shine with the radiance of the divine, they must be transparent to immediate, internal, and highly personal experience.

Practice: Sunrise, Sunset, Symbols

Take time today to witness either the sunrise or the sunset. It is important that you don't substitute an "imagined" sunrise or sunset—really go outside and engage in nature. As you experience either the sunrise or sunset, take note of your feelings and your state of mind. After this, take time to commit your thoughts to paper regarding these questions:

- What did you experience internally as you witnessed this event?
- From this experience, what do you imagine this sunrise or sunset could symbolize?
- Now think about a symbol from a spiritual path from your past. Spend time contemplating this symbol's meaning. What could this symbol mean for you today?

Day 8

Meditation

Meditation is a word that most of us have heard in reference to spiritual practices. The trouble is that most of us think it applies to someone else. When we first hear the word, many of us imagine bald-headed monks, the wearing of scarlet and saffron robes, or the chanting of mantras high in the mountains of Tibet to the sound of gongs. BONG! Is that what you think? Then you're wrong.

Witches worth their broom-bristles know how to meditate. If you are new to the Craft or to mystical practices in general, you have probably never learned this skill. It's time you hunkered down to the *zafu* (a meditation cushion, see Day 10 for method) and learned how to do it. It is an important mystic art as well as a basic staple of magical doings. Aside from the fact that regular meditation can lead to profound insights and life-changing understanding, it also has its more mundane uses. It helps you to relax; it promotes good sleep, better concentration, and improved overall health. It almost sounds too good to be true!

There are probably as many ways to meditate as there are words written on this page. Each style of meditation has common elements yet each requires a unique approach. Some common elements of all meditation techniques are that they all can lead to both personal and universal insight, and each requires focused attention. Here are some of the ways that meditation techniques are distinctive and unique.

Eastern Methods

Meditation techniques that come to us from the East—in particular from China, Japan, and India—lead the practitioner toward physical and mental stillness. Once you learn to intentionally still the associative, rational, and cognitive churnings of the mind, you begin to experience multidirectional consciousness. In other words, you align your *internal* world of perceptions with the *external* world, and form a single unifying reality. The result is that one is able to perceive the unity of life and the imminence of deity.

Eastern styles of meditation do not require that you create mental stillness by blocking out your thoughts. Instead, they suggest that you observe your thought processes in a detached way. In other words, you should allow your thoughts to exist naturally, but try not to engage in any of them. Some specific techniques include recitation of mantras, focusing attention on the breath, or focusing one's vision on an object like a candle flame. Although this type of meditative practice can be difficult for some Westerners, its devotees refer to it as "the quick path" to spiritual empowerment.

Western Methods

In the West we have television timing. We like action—and lots of it. Westerners also like to think of the world in terms of scientific truths and objective reality. We tend toward thinking in straight, logical lines rather than in endless Eastern loops. We feel comforted whenever we can understand the logic behind point A leading directly to point B. We believe that time is valuable and that it can be wasted. Of course, none of our ideas about the world are truth-in-fact, but since they are part of the culture in which we live, they do influence our meditative style.

Like our Eastern counterpart's, the goal of the Western style of meditation is that of bypassing the critical thinking mind and its processes. But instead of doing so with stillness, it accomplishes the same task with activity and imagery. We like to see and hear things in our meditations, so Western styles of meditation often include what is known as guided imagery. A guided imagery meditation is something like a controlled, planned dream through which someone else leads you. Guided imagery meditations work to evoke some response from you at a deep mind level. Examples of guided imagery include using your imagination to envision world peace or imagining a healing golden glow that surrounds and nurtures you.

Exercise: Meditation Temperaments

To assess which style suits you best, consider the following questions:

- Do you like your life to be perfectly organized or do you not mind a bit of chaos?
- Do you respond to most queries with action or with contemplation?
- Are you active and mobile, or are you laid back and sedate?
- Do you believe that every question has a definite, logical answer, or do you think that questions can sometimes beget more questions?
- Are you naturally *internally* focused or *externally* focused?
- Are you naturally patient or not?
- Are you strong willed, decisive, and direct? Or are you easy going and more indirect in your approach to people and tasks?

Consider your answers and decide which style might be best suited to your temperament before you begin with the meditation exercises tomorrow. Individuals who consider themselves to be organized, action-oriented, mobile, and logical might try the Western types of meditations techniques. Those of you who see yourselves as laid back, contemplative, less active, and nonlinear might try the Eastern meditation methods.

Day 9

Meditational Breathing

Take a deep breath. Don't hold back. Go ahead; fill your lungs and feel them expand. Once you've done this, you've already begun your most basic lesson in spiritual empowerment. Breathing is essential for life. It is also essential for magic.

Does it seem a little mundane? Great. Breathing is not only grounding, but it is the basis of many spiritual disciplines that focus on acquiring and directing magical power. The practitioners of hatha yoga rely on the effects of breathing to stimulate *prana*, the life energy. Once the life energy is flowing it leads to the rising of the *kundalini*—the force that awakens and brings strong magical force to you. Success in many martial arts, such as akido, tai chi and qui gong, depends on the practitioner tapping into his or her spiritual energy, also known as *chi* or *ki*, through specialized breath control techniques. In Hawaii, the master of magical power, the *kahuna*, relies on ritualized breathing methods that help control the flow of both physical and psychic energy.

Good, deep breathing also has healthful benefits. It helps you to relax. A good breath contributes to sustaining the body by nourishing the blood supply and the cells with oxygen. In essence, human life needs air.

Impressive, isn't it? A little breathing goes a long way in magical practices. And if you're planning to live your life energetically, healthfully, and magically you'd better get used to doing it well. Speaking of breathing: have you begun to notice your own breath yet? If not, take a moment and sense how you're breathing right now. Do not alter the quality of your breathing. Simply follow it. Is it short and shallow? Is it deep? Is it regular and rhythmic? Where does the breath feel as though it reaches? Your stomach? Your chest? Your throat?

The magical ceremonies of Wicca typically begin and end in the direction of the east, which symbolically corresponds to the element of air. It is fitting that your journey along the mystic path of Wicca begins with air and with breathing. Mastering breath control is your first act of empowerment.

Exercise: Powerful Breathing

Take a slow, deep breath. As you do notice what happens. Does your rib cage hike up and cause your shoulders to wrap around your ears? Does it feel as though it stops short in your throat? That's improper breathing. Don't worry, most of us who lead stressful, fast-paced lives do that. Let's jump right in and learn the secret of a powerful, magical breath.

As you take your next slow, deep breath, focus your attention on drawing the air in and down. You want to create the sensation that your belly fills with air as your back expands in the process. As you exhale, allow the breath to go naturally. Now that's good breathing.

DAY 10

Meditational Sitting

Sitting meditations are based in a very old shamanic technique. The technique attempts to immobilize the body so that the mind can begin to clarify. The magical, multidirectional human consciousness begins to deepen in the process and this, in turn, creates spiritual empowerment.

There are two basic variations of sitting meditation. One variation is sitting on a specialized floor cushion (sometimes called a zafu), and the other method is to meditate while sitting in a chair.

To do the cushion-on-the-floor method, you must first locate and purchase a zafu. Zafus are sold at most well-stocked mind-body-spirit shops. Zafus are typically round, approximately 15 to 20 inches in diameter, and about four inches thick. Firmly packed cotton, buckwheat hulls, or beans are typical zafu fillers. Try sitting on several types before you commit to buying a cushion, remembering that you two will be spending many magical hours together.

Successfully arranging the body on a zafu takes a little practice. The meditator sits on the front third of the cushion, so that the pelvis tilts slightly forward. Both knees should touch the ground and the legs should be arranged in a loose "Indian style," so that one leg is folded in front of the other. Finally, there should be equal weight distribution on your rear end and both knees, so that there is a tripod effect. But wait, that's not all. Here is how you should arrange your other body parts while doing sitting meditation:

- Spine: elongated
- Head: straight, level; not tilted forward or back.
- Teeth: together, lightly
- Tongue: tip pressed lightly to the roof of the mouth behind front teeth (to avoid excess saliva buildup while sitting)
- Shoulders: down, relaxed
- Arms: relaxed and arranged so that wrists rest in the lap
- Hands: resting one on top of the other, palms up, thumbs touching slightly

The only difference between chair and cushion sitting is that your legs should be bent at the knees comfortably and your feet should be placed flat on the floor. Allow your back to rest on the chair's backrest, keeping the spine aligned and straight.

Practice: Wall Gazing

To begin, sit on either your cushion or chair while facing a blank wall. Sit so that you are at least two feet from the wall's surface. Assume your usual sitting posture. Look downward at about a 45-degree angle. Soften your focus until the wall feels insubstantial, almost as though it has lost its solidity.

Allow your attention to settle on your breathing. Try not to breathe deeply or erratically—simply breathe as you normally do. Begin to count each exhalation, from one up to ten. If you notice that your attention drifts from the counting and you become caught up in memories, future planning, emotions, or situations outside of your direct experience, start counting over. Practice this meditation technique today and for the next several days until you feel as though your mind is settling on simply counting.

Next, let's focus on the exhalation. Practice releasing your breath just as slowly as you've inhaled it. Feels pretty good, doesn't it? Notice how your tension just seems to melt away? The next time you face a stressful situation, take time to breathe deeply and slowly and you'll quickly regain your composure. Just get cut off on the freeway? Breathe. Is your boss on your case? Breathe. It will soon pass and you'll be all the more relaxed in the meantime.

Practice powerful breathing at least once daily, for three to five minutes at a time. A deeply relaxed state of mind and powerful energy raised by proper breathing is what Wiccans need to successfully employ their craft. Powerful breathing is the first step toward a thriving magical practice.

DAY 11

Meditational Walking

Walking in meditation is another effective method for opening the magical senses and empowering the spirit. In walking meditation, you aim your practice toward a specific end, such as raising magical energy to achieve some specific goal, opening the sixth sense so that you increase psychic ability, or gaining spiritual insight on some matter in your life. You would normally conduct walking mediation during a Wiccan ritual; however the ritual context is not necessary for this meditation technique to be effective. In a ritual context, walking meditations might take place, for example, within a spiral design you map out on the ground, within a labyrinth, or at specific symbolic times of the year.

A Word to the Wise: Labyrinths are a form of *Mandala* (a Sanskrit word that roughly means "a circle that contains essence, or spirit"). A labyrinth is a design usually marked upon the ground that conveys spiritual and numerological symbolism. Labyrinths are usually created to have a single winding pathway within a circular design. The pathway is traditionally composed of either 7, 11, or 12 circuits that spiral inward to a center. The labyrinth is a universal symbol of transformation that spiritual practitioners can use to represent an individual's pilgrimage to his or her own center point, which is the heart of divinity.[9]

The focal point of walking meditation can be one of several options that depend on the purpose of the meditation. For instance you might focus on the sensations of your body, such as the feelings you experience as your weight shifts from one leg to another. You might focus on counting your breaths. Or you might count your steps, counting in rounds from one to ten.

Not every type of walking meditation is suited to every personality. There are two specific styles of walking meditation for you to consider: *sunwalking* and *moonwalking*. Sunwalking is a brisk, gentle forward movement. The sunwalking stride is quick and long, and it is best suited to folks who usually have a directed, logical, linear mental focus. In moonwalking, each step is half the length of the foot. There is a pause between steps that lasts approximately three breaths to allow you to integrate the energy of each step you take. Moonwalking is best suited to folks who have a contemplative, creative, nonlinear mental energy.

Exercise: Moon or Sun?

Determining whether you are naturally a Sun or Moon walker is a simple process. Below is a list of some solar and lunar qualities. Circle the qualities that best describe you.

Solar	*Lunar*
Fiery: Expressive	Mellow: Contemplative
Fast paced: Active	Serene: Sluggish
Impatient: Moving	Forgiving: Tranquil
Overt: Frenetic	Discrete: Secretive
Sexual: Passionate	Sensual: Emotional
Cerebral: Analytical	Empathic: Compassionate
Logical: Reasonable	Intuitive: Introverted

Whichever category holds the most markings represents your natural type, either solar or lunar. If your markings are evenly distributed, you have integrated energy and can use either method with success.

DAY 12

Moonwalking and Sunwalking

Whether you naturally align with solar or lunar energy, today take some time to experience both the solar and lunar method of walking meditation.

Moonwalking

For this exercise, find a place where you can be undisturbed for up to twenty minutes. You can practice moonwalking either indoors or outdoors in some natural setting. The best time to practice moonwalking is at night, under the energetic influences of the moon.

To begin, stand straight, feet together. While holding your head straight, squarely above your shoulders, lower your gaze so that you are looking down at about a 45-degree angle. Place your left hand on your abdomen, just above the navel. Place the right hand over the left so that your knuckles overlap and align. This hand posture is one that represents (and evokes) containment and protection.

Allow your breathing to be natural and rhythmic. Turn your attention to the weight of your body. Feel the pull of gravity and where your body supports itself. Wherever you sense tension, release it by taking a deep breath and imagining the muscles relaxing as you exhale.

Step forward with your left foot about half the length of your right foot. Feel the weight of your body shift as you step forward. Breathe naturally, but wait for at least three exhalations before you step forward with your right foot. Focus your attention now on your steps. Count each step as you moonwalk forward, counting from one to ten. If you catch yourself thinking, start counting again from the number one. Try not to allow counting to disrupt your stepping forward.

Sunwalking

To begin, find a place where you can be undisturbed for up to twenty minutes. As with moonwalking, you can practice sunwalking either indoors or in some natural setting. Try this exercise during the day, under the influence of the sun.

Because you will cover more ground in twenty minutes of meditation, it is important to find either a long, level stretch of walking area, or to mark out a meditational walking circle. If you choose to practice sunwalking in a circle, mark out a nine-foot diameter space, using a four-and-a-half-foot length of cord to demarcate the circumference. Indicate your circular path with stones, candles, seashells or some other aesthetically pleasing and spiritually awakening items.

As in your moonwalking exercise, begin by standing straight, with your feet together. Hold your head erect and lower your gaze so that you are looking down at about a 45-degree angle. Place your right hand over your left so that your knuckles overlap and align as they rest on your abdomen.

Allow your breathing to be natural and rhythmic. Turn your attention to the weight of your body. Feel the pull of gravity and where your body supports itself. Wherever you sense tension, release it by taking a deep breath and imagining the muscles relaxing as you exhale.

Begin to walk forward, stepping first with your right foot. Establish a brisk but relaxed pace. Once you have set your pace, try not to change it. Focus your attention now on your steps. Count each step as you move forward, counting from one to ten. If you catch yourself thinking, start the count again from the number one. Once you reach the tenth count, return to one and continue the count in rounds of ten. Do not disrupt your stepping forward when you renew the count.

Day 13

Guided Imagery Meditations

Guided imagery is the last magical meditation method that you will use in your year and a day study. Guided imagery is like a dream that someone else creates for you. Typically, the meditator begins by closing the eyes. A guide invites the meditator to visualize or imagine a series of images that channel the meditator toward a particular experience.

A skillful guided imagery meditation is one that will draw you near to a goal such as healing, evoking magical power, insight, or releasing old, limited ways of thinking.

Exercise: Finding Your Power Place

The guided imagery meditation that follows is the foundation for many other meditations presented later in this book. You can either try this guided imagery meditation by having a friend read it to you, or by recording it on a tape player for later use.

Reader:

Find a comfortable sitting position, or lie flat on your back on the ground. Close your eyes. Take several deep breaths. Mentally scan your body for tension, starting at your feet and working your way up to your head. With each exhalation, imagine that you release any tension that you have sensed in your body.

Once you have released any noticed tension, shift your attention back to your breathing. Begin to take deep, slow breaths. Inhale and exhale slowly. Imagine now that a bright white mist begins to form at your feet. With each inhalation, the mist is drawn up around your body and begins to spiral. As you draw the mist upward you feel warm and comforted. Continue to see the mist climbing your body with each inhalation until it envelops you completely.

Once you are cloaked in this magical mist, you begin to feel weightless. Your usual sense of time and place slips away from you. All that is left is a feeling of floating inside this soft, glowing, white mist.

Soon you recognize that you are moving. You cannot sense the direction, whether forward or back, up or down, but you feel movement as the mist transports you across time and space. It is taking you to your place of power. Allow the mist to move you and it will stop when you have arrived at your power place.

(Reader: pause for a moment.)

When movement has stopped, the mist begins to clear to reveal a landscape. Where are you? Are you on a desert mesa? Are you stationed by a shady mountain stream? Are you on the beach near a sparking sea? Whatever your surroundings, note them in detail now. As you explore this place you will find a particular spot in the landscape that draws your attention. Go to that spot and sit there.

This is your power place. As you sit here, you are able regenerate your energy; you are able to relax and cultivate a sense of peace. You are safe here. You gather magical power here. This is your spiritual home.

Stay here for as long as you need. When you are ready to return, imagine that you gesture with one of your hands in a spiral motion near your feet. As you do this, the white spiraling mist will appear again and will climb your body. As the mist covers you, you lose the sense of time and place again. The feeling of motion returns, and the mist transports you rapidly back to the place where you began.

(Reader: pause for a moment.)

Once you have arrived back in the place where you began, open your eyes. Take a few moments to recount your experience.

Day 14

Re-Thinking God

There is a monotheistic philosophy of deity that operates behind the scenes in most of our mainstream religious thinking. It not only permeates religion, but popular culture as well. Monotheistic religions propose that if you are a reasonable person, it should be clear to you that there is an intelligence behind the design of the universe. After all, "Figs do not grow on thistles. Grapes do not grow on thorns."

At this point, an unwarranted leap in logic takes place. Monotheistic religious paths usually jump to the conclusion that the intelligence behind the scenes is, in fact, a specific, singular god—the Biblical Yahweh, for instance. Along with this assertion comes the belief that this god governs all affairs, much like a monarchy, and he has some definite opinions and regulations about how things "should be." Monotheistic religions (which are usually those of "the book"[10]) therefore conclude that human beings should be vigilant lest they violate the fundamental grain of the universe, as established by this watchful (and often vengeful) god.

Does this mythology shape your worldview? You bet it does. Joseph Campbell says, "What if the Lord's Prayer began with 'Our Mother' instead of 'Our Father'?" The gender of deity, its location, presumed purpose, and its number are all features that shape how we live and act in the world. Now let's pull the rug out from beneath ourselves and wonder about a "god" that is nothing like what we might suppose.

There is an old joke about the person who has a near-death experience and who comes back to tell the tale. When asked if he saw god, he says, "yes." When asked for a description, he says, "she's black." This story amuses us because, in the back of our minds, many of us hold onto the image of god as an old white man with a long beard. This is an institutionalized, well-disseminated cultural image that many of us take for granted. It rarely occurs to us that god may be something else entirely. Perhaps god is not something that we can understand through rationalization or through philosophical inquiry.

A Word to the Wise: In Wicca, the divine is not a person, nor is the divine something that is "greater than" each of us. Wiccans view the divine as an energy that manifests through us at all times. It is who and what we are. In addition to that, it is a good practice to begin deconstructing and closely observing cultural customs that incite emotional or mechanical reactions.

Take time today to contemplate and commit to paper your thoughts about the following questions:

- What images of god did you hold as a child?
- How have these childhood images influenced your understanding of the divine today?
- Are the images of god that you know actually representative of god's fundamental nature?
- Are images of god important? Why?
- What is the purpose of believing in deity?
- Do we cheat ourselves at any level by characterizing god through image? Why? Why not?
- Does it bother you to see the word "god" not capitalized in this book? Why?
- Does the word "god" need capitalization?
- What automatic, conditioned responses do you have in relation to words, letters, and grammatical formalities?

Day 15

Divine Polarity

The universe is a singular "great energy," in the Witches' world view. People across the globe have tried to give this unifying energy names. They've tried "god," "Tao," "Tathata," and "Great Spirit," to name only a few, but no words adequately describe this spiritual energy, which binds together the entire phenomenal world.

The very nature of spiritual energy is dichotomous. Just like electrical current, spiritual energy manifests in a natural balance of waves and troughs. It reveals itself as hot and cold, on and off, light and dark, life and death. As the Chinese say, the single energy of the universe is both Yin and Yang.[11] Witches symbolize their understanding of this divine energy in male and female terms—as both god and goddess.

That is not to say that Witches believe deity literally has either male or female genitalia. Rather, god and goddess are symbolic representations of how nature expresses this divine energy. "As above, so below," is one of the most basic magical axioms, and Witches understand that nature is a direct reflection of spiritual energy. In other words, Witches view nature in all of its manifestations as an expression of the divine.

A Word to the Wise: The noted psychoanalyst Carl Jung wrote that each of us carries gender traits that are the opposite of our physical gender characteristics. For example, if you are male, you have an anima or internalized feminine nature—if you are female, you contain the animus, or internalized male nature. In order to have appropriately balanced mental health, the external physical gender of the individual should be balanced by his or her internal polar counterpart.

A Witch's Brief Guide to Polarity

god	*goddess*
Male	Female
Sun	Moon
Expanding	Contracting
Light	Dark
Yang	Yin
Active	Passive
External	Internal
Conscious Mind	Unconscious Mind
Thinking	Dreaming
Hard	Soft
Warm	Cool
Linear	Nonlinear
Direct	Indirect
Life	Death
Day	Night
Positive	Negative
Square/angled	Round
Speaking	Listening
Doing	Being

Exercise: Exploring Polarity

As with all Wiccan symbols, the energies and the polarity of god and goddess represent aspects that reside within all of us. It does not matter if you have male or female physical characteristics; every human being has qualities and energies that express both the god and goddess. Let's find out now how you express them.

- Look at the brief guide to polarity above. As you consider the very short list of god and goddess energy attributes, what other words might you add to both sides of the list? Take time now to develop a more comprehensive list for yourself.

- Take out paper and pen and make a list of qualities that represent your "god" energy. Then make a list of qualities that represent your "goddess" energy.
- Review both lists to determine if you seem to express one side of the divine polarity more than the other. Which aspect do you most express in your daily life? Which energy gets least expressed in your daily life?

Day 16

Sun and Moon: Divine Polarity in the Sky

For Witches, the sun and the moon are two basic and yet spiritually fundamental phenomena in nature that symbolize the mystical polarity of god and goddess energies. The sun and moon's interplay maintains life upon our planet, but it also symbolizes the basic truth that all of life exists in a state of interdependence. The sun radiates energy and vitality. Without the sun there would be no light, and subsequently no life, on this planet. The light of the sun gives life to the plant world, and in turn the plants give life to the animal world. Likewise, the moon reflects the sun's light and caresses the earth with a reflective glow that allows time for life on the planet to rest and rejuvenate itself. Without the regular rhythm of night punctuated by the appearance of the moon, life would soon wither and die.

In Wicca, the sun represents masculine, active, or god energy. The moon represents feminine, receptive, goddess energy. The natural interplay of sun and moon gives rise to the Wiccan mythology suggesting that god and goddess not only maintain all life, but infuse it. In reality, the mythology is true. When you eat something, you eat the light of sun and moon (as well as all other natural phenomena that come together to form your food, such as rain, wind, soil, etc.). You cannot survive without these heavenly luminaries, and, in fact, they form and nurture your very body and mind.

Exercise: Solar and Lunar

Use the list you developed in yesterday's exercise to help you think of your life in four basic categories: your thoughts, your activity, your feelings, and your body. Consider whether the sun or the moon best represents your energy in each of the four categories. For example, someone whose thoughts are solar would have linear, analytical thinking much of the time. Someone whose thoughts were lunar would have more intuitive and circular thinking processes. Below is a list of words that can help you discover your own symbolic representational energies of both moon and sun in your four categories.

Sun: Active, lively, vigorous, dynamic, direct, orderly, energetic, bold, assertive, proactive, confident, assured, logical, rational, careful, sequential, cheery, high-spirited, joyful, vain, haughty, pompous, hot-headed, muscular, angular, thin, firm.

Moon: Receptive, indirect, passive, reflexive, reactive, subtle, fine, understated, circular, inclusive, intuitive, spontaneous, holistic, reflective, moderate, introspective, moody, disorganized, insecure, timid, apprehensive, emotional, touchy, round, soft, plump.

Day 17

Tracking the Sun and Moon

How attuned are you to the cycling of the Sun and Moon? What season is it outside—right now? Do you know the dates of when one season passes and when the next begins? Do you know the moon's phase? If you are like most people, you rarely take notice of the passage of the moon through her monthly cycles, or the sun as it moves through its annual progression of solstices and equinoxes. Most of us take note of the season and details such as the patterns of weather, heat or cold, only when it affects our health or recreational possibilities. But in the world of Witchcraft, the stage and location in the heavens of the sun and moon signify magical and spiritual energy tides.

Because of this, Witches place great attention to the cycling of these two magical luminaries. In Wicca, there are eight seasonal festivals, or Sabbats, that occur as the sun progresses through the seasons of the year. Likewise, as the moon gains and sheds light throughout its 28-day cycle, Witches plan their Esbats, their magical lunar celebrations.

Keeping track of the sun and moon are basic to Wiccan practice and folks new to the path would be wise to attend to these cycles. To begin, check your local newspaper to find out the moon's current phase. The waxing moon is from the first phase to the end of the second phase. The full moon rises during the end of the second phase. The waning moon occurs during the third and the fourth moon phases.

The four lunar phases.

The seasons occur as the sun progresses through the solstices and equinoxes. The Winter Solstice occurs when the sun enters the astrological sign of Capricorn (usually between December 20–23). Spring Equinox occurs when the sun enters the sign of Aries (between March 20–23). Summer Solstice happens as the sun enters the sign of Cancer (between June 20–23), and the Fall Equinox happens when the sun enters Libra (somewhere between September 20–23).

Exercise: Sun and Moon Cycles

The Farmer's Almanac (available at most bookstores and through online services) can tell you when the seasons change. You can also check with an astrological ephemeris, which charts the passage of the sun and the planets of the solar system as they progress through the twelve constellations.

In later days you will discover the importance of knowing these luminaries and their rhythms, but for now, develop a habit of knowing the cycles of the sun and moon on a regular basis. This alone will begin the process of attuning you to the energies of the goddess and god.

Day 18

Meeting the Goddess: Maiden

In Wiccan mythology, goddess energy manifests itself in three symbolic forms: the *maiden*, the *mother*, and the *crone*. These three aspects are also the common stages through which all women pass in their lifetime. But more than this, they are symbols that represent the internal stages of consciousness that are common to all human beings, regardless of gender. Each of these aspects has its own internal polarity—a light and a dark side, if you will. Over the next several days you will learn about each of these symbols and uncover their expression in your own life.

The first of the goddess' aspects is the *maiden*. The goddess in this aspect represents youth, newness, beginnings, brilliance, and simplicity. The maiden aligns with several symbolic correspondences such as springtime, the compass direction of east, and sunrise. The maiden represents potential. She is not partial to the direction that potential manifests itself. All potential is the maiden. She is the future, creativity, and fecundity. She represents the seed, newly planted into the soil, full of potential but not yet sprouted. The maiden is that part in each of us that is our innocence, purity, and raw energy.

The maiden also has a dark, shadowy side. In her dark aspect, the maiden cannot realize potential. Stuck in her own youth, the maiden in her shadow aspect can be a dilettante, lacking in depth. This dark maiden energy, residing within each of us, can represent our inability to mature with time. In this darker aspect she can represent a perpetual unworldliness, childishness, internalized fear, and overdependence upon other people.

Some maiden goddesses in mythology include: Pandora, Persephone, Arachne, Venus/Aphrodite, Kore, Tana, Ariadne, Flora, Electra, Athena, Brigid, Branwen, and Gaia.

Table of Correspondences: The Maiden

The practices of Wicca rely principally on the workings of the deep unconscious mind and the channeling of subtle energies that reside therein. The unconscious mind speaks in symbol and image and therefore the best way to access this realm is through symbolic means. Because of this, symbolic correspondences are key spiritual points in Witchcraft practice. Each set of symbols in the Craft connects us to specific spiritual, energetic tides or fields. They also connect us to aspects of our own lives, our personalities and experiences. Symbolic correspondences bridge your own experience of the world and physical reality.

Take time today to commit to memory the following magical correspondences that evoke Maiden energies.

Lunar Phase: New

Seasonal Phase: Late winter/early spring

Color: Orange

Pagan Celebration: Imbolc, February 2

Direction: Northeast

Time: The darkness that precedes the dawn

Incense: Myrrh, orris root

Essential Oils: Heather and basil

Magical Number: 2

Vocalization: ū (as in you)

Herbs: Angelica, bay laurel

Planet: Moon

Body Part: Sexual organs

Chakra: 2nd—Genitals/womb

Exercise: Knowing Your Maiden

Think about your own maiden traits. On a single piece of paper, draw a line down the center. On one side write down your personality traits (no matter if you are physically male or female) that reflect positive maiden qualities. On the other side of the page, write down any shadowy maiden qualities you might recognize in yourself. If you do not note any of the maiden's qualities in your life, this is an archetypal energy that might require balancing and integration in order for you to claim your full potential and power as a Witch. Over the next few days, you will learn how to evoke these qualities into your life.

The Chakras

Chakras are seven wheel-like energy centers that reside within the body. Anodea Judith, author of *Wheels of Life*, describes chakras as "Swirling intersections of vital force [life-energy]."[12] Each of the chakras governs aspects of our consciousness.

The Chakras or energy centers of the body.

Locations of the Chakras

- The point between anus and genitals—the root or 1st chakra
- Just above genitals—2nd or genital chakra

- Just below navel—3rd or solar plexus chakra
- Center of chest—4th or heart chakra
- Hollow or base of throat—5th or throat chakra
- Center of brow, between eyes—6th chakra, pineal or third-eye chakra
- Top of head—7th or crown chakra

What Each Chakra Governs

1st—root, grounding, connection to earth
2nd—sexual activity
3rd—anger, mastery, control
4th—love, compassion
5th—communication
6th—conscious awareness, psychic activity
7th—connection with deity

Day 19

Exercise: Calling on the Maiden

Pick or buy fresh flowers today. Place them in front of you. Close your eyes and take several deep breaths. Smell the sweet scent of the flowers in front of you. Relax your body from head to toe with each exhalation. Once you are relaxed fully, imagine that you stand in a vast, grassy field facing the east. It is dawn. With your spirit-voice, internally chant the name of one maiden goddess. Watch for her to appear on the horizon, holding flowers.

She will approach you and hand you several flowers, one at a time. With each flower she gives you, she will name a trait that is important for you to develop in order to access her power. Once she finishes handing you flowers, bid her farewell. Return to the place where you began your journey and open your eyes.

For the remainder of the day embrace the traits or qualities the maiden has given to you.

The "cosmic Yoni" is a term that refers to the vulva of the goddess. It is the personification of the female principle in nature.

Day 20

The Maiden: Intonation

In magical parlance, *intonation* means to vocalize. Vocalization for magical purposes usually involves resonating or vibrating a particular sound so that it feels as though it originates from deep within. When you intone a sound or word, it may feel as though the sound emerges from your diaphragm, which is an area just below your navel and just above the pelvis. Today's working will involve intoning a sound that will invoke the maiden's energies.

What You'll Need:

- An orange candle
- A compass

To begin, look in a local newspaper or in an almanac to find the exact time of dawn today. Set your alarm clock so that you are awakened one hour prior to dawn. Use your compass to locate the northeast and find a comfortable sitting position while facing that direction. Be sure you are sitting in such a way that your spine is aligned and balanced—perpendicular to the floor. Set the orange candle before you, light it and cast your gaze upon the flame. Take a deep breath that expands the lungs and fills the belly as well. As you exhale, begin to vocalize the sound "u" (which should sound like "you"). Sustain the sound until all air vacates your lungs. Then allow the inhalation to arise from this emptiness, and again fill your lungs to capacity. Repeat the intonation a second time. When you finish the second intonation, sit in silence for 15 or 20 minutes to allow the essence of this intonation to realign your consciousness. Extinguish the candle when finished.

Day 21

The Maiden: Magical Pass

A magical pass is a hand gesture that a Witch uses to symbolize and therefore invoke specific spiritual energies. Here is the magical pass for the maiden. Begin by facing the northeast. Stand with your arms at your side, palms flat, facing behind you. Your thumbs should both be touching your outer thighs.

Bend the elbows so that only your forearms move. Open the thumbs so that they are at a 90-degree angle with the forefinger. Bring the hands together so that the tips of both thumbs and forefingers touch. The hands should meet in front of the body at the genital area. The opening that the two hands create represent the cosmic yoni, a term that refers to the vulva of the goddess. It is the personification of the female principle in nature.

Take time today to practice this magical pass and sense what energies it invokes for you.

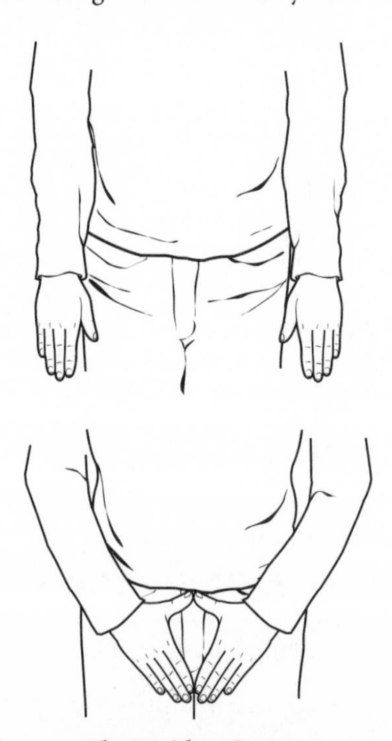

The Maiden Gesture.

DAY 22

The Maiden: Invocation Prayer

In the world of Witches an invocation is a type of *summoning.* Witches can summon entities, energy forces, or aspects of the god and goddess to achieve particular purposes. Witches usually invoke the gods within a formal sacred space, the magic circle, since the presence of the gods has a powerful, spiritually electrical effect. Witches usually invoke the Old Ones using a combination of gesture, sound, and symbol. The invocation you will learn today (and those you will find over the next weeks) are only part of a full ritual invocation process. The entire process involves creating sacred space, using specialized magical tools, gestures, sounds, and symbols. Over the course of the year and a day, you will learn the full process. For now, take time to practice the invocation words and gestures. In reciting these words, you may notice a change in your personal energy, or the energy of the room.

What You'll Need:

- An orange candle
- Myrrh or orris root to burn as an incense

Stand facing the northeast. Light the candle and set it on a table before you. Ignite self-lighting charcoal (such as Three-Kings), then sprinkle loose incense on the hot coals. Practice the magical pass of the maiden, and hold your arms in this position while you say:

> ***By Persephone and Pandora,***
> ***By Ariadne and Athena,***
> ***By Brigid and Branwen,***
> ***And the countless names of power,***
> ***By the crescent moon and horn,***
> ***Come ye Maiden goddess,***
> ***Thy Holy Rites reborn!***

When you are finished sit where you are, close your eyes, and sense the maiden goddess' presence.

DAY 23

Meeting the Goddess: Mother

The mother is the second of the goddess' three aspects. In her mother aspect, the goddess represents birth and nurturing. She is the archetype of actualized potential. The seed that was planted in the maiden phase of energy has come to fruition. She is no longer the bud of potential, but the full, fragrant bloom, the ripened orchards, and the full sway of summertime. The mother aligns with the compass directions of south and west. She aligns with energy and the full power of growth and adult maturity. The goddess in this aspect also represents compassion and understanding. She is the earth-mother in all of us—caring, forgiving, receptive, and open to change. She is the actualization of creativity and of fecundity.

The mother also has a dark side. When we hold internally to our own mothering archetype, rather than allowing the free flow of energies in our life, she can represent our potential to smother and to encourage dependence in other people. The dark side of the mother is a belief in one's own compassion, but expressed in a self-serving way. It may not be overt, and certainly when we have this aspect in our personality, we entertain ourselves with kind intentions. However, it is important to know that the dark aspect of the mother does not allow people around us to live independently and to their fullest potential.

Some mother goddesses in mythology include: Demeter, Io, Cerridwen, Nut, Melusine, Arianrhod, Isis, Aradia, Ceres, Dana, Hecket, Ishtar, Artemis, Boann, and Astarte.

Table of Correspondences: The Mother

Take time today to commit to memory these magical correspondences that evoke mother energies.

Lunar Phase: Fall

Seasonal Phase: Late summer/early fall

Color: Green

Pagan Celebration: Lughnassadh, August 2

Direction: Southwest

Time: Late afternoon

Incense: Meadowsweet and oak

Essential Oils: Lotus, cucumber

Magical Number: 4

Vocalization: ā (as in say)

Herbs: Hollyhock, frankincense

Planet: Venus

Body Part: Heart, lungs, hands

Chakra: 4th—heart, center of chest

Exercise: Knowing Your Mother

Consider your own motherly traits. On a single piece of paper, draw a line down the center. On one side write down your personality traits (no matter if you are physically male or female) that reflect positive mother qualities. On the other side of the page, write down any shadowy mother qualities you might recognize in yourself. If you do not note any of the mother's qualities in your life, this is an archetypal energy that might require balancing and integration in order for you to claim your full potential and power as a Witch. Over the next few days, you will learn how to evoke her qualities into your life.

The archetypal energy of the mother can present unique challenges and opportunities, especially for those who've had difficulty developing a strong or productive relationship with their own mothers. Explore this archetype—the mother as a goddess—and take time to question your own feelings about mothers and your relationships with mothers. How clear a connection to this energy can you establish? Do you sense emotional blockages in your way, or internal neediness or clinging when thinking of "mother"? What practical steps might you take to achieve balanced accord with the *energy of mothers* in your life?

Day 24

Exercise: Calling on the Mother

Indulge in comfort foods today regardless of any diet you may be on. Eat familiar foods that nourish your soul. Macaroni and cheese, apple pie, and ice cream are all comfort foods that many folks associate with the principle, the symbol, of "mom." While you eat this food, maintain a sense of attention on how this food might bring forward your own maternal instincts. Perhaps it simply reminds you of home or makes you want to be loved and nurtured. Maybe it reminds you of something you've lacked in childhood. Try to honor and observed with reverence whatever it is that comes up for you while eating this food.

When you have finished eating, close your eyes and take several deep breaths. Relax your body from head to toe with each exhalation. Once you are relaxed fully, imagine that you stand near a beautiful waterfall that faces the southwest. It is late afternoon. With your spirit-voice, internally intone the name of a mother goddess. Watch as the waterfall parts and she walks through it toward you.

She will take your hand and place another of her hands on your heart. Feel your heart soften and fill with love and compassion. Once she finishes touching your heart, bid this holy mother farewell. She will disappear again into the waterfall. Once she has vanished, return to the place where you began your journey and open your eyes.

For the remainder of the day, embrace the compassion and love you felt from the mother goddess and allow that compassion to inform your actions.

Day 25

The Mother: Intonation

Today's working will involve intoning sound that will invoke the energies of the mother.

What You'll Need:

- A 5–6 inch green taper candle
- A compass

Set your alarm clock so that you know to begin this exercise in the late afternoon today, at approximately 3:00 or 4:00 PM. Using your compass, locate the southwest and sit in a comfortable position facing this direction. Set the green candle before you and light it. Set your gaze upon the candle flame. Take a deep breath, expanding both the lungs and the belly. As you exhale, begin to vocalize the sound "ā" (as in "say"). Sustain the sound until all breath vacates your lungs. Allow the inhalation to arise from this emptiness you create from the vacated lungs, and then again fill your lungs to capacity. Repeat the intonation three more times, which will make a total of four intonations. After you complete the fourth intonation, sit in silence for 15 or 20 minutes and allow the essence of this intonation to reverberate your consciousness.

Day 26

The Mother: Magical Pass

Begin this practice by facing the southwest. Stand with your hands placed on your chest. Set the right hand on the right breast and the left hand on the left breast. The tips of the middle fingers of the right and left hands should be touching lightly. Elbows should be raised from the sides and your forearms should be straight lines perpendicular to the floor. Open the arms now so that the palms of the hands face front and are at the level of the hips. The arms should be at 45-degree angles to the trunk of your body.

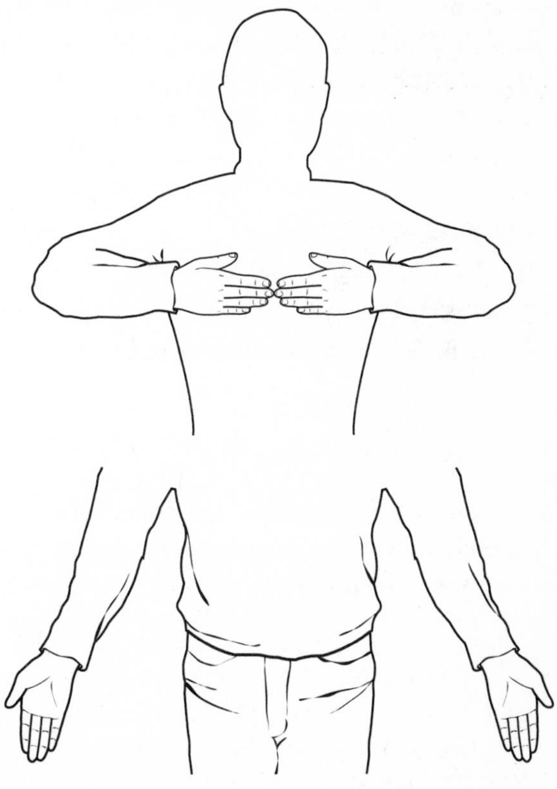

Steps 1 and 2 of the Magical Pass of the Mother.

Practice this magical pass with a heightened sense of inner attention and discover what energies it invokes for you.

Day 27

The Mother: Invocation Prayer

Today you will practice the mother's invocation words and gestures. As you recite this invocation, you may notice a change in either your own energy or the energy of your immediate environment.

What You'll Need:

- A green candle
- A blend of dried meadowsweet and oak bark to burn as an incense
- A compass

Use the compass to find the southwest. Face that direction. Light the candle and set it on a table before you. Ignite a self-lighting charcoal and then sprinkle the loose incense on the hot coal.

Practice the magical pass of the mother, and hold your arms in this position while you say:

> *By Demeter and Dana,*
> *By Aradia and Astarte,*
> *By Cerridwen and Ceres,*
> *And the countless names of power,*
> *By the full moon and branched horn,*
> *Come ye Mother goddess,*
> *Thy Holy Rites reborn!*

When you are finished with this invocational prayer, sit where you are, close your eyes, and sense the mother goddess' presence.

Day 28

Meeting the Goddess: The Crone

The crone is the goddess' third aspect. In her crone aspect, the goddess represents repose, wisdom and decline. Beyond her childbearing years, the crone is the archetype of female power turned inward. She is no longer the fragrant, full bloom, but she's brimming with the seeds of wisdom. She's ready to teach others the mysteries of what lies beyond death and the inner secrets of magic, if only we would listen. You can't pull the wool over those old, weathered eyes; she has been around the block a few times already and she is the personification of common sense and seasoned practicality.

The goddess in this aspect also represents justice and the reaping of whatever harvest we have planted. Sometimes what we reap is not exactly the thing for which we hoped. But the crone does not rely on hope. At the end of her life cycle, what need has she of hopes and dreams? The crone represents life lived beyond the crutch of hoping, wishing, and dreaming. She is an all-or-nothing lady. She is the old woman in all of us, she who sits by the hearth and who can foretell the future. Maybe she's just telling us things we don't really want to know, but that we need to know in order to grow and change. She is the manifestation of internal movement and mystic insight. She is there whenever you act in a level-headed, rational, responsible way.

The crone also has a dark side. When we cling to our own internal crone energy, without allowing a natural flow of energies of all kinds, she can represent bitterness, and self-sufficiency to the point of isolation. When we have dark crone energies in our personality, we might believe that we need to "set the record straight," set endless boundaries with other people, and criticize without noting much of anything positive. In her dark aspect, the crone can be our potential to cut ourselves off from other people, to judge harshly, or simply to carp.

Some crone goddesses in mythology include: Hecate, Spider Woman, Sophia, Kali, Circe, Hera, Fea, Hel, Sekhmet, Inanna, Discordia, Lilith, Minerva, Rhiannon, and Fortuna.

Table of Correspondences: The Crone

Commit to memory the following magical correspondences that evoke crone's energies.

Lunar Phase: Waning/dark

Seasonal Phase: Late fall/ winter

Color: Indigo

Pagan Celebration: Samhain, October 31

Direction: West

Time: Dusk

Incense: Mugwort and star anise

Essential Oils: sage, cedar

Magical Number: 6

Vocalization: Mmm

Herbs: Nightshade, fly agaric

Planet: Saturn, Jupiter

Body Part: Eyes

Chakra: 6th—pineal, at the center of the brow

Exercise: Knowing Your Crone

Consider your own crone traits. On a single piece of paper, draw a line down the center. On one side write down your personality traits (no matter if you are physically male or female) that reflect positive crone qualities. On the other side of the page, write down any shadowy crone qualities you might recognize in yourself. If you do not note any of the crone's qualities in your life, this is an archetypal energy that might require balancing and integration in order for you to claim your full potential and power as a Witch. Over the next few days, you will learn how to evoke these qualities into your life.

Day 29

Exercise: Calling on the Crone

Sit by the hearth at night and build a cheery fire. Don't worry if it is the middle of summer—make the fire anyway. If you live in a home without a fireplace, sit in a corner of your home during the night and light several candles. Watch the flicker and dance of the flames until you feel your eyes becoming heavy. Close your eyes and take several deep breaths. Relax your body from head to toe with each exhalation. Once you are relaxed fully, imagine that you are standing in the dark outside of a rickety wooden cottage in the middle of a dense forest. It is midnight. With your spirit-voice, internally intone the name of a crone goddess. Watch as the door of the cottage opens and an old woman walks toward you.

In her hands she holds a magic mirror. This is the mirror that reveals your wisest self. She silently holds up the mirror to your eyes and an image appears. It is the image of you acting throughout your day from a center of wisdom. She then whispers a word that represents a trait you must accrue to become your wisest self. Listen. After she speaks, she turns silently away and disappears into her cottage. Once she has, you will return to the place where you began your journey, seated in the chair before the fire (or candles), and open your eyes.

For the next twenty-four hours, try to live by the wise rule of the crone, guided by her magical word.

A Word to the Wise: After you light a self-igniting charcoal, you will notice that it sputters and sparks for a few minutes. Once this initial activity is over the coal will continue to heat up. It is usually best to wait for a few more minutes until the coal is at least white on its edges before it is hot enough to burn your incense.

Day 30

The Crone: Intonation

What You'll Need

- A 5–6 inch indigo taper candle
- A compass

Set your alarm clock so that you know to begin this exercise at dusk. Take out your compass, locate the west, and place a cushion on the floor or set a chair so that when you sit you will face this direction. Set the indigo candle before you, light it and set your gaze upon the candle flame. Take a deep breath, expanding the lungs and the belly. As you exhale, begin to vocalize the sound "mmmm." Sustain the sound until all breath vacates your lungs. Allow the inhalation to arise from this emptiness you create from the vacated lungs, and then again fill your lungs to capacity. Repeat the intonation five more times, making a total of six intonations. When you complete the sixth intonation, sit in silence for 15 or 20 minutes and allow the essence of this intonation to change your consciousness.

Days 30-60

Magical Items to Gather

You will need the following magical items during the next 30 days of training:

Day 32

- A 5–6 inch indigo taper candle
- ¼ ounce of an herbal blend consisting of equal parts dried mugwort and star anise
- A compass (you'll also need this tool on days 38, 40, 43, 45, 48, and 50)

Day 33

- A 5–6 inch yellow taper candle

Day 38

- A 5–6 inch yellow or gold taper candle

Day 40

- A 5–6 inch yellow taper candle
- ¼ ounce of an herbal blend consisting of dried cinnamon bark and pine bark

Day 43

- A 5–6 inch red taper candle

Day 45

- A 5–6 inch red taper candle
- ¼ ounce of an herbal blend consisting of frankincense and benzoin

Day 48

- A 5–6 inch violet or black taper candle

Day 50

- A 5–6 inch violet or black taper candle
- ¼ ounce dried white sage

Day 51

- Four yellow or gold candles

- An essential oil of one of the following herbs: chamomile, clove, cinnamon, bergamot, or rosemary
- Cornmeal

Day 52

- Four 5–6 inch silver or white taper candles
- Sea salt and poppy seeds
- An essential oil of one of the following herbs: cucumber, rose, hyssop, lily, nutmeg

Day 58

- Family photos of deceased relatives
- An altar cloth—can be made of any material, preferably a dark color
- Flowers—just a few to fill a small vase
- Candles—tea lights or candles of any shape or size
- Fresh basil—at least five or six leaves
- Dried mandrake root—usually available at any herbal shop; see the guide in the back
- Small bowl of water
- Dish with a small mound of salt (about 1 tablespoon)

Day 59

- A 5–6 inch black taper candle
- A pendulum (if you don't know what this is, skip ahead and read the description in Day 59)

A Word to the Wise: Essential oils are viscous distillations of various fragrant herbs and flowers. The sense of smell is powerful; fragrance experts believe essential oils produce an effect called "aromachology," a psychological effect of ambient odors. Some scents are believed to deeply influence psychological, physical, and spiritual change.

Day 31

The Crone: Magical Pass

To begin the magical pass for the crone, stand facing the west. Stand with your hands at your sides, palms flat, facing behind you. Bend the arms at the elbows and raise the arms so that your hands can rest, palms open, crossed on your chest. The right hand should be resting on the left breast and the left hand should be resting on the right breast. Witches also call this ritual posture the *Osiris Position.*

As you practice this magical pass, attend to whatever sensations or energies it seems to awaken in you.

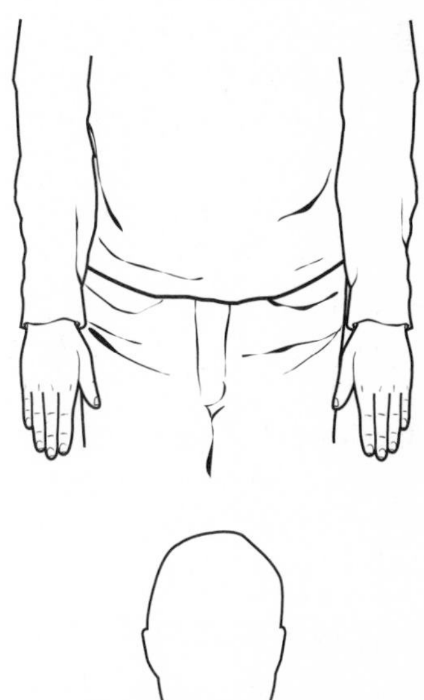

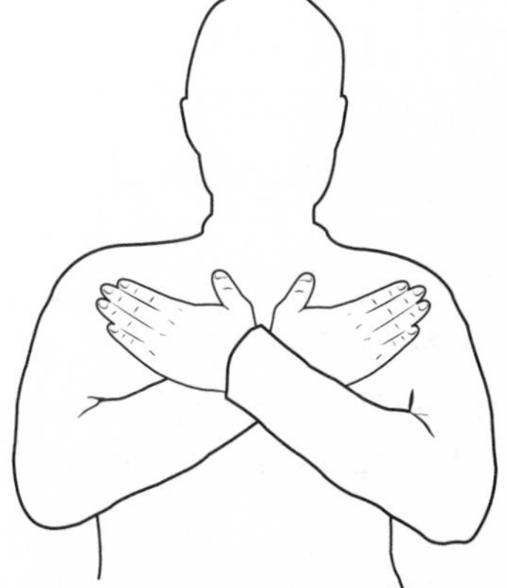

The Magical Pass for the Crone (the Osiris Position).

Day 32

The Crone: Invocation Prayer

As you recite the crone's invocation, you may notice changes in your physical energy, your mood, your awareness and sensation, or you might even notice changes in the energy of your immediate environment. Whatever the result of this practice, stay open and aware of its influences.

What You'll Need:

- An indigo candle
- A blend of dried mugwort and star anise to burn as an incense
- A compass

Use the compass to find the west and then stand facing that direction. Light the indigo candle and set it on a table or the floor in front of you. Ignite a self-lighting charcoal and then sprinkle on the hot coal the loose incense you made from dried mugwort and star anise.

As the smoke rises, practice the crone's magical pass and then hold your arms in this position while you say:

By Hecate and Hel,
By Sophia and Sekhmet,
By Inanna and Rhiannon,
And the countless names of power,
By the dark moon and buckled horn,
Come ye Crone goddess,
Thy Holy Rites reborn!

When you are finished with the crone's prayer, sit on the ground or in a chair near the indigo candle, close your eyes, and sense the crone goddess' presence. When you are finished, extinguish the candle.

Day 33

Contemplative Day: The Center of Knowledge

What is a "Contemplative Day"? Each month within your year of training, you will experience a retreat day of inner reflection during which you are encouraged to explore specific themes through your nonlinear, spiritual mind. As you have discovered in previous days, Wicca is a mystical path that places great emphasis on (and value in) direct experiential learning. While the formal acquisition of knowledge through conventional, linear, intellectual processes is important, your most important spiritual experience emerges from direct nonrational means. The Craft is chock-full of philosophical underpinnings and the contemplative days you will encounter each month facilitate your direct spiritual understanding of these points.

Meditative Question: What is at the center of knowledge?

Symbolic Color: Yellow

Symbolic Direction: East

Contemplation

Is knowledge an end in itself? How far can knowledge take you? The old magical saying is that there is "power in knowledge." But are there limits to such a power? Does knowledge affect the spirit? Does it change who or what you are at the core? Does it change the essential character of nature? Like a series of Chinese boxes nestled one inside of the next, the contemplative question posed this month explores a great breadth of themes. What may surprise you is what emerges from your own inner core as you discover what lies at the center of knowledge. Is it truth? Is it freedom? Let's find out together.

How to Use the Contemplative Question

To begin working with any of the contemplative questions, you should first find a comfortable meditative sitting position in a quiet space. Since this month's question symbolically aligns with the compass direction of east, you should arrange your chair or zafu so that you can sit facing that direction. Light a candle, set it in front of you, and sit approximately two feet away from the flame. Since this month's question symbolically aligns with the color yellow, you should choose a yellow candle for this contemplation.

Wicca is a system that embraces sympathetic magic. Sympathetic magic begins with (as one alchemical postulation states) the premise of "As above, so below," meaning that unseen forces align with seen forces. If you can make changes in the physical world, you make changes spiritually. The reverse holds true as well; if you can make changes at the level of spirit, they will manifest as changes in the physical world. Therefore, many Western magical systems enumerate correspondences between the seen and unseen. These correspondences reputedly align the user with specific aspects of spiritual power. For example, facing east reputedly aligns one with the spiritual essences of that compass direction, which include such attributes as beginnings, newness, awakenings, hope, optimism, and faith. You will learn more specifics about magic and the use of correspondences later in your year, but as the year progresses, you will learn many of these magical alignments.

As you sit comfortably and settle your consciousness, cast your gaze upon the flickering candle. Imagine that you hold the contemplative question firmly in the abdominal region. Imagine that you apply pressure to the question as though you were internally gripping an imaginary yellow ball with your abdominal muscles. Relax your shoulders and arms and breathe normally. Sit with this internal "holding" of the contemplative question for 20 minutes. If you should notice extraneous thoughts intruding as you concentrate on holding your contemplative question, simply maintain awareness that thoughts are coming and going in the mind, but quickly shift your focus back to holding the question.

Try not to solve the question through rational means of any sort. Just hold the question internally until an intuitive answer emerges. It is important to note that an answer to the contemplation may not emerge in one 20-minute sitting alone. You may not intuit an answer in direct response to your meditative inquiry. It may occur to you hours, days, or weeks later. It may occur to you as you take a shower or stand in line at the grocery store. For this reason it is important to merge with the contemplative question and engage it through each of your everyday tasks. Be prepared to receive an intuitive answer at any given moment. Give this process time and eventually a shift in your perception will take place through which you will realize your own answer.

Day 34

Devotional Day: Honoring Isis

During your year and a day you will encounter what I have termed "Devotional Days." During each of these days, you will encounter the spiritual essence of particular goddesses and gods from around the globe. Let us explore the first of these devotions by honoring Isis.

Table of Correspondences: Isis

Symbols: The magic circle, women's bodies, the cosmos, nighttime sky, throne

Tools: The magic wand

Magical Essences/Herbs: Papyrus, storax, willow, lily, and ivy

Direction: Isis is aligned with the center.

She Rules: All compass directions, elements, and powers

Animal Symbols: Cow, swallow, sphinx, lion, and eagle

Sacred Foods: Bread and wine

Magical Stones: Quartz, star sapphire, and amethyst

The ancient Egyptian goddess Isis is perhaps one of the most complete and all-encompassing figures in myth and symbolism. The cult of Isis was popular through the Old, Middle, and New Kingdoms of ancient Egypt. Her worship continued past the end of Pharaohic Egypt. Because of her popularity in the ancient world, other minor goddesses throughout the Mediterranean region and across the continent gradually assimilated Isis' qualities. For example, to the Greeks and Romans, the image of Isis was transformed into "the star of the sea," who was patroness of travelers.

Isis is a goddess of sky and earth. Her archetypal aspects included the "dutiful wife," the "grieving widow" and the "protector of the dead." She was the female counterpart to the god Osiris. In this sense, Isis represented the life principle while Osiris represented death. Her myths describe her as the embalmer and guardian of Osiris. She was an enchantress and a goddess of magic. Together with the god Thoth, she was a teacher of the healing arts, of balms and medicines.

Isis is a goddess of the entire life cycle: birth, growth, and cessation. There are no gaps between one's own life and Isis'. The ancients believed that all things emerged from her. In mythic terms, Isis is your very body and spirit. Each of us, and everything seen is her body, mind, and spirit.

Isis rules all natural magic. When you tap into her spiritual energies, you also evoke your ability to become one with the natural world, with both sky and earth, life and death. Rely on Isis when magical aid becomes necessary in your life. The ancients believed that Isis had the power to bestow boons upon those who humbly sought her assistance.

Isis Practice

In honoring Isis today, create an altar to her using the various symbols, images, candles, and incense that evoke her presence. Once you have created your altar, take time to face it and slowly, vocally intone her name, one syllable at a time (I-sis), until you feel or sense her presence surrounding you. Once you become aware of her energies filling your magical space, spend some time contemplating what it might mean to align with this aspect of deity. Take time to ask Isis what it would mean to live life through her energy and listen for her answer. Spend the day honoring this goddess by fulfilling another person's desire.

Day 35

Day of Silence and Review

Sporadically throughout your year and a day of training, you will encounter a "Day of Silence." Witches observe regular periods of silence for three reasons. First, the observance of silence most likely emerged from the Renaissance, when anyone found to be a practitioner of the Old Religion was subject to officially sanctioned torture and death. Silence meant safety for oneself and one's family.

Second, Witches observe silence because truth, power, and spirit (all of which are multidirectional and nonlinear) cannot be adequately placed into one-at-a-time words and descriptions. How can one ever hope to explain personal spiritual revelation? Words fall short of experience.

Third, Witches have found that silence is a method of preserving one's personal magical power. The water from a dam can be channeled to generate electricity, as long as the dam contains an adequate reserve of water. Days of silence help Witches to restore their spiritual resources.

Today, you will begin to learn firsthand the power of your own silence. It is best if you can maintain complete silence throughout the day. However, since this is not generally possible for many contemporary practitioners, it is necessary to adapt this practice. During the normal course of your day, limit your utterances to only that which is necessary. As you observe silence at whatever level possible for you, focus your attention on your thoughts. Do not attempt to limit your critical thinking; simply observe your mental activity. When the day is complete, answer these questions:

- Was it difficult to maintain silence?
- When did I most want to verbally communicate?
- Did silence help me to notice what was going on in my own body, mind, or spirit?
- Did I have times when mental activity increased or decreased?
- Did I have times when physical activity increased or decreased in response to silence?
- How might periodic observances of silence be beneficial to me?

DAY 36

Meeting the God: The Inseminator

Just as the goddess reveals her wisdom and power through three distinct aspects, so does the male counterpart of divinity. The first of the god's aspects, the *inseminator,* is his most youthful. In this aspect, the god represents youthful exuberance, pure undirected energy, and a sense of play. The inseminator is the bold youth, full of foolish bravery and carefree charm. He is the archetype of youthful, active, outwardly directed power. He is boisterous, sexually motivated, and extroverted as he faces the world. Let's face it; the inseminator is the party boy or party girl in each of us! The inseminator in all of us just wants to get down and have a little fun. Okay, maybe a lot of fun. This archetype represents the wildness of fire and spontaneity in all of us, no matter our physical gender. He does not know what lies ahead of him in life, therefore he has no obstacles. The inseminator knows no limits; all things are possible to him. He is the energy of one who won't learn from other people; he must learn from doing and experiencing for himself. Like the maiden, his energy represents simplicity and purity of heart.

The god in this aspect represents your enthusiasm, your physical strength, energy, and optimism. He is the part in each of us that is motivated by sexual and energetic drives. He is there when we accomplish what others say is impossible and when we feel the urge to clown around.

The inseminator also has a dark side. The dark side emerges when we (consciously or not) cling to our own internal inseminator energies rather than allow a free, natural flow of energetic expression in our lives. In his dark aspects, he can represent our wild destructiveness, a lack of impulse control, a lack of constructive direction, indolence, and our potential for flagrant self-indulgence. In his dark aspect, the inseminator can represent our potential to be driven blindly by physical urges and impulses.

Some inseminator gods in mythology include: Pan, Eros, Dionysus, Cupid, Enki, Gwion, Loki, Hermes, Janicot, Iacchus, Adonis, Mabon, Lugh, Prometheus, Dianus, Raven, Faunus, Shiva, Taliesin.

Table of Correspondences: The Inseminator

Commit to memory the magical correspondences that evoke the inseminator's energies:

Solar Phase: Waxing year

Seasonal Phase: Spring

Color: Gold/yellow

Pagan Celebration: Beltane, May 1

Direction: East

Time: Morning

Incense: Cinnamon or pine

Essential Oils: Carnation, cinnamon

Magical Number: 3

Vocalization: "ah" (as in caught)

Herbs: Woodruff, hops

Planet: Mars/Sun

Body Part: Muscles

Chakra: 3rd—Solar plexus, between navel and stomach

Exercise: Knowing the Inseminator God

Think about your own inseminator traits. On a single piece of paper, draw a line down the center. On one side write down your personality traits (no matter if you are physically male or female) that reflect positive inseminator qualities. On the other side of the page, write down any shadowy inseminator qualities you might recognize in yourself. If you do not note any of the inseminator's qualities in your life, you need to get out and enjoy things a bit more! You will find it spiritually beneficial to spend time cultivating this archetypal energy. In the days that follow, you will learn methods for invoking this energy. Use these methods to invoke the inseminator in you whenever you need a boost of energy or if you simply need to lighten up.

Day 37

Exercise: Calling On the Inseminator

Here is an exercise that will get your sexual attention. Oh come on, don't be a prude! Try this exercise to expand your consciousness, for goddess' sake.

Find a comfortable position, either sitting or lying down. Close your eyes and take several deep breaths. Relax your body from head to toe with each exhalation. Once you are relaxed fully, visualize yourself engaged in sexual activity with a partner. With your spirit-voice, internally intone the name of an inseminator god. Soon he will appear before you as you engage in your fantasy sexual activity.

Look into the eyes of your imaginary sexual partner and you will notice a flame, a wild energy there. This is the energetic expression of this deity. Continue the imagined sexual act and soon you will hear a word that represents your own inseminator energy. After you hear the word, immediately return your awareness to your physical body and then open your eyes.

Remember the word you learned in your vision and act from that word for the entirety of the day.

Here are some questions you might consider:

- Was I either unduly drawn toward or did I feel repulsed by this visualization?
- What might be some contributing factors to my feelings about this exercise?
- What are my experiences with sexuality?
- Should religion and sexuality ever find common ground? Why? Why not?

Day 38

The Inseminator: Intonation

What You'll Need:

- A yellow or gold candle
- A compass

Set an alarm clock so that you know to begin this exercise during the sunlit morning hours today. Use your compass to locate the east and place a cushion on the floor or set a chair so that you can sit facing this direction. Light the yellow or gold candle and set it in front of you so that you can gaze upon the candle's flame. Take a deep breath that not only expands the lungs but fills the belly as well. As you exhale, begin to vocalize the sound "ah" (like the vowel sound in the word *caught*). Sustain the sound until all breath vacates your lungs. Allow the next inhalation to arise from the empty feeling you create in your lungs. Then fill your lungs to capacity and repeat the intonation. Practice the inseminator's intonation for a total of three breaths. When you complete the third intonation, sit in silence for 15 or 20 minutes and allow the essence of this intonation to realign your consciousness.

Day 39

The Inseminator: Magical Pass

Begin by facing the east. Stand with your hands at your sides, palms flat, facing behind you. Bend the arms at the elbows and raise the hands so that they are level with your ears. Hands should be approximately eight inches away from the ears on either side of the head. With both of your hands, extend the forefinger and little finger, and close together the remaining fingers and thumb. This forms the Witch's "stang" (symbolizing the antlers of the young horned god).

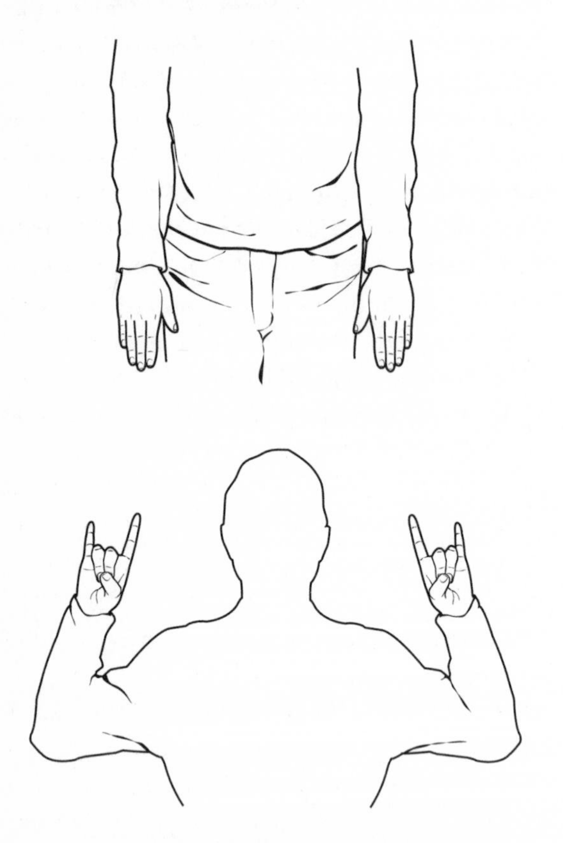

The Inseminator Position

As you practice this magical pass, focus your awareness on any sensations, thoughts, feelings, or energies that it may evoke for you.

A Word to the Wise: The horned god is an ancient pagan deity that predates Christianity and any of its angelic hierarchy. Witches do not either worship or acknowledge the deities or demons of the Christian religion. The horned god as an archetype links back in history to the hunter-gatherer societies. Based on archeological evidence such as cave paintings and clay renderings, historians have determined that the roles and tasks of men and women were commonly divided in the ancient traditional communities. Women were predominantly responsible for gathering, community building, and the raising of children. Men were assigned the responsibilities of tracking and killing food animals. In these Old European cultures, bison and deer were often the most hunted food sources. Villagers relied on tribal shamans to spiritually *call* the food animals to them in the hunt. One common custom in shamanic animal-magic was to dress in the skins (and antlers) of the hunted food animal. Shamans and villagers believed that this activity done in a ritual context would summon the herd animals. Thus, the antlers or "horns" of the shaman became linked with men's rites, magic, and divine activity.

The horned-god is another name for the male divinity in the Witches' pantheon.

Day 40

The Inseminator: Invocation Prayer

As you recite this invocation today, you may notice a change in either your own energy or the energy of your immediate environment. Again, be sure to focus your awareness on the process that is happening to you both internally and externally.

What You'll Need:

- A yellow candle
- A blend of dried cinnamon bark and pine to burn as an incense
- A compass

Use the compass to find the east. Face that direction. Light the candle and set it on a table before you. Ignite a self-lighting charcoal and then sprinkle the dried cinnamon bark and pine onto the hot charcoal. Wait for this to smolder.

Assume the inseminator's magical pass, and hold your arms in this position while you say:

By Pan and Prometheus,
By Dionysus and Dianus,
By Loki and Llugh,
And the countless names of power,
By the morning sun, by hoof and horn,
Come ye fertile god,
Thy Holy Rites reborn!

When you are finished with this invocational prayer, sit where you are, close your eyes and sense the inseminator god's presence. Set the candle someplace where it can safely burn completely out.

Day 41

Meeting the God: The Provider

The *provider* is the god's second aspect. The provider represents the god in his maturity, at his zenith of power. In his provider aspect, the god represents self-sufficiency. He is able to care for himself and others. The provider represents action done because action is needed. There is no hidden motive behind the actions of the provider. He does that which needs doing. Societal, communal, or tribal benefit is often the reward of his action. The provider is the active principle, the individual involved in the concerns of building community, and preparing and protecting the space into which the next generation will come. The provider is the vehicle of society. He is the archetype of adult male power: he is focused, attentive to what is needed, active and purposeful. He represents the growth-movement of all life. You can find him in the ripening of the fields and in the consequences of your own actions. The provider in each of us understands the brevity of human life and the value of each action you take in this moment.

The provider represents our drives to complete what has been started, to provide what is needed, and to be self-reliant. He is the part of every man or woman that becomes motivated to accomplish. We can see his energy when someone demonstrates a paternal concern for other people. The provider in each of us notices societal/social limits, guidelines and structure, and understands the benefits of honoring these limits. On the flip side, the provider is also that part of each man or woman that understands the importance of challenging the limits so that new frontiers can open in a way that benefits the whole of society. The provider is the manifestation of the sun's vital energy and an energized, focused mind.

The provider also has a dark side. This shadowy side emerges when we (consciously or not) cling to our own internal provider energies rather than allow a free, natural flow—a variety of energetic expression in our lives. When we hold to this energy, the dark provider can represent our blind ambitions and self-reliance taken to the point of self-serving. The provider in his dark side can represent our anger and impatience. It can be our insistence on social rules, regulations, and norms. In his dark aspect, the provider can be our potential to inflexibly identify with the rules of our society, our jobs, or organizations.

Provider gods throughout the world include: Sol, Cernunnos, Herne, Ra, Zeus, Dyaus, Yahweh, Apollo, Ares, El, Helios, Jupiter, Mars, Neptune, Nereus, Oak King, Nick, Odin, Saturn, Sin, Thor, Thoth, Wotan.

Table of Correspondences: The Provider

Commit to memory the following magical correspondences that evoke the provider's energies.

Solar Phase: Full midday sun

Seasonal Phase: Summer

Color: Red

Pagan Celebration: Summer Solstice

Direction: South

Time: Noon

Incense: Frankincense

Essential Oils: Frankincense, chamomile, benzoin, patchouli

Magical Number: 5

Vocalization: ē (as in heat)

Herbs: Chamomile, hemp

Planet: Mercury/Sun

Body Part: Neck, throat

Chakra: 5th—Throat, at the hollow point/base of throat

Exercise: Knowing Your Provider

Consider your own provider traits. On a single piece of paper, draw a line down the center. On one side write down your personality traits (no matter if you are physically male or female) that reflect positive provider qualities. On the other side of the page, write down any shadowy provider qualities you might recognize in yourself. If you do not note any of the provider's qualities in your life, this is an archetypal energy that requires balancing in order for you to claim your full potential and power.

Just as you might have discovered unfinished business with the archetype of *the mother,* you may have difficulties with the provider if you have lingering issues with adult males or father figures. When exploring the provider archetype, *the father* as a god, question your own feelings about fathers—and your relationships with father figures in your own life. How clear a connection to this energy can you establish if you have psychological roadblocks in your way—either in casting and framing the father as a particularly desirable figure or in rejecting the adult male figure? Also, be sure to examine your relationship, your thoughts and feelings about male divinities. Is Wicca a way for you to escape male divinities?

Day 42

Exercise: Calling on the Provider

Be observant today and take note of the needs of others. Attempt to take actions that benefit other people today. Instead of seeking approval or reward, simply perform actions that benefit other people because action is needed. As you perform actions that benefit others, take note of how you feel. What changes in your mind, body, and spirit do you perceive?

Call your father on the telephone or converse with a father figure. Find out what is important to him and what makes him tick. After this conversation, think about what he said. What from this conversation can you use as a guide today? What from this conversation made you uncomfortable? Why do you suppose you felt discomfort or not? Is there anything in this male power symbol that stirs your emotions in one direction or another? Now think about your family life. What was your relationship to your own father (or other father figure)? Can you draw parallels from your own father to the image of the provider?

Day 43

The Provider: Intonation

Today's working will involve intoning sound that will invoke the energies of the provider.

What You'll Need:

- A red taper candle
- A compass

Set an alarm clock so that you know to begin this exercise at noon today. Use a compass to locate the south and find a comfortable seated position facing this direction. Set the red candle before you and light it. Set your gaze upon the candle flame. Take a deep breath, expanding both lungs and belly. On the exhalation, vocalize the sound "ē" (as in the vowel sound in *heat.*) Sustain the sound until all breath vacates your lungs. Allow the next inhalation to arise from the empty feeling you create in your lungs. Then fill your lungs to capacity and repeat the intonation. Practice the provider's intonation for a total of five breaths. When you complete the fifth intonation, sit in silence for 15 or 20 minutes and allow the essence of this intonation to realign your consciousness.

Day 44

The Provider: Magical Pass

Stand facing the south. Begin with your hands at your sides, palms flat, facing in front of you. Bend the right arm at the elbow and raise the right hand so that the palm faces out and is level with your right cheek. The left hand remains open at the left hip. Close the little finger and ring finger of both hands, which creates the hand gesture of esotericism. This pose has some similarities with the well-known "Baphomet" image of the Knights Templar.[13] As you practice this magical pass, sense what energies it invokes for you.

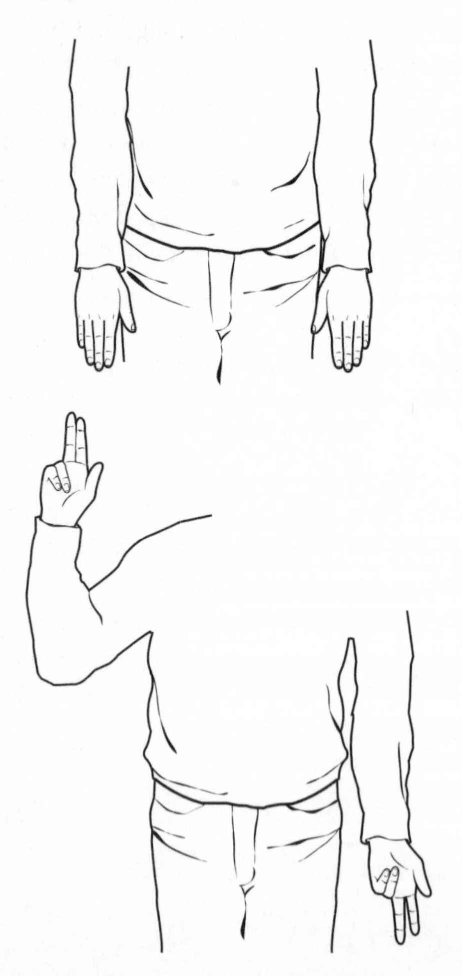

The hand gesture of Esotericism.

Day 45

The Provider: Invocation Prayer

As you recite this invocation, you may notice a change in either your own energy or the energy of your immediate environment. Simply remain aware of your process both internally and externally.

What You'll Need:

- A red candle
- A blend of frankincense and benzoin to burn as incense
- A compass

Use the compass to find the south. Face that direction. Light the candle and set it on a table before you. Ignite a self-lighting charcoal and then sprinkle the frankincense and benzoin onto the hot charcoal.

Practice the provider's magical pass and hold your arms in this position while you say:

By the Oak King and Odin,
By Herne and Helios,
By Thoth and Thor,
And the countless names of power,
By the noonday sun, by hoof and horn,
Come ye father god,
Thy Holy Rites reborn!

When you are finished with this invocational prayer, sit where you are, close your eyes, and sense the provider god's presence. When you are finished, extinguish the candle.

Day 46

Meeting the God: The Sage

The sage is the third of the god's aspects. He represents the human energy that is past its physical zenith. The sage represents the once outwardly directed energy that is now turned inward. In his sage aspect, the god represents our human ability to become self-reflective and to develop wisdom and spiritual power. The god here represents prophetic vision and good counsel given to others. He is the one who presides over the rites and ceremonies that mark the passages of time and the seasons of human life. He is the teller—and the keeper—of secrets. He is the wisdom of the great wheel of the year itself. He knows what actions to take and when to take them. He is reflective and meditative. The sage in each of us is the weaver of stories by the hearth, he is our ability to laugh at a lifetime of mistakes, he is that part of us that sees through the facades of other people.

The god in this aspect represents our ability to turn inward and to learn that the deepest secrets of the magical path have been here, in front of us, all along. The sage does not move to the rhythms of the earthly seasons, but rather to the seasons of spirit and intuition. The sage sets no limits or time frames upon tasks. He understands that life is a journey, not a destination. He is the manifestation of the serenity that comes with deep reflection and the dissolution of all personal requirements and fears.

The sage, too, has a dark side. When we cling to our own internal "sage" energies, he can represent the expansion of consciousness beyond that which has any practical value. The sage here can represent our foolish inability to protect ourselves in the face of actual danger. In his dark aspect, the sage can be our potential to ruminate on our past or to become acerbic or grim.

Some sage gods in mythology include: Thoth, Woden, Dagda, Arawyn, Llugh, Osiris, Pluto, Saturn, Beli, Mandred, Oghma, Balor, Farbanti, Kronos, Minos, Hades, Anubis, Set, Harpocrates.

Table of Correspondences: The Sage

Commit to memory the following magical correspondences that evoke the sage's energies.

Solar Phase: Waning Sun

Seasonal Phase: Winter

Color: Violet or black

Pagan Celebration: Winter Solstice, December 21

Direction: North

Time: Midnight

Incense: White sage (also called desert sag)

Essential Oils: Sage, lotus, pine

Magical Number: 7

Vocalization: Nnnn

Herbs: Holly, mistletoe, pine

Planet: Uranus/Sun

Body Part: Head, brain

Chakra: 7th—crown, at the top of the head

Exercise: Knowing your Sage

Consider your own sage traits. On a single piece of paper, draw a line down the center. On one side write down your personality traits (no matter if you are physically male or female) that reflect positive sage qualities. On the other side of the page, write down any shadowy sage qualities you might recognize in yourself. If you do not note any of the sage's qualities in your life, this is an archetypal energy that requires balancing in order for you to claim your full potential and power.

DAY 47

Exercise: Calling on the Sage

If you talk all the time, you have few opportunities to listen. The sage is about the wisdom that comes from bearing witness to life, to people, to events. His are the arts of "listening much" and "speaking little." The sage represents the ability to observe life without judgment or internal comment. Through this power, one is able to see nature unfold, just as it is—not as one wants, hopes, or dreads.

In honor of living your life according to the sage's principle, allow the silence of the day to fill you. Focus your attention on the environmental sounds that pervade your life: the voices of other people, the sounds of birds, a wind chime, the music from a neighbor's house. Speak only when spoken to, and at the end of the day take note of how this exercise made you feel. Are you more peaceful? Do you feel agitated? Do you feel energized or exhausted? How does your ordinary state of mind appear to you when confronted with stillness? Did this process help you to tap your intuitive wisdom?

DAY 48

The Sage: Intonation

What You'll Need:

- A violet or black candle
- A compass

Set an alarm clock so that you know to begin this exercise at midnight tonight. Find a comfortable sitting position while facing the north. Set the violet candle before you and light it. Set your gaze upon the candle flame. Take a deep breath, filling both the lungs and the belly. As you exhale, vocalize the sound "nnnn." Sustain the sound until all breath vacates your lungs. Allow the inhalation to arise from this emptiness you create from the vacated lungs, and then again fill your lungs to capacity. Repeat the intonation six more times, which will make a total of seven intonations. When you complete the seventh intonation, sit in silence for 15 or 20 minutes and allow the essence of this intonation to realign your consciousness. When finished, extinguish the candle.

Day 49

The Sage: Magical Pass

Begin by facing the north. Stand with your hands at your sides, palms flat, facing in front of you. Bend the arms at the elbows and raise the arms so that your hands can rest, palms open, crossed on your chest. The right hand should be resting on the left breast and the left hand should be resting on the right breast. This is the same Osiris position that you learned for the crone's magical pass. Symbolically speaking, the double use of the Osiris position indicates that in old age, there is a blending of energies that were once quite separate, as well as a blurring of gender lines. As you practice this magical pass today, focus your awareness on thoughts, sensations, feelings, and energies that it may evoke for you.

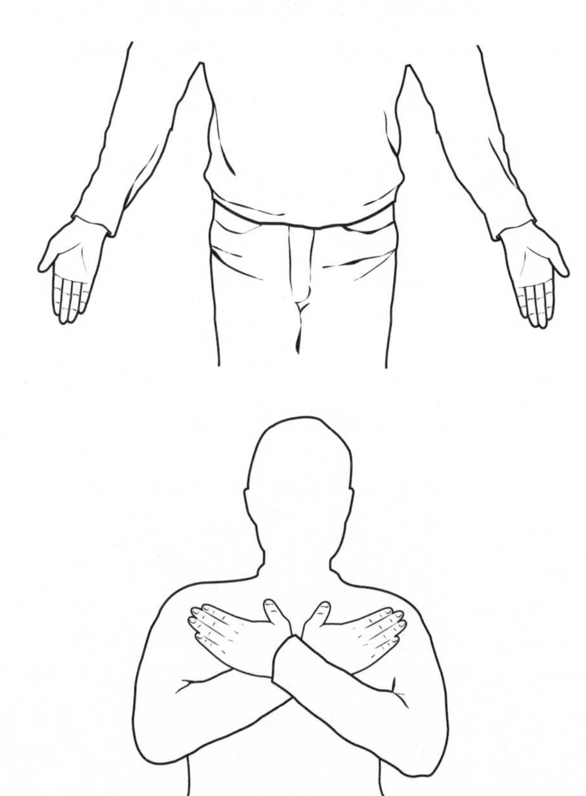

The Sage Magical Pass.

Day 50

The Sage: Invocation Prayer

What You'll Need

- A violet or black candle
- Dried white sage to burn as an incense
- A compass

Use the compass to find the north. Face that direction. Light the candle and set it on a table before you. Ignite a self-lighting charcoal and then sprinkle the white sage on the hot coal.

A Word to the Wise: After you light a self-igniting charcoal, you will first notice that it sputters and sparks for a few minutes. Once this initial activity is over, the coal will continue to heat up. It is usually best to wait for a few more minutes until the coal is at least white on its edges before it is hot enough to burn your incense.

Practice the magical pass of the sage, and hold your arms in this position while you say:

By Arawyn and Anubis,
By Beli and Balor,
By Osiris and Oghma,
And the countless names of power,
By the absence of sun, by hoof and horn,
Come ye Sage god,
Thy Holy Rites reborn!

When you are finished with this invocational prayer, sit where you are, close your eyes, and sense the sage god's presence. When finished, extinguish the candle.

DAY 51

Finding the God and Goddess in Your Life

Because Wicca is a mystical, shamanic path, establishing a direct link to the divine is a key practice. One way that Witches begin building a bridge to the divine is by approaching it through a sense of *wonder*. In other words, they set aside all of their preconceived notions about god or goddess. Certainly, as you have done in past days, you might learn specific correspondences and symbolic representations of various deity forms. But these references are not deity themselves. They are, as one Eastern mystic said, "a finger pointing to the moon" rather than the moon itself. In order to know the gods directly, it is important that you begin by opening your consciousness to include any and all possibilities. This then leads someone to wonder, "What is divine?" Is the sacred dimension something that stands over and above everyday life? Over the next two days you will experience these energies of the god and goddess as manifestations of your everyday life. Let us begin with the god.

Practice: A Day in the Life of the God

What You'll Need:

- Four yellow or gold candles
- An essential oil of one of the following herbs: chamomile, clove, cinnamon, bergamot, or rosemary
- Cornmeal

Despite your physical form, gender or gender-based personality traits, this is a good exercise in which to engage to begin the process of incorporating the divine masculine energy into your life. It doesn't matter if you are the roughest leatherneck around or the laciest frill-seeker—this exercise will hold power and can open you to significant self-understanding.

Allow yourself some time early in the morning to begin this all-day spiritual task. Begin by making a list of personal traits that you feel represent your own god or spiritually masculine characteristics. Your list can include any traits from your physical body (especially if you are male), to your thought processes, activities, actions, and feelings. This list of personal associations with the god energy does not necessarily need to align with the archetypal, symbolic qualities of the god as described in our explorations of this energy. The list should only relate to your own experiences and personal associations with masculine energy.

Once you have your list, mark out a small circle (4-foot diameter) on the floor (or ground) using the cornmeal. Place the four yellow/gold candles at each of the four compass points (north, east, south and west). Find a comfortable sitting position and then anoint yourself with the essential oil at each of your seven chakra (or body-energy) points. For easy reference, here again are the chakra points:

- The point between anus and genitals
- Just above genitals
- Just below the navel
- Center of chest
- Hollow or base of throat
- Center of brow, between eyes
- Top of head

Light the four candles. Now close your eyes and begin to focus on your breathing. As you inhale, focus on expanding the solar plexus region around the navel. Begin to relax your body and imagine that any muscle tension you detect drops away from you so that the earth absorbs it.

Imagine that the solar plexus region of your body begins to radiate a bright, golden light. This is your energetic connection to the god. Allow this radiating light to expand and grow with each inhaled breath. As the golden light grows, imagine that it fills your entire being. Continue to breathe and watch the energy grow until your entire body is flooded with this golden energy. When you have finished, open your eyes. How do you feel?

Take a few moments to stay centered in this energy before you begin your usual daily routine. When you are ready, extinguish the candles. Sweep up the cornmeal, take it outside, and bury it in the ground. Put away all ritual items and go on with your day.

For the rest of the day, pay close attention to the god aspects of your personality, actions, or communication style. Complete all of your usual daily tasks from the center of this golden light that permeates your entire being. Allow the golden light to direct you in your tasks and to inform your decision-making.

If you feel as though you have somehow lost your connection to the god energy during the day, repeat the guided imagery exercise and anoint yourself with your essential oil. Take time at the end of the day to journal about your experiences or to share them with a friend.

A Word to the Wise: When this book refers to the "divine" it is in reference to the one universal power that manifests as god, goddess, me, you, a flower, and anything else you can name. The divine is the invisible energy that supports and manifests as anything that can be named.

Day 52

A Day in the Life of the Goddess

What You'll Need:

- Four silver or white candles
- A mixture of sea salt and poppy seeds
- An essential oil of one of the following herbs: cucumber, rose, hyssop, lily, nutmeg

Today you will learn how to fill your being with the divine energy flow of the goddess. You will also learn how you might integrate this goddess energy into your daily routine. Again, regardless of your physical characteristics, gender, or traits, this spiritual exercise will awaken your internal goddess energies. In my experience over the years of working with a wide variety of magical aspirants, I have noticed a tendency of men in particular (not all men, mind you; this isn't a sweeping generalization) to shy away from regularly tapping into their divine feminine energy, but it is important for practicing Witches to draw power from all aspects of deity.

Again, this is an all-day practice, so set time aside in the morning to begin this process. Begin by making a list of your traits that you feel represent your personal connection to the goddess or spiritually feminine aspects. Again, list any traits from your physical body (especially if you are female), as well as your thought processes, activities, actions, and feelings.

Once you have your list, mark out a 4-foot diameter circle on the floor (or ground), using the mixture of sea salt and poppyseeds. Place the four white/silver candles at each of the four compass points (north, east, south, and west). Find a comfortable sitting position and then anoint yourself with the essential oil at each of your seven chakra points.

Light the four candles. Now close your eyes and begin to focus on your breathing. As you inhale, expand the heart region around the center of the chest. Relax your body and imagine that any muscle tension you detect drops away from you and is absorbed by the earth.

Imagine that your heart region begins to radiate a bright, silvery light. This light represents the goddess' energy within you. Allow this energy to expand and to grow with each inhalation. As the silver light grows, imagine that it fills your entire being. Continue to breathe and watch the energy grow until your entire body is flooded with this silvery goddess energy.

When you have finished, open your eyes. Take time to assess how you feel now that you have attuned yourself with this divine feminine energy. Take a few moments to stay centered in this energy before you begin your usual daily routine. When you sense that you are ready to begin your day, extinguish the candles. Sweep up the sea salt and poppyseed mixture and take it outside; bury it in the ground.

For the rest of the day, pay close attention to the goddess aspects of your personality, actions, or communication style. Complete all of your usual daily tasks from the center of this silvery light that permeates your entire being. Allow the silver light to direct you in your tasks and to inform your decision making. At the end of the day, take time to journal about your experiences, to discuss them with a friend.

A Word to the Wise: Mystical power flows naturally only when an individual opens his or her consciousness fully. Opening in this way is not instantaneous. It takes time, personal motivation, and a lot of introspection to move one's consciousness in a direction that is freer of the influences of classifications, judgments, and mental associations (such as gender, social role, cultural orientation, geographic location, and so on).

Day 53

Seasons of Spirit

Spirit develops much like the changing of the seasons. In the environment we notice that the turn of seasons ushers in changes of growth, warmth, and light. The briskness of autumn follows upon the lazy, leafy days of summer. There is a simple wholesome purity in this seasonal process. And in many ways, this same simplicity applies to our own lives. Wiccans take note of this and see the four seasons of our planet as metaphors for human spiritual development.

Some of the features that share commonality with spiritual development are:

- Both spiritual and seasonal progressions are cyclical. There is no forward movement per se. Both represent perpetual cycles of change.
- Both the changing seasons and spiritual development are a process of unfolding. Seasonal changes come upon us gradually, in tune with the right planetary conditions. Similarly, your spiritual understanding unfolds in a gradual manner, facilitated by certain conditions such as regular spiritual practices.
- The seasons do not strive to change their inherent nature. Winter does not try to be something more or less than cold, rainy, or snowy. It realizes its full potential by being itself fully. Similarly, you express your greatest spiritual power by being what you are completely. Repressing your fullest expression is a dark, unhealthy, and magically destructive path.
- All that ever changes about the seasons is your experience of them. The same holds true of spiritual changes. You can live in reaction to the seasons, loving or hating them, or you can live in harmony with them, learning from their pace, their rhythm, their very presence. Similarly, you can live in reaction to your own true nature by either loving or hating yourself—or you can simply accept what is.

Exercise: Learning Your Season

Today's task involves determining your individual spiritual season. To begin, review the list below that describes the seasons as metaphors for your current spiritual life phase.

- *Spring:* newness, beginnings, birth, potential, seeding, awakening, freshness, individual way
- *Summer:* achievement, fruition, full potential, activity, growth, externalized expression, group way
- *Fall:* ripening, wisdom, maturity, reaping, receiving, realization, gratitude, reflection
- *Winter:* silence, internal expression, inward movement, release, repose

Perhaps you have additional or alternative seasonal associations. If you do, please take time to add those to the words listed above. As you consider your life as it is right now, which season seems to represent your current phase? Which represents your spiritual life? Honor your seasonal phases today by dressing in seasonal colors, eating seasonal foods, or listening to music you associate with your season. It is a good practice to periodically note your current spiritual season, so be sure to try this exercise again—perhaps at the time of the next full moon.

Day 54

Celebrating Life's Seasons

A Witch is keenly focused on the simple experiences of living in the world. Witches follow their heartbeat, their intuition, their dreams, and sensations. They live their lives in this way because they know that experiences of simplicity tune them into the cycles of the natural world. That is where the Witch finds power and spiritual unfoldment.

Because of this, Witches mark the passage of the natural seasons with celebrations, rituals, and magical doings. Aside from the more formal observations of specific ceremonial days, Witches take time to celebrate each day of their lives. The celebrations of everyday life allow the Witch a simple spiritual perspective from which to look back at where she has been and to look ahead at where she is going. All the while, her daily celebrations are about what is happening right now. Witches celebrate their times of happiness and mark their moments of pain and regret. They observe their laughter, their fears, their anger, and their ecstasy. They commemorate the grand parade in which we all participate.

Taking up the practice of noting and celebrating where you are in your life right now is a powerful step on your own spiritual path. Not only is celebrating each day a centering activity, it also helps you to recognize the value of each day. With each sunrise you can find another opportunity to open up to the wonder and magic of your life.

Practice: Celebrating the Moment

Begin this exercise by listing those aspects of your life that deserve or require recognition. If you have nothing that you can list, consider what that might mean. Are you cultivating an authentic, multifaceted life? If you have nothing that you consider worth honoring, consider how you might have arrived at this point in your life, or how this perception might have emerged.

It is easy to get caught up in the grind of our work, the headaches of traffic, managing our social obligations and our families. Before long, we lose touch with the experiences of simply being in the world that can bring us joy. For example, we lose track of the importance of simple pleasures like a cool breeze on a hot day or the laughter of our children. Maybe we've lost track of how to savor a spoonful of ice cream, or the sensuality of a hot bath. The purpose of today's activity is to open your sense of wonder and appreciation about the simple delights of living.

Sometime today, pause to breathe deeply and to appreciate a simple quiet moment. Perhaps you can enjoy the sunset, a beautiful cloud formation, or the purr of a cat. Find some aspect of your daily experience that can become a point of celebration. When you build upon such moments, life begins to take on greater meaning—and ultimately, magical power.

DAY 55

Sabbats: Wheel of the Year

In honor of the changing spiritual seasons of our lives, Witches celebrate eight annual seasonal celebrations that they call *sabbats*. The word "sabbat" is itself the subject of speculation. Some scholars believe that the word may have its origins in the Hebrew *shabbathi*, which refers to the planet Saturn. Other accounts suggest that the word has its origins in the rites of Dionysus, whose celebrants would cry out "*Sabai!*" during the height of ecstatic trance. Some scholars trace the word back to Witch trial testimonies of the sixteenth century. In one French account, an accused Witch stated that her coven would chant, "*Har, har, Hou, Hou, danse ici, danse là, joue ici, joue là. Sabbat, sabbat!*"

Whatever the true origins of the word, the Witches' sabbats mark eight annual passages of earthly and spiritual energy. Together, these eight sabbats comprise the Witch's *wheel of the year*. Each of the celebrations belongs to one of two major categories: they are either one of the *greater* or *lesser* sabbats. The lesser sabbats typically mark the passage of the sun through the heavens in the course of a year. Each of the four seasons begins when the sun enters into one of the cardinal astronomical constellations. These four seasonal celebrations are the solstices and equinoxes. The dates of the solstices and equinoxes vary from year to year because the earth does not orbit around the sun in a perfect circle of 360 degrees. The Winter Solstice begins when the sun enters the sign of Capricorn. Spring Equinox marks when the sun enters Aries. Summer Solstice starts when the sun enters Cancer, and the Fall Equinox is when the sun enters the constellation of Libra.

The remaining four sabbats—Samhain, Imbolc, Beltane, and Lammas—are the greater sabbats. In Wiccan lore, these sabbats are "as old as time itself."

The greater sabbats are on fixed calendar dates, unlike the solstices and Equinoxes. The ancients of Old Europe positioned these celebrations on days that coincided with their agricultural cycles of planting, growth, and harvesting. The greater sabbats are rooted deep within the rhythms of the earth herself. Since the four greater sabbats align with the cycles of the earth, Witches believe that they are feminine in their character and energy. The solstices and equinoxes, marked by the sun's passages, are masculine in their energies.

Here are the eight sabbats in their order, their type and energy. Take time to memorize the sabbat names and dates. In the coming days you will learn more about the meaning of each of these sabbats.

Samhain (pronounced: *SOW-en*), October 31, a greater sabbat, feminine

Winter Solstice, December 19–23 (when the sun enters Capricorn), a lesser sabbat, masculine

Imbolc, February 2, a greater sabbat, feminine

Spring Equinox, March 19–23 (when the sun enters Aries), a lesser sabbat, masculine

Beltane, May 1, a greater sabbat, feminine

Summer Solstice, June 19–23 (when the sun enters Cancer), a lesser sabbat, masculine

Lammas, August 1, a greater sabbat, feminine

Fall Equinox, September 19 –23 (when sun enters Libra), a lesser sabbat, masculine

Day 56

Samhain

Samhain, Hallows, or "Halloween" is an annual festival of death that occurs at the conclusion of the Celtic agricultural cycle. It also marks the Celtic New Year. Samhain is a Gaelic word that means "summer's end." Wisely, the ancient Celts noted that endings and beginnings were united. What is an end? What is a beginning? These were the mysteries that our ancient ancestors acknowledged through the rituals and activities of Samhain.

In Old Europe, Samhain was a time in which the herds were thinned through ritualized slaughter. Only the strong and the hearty survived the harsh Northern European winters, and herdsmen believed that slaughter of the weak and feeble saved animals from the cruelty of the winter frosts. Farmers would be sure to collect their crops before Samhain. Otherwise whatever was left behind was considered untouchable and fit only for night-spirits, fairies, and otherworldly beings that could easily slip through the veils of death into our world at Samhain. Some rural folk believed that whatever remained in the fields after Samhain was cursed. It was an omen of foreboding for whoever ate food harvested after Samhain.

Lighting of hearth fires and bonfires on the highest ground near to the home was another old Samhain practice. In Scotland, the hearth fire was called *Samhnagan*. In James Frazer's *The Golden Bough*, he describes an unusual custom associated with the bonfires. Once the last spark of the ritual bonfire became extinguished, people would run about shouting, "The cropped black sow, seize the hindmost." What seems to be an incomprehensible statement in modern English makes some sense when one understands both the older forms of the language as well as the fact that the sow is the totem animal of Cerridwen, a Celtic crone-goddess who presides over the rites of Samhain. Essentially, the statement was one of warning, telling the folk to run and hide before the crone, the death figure, finds them.

Contemporary pagans believe that the boundary separating the world of the living and that of the "Mighty Dead" is thin at the time of Samhain. Because of this thinning of the veil, tradition holds that communication with deceased loved ones is possible at this time of the year. At Samhain, Witches make offerings and build altars to pay homage to the dead. Part of their rituals include a *dumb supper*, which is a meal prepared for the spirit world. The dumb supper includes setting out a plate filled with the finest foods to feed the spirits of loved ones. The food may appear to go untouched through the meal, but Witches believe that the dead eat the essence of the food. The name of the meal comes from the practice of eating mutely, in ritual silence, during the meal shared with the spirit world.

Witches traditionally associate the feast of Samhain with two specific aspects of deity: the crone (or the hag) and the Lord of Death, who is also the Lord of the Underworld. Each of these aspects of deity signifies the process of human aging, cessation of life and death itself. The crone and the Lord of Death represent the wisdom that comes with age and the mysteries of passage through to the *Summerland*, the Witches' mythic place of rest and regeneration after death.

Practice: Exploring Samhain

- Take out some paper and journal about your past memories of Halloween.
- How does it feel to celebrate death?
- Is death something to celebrate? Why or why not?
- How does death touch your life in this moment?
- How did it feel to think about death today? From where do your reactions about death come?

Day 57

Samhain's Meaning

Why do Witches celebrate death? To folks who are new to the Craft, the celebration may feel morbid, frightening or distasteful. However, it is important to remember that it is a lifetime of conditioning that tells you that death is morbid or frightening. These are learned concepts about death.

So what is the right attitude to take about death? The most powerful position you can take is one void of opinion. This means that you consciously make an effort to hold no associations at all with death. When you clear your mind of everything you have learned about death, it unfolds as a simple, natural process. When you come to this more neutral understanding, death holds no power over you.

Witches do not believe that death is the end of life. The spirit, the immortal part of you, survives death. Wiccan myth says that the spirit journeys to the Summerland, a place of endless bounty and feasting. There, you reunite with loved ones that have already passed over. Witch lore states that your time in the Summerland is one of rejuvenation, so that you can replenish yourself before re-entering the world of physical form.

Witches believe in reincarnation not as a symbol, but as a literal fact. Although the concept of reincarnation may, upon first encounter, appear to be eastern in origin, it is a belief common to many spiritual traditions around the globe. One can find historical evidence for belief in reincarnation throughout Old Europe and later in the classical world of Greece and Rome. For example, Julius Caesar said of the Druids, "They wish to inculcate this as one of their leading tenets, that souls do not become extinct, but pass after death from one body to another . . . ." The Greek Pythagoras also believed in the transmigration of the spirit from one body to another: "The spirit wanders now here, now there and occupies whatever frame it pleases." Contemporary Witches base their beliefs on these ancient western notions of reincarnation. Contemporary Witches have added lore to classical western reincarnation beliefs. In particular, modern Witches believe that the purpose of reincarnation is that of spiritual learning.

If we contemplate the symbolic level of Samhain, we discover that it is directing our attention to the theme of endings. It is about ending one phase of our lives and beginning another. But if we consider this thing we call "endings" rather closely, we can see that it is a concept, an invention. Does anything ever really end? Perhaps, more appropriately, one might say that all things in life have their progression. People, events, conditions of life transform from one moment to the next. In that sense, each moment is an ending and a beginning. Samhain is a time to contemplate these truths and to gain insight into how they affect your life.

- Take time to journal about your thoughts and feelings about death. Sit down with paper and pen and simply free-associate about death for five minutes. Set a timer and do not allow the pen to stop during the five minutes. Just keep on writing, even when you have nothing to write about. Say whatever is coming to you and even if initially you experience writer's block, you'll move through it to reveal your deepest insights and understandings.
- Make a list of every deceased person you have known or that has been part of your life. Examine the list and, if possible, visualize each person whose name appears on it.
- Imagine your own name appearing on the list and then add it in writing.
- Post this list near you and refer to it throughout the day.
- Take note of how it feels to periodically refer to deceased persons throughout your day.

Day 58

Samhain: Ancestor Practice

Witches honor the departed members of their family tree, but in a wider sense, they also honor all creatures as branches and roots of the wider existential tree. These are the Witches' ancestors.

Ancestor practices are some of the very oldest religious observances worldwide as evidenced by ancestral shrines found in Neolithic archeological sites. In primal cultures across the globe, tribal folk called upon their departed ancestors to bring magical aid and teaching from the spirit world.

Witches pay homage to their ancestors as part of their contemporary Samhain practices. One growing custom among contemporary pagans is the building of ancestral shrines on Samhain. Although it may not be Samhain today, our practice will focus on this custom of creating a magical ancestral shrine.

What You'll Need:

- Family photos of deceased relatives
- An altar cloth
- Flowers
- Candles
- Fresh basil
- Dried mandrake root
- Bowl of water
- Dish of salt

To begin this practice, leaf through your old family photo albums. Rummage through that old box of family memorabilia. Look for photographs and items that were once part of your deceased relative's lives. If you cannot find anything suitable, take time to write a memory of each deceased ancestor you can recall. You needn't spend hours on writing, simply put a few memories down on paper.

Next, find a table in the westernmost part of your house and use this as your altar. Lay out a beautiful altar cloth of any color. Spread out on the cloth the photos and other items that were once your ancestor's belongings.

Now you should be creative. Add to the altar fresh flowers, or scatter flower petals. Arrange some fresh basil and dried mandrake, two traditional death herbs. Light tea lights or candles. Hang tiny white Christmas tree lights around. Drape your photos with sheer fabrics. Set out toys or trinkets that are beautiful or symbolic to you in some way. You might also add in foods or items that the ancestor once enjoyed. Light some pleasing incense.

When you have finished decorating your altar, sit in front of it and take time to silently thank the ancestors for being part of your journey in this world. Allow the candles to burn completely out. Since you will use the altar again for tomorrow's spiritual work, try to leave the altar undisturbed. For the remainder of the day, keep thoughts of your ancestors in your mind.

Day 59

Samhain: Ancestor Divination

Witches consider Samhain the perfect time to commune with departed loved ones since the worlds of the living and the "Mighty Dead" are not too far apart. Witches seek the advice or the teachings of their ancestors through divination methods.

A Word to the Wise: You will learn many more divination techniques and their background later in your training. For now, it is important to know that divination is a practice through which you obtain information from spiritual sources. The word *divination* comes from the word *divine*, a literal reference to deity suggesting that the spiritual information one obtains comes from divine sources.

Practice this divination method today and be sure to include this method as part of your Samhain celebration on October 31.

What You'll Need:

- Your ancestor shrine
- Two pieces of paper, one with the word "yes" and the other with the word "no" written on it
- A 5–6 inch black taper candle
- A pendulum

Before you begin, either buy or create a pendulum. A pendulum is a divination tool that consists of a small weight tied to a length of cord. To create your own: cut a 13-inch length of string or thin cord. Tie a ring or similar small, weighted object to one end of the cord. Some objects that people use to make pendulums include crystals, I-Ching coins, stones with holes in them—even plain metal washers will do. If you would like to purchase a pendulum, check the resources section at the back of this book.

Begin this practice by standing in front of your ancestral shrine. Hold your left hand, palm down, over the photos and memorabilia of your departed loved ones. Grip the pendulum's length of string between the thumb and forefinger of your left hand. Hold the pendulum over your ancestral memorabilia. Say, "Which of my departed ones will speak and teach?" Now state the names of each departed ancestor. Be sure to pause at least 60 seconds between the names you recite and watch the pendulum for movement. If it begins to swing, then the loved one you last named is one who will teach and guide you during this exercise.

If you have a photo of the ancestor who wishes to teach, place it before you now. If not, use a pin or a knife to inscribe the name of the person along the length of a black taper candle. Light the candle and set it before you on the ancestral altar. Now take out two pieces of paper. On one paper write the word "yes," on the other write the word "no." Set them before you on the shrine, close your eyes, and then imagine your ancestor's face. As you visualize your ancestor, recite the following incantation, which is based on old European death chants.

Death swims on the water
Summer will soon be here
And do thou, O holy________
[name of ancestor],
Give us a good year.
Speak this night of sabbat
Although the hour is late,
And do thou, O holy________
[name of ancestor],
Tell us fortune's fate.

Ask any specific yes or no question at this time. Once you ask the question aloud, hold the pendulum over the papers that say "yes" and "no." When the pendulum swings over one of the words, this represents your answer. When you have asked each question you have in mind, simply leave the shrine and allow the black candle to burn out completely.

DAYS 60-90

Magical Items to Gather

You will need the following magical items during the next 30 days of training:

Day 61

- A 5–6 inch red taper candle

Day 64

- ¼ ounce dried and powdered acorns or dried white oak bark
- ¼ ounce dried Dittany of Crete
- ¼ ounce cedar (bark chips or powdered bark)
- Powdered sandalwood
- Sage essential oil
- Patchouli essential oil
- Vegetable glycerin
- ⅛ ounce dried mullein leaves
- ⅛ ounce dried wormwood (leaf)

Day 71

- Pencil, pen, markers, crayons, or any other favorite drawing utensil

Day 72

- Two 4 x 4 inch squares of paper
- A red ink pen
- Dried holly (mistletoe, pine, or some other evergreen herb)
- Dried powdered oak (or a perennial herb such as lavender)
- A small burning vessel, such as an iron pot

Day 73

- A 5–6 inch red taper candle
- Small amount of dried pine or pine needles
- Self-igniting charcoal/matches

Day 74

- 2 pints brown ale
- ½ pint dry sherry (or dry white wine)
- 3 ounces sugar
- 3–4 apples
- ½ lemon
- ¼ teaspoon ground cinnamon
- ¼ teaspoon ground ginger
- ¼ teaspoon ground nutmeg

Day 76

- ¼ ounce dried mistletoe
- Gold leaf (a few sheets)
- Vegetable glycerin
- A 6 x 6 inch square of green cloth
- Gold thread
- A sewing needle
- Pine essential oil (optional)

Day 77

- ¼ ounce powdered sandalwood
- ¼ ounce dried pine bark (or dried cedar bark)
- Several crushed, dried pine needles
- Vegetable glycerin
- Pine essential oil
- Rosemary essential oil
- Bay essential oil
- Twelve frankincense "tears" (or pieces of resin)

Day 78

- A piece of blank paper about 4 x 4 inches square
- A pen with red ink (or a quill pen with dragon's blood ink)
- A small piece of cheese, bread, or fruit

Day 80

- A bucket that contains milk and water
- A broom

Day 82

- Five taper candles, one yellow, one red, one blue, one green, and one white
- A pin or sharp-edged knife

Day 83

- A small piece of wool (perhaps from a spool of wool yarn)
- A sack of birdseed
- Flax seed (optional)
- An iron pot, a large cooking pot, or a cauldron large enough to accommodate all five upright candles
- The ash you collected from burning your Yule log

Day 86

- ¼ ounce white sage, cedar, or frankincense resin

Day 90

- 1 ounce powdered sandalwood
- 1 teaspoon dry bay laurel
- 3 teaspoons myrrh powder or resin pieces
- 1 teaspoon dried coltsfoot (leaf or flower)
- Vegetable glycerin
- Myrrh essential oil
- Basil essential oil
- Bay essential oil

Day 60

Samhain: The Bagabi Chant

One important practice during Samhain is chanting the *Bagabi* incantation. Scholars suggest that the Bagabi was written in a long-dead version of the Basque language. There are several versions of the Bagabi incantation that circulate within the Wiccan community and with this distribution, the chant has acquired some changes. The oldest verified version of the text comes from the thirteenth-century troubadour Rutebeuf's manuscript, which is now part of the permanent collection of the Bibliothéque Nationale in Paris.

On Samhain, Witches traditionally chant the Bagabi incantation while walking widdershins, (which means counterclockwise in Wiccan parlance) around the inner perimeter of a magical ritual space that they create. This widdershins movement ritually symbolizes the state of death as a counter-movement to life. In combination, both the widdershins movement and ancient sounds of the Bagabi form a great mandala, a magnificent symbol of the interplay between the principles of life and death.

In today's practice, chant the Bagabi incantation, and simultaneously walk, taking one small step for each word you recite. You will be combining the practice of moonwalking—which you learned in earlier lessons—and chanting. In some covens, a drum is beaten for each step participants take while chanting the Bagabi. If you know someone who might drum for you, you can try this technique out.

As you attempt to chant the Bagabi (and I say attempt, because the words are difficult for everyone to pronounce!) do not focus on the words themselves. Focus your attention on what the chant seems to evoke for you. If you focus on pronunciation, you will miss the point of the practice. Move into the heart of the practice, which is all about evoking the interplay between the opposing energies of endings and beginnings.

Bagabi laca bachabe
Lamac cahi achabe
Karrelyos
Lamac lamec bachalyas
Cabahagy sabalyos
Baryolas
Lagozatha cabyolas
Harrahya!
Palas aron ozinomas
Baske bano tudan dona
Geheamed cla orlay
Berec he pantaras tay.

When you are finished with the chant, sit down and sense any changes of energy within the physical environment, or within yourself. Take time to journal about your experiences or talk about the experience with a friend.

Day 61

Contemplative Day: Learning About Power

Meditative Question: What is power?

Symbolic Color: Red

Symbolic Direction: South

Contemplation

Power is an important issue in Wiccan spiritual exploration. Power, who has it and who does not, is an issue that permeates and charges the stratification of most Western cultures. Eco-feminist and author Starhawk explains that power in our culture assumes three distinct forms. Our power forms include "power over," "power with," and "power from within."[14]

Power over is a model with which Westerners have the most familiarity and it is a structure that is highly removed from the patterns of nature. Power over operates from the premise of domination, force, containment, control, authority, and compliance. In this model, someone (or perhaps a group) in charge determines the rules, the order, and the common good for everyone else. Suppression of one's own experience, voice, and wisdom, as well as obedience to a central authority, are the hallmarks of power over. Many Western religious paths that feature a one-and-only-god, spiritual regulations, and hierarchy for the religious community operate from this authoritarian and patriarchal postulation.

By dismantling stratified power structures, *power with* is a model that turns "top-down" authority on its side. Power with encourages shared, interdependent power and functions similarly to the symbiotic and interdependent systems found in nature. In power with, the strengths of many individuals are braided together, community welfare becomes a focus, and authority becomes a grassroots, localized affair. The heart of Wicca and other mystical spiritual traditions rests securely in this more matriarchal form of power sharing. Power with generally starts from an individual's understanding that he or she is part of a vast, cosmic whole; this is the premise of *power from within*. In considering the three models of power, which ones do you identify as operating in your life, your family, community, friendships, relationships, and work?

Today's mystic contemplation allows you to discover your own links to and understanding of power. Where does power come from? Where does it go? Is power real? After focused contemplation of these matters, you may arrive at your own conclusions.

To begin working with this contemplative question, find a comfortable, meditative sitting position in a quiet space while facing the south. Light a red candle, set it before you, and cast your gaze upon the flickering flame. Meanwhile, hold the meditative question firmly, as though you were gripping it with your abdominal muscles. Relax your shoulders and arms and breathe normally. Sit holding the question for 20 minutes or more.

Instead of trying to logically answer the question at the conclusion of one meditative sitting, work to absorb the question into your spiritual center. Allow your body, mind, and spirit to become this question and take it with you into the world. Eat, sleep, work, and play as the question. Over time, a shift in your perception will take place and you will realize your own answer.

Day 62

Devotional Day: Honoring Cerridwen

Table of Correspondences: Cerridwen

Symbols: The cauldron, the old woman, hearth fire, the moon

Tools: The cauldron, the broom

Magical Essences/Herbs: Sandalwood, sage, henbane, hemp

Direction: Cerridwen is aligned with the north

She Rules: Wisdom, longevity, knowledge, the occult, shape-shifting

Animal Symbols: Sow, greyhound, otter, hawk, hen

Sacred Foods: "Greal," corn

Magical Stones: Moonstone

Cerridwen is a Welsh triple goddess; she represents all three stages of the goddess' powers (maiden, mother, and crone). She is the lady of the cauldron of change and of wisdom. She is the patroness of shape-shifting, Witchery, and all magical knowledge. In Celtic myth, Cerridwen had a cauldron called *Amen*, filled with a brew of six magical herbs, which she called *greal*. As the story goes, she asked her apprentice, Gwion, to stir her cauldron of greal. Cerridwen then stepped away, and Gwion tasted the cauldron's contents. When he did, he was filled with knowledge. When she discovered what Gwion had done, she pursued him in various animal guises.[15] One source suggests this mythic chase sequence links to the ancient initiation rites of Druids.[16]

Wiccans associate the goddess Cerridwen with inspiration itself. Cerridwen is the goddess who rules wisdom and hidden knowledge revealed only through initiation. When you tap into the archetypal energies of Cerridwen, you evoke the ability to change consciousness. Once you assume Cerridwen's consciousness, lore says that you are able to adopt the various powers of the animal world.

Rely on Cerridwen when you've run out of ideas and you need inspiration. Cerridwen serves to remind us that nothing is static; life evolves from one moment to the next. She embodies the insight of Charles Dickens, who said "Change begets change."

Cerridwen Practice

Build an altar in Cerridwen's honor today. When the altar is complete, face it and intone her name one syllable at a time (pronounced: *KER-i-dwen*) until you sense her energies surrounding you. Once she has arrived, spend some time contemplating what it might mean to serve her. Internally ask Cerridwen what it would mean to live life through her energy. Listen for her answer and follow her advice.

Day 63

Day of Silence and Review

Today, as you observe silence, focus your attention on your thoughts. It may take your highly concentrated efforts, but attempt to observe your mental activity without trying to control it. When the day is complete, answer these questions:

- What were the most frequent kinds of thoughts I had today?
- Did my thoughts influence my emotions today?
- Did my thoughts influence my energy?
- Did I have times when mental activity increased or decreased?
- How might maintaining awareness of what I think about be of benefit?
- Have I improved in my ability to remain silent since my first attempt?

Review

For today's practice, take time to ask yourself the following:

- Of the information I have learned up to now, what stands out as most vital?
- What information seems least relevant to my current spiritual development?
- Which of the practices seemed to move me spiritually, and which had little impact?
- Of the information I have learned so far, what would be best to review? (Take time to review it now.)

Day 64

Samhain Incense and Oil

Witches make their own magical incense and essential oil blends that spiritually align with the energies of each sabbat. Witches make these special magical blends to use during their sabbat celebrations in consecration of the participants and as an offering to the Old Ones, the gods of the Craft. Burn the Samhain incense that you'll make today at your Hallows ritual, or at any time that you want to evoke the energies and insights of Samhain.

Samhain Incense

What You'll Need:

- 1 part dried powdered acorns or white oak bark
- 1 part cedar (bark chips or powdered bark)
- 2 parts powdered sandalwood
- 5 drops sage essential oil
- 3 drops patchouli
- ¼ cup vegetable glycerin
- A medium-sized mixing bowl

Mix the dry ingredients together in a bowl. Add vegetable glycerin and mix until it has the consistency of coarse cornmeal. Add the drops of essential oil. Mix thoroughly. Allow the mix to settle and dry for at least three to six hours before burning on hot coals.

Samhain Oil

Again, the magical oil of Samhain evokes the energies and influences of this spiritual tide. When you are finished making the oil, use it to anoint yourself today. Then note any changes you may sense in your consciousness or physical energy levels.

What You'll Need:

- ⅛ cup vegetable glycerin (or grape-seed oil)
- 5 drops sage essential oil
- 5 drops patchouli
- Pinch of dried mullein
- Pinch of dried wormwood (leaf)

Find a one-ounce bottle and fill it *half* way with vegetable glycerin. Add plain water until the bottle is three-quarters full. Add the drops of sage and patchouli essential oils. Now add the dried mullein and wormwood to the bottle. Shake it up before you use it to assure a proper blend.

Day 65

Samhain: Funeral Arrangements

Make time today to discuss your death arrangements (funeral, burial, cremation, etc.) with a spouse, friend, or family member. Then take practical action: complete your will, write your eulogy, and plan the funeral arrangements in practical terms. At the end of the day, reflect on these questions:

- Did you procrastinate on these tasks today? Why? Why not?
- Did you feel these tasks were important or relevant to your life right now? Why? Why not?
- How might engaging in these tasks hold power for you in both practical and spiritual terms?

Day 66

Samhain Meditation

Samhain is a magical energy tide that unites your personal spiritual process, your individual energy system, with the universal. Each of the sabbats offers us opportunities to shift our consciousness from personal concerns to those that are universal, collective and archetypal. They offer us the chance to move from an ordinary to a mythic mindset.

For best results with this guided imagery, have someone else read the text out loud to you while you meditate. Or you might create an audio recording in your own voice that you can play back later.

Reader

Lie down. Cross your arms in the Osiris Position (the crone/sage magical pass). Close your eyes and take several deep breaths. Focus attention on your breath. Follow the trail of your breath down into your chest. Now trail it down even further, into your solar plexus. Feel the life that this breath gives your body. Sense the energies of your body as they manifest in your chest and abdomen. Allow this awareness to spread, feeling the inner body's energy, its vibration downward to your pelvis and upward to your neck and shoulders. Now spread this awareness of energy further to include your arms and legs. Now include your hands and feet. Now feel it in your neck and head.

Hold this awareness of your whole body vibrating with the energies of life. Imagine now that you feel a hand that very gently touches, even caresses your own hands. Visually follow the length of the hand, arm, shoulder, neck, and face of the figure that touches you. Is this figure male or female?

***(Reader:** pause for a moment.)*

What is this figure wearing?

***(Reader:** pause for a moment.)*

This figure is death—your death. Ask this figure to tell you the lesson it holds for you.

***(Reader:** pause for a moment.)*

Now ask how you might best and most powerfully live your life.

***(Reader:** pause for a moment.)*

After you hear the response, ask any other question you might have.

***(Reader:** pause for a moment.)*

Once you receive your answers, it is time to return to the waking world. Bid this death-figure farewell and it will vanish from your vision. Now it is time to return to your physical body. Feel your awareness filling your physical senses and then slowly stretch your arms and legs. Open your eyes.

When you feel that you are fully present, take time to journal about what it was you saw in your magical journey. How did death tell you to conduct your life? Be sure to live as closely as possible to death's advice.

Day 67

Samhain: Graveside Observance

Have you been stuck in the house lately? Well, let's break that cycle of gloomy isolation and do something fun! For example, let's take a field trip to a graveyard in your community. Honestly. Find out the location of your nearest graveyard and go visit it. Bring a stick of incense with you (along with a lighter or matches) or some other small token—such as fruit or a loaf of bread—for an offering. Once you are at the graveyard, take some time to wander through the gravestones. Open all of your senses and take in the whole experience. What bodily sensations do you experience as you walk through the cemetery? Do you sense any tightening or constriction in the body? Where are you constricting? Do you feel emotions stirring of any sort? What are they and to what do you attribute them?

Continue wandering, simply viewing each of the gravestones as you walk. When one seems to draw your attention, sit down in front of it. Place the incense or food offering in front of the stone you have selected and sit silently in front of the grave. Look at the stone and learn the name of the person who lies there. Imagine that it is your own name that will one day be on a similar stone. Contemplate the limited time you have on this planet.

When you are finished, thank the person who is buried in the grave. Now leave the site, never looking back. Take time to journal about whatever insights regarding your life and your death may have arisen during your graveside observance. Now, wasn't that fun?

Day 68

Yule

When the sun enters the sign of Capricorn, anywhere from December 19 to 23, you have also officially entered Winter. Witches call this second celebration in the sabbat calendar alternately *Winter Solstice, Midwinter*, and *Yule.* The word Yule comes from the Norse *Iul*, which means "wheel."

Yule marks the rebirth of the sun—the "great wheel" of the sky. From the time of the Summer Solstice to that of Winter, the days become progressively and visibly shorter in the northern hemisphere. The Winter Solstice is the shortest day of the year in terms of daylight hours. Imagine how feared this time would be for the tribal folk of Old Europe. As the days became shorter, the crops in the fields would die out. The darkness of night with its myriad spirits and goblins would reign supreme during this tide. The rites of our ancient ancestors were often aimed at coaxing the sun, "Return, O return . . . " to bring back light and life into their world.

There are two dominant mythic themes that represent the interplay of the energies of birth and death at Yule. The first is the battle between the Holly and Oak Kings. Holly is an evergreen that can survive the harshness of Winter's chill and it represents the winter-tide. The King of the Holly is the Winter King, the Underworld Lord of the waning year. He represents the death principle. On the flip side is the leafy, deciduous oak tree that comes into its full power during the summer months. The Oak King is the Lord of the waxing year, the time when the daylight hours grow. He represents the life principle.

A Word to the Wise: Ritualized enactments of these mythic themes are called Mystery Plays.

During the Winter Solstice, Witches join together to ritually enact the mythic battle between the opposing forces of holly and oak. The Oak King reigns victorious; the life principle wins over death at Yule and the celebrations and symbols of Yule reaffirm this life principle.

Yule's second mythic theme is that of the child-sun, who is born of the "white lady," the "snow hag" of winter. This myth tells how the sun is reborn at the moment of greatest darkness on the night of Yule. In British traditional covens, the High Priest calls upon the goddess to "bring forth the child of promise" at the exact moment of the night's greatest darkness.

And what would Yuletide be without the appearance of the familiar "Santa Claus" figure? The Jolly Red Elf takes his name from the Christian Saint Nicholas. However the Christian figure has his origins in the pagan past. The name Nicholas itself is not a mistake as it is rooted in the name "Old Nick," a reference to Nik (also Woden), who is an old Scandinavian Holly-King god. The myths of Nik describe him flying on the back of a horse through the night sky instead of being pulled by the familiar reindeer (animals which are, incidentally, another symbol for the pagan horned god.)

The evergreens that we use to decorate our homes at Yule—such as pine, mistletoe, and holly—are pagan symbols of everlasting life. These plants became symbolic of the eternal life principle, since all of these evergreens thrived at the seeming center of death. Mistletoe was reputedly a highly respected magical herb for Druids who collected it only at their high holy days of Midsummer and Midwinter. The Druid priests would use a golden sickle to harvest mistletoe from oak trees, which they regarded as teachers and sacred beings. Ancient reports describe how the Druids would devise elaborate means to assure that they would cut the herb without touching it with their hands. They could allow cut mistletoe to drop onto a white cloth, and an officiating priest would sacrifice a bull or another sacred animal as a token exchange to the tree for its gift of mistletoe.

Contemporary Witches use mistletoe in their Midwinter spells and, of course, they suspend it over a doorway under which they kiss someone to assure a lasting love.

Practice: Yule Questions

- Spend some time today journaling about your winter holiday memories.
- What is it about the winter months that you enjoy? What are your least favorite aspects of winter?
- As you contemplate your past memories about winter, what are the dominant feelings that emerge?
- How did you feel after reading about the historical roots of Yule? Was this information startling or disorienting? Or did you find it settling and comforting? Why?
- Which of the old Yule customs have you (knowingly or not) observed in your lifetime?
- Which of the holiday customs from your memory are the most powerful?
- How might you incorporate or adapt some of your traditional winter holiday customs to your new Yule observances?

Yule: Solar Practice

Find time to sit in the sunlight today and feel its warmth against your skin. If the weather does not permit this activity, start a hearth fire or light up a dozen candles and arrange them in a grouping on a table. Now close your eyes and feel the warmth of the fire, the warmth of the sun. Whether you sit before a fire or outside in the sunlight, imagine that you absorb the sun's warming energy with each inhaled breath. Become one with the heat-energy.

When you have finished this exercise, journal about your experience and any energetic changes you experienced.

Day 69

The Meaning of Yule

Imagine the cosmic event of Yule. Go ahead. Close your eyes and see it all happening. From out of the deepest, darkest night of the year comes a "newborn" sun, full of promise for days of greater light and warmth. It is this event that symbolically reminds us that light comes out of our darkness, the chaos of our lives, the heartbreak and the pain we sometimes endure. Yule is about promise. It teaches us the lesson of the mythic Phoenix that rises out of the ashes of what appears to be complete destruction. The continual rebirth of the sun illustrates for us that destruction is a fantasy. Life and energy go on eternally.

Because the new solar light emerges from darkness, we also see that life may be full of seemingly opposite and complementary components. For example, there may be a hint of sadness in a moment of joy. Or there may be a glimmer of hope in despair. Life is a mix of these things, and nothing can remove itself from the mix entirely. We live in a sphere of duality. There is up and down, light and dark, life and death, etc. The Winter Solstice reminds us that even in our darkest hour, we can find a spark of light. Our task as Witches is to always search for that spark (not only for ourselves, but for other people too) and to help it grow into a blazing sun.

Many of the magical workings you will encounter in the course of the next several days have their roots in the essence of Yule, facing darkness and transforming it into light.

Practice: Darkness Exercise

Go outside at night and fix your gaze upon the vast night sky. Now bring to mind a negative or destructive situation in your life. Feel all of the emotions that this situation stirs up. Take your time with this so that you feel everything intensely. Once you are at the peak of your emotions, begin to exhale deeply. Imagine that with each exhalation, the negativity of the situation you imagined leaves you and dissipates in the vastness of space. Continue with this practice until you are completely drained of negative feelings.

A Word to the Wise: If you cannot go outside, gaze at the night sky though a window. Or you might simply close all of your windows and doors and sit in a room in which you are completely surrounded by darkness.

Once you are drained of the negativity, stop the exhalations. Close your eyes and sense the vast emptiness, the spaciousness you have created inside of you. Now imagine that a glow of light emerges from this empty space within you. The glow becomes brighter and larger until it fills you completely. From this glow comes a word or a phrase that will tell you the bright spot in your negative situation. Listen closely. How might the word you receive change your perspective on this difficult situation in your life?

Use this technique whenever you face darkness or difficulties in your life.

Day 70

Yule: Banishing Winter Shadows

Since the theme of Yule focuses on the return of the sun, light, joy, and life, Witches use this tide to engage in practices aimed at dispelling darkness, in the form of shadows, from their lives. In the Witch's world, *shadows* refer to aspects of your life experience that you have not fully explored or that you might even overtly deny. These denied and fragmented parts of your total life experience take on a powerful, even uncontrollable force. There is no shame in having shadows—we all have them to varying degrees. It is simply a part of being human.

A Word to the Wise: In spiritual terms, darkness is only one of a variety of natural human states. To judge darkness as bad or wrong is akin to judging whether up is better than down, or whether blue is better than red. Judgment of your natural emotional states hinders your spiritual progress and your psychological health. It incites guilt and does not belong at all in Witches' magical practices.

But from where do shadows come? Shadows emerge from every corner of our lives. We unwittingly fashion our own shadows out of taboos, both personal and cultural. They are our unexorcised emotional burdens, our unexamined sadness, fear, anger, and other dark (but purely natural) emotional states. We also make up shadows when we suppress natural feelings that arise from traumatic experiences such as a death in the family, a brush with danger, or a frightening ordeal. These unexamined emotional states fester over time and result in dark and often disturbing behaviors.

Shadows also emerge from our cultural standards or rules that regulate behavior by social agreement on what is acceptable and unacceptable. Cultural standards can create rigid behaviors and strong emotional reactions—especially when you observe someone within your culture abandoning the agreed-upon rules. For example, imagine that in your culture, the word "please" should politely precede a request. If someone does not respect the rule that you have learned (and to which you are accustomed), then you may experience feelings of frustration, offense, or confusion. In reality, this was only a rule that a social group agreed was real. The rules we learn from culture are often those reinforced in our families and they are strong enough to create *illusory* emotional states. In other words, we can experience joy or sorrow simply because of made-up rules, but these rules are so powerful and pervasive that they can dissolve relationships, cause stress, and even push us toward self-destruction.

At the time of Yule, certain Witchcraft practices involve encounters with shadow, penetrating its reality and seeing it for what it is (which is nothing substantive at all). Our magical work over the next several days will introduce you to your shadows so that you can further your own work with these energies.

Practice: Knowing the Rules

- Make a list of at least ten socially enforced rules that you have learned from living in your culture of origin. For example, your culture may tell you that men are supposed to be the main financial supporters to a family. Or it may tell you that it is shameful to have sex outside of marriage. After you have compiled your list of cultural rules, take time to journal about how each one has affected you both positively and negatively.
- Make a similar list of 5–10 rules that you are supposed to follow as a member of your gender. When you have your list, take time to journal about how these rules have affected you.
- Now make a list of rules that you are supposed to follow as a member of your family. Then journal about how these rules have affected you.

Day 71

Yule: Finding Shadow

To begin this exercise, sit quietly for a moment with pen and paper. Jot down your three most negative traits. Okay, most of us have a few more than three—but three will keep you busy enough for a while. Select one of these negative traits for this exercise. Next, find a comfortable position, either sitting in a chair or lying down. Close your eyes and take several deep breaths. Imagine that you can see the word of your chosen negative trait in bold letters, floating before you. The letters soon dissipate and become a misty dark color. The color begins to swirl and form a vortex before you, which sweeps you up and carries you through time and space.

Soon you are through the vortex and find yourself in front of an old wooden door. Open the door and walk into this dimly lit chamber. There on the far wall of the chamber is a mask, glowing with an unearthly light. This is the mask of your shadow. Go to the mask, lift it off the wall, and examine it. Place it against your face and you will notice that it fits perfectly. After you place it on your face, ask how this shadow affects your life. Remember what the mask tells you. Then ask what it is you are doing to keep this mask alive. Listen for the response and remember it.

After you have learned the function of this shadow, take the mask off, place it back on the wall and leave the chamber. When you open the chamber door, you are greeted by the same swirling vortex that transported you here. Step into the vortex and allow it to bring you back to the place where you began this journey. Once you feel that you have arrived back to your body, open your eyes. Take a moment to contemplate what it was you learned in the shadow chamber.

- Use a pencil, pen, markers, crayons, or whatever you choose to draw the shadow mask you saw
- Somewhere on the page, write down the name of this shadow mask
- Write down how the mask affects your life
- Contemplate how you might affect the life of the mask; in other words, what are you doing in your life that might be energizing this mask and allowing it to have power? (note: this is a difficult question to answer; it requires candidness and introspection)
- Keep the mask imagery near you for the remainder of the day

Confronting your shadow masks and knowing their names, examining what it is they do in your life, is often enough to disperse them. Continue to shine the light of your focused awareness on this shadow until it no longer holds power in your life.[17]

Day 72

Yule: The Mortal and the Immortal

During the Winter Solstice, the "birth" of the sun from the darkness of the longest night holds deep archetypal symbolism that can instruct us on the way to live our lives. The solar solstice activity symbolizes the interplay between the polar opposites of life and death, as well as the issues of mortality and immortality. In symbolic terms, the darkness of winter's longest night can represent our human, mortal state. Just like our human body, the dark tide of midwinter eventually passes. What is born at the moment of winter's passing? Daylight. The sun is reborn. The light of day and, specifically, the sun, are symbols that cross-culturally represent the immortal dimension. This is because the sun is a constant source of light in the heavens, which means that, symbolically, it is an importal light.

The popular European myth of the Holly and Oak King battle also represents this interplay between mortal and immortal. As we learned earlier, the Holly King represents the dark half of the year and the cycles of death and return, while the Oak King represents the seasons of light and life. In their mythic battle, the Holly King relinquishes power to the Oak King at the time of the Winter Solstice. In essence, the symbols reaffirms to us that darkness gives way to light at Yule. The mortal yields to the immortal.

Interestingly enough, it is only within the Western mythologies that we can find the two primal forces of life and death, mortal and immortal in a state of *conflict*. This may well be the result of ancient Greek philosophies that portrayed spirit and matter as discrete, separate, and conflicting forms. In contrast, Eastern myths and symbols express an understanding of the natural interplay between the forces of life and death, mortal and immortal, spirit and matter. Life and death, spirit and matter form a single continuum in Taoist philosophy, for example. The familiar yin-yang symbol from Asia also illustrates the two aspects of mortal and immortal in natural union and harmony, with light and dark energies wrapped around, embracing one another. In essence, this symbol portrays polar opposites as being both "two" (that is to say, distinct) and "one" (meaning that they are also indistinct). In the realm of spirit there is no differentiation, all opposites collide and unify. On the everyday, mundane level, differentiation is clear and distinct.

In the spiritual realm, there is neither mortal nor immortal. There is only this constant, unnamable, unformed energy that is always ready to assume a new form. It may become a human being, a plant, an animal, a rock or anything else that is ready to come into existence. In the ordinary physical realm, you come to know the undifferentiated life energy through its many distinct forms.

In today's magical working, you will experience the dual forces of light and dark, mortal and immortal residing with you.

What You'll Need

- Two 4 x 4 inch squares of paper
- A red ink pen
- Dried holly (or pine or other evergreen herb)
- Dried powdered oak (or a perennial herb such as lavender)
- A small burning vessel such as an iron pot

To begin, close your eyes and take several deep breaths. Relax your body completely. Imagine that you stand before two wooden boxes. One box is made of light-colored wood and the other is made of dark wood. Open the dark-wood box and you will find a single word that represents your mortal nature. This word represents the part of you that will pass with time. Remember the word. Now open the light-colored box. Inside you will find a single word that represents your immortal nature. Remember the word.

When you have seen both words, open your eyes. Use your pen to write the words, one on each 4 x 4 inch square of paper. Take a pinch of the powdered oak (or perennial herb) and place it at the center of the paper with your immortal word written upon it. Now fold the paper into a tight bundle. Take a pinch of the evergreen herb and place it at the center of the paper with your mortal word written on it. Fold this paper into a tight bundle. Use a length of string to tie the two bundles together. Light a match and set the two tied bundles on fire, allowing them to burn in the iron pot.

Watch as the two aspects of mortal and immortal become one ash. Keep this magical ash in a small container (or even plastic baggie, if that is easier) for a future ritual working.

Day 73

Yule: Invocation

What You'll Need

- A red taper candle
- Incense made from dried pine wood or pine needles
- Self-igniting charcoal/matches

Begin this invocation practice during nighttime hours. Find a quiet, secluded spot and turn off all of the lights. Light your red taper candle. Light some self-igniting charcoal. Allow the coal to get hot (it will be white around the edges). Then sprinkle the pine (either the wood or shavings) on top and allow this to smolder. Hold your hands, palms open and forward, fingers spread and reaching for the sky. Orient the palms of your hands toward the flame. As you practice this chant, allow your mind to incrementally focus less on the words and begin to open to the feeling behind the chant. When you practice this chant long enough, you can lose yourself in it, becoming one with the sound. This, then, becomes a practice to awaken and to bind your own mortal and immortal natures as one.

> *Queen of the Moon! Queen of the Sun!*
> *Thy nightly labor hath begun.*
> *Queen of the Heavens! Queen of the Night!*
> *Lend thy power, lend thy might!*
> *Queen of the Waters! Queen of the Earth!*
> *Bring to us the Child of rebirth!*
> *It is the Great Mother that giveth birth;*
> *The Golden Sun who is born again.*
> *Darkness and tears are set aside,*
> *And the Lord of Life shall commeth then!*
> *Io! Evohe! Io! Evohe! Io! Evohe!*[18]

After chanting, extinguish the candle and the incense. Put all ritual items away. Take time to sit and sense what changes this invocation may have brought about.

DAY 74

Yule: Wassail

Making wassail is a favorite Yuletide pagan custom. This traditionally spiced ale (or mulled wine) filled with magical solar herbs has its origins in Saxon history. The word "wassail" was a salutation for the ancient Saxons. It literally meant "be in good health." By the twelfth century, the Danes had introduced the term to the Britons as a drinking toast. As time went by, Britons used the word in reference to the drink in which the toast was offered. The magical spices and herbs that infuse the wassail invoke the energies of the sun in anyone who drinks it.

Christmas Eve and Twelfth Night (another winter holiday) became the traditional times that celebrants would drink wassail. One twelfth-night tradition involved invoking the gods to bless the apple trees that would bear the crop from which next year's cider would be made. Ancient celebrants would invoke the solar deities by soaking small pieces of bread in cider and placing them around the apple trees. They would then sing special wassailing songs that would encourage the tree to bear fruit.

What You'll Need

- 2 pints brown ale
- ½ pint dry sherry (or dry white wine)
- 3 ounces sugar
- 3–4 apples
- ½ lemon
- ¼ teaspoon ground cinnamon
- ¼ teaspoon ground ginger
- ¼ teaspoon ground nutmeg

Preheat your oven to 350° F (180° C). Wash, peel, and core the apples. Place the apples, sugar, and 4 tablespoons of the brown ale into a glass baking dish or heat-resistant bowl and bake this together for 25–30 minutes, or until the apples are tender. Peel the lemon rind, removing only the bright outer layer. Remove the apples and their collected juices from the oven and set aside. On top of the stove, set out a large pot, and add to it the remaining ale, sherry or wine, lemon peel, cinnamon, ginger and nutmeg. Mix this together and simmer gently over a low flame for 10–15 minutes. Add the apples and juices and serve immediately.

◐ **A Word to the Wise:** If you are planning your own Yule gathering and intend to serve wassail, it is always a considerate gesture to offer guests a non-enabling beverage.

Non-alcoholic Wassail

What You'll Need:

- 1 gallon apple cider
- ½ gallon orange juice
- 1 pint cranberry juice
- 4 cinnamon sticks
- 24 allspice berries
- 36 cloves
- 1 large orange
- 1 cup brown sugar

Press cloves into the orange. Combine all ingredients in a pot and boil it over high heat for 5–7 minutes. Reduce the heat and simmer for 45 minutes to 1 hour.

Day 75

Yule Log

Burning huge communal bonfires was another ancient Yule custom. Pagan folk would first select trees that they considered to be sacred. Each household would cut down a sacred tree and add it to the communal fire. Some of the trees sacred to the ancient Europeans included birch, oak, holly, pine, and willow. Pagan folk believed that while the wood burned, it imparted some special or magical influence.

The hearth fire replaced the customary outdoor bonfire over the course of time. Because of this change, pagan folks typically burned only a section of the tree—a Yule log—instead of the entire tree. New magical traditions arose with this change. For example, pagan folk would first select a tree for logging on the land of the home where it would be burned. Like other magical tools, the Yule log was not a thing to purchase. It could, perhaps, be a gift.

Families would cut Yule logs from the thickest parts of the tree. Sometimes huge roots or giant stumps found their way to the hearth. After cutting the log, the householder would then ceremonially drag it across his or her land for luck. Once the log made its way to the hearth, family members and neighbors might then decorate it with sprigs of holly, pine needles, and berries. The master of the house would sprinkle the log with oil, salt, and cider or wassail. A young girl would then ceremonially kindle the log, and attendants would keep it burning over the course of twelve nights. In other accounts, the log was supposed to last for twelve hours; it was considered an evil omen if the log extinguished before the end of twelve hours.[19]

A family would then, customarily, preserve a piece of the log from the fire. This piece of wood served as kindling for the next year's Yule log. In the rural parts of Europe, a farmer might attach the piece of unburned Yule log to his plow to assure a bountiful harvest. The early Europeans also believed that they could bless their crops by mixing the ash from the incinerated Yule log into the soil just before seeding. Pagan folk might also keep the ash in their homes as protection from lightning, malevolent forces, or from evil spirits.

For today's practice, select one of the magical woods listed below, based on its magical influence:

Magical Wood / Magical Influence

Aspen: Invokes universal understanding and compassion

Birch: New beginnings, a fresh start, new ideas, new projects

Holly : Inspires visions and reveals past lives

Oak: Evokes the power of the sun and brings healing, strength, and wisdom

Pine: Invokes the energies of prosperity and growth

Willow: Invokes the triple goddess' aid, psychic power

You won't need an entire log for this activity. You can use a branch or even a twig. Sprinkle the wood with salt and rub it vigorously with olive oil. Cut off one end of the branch and save it as kindling for your Yule log this winter. Burn the rest of the log in order to release the wood's magical virtues. When you are finished, place the ash in a small bundle that you make from a red square of cloth. Tie the bundle with green thread and hang it near the hearth to keep away unwanted forces. Be sure to save this ash, as you will use it in future ritual work.

Day 76

Yule: Mistletoe Charm

In the ancient Celtic world, mistletoe was an herb that represented immortality. It was a panacea for the Druids who would grind the herb and infuse it into elixirs and curative potions. It is little wonder the Druids died out, as mistletoe is a highly poisonous herb! Today, you will make a charm for long life using dried mistletoe.

What You'll Need:

- ¼ ounce dried mistletoe
- Gold leaf
- Vegetable glycerin
- A 6 x 6 inch square of green cloth
- Gold thread
- A sewing needle (or if you lack sewing ability, use a fabric pen)
- Pine essential oil (optional)

In a shallow mixing bowl, stir together the mistletoe and three tablespoons of the vegetable glycerin. Add the glycerin, one tablespoon at a time, since you will use only enough to coat all of the mistletoe. Now add a few leaves of the gold leaf. Use a fork or a whisk to blend the gold and the mistletoe. The glycerin should act as a binding agent and cause the gold leaf to distribute evenly and to coat the mistletoe. Set this aside.

Use the needle and gold thread to stitch the magical symbol of the sun (⨀) onto one side of the green cloth. If you are unfamiliar with sewing and don't want to learn now, then try using a fabric pen to make the markings on the cloth. Make the symbol by stitching (or drawing) a perfect 2-inch circle. Inside of this circle, at the center point, make a smaller ¼-inch circle. Use your needle and thread (or again, use your fabric pen) to stitch words that represent the everlasting qualities you might desire in your life. For example, you might stitch simple words such as *love*, or *joy*, or *wealth*.

Lay the cloth flat so that the words and the sigil are face down, toward your work surface. Place your gold-leafed mistletoe into the center of the cloth. Fold the cloth in half and stitch around the outside to seal in the golden mistletoe. Set the bundle in a place of prominence so that you can see it often.

Anoint this magical charm with pine oil at the center of the sun symbol at least once a month for a strengthened effect.

A Word to the Wise: Please exercise caution when handling mistletoe. During and after handling, do not touch your face, nose, eyes, or mouth. If you accidentally ingest mistletoe, immediately contact your local poison control.

Tradition says that you can additionally use this charm to increase the fidelity of a lover or the longevity of a relationship. To do this, hold the bag of mistletoe at the level of your chest (your heart chakra). Bring your lover or spouse close so that you hold the bag between both of your chests. Now kiss to seal the magic.

Day 77

Yule: Incense and Oil

Burn this Yule Incense at your Yule ritual, or at any time that you want to bring about the energies and insights of the Yule season.

What You'll Need:

- A handful of powdered sandalwood
- Dried pine wood or bark (or dried cedar wood chips)
- Crushed, dried pine needles
- Vegetable glycerin
- 3 drops pine essential oil
- 4 drops rosemary essential oil
- 2 drops bay essential oil
- Twelve small frankincense chunks

In a medium-sized bowl, place your powdered sandalwood. Stir in about two tablespoons of vegetable glycerin. Add the tablespoons one at a time, and then mix with a metal whisk or a fork. You simply want to create a soft, fluffy, compound. Do not add in the second tablespoon of glycerin, if it feels like it would be too much, causing the incense to be too wet.

Now add in the essential oils and whisk. Add the frankincense pieces and stir them in. Finally add the other dry ingredients. Wait for at least a day for the compound to settle before you sprinkle it on hot coals.

A Word to the Wise: Witches traditionally call the small bead-like pieces of resinous incenses (such as frankincense) "tears."

Yule Oil

Use this oil to anoint attendees of your Yule ritual. You can also use this oil any time that you want to awaken the insights and mysteries of the Yule season. This oil awakens the magical energies of immortality, long life, and knowledge of what lies beyond death.

What You'll Need:

- Vegetable glycerin (or a carrier oil such as grape seed oil)
- 6 drops pine essential oil
- 8 drops rosemary essential oil
- 2 drops bay essential oil
- Twelve frankincense tears

Find a one-ounce bottle. Fill the bottle *half* way with vegetable glycerin. Add plain water until the bottle is three-quarters full. Add your essential oils and your frankincense tears. Close the lid and shake the bottle. After you have created this oil, anoint yourself with it and see what changes it evokes for you.

Day 78

Imbolc

Imbolc is the second of the Greater Sabbats in the Witches' Wheel of the Year. Imbolc is an Irish Gaelic word which is pronounced *im'-molk*. Other variations of this festival's name include the Gaelic *Imbolg* and the English *Candlemas*. Imbolc celebrates the official end of the "dead time," the period from October 31 to February 2 during which Witches perform very little magic and no initiatory rites. This dead time coincided with the "death" of the sun, the light of day, and subsequently all perennial plant life. Pagan folk could see that daylight hours were visibly longer at Imbolc and country folk and Witches alike celebrated this turn of events as one of awakening for the earth's energies.

Along with this extended daylight came the promise of spring and the renewal of life. Imbolc is a celebration of the first stirrings of the earth. In northern and western Europe, the ground is often still frozen or snow covered in early February. The return of light, the lengthening days signaled promise of the long growing season of the still-distant Summer.

The ancient Celts favored Brigid, the triple goddess of wells and springs, as the patroness of Imbolc. Devotees of Brigid believed she could bring fertility, and they lit candles in her honor to mark the growth of light and the coming change of season. So popular was Brigid's worship that she is still the patron deity of contemporary Druidic circles.

Ancient celebrants made "Saint" Brigid's Crosses from new rushes and hung them near the pens of farm animals to assure their growth and fertility. After the celebrants wove their crosses, they would carefully bury whatever rushes remained. Ancient celebrants might also make dollies from oat sheaves or corn-husks. One old custom consisted of dressing the oat or corn dolly in woman's attire and then placing it in a "Brigid's Bed" (usually a simple basket) along with a phallic symbol. Pagan folk believed that the custom assured a fruitful and prosperous year.

At the time of Imbolc (which literally means "in milk") the ancient pagan folk noticed that female herd animals usually gave birth and suckled their young. This "lactation" period signaled the rebirth of the earth energies and the promise of spring and summer. The suckling of young, birth, and fecundity of the animal world gave rise to several pagan customs. One practice involved pouring the first pail of cow's milk on the ground to assure a prosperous spring. It was also a day set aside for the blessing of plows and other agricultural tools. In one custom, farmers would wash their spades and other tools in fresh cow's milk, again to assure bounty. In areas where the weather permitted, the plough might be dragged from one home to another. Yet another account tells of farmers pouring whiskey over their ploughs to assure blessings and a bountiful harvest.

The English language borrowed and shortened the word "whiskey" from the Irish Gaelic word *usquebaugh,* or *uisce beatha* and Scottish Gaelic *uisge beatha.* This compound descends from Old Irish *uisce,* "water," and *bethad,* "of life," meaning literally "water of life." Ancient pagan folks poured whiskey over their ploughs in order to give life to the land.

Celebrants also made small food offerings to the fairy folk, who they believed blessed the fields with their magic and assured a good crop. Farmers might make the offerings to fairies by placing cheese or bread on a plough and then leaving it unattended in the fields.

Although customs varied from one region to another, the celebration was important for the ancient agrarian societies since it symbolically prepared the way for the earth's fecundity.

Practice: Fairy Offerings

What You'll Need:

- A piece of blank paper about 4 x 4 inches square
- A pen with red ink (or a quill pen with dragon's blood ink)
- A small piece of cheese, bread, or fruit

To begin, use your red ink pen to write a wish you might have on the blank piece of paper. The lore of fairies indicates that they grant wishes for healing, fertility, or general blessing. Go outdoors at dusk and place the paper with your wish written upon it on the ground near a fern or a flowering plant, both of which are favorite places for fairies. If there are no flowering plants or ferns nearby, place the paper in some place hidden, such as in a shadow where it will go unnoticed by humans. Place your food offering on top of the paper, then turn and walk away, making sure not to look back at the site. Return to the offering site in a few days to reclaim the wish paper. Once you have it, burn it and scatter the ashes near your front door. If the paper is missing, know that the fairies have taken it. Word has it that the fairies work cheaply, so know that the fairies have noted your wish and they will grant it in return for your food offering.

A Word to the Wise: The English word "fairy" traces its roots to the Old French *fae,* and from Vulgar Latin *Fata,* the name of the goddess of fate.)

Day 79

The Meaning of Imbolc

When thinking about Imbolc and learning to decipher its inner meaning for our contemporary lives, it is important for us to first consider the sabbat name itself. As you learned yesterday, the word Imbolc literally means "in milk." One of the primary mythic themes of the great wheel of the year is that of succor; it is the celebration of consuming nourishment from the goddess' body. Since the dawn of time, one of the primary images of the goddess is that of "she-who-nourishes." Mythologist Joseph Campbell writes that the ancient goddess myths and rituals can inform us how we might come into perfect union with the female principle and her unique, spiritual form of nourishment. Regarding this, Campbell states:

"[The] woman with her baby is the basic image of mythology. The first experience of anybody is the mother's body. And what Le Debleu called participation mystique, mystic participation between the mother and child and the child and the mother, is the final happy land."[20]

Milk holds tremendous symbolic value as a basic nourishment. We first experience milk as children, whether we are bottle or breast-fed. Both literally and symbolically, we are children of the goddess, children of the earth. We rely on this great mother to sustain our lives, just as the infant relies upon the mother to nourish with milk. It is important at this time of year to honor the earth and acknowledge our direct reliance upon her.

Imbolc is also an important time for you to get in touch with whatever nourishes your soul. Have you left your interest in art or music behind so that you can focus seriously on your real work, your career, monetary gain, or daily routine? What nourishing interests have you abandoned—no matter what they are—simply because you cannot seem to find the time for them?

The goddess bids you to awaken to your *whole* self. Feed yourself with the nourishment of enjoyment, the sustenance of life. You are not complete when you repress your talents, your interests, your sense of fun and curiosity. Imbolc is a time to return to simple pleasures, good food, good sex, good friendships, and whatever nurtures your tender soul. These are what quicken the flame of Candlemas, and what stir the seeds of full potential within you.

The earth first awakens at Imbolc, according to Wiccan lore. Likewise, the festival should be about your own awakening. But to what must you awaken? Awakening always consists of becoming present to life as it unfolds before you. Life is not something that is *happening* to you. It is something that you *are*. Don't hold back at Imbolc. Join in. Become one with life that is happening right now. Use all of the ingredients of your life. Once you connect wholly with life, you find that even without trying, the goddess' nourishment is there in abundance.

Imbolc Practice: My Favorite Things

What's been missing from your life? It is easy to lose track of what is important to us when we shift our attention to family, children, work, and responsibilities. These are important, but since you don't get a second chance at this lifetime, you might consider making room in your life for the things that bring personal enjoyment—things that nourish your soul. What are your favorite foods, hobbies, types of friends, clothing, etc.? Make a comprehensive list of these items and attributes. Once the list is complete, review it to see how many of the listed items are part of your life right now. Check off the words that currently apply to your life and spend the day actualizing parts of the list. Go to a dance class. Write a poem or a story and read it to a friend. Try out a new recipe; or better yet, enroll in chef school. Start learning a new language, paint, sculpt, or create an origami figure. Bring back the "Funky Chicken"; just do something that awakens your innate sense of joy and enthusiasm.

Day 80

Imbolc: Blessing the Earth

Imbolc is a time for preparing the earth for plowing, seeding, and growth. Naturally, blessing the earth, the source of all sustenance, is one of the Witches' favorite activities of this seasonal tide. Today, you will practice blessing the earth, preparing it to become verdant. In the process of this rite, you bless your own life.

What You'll Need:

- A bucket that contains milk and water
- A broom

I have based this magical working on an old Witches' custom for changing the weather. To begin, fill a bucket halfway with warm water. To this add some milk. Add just enough milk so that the water becomes white and opaque. Go someplace outdoors (the best place would be on some land adjacent to your home). Set the bucket at your side and dip the broom bristles in the milk-water.

A Word to the Wise: This isn't the most discrete ritual to perform out of doors—if you're the bashful type, try this subtler alternative version of the rite:

Gather a bundle of twigs from a local tree to represent the broom. Be sure to gather living twigs, rather then ones that have fallen dead to the ground. Fill a cup or small glass with the milk/water mixture. Take the twigs and milk outside and perform the rite internally—meaning, read the words from the ritual silently, but follow through with the ritual actions.

Face the east and shake the broom over your head toward the east, flinging the milk-water in that direction. As you do this, say:

To the East: Renewal!

Dip the broom bristles again and then fling the milk-water overhead, toward the south, saying:

To the South: Warmth and heat!

Dip the broom bristles again and then fling the milk-water overhead, toward the west, saying:

To the West: Succulence!

Dip the broom bristles again and then fling the milk-water overhead, toward the north, saying:

To the North: Growth! Abundance! Fertility!

As you say the last word, spill the entire bucket and its contents onto the ground. The rite is finished.

Did you change the weather? Or did you change your consciousness?

Day 81

Imbolc Meditation: Seeds of Potential

When one considers early agrarian life in Old Europe, it becomes an easy matter to understand how the cyclical patterns of the plant world took on an important mystical focus for our ancestors. The changing seasons and their effect on the growth of food crops became a powerful metaphor for the ancients. The passage of the seasons, which affected the birth, growth, and propagation of crops, also represented the basic pattern for a human life.

Seeds usually scatter after a plant dies, but seeds are points of potential. They are unformed life. Rituals that involve the planting of seeds at Imbolc represent setting potential into motion. The seed rituals of Imbolc symbolize the principle that death is really an illusion; life always continues, sometimes in a hidden or an unseen form.

In today's mystical working, you will identify your own inner (possibly hidden) seeds of potential.

Meditation

General directions for guided imagery meditations are included in the text for Day 13 (page 18).

Reader:

Find a comfortable sitting or lying position and close your eyes. After several deep, slow breaths, imagine that you stand before a great stretch of freshly ploughed farm land. The soil is rich and dark. Reach down and feel the cool, sticky, dampness of the soil. Inhale the dark, earthy scent. Now cast your gaze into the center of the field. There you will notice a golden glow that you had not noticed before. Walk through the field to the golden glow.

(Reader: pause for a moment.)

When you reach the glow, you notice that it is a golden sack, lying on the soil. It is a seed sack. These are the seeds of your greatest potential. Pick up the sack and you will find a word written on it that represents your potential. Imagine now that you plant these seeds all over the field. As you plant each seed, the earth takes on a golden glow.

(Reader: pause for a moment.)

When you are finished, slowly return to the place where your body rests comfortably. Open your eyes and take time to contemplate your visions. Write down the word that represents your potential. You will use this in tomorrow's exercise.

DAY 82

Imbolc: Sacred Inscriptions

What You'll Need:

- Five taper candles (any length, but short ones are best): one yellow, one red, one blue, one green, and one white
- A pin or sharp-edged knife

Take a look at the word (or words) that you saw in yesterday's guided imagery meditation. Deeply consider this word which represents your potential. While you contemplate the word, use a sharp knife or a pin to engrave this word onto the white candle. Next, you will develop a list of four other words that represent the four elemental energies surrounding this potential. You will learn more about the four elements later on in the year, but for now:

- Write one word that represents the state of mind you would need to realize your potential. Engrave this word onto the yellow candle.
- Write a word that represents action you would take to realize this potential. Engrave this word onto the red candle.
- Write a word that represents the feeling underlying your potential. Engrave this word onto the blue candle.
- Write one word that represents a type of behavior you might omit in order to achieve your potential. (For example, if you wanted to make more money, you might omit overspending.) Engrave this on the green candle.

Set aside these inscribed candles for tomorrow's ritual working.

Day 83

Imbolc: Seeds Ritual

What You'll Need:

- The five candles you inscribed yesterday
- A sack of birdseed
- A small piece of wool (perhaps from a spool of wool yarn)
- Flax seed (optional)
- An iron pot, a large cooking pot, ora cauldron large enough to accommodate all five upright candles
- The ash you collected from burning your Yule log

To begin, fill your iron pot, cooking pot, or cauldron with birdseed. Fill the pot just enough so that your candles will stand upright when you wedge them in. Try this out before you begin the rite. Once the pot is filled with birdseed, sprinkle in some of the ash from your Yule log. Be sure to retain some of this ash for another ritual. Add in a small amount of milk and water. Now add in your piece of wool (and if you have it, flax seed), saying this old English incantation:

Iron, water, wool and blood
Ash, milk, and flax-thread,
Here, the countless masks made bare,
And seed is but bird's bread!

Place all five candles in your right hand and use them to stir the pot of seed and ash, using the candles. Stir the pot three times clockwise.

Then light the yellow candle, saying:

In thought I change with the birth of light.

Place it in the birdseed along the easternmost edge of the pot. Light the red candle, saying:

In action I change with the birth of light.

Place it in the birdseed along the southernmost edge of the pot. Light the blue candle, saying:

In feeling I change with the birth of light.

Place it in the birdseed along the westernmost edge of the pot. Light the green candle, saying:

In silence I change with the birth of light.

Place it in the birdseed along the northernmost edge of the pot. Light the while candle, saying:

My soul will change with the birth of light!

Place the white candle in the center of the pot. Stay with the candles and allow them to burn almost completely out. Be sure to exercise caution during this operation. Blow out the candles if they threaten to ignite the birdseed. After blowing out the candles, wait a few moments for the melted candle wax to solidify and then take it out of the pot. Scatter the seeds in an open area so that the birds can eat them and thus carry your spell to the four quarters of the globe.

Day 84

Imbolc: Preparing Sacred Space

The theme of Imbolc is preparing the way for fertility. One of these preparations is the creation of sacred space. In magical terms, all space is really sacred space, but there are specific spaces—for example, a ritual room, a temple, or a church—that are set aside for religious activity. Communities generally refer to these as sacred spaces. Because Wicca is a path that does not separate the religious from the secular life, it extends the definition of sacred space to include one's home, office, or any space that one might want to set aside with spiritual blessings and protections.

Because of the natural symbolic connection between the goddess and the archetype of home, a Witch's primary sacred space is the home. It is therefore important to foster this sacred sense in our homes. The first step in this process is always evaluation of your existing household environment. Remembering that in sympathetic magic we believe "As above, so below," it is a simple matter to note that the home environment represents an intersection between our inner and outer realities. This means that how we decorate our rooms, our choice of color, fabric, texture, object placement—each of these aspects of our homes is a representation of our internal state of affairs.

Take time today to ask yourself these questions:

- Is my home a mess?
- Is it militarily spotless?
- Is it cluttered or dark?
- Is it sterile?
- Is it warm?
- Is it adult or childlike?
- Is it somewhere "in between?"
- What is your home saying about *your* internal world?

Take time to contemplate what your home environment might be communicating. This is a difficult task to undertake. It requires a certain amount of detachment and objectivity. Like most of us, your home interior may never make the cover of *House Beautiful*, but it should reflect a modicum of attentiveness, cleanliness, and orderliness. A tidy, well-managed household is also one that allows for a natural flow of energy. When your home's energy flows, it is balanced, serene, and free of clutter. Health and abundance are sure to emanate from such an environment. In the coming days, you will learn a few basic principles that can help make your home energetic, magical, and sacred.

Day 85

Imbolc: Straightening Up

Find some part of your home that has become a mess. Maybe you are like me and you scrape the contents of your desk into drawers until they are overflowing. Perhaps you have a closet that has taken on a life of its own. How is the garage or storage space? What is going on in your checkbook? Dare you peek in the attic or cellar? Before you do anything about the mess you find, take time to contemplate it. Sit in front of the clutter and ask yourself how this happened. What part did you play in allowing clutter to take over? Was there fear? Anger? Was there sadness underneath it all? Take time to fully examine your feelings. Now take time to explore how you might feel right now facing the prospect of clearing away the clutter. You might take time to commit your feelings and thoughts to paper. That process in itself clears away some mental clutter.

Now go through the physical mess. Clear away things that have no use to you any more. Why are you still holding onto these things? Find at least three things in this clutter that have some value, but that you do not use regularly. These are things that you should give away. After you have straightened out the mess, take time to stand back and admire your work. What effect did clearing away the clutter have on your mind and spirit? Almost everyone can notice a difference in energy before and after cleaning a space. Explore your experience now.

Day 86

Imbolc: Clearing Harmful Energies

Before you can bless your home and renew its energies, it is a good spiritual practice to clear out any harmful or destructive energy forms. Energy moves naturally in waves and patterns, and often we block the free flow of energy in enclosed spaces with clutter, closed doors, a lack of ventilation, obstructed light, and we evoke a generally chaotic feel by haphazard placement of our belongings. When we block the free flow of energy in a home, it becomes stagnant and unhealthy. The energy can take on a life of its own and wreak havoc with health, finances, relationships, and more.

Fortunately, Wiccans have many methods for clearing these blocked energies. These methods range from ritual spellwork and other specialized magical methods (which you will learn later on in the year) to simple but highly effective techniques that do not require any specialized knowledge or abilities. Over the next several days, you will have the opportunity to try out many of these simple, easy, and effective methods.

The first method calls for clearing your space with representations of each of the four basic elements that compose all of life: air, fire, water, and earth. Today you will begin with clearing your home with the element of air. Lighting certain types of incense is the simplest method to cleanse a space with air. Some air-cleansing incenses include:

- *Important:* White sage, cedar, frankincense.
- *Always Useful:* Dragon's blood resin, white copal.
- *In a Pinch:* Prepared incenses such as Nag Champa or just plain sandalwood.

How to Cleanse with Incense

Light some incense and stand at the front door of your house. Move clockwise through the building, going from one room to the next, always in a clockwise manner. As you walk through your building, imagine that the sacred smoke is clearing away all stagnant energies. When you return to the front door, extinguish the incense. Stand there with your eyes closed and breathe deeply. With each exhalation, imagine that you emit a bright yellow light that fills the entire house. Once you have completed this visualization, open your eyes.

How does the house feel to you after cleansing by the element of air?

Other Air Cleansing Techniques

- Turn on an air purifier regularly
- Use an ozone generator to neutralize toxic gases and odors
- Open all of the windows of your home regularly, for at least one hour at a time

Day 87

Imbolc: Clearing Space with Fire

Today you learn how to clear your home with the element of fire. Fire techniques bring a decidedly active quality to purifying the energies of your home. Fire is a direct and immediate element that clears a sacred space rapidly.

How to Cleanse with Fire

Light a red or white candle and stand at the front door of your house. Move clockwise through the building, going from one room to the next. As you walk through your building, imagine that the energy of the candle flame is clearing away all stagnant forces within each room. When you return to the front door, extinguish the candle. Stand there with your eyes closed and breathe deeply. With each exhalation, imagine that you emit a bright red light that fills the entire house. Once you have completed this visualization, open your eyes.

How does the house feel to you with cleansing by the element of fire?

Other Fire Cleansing Techniques

- Light a fire in your fireplace; as you watch the flames, clear your mind (but while you are there, open yourself to receiving messages or visions from the realms of spirit)
- Light candles in various rooms of your home regularly, for at least one hour at a time; again, be sure to attend to open flames; not only is it unsafe to leave a fire unattended, but Wiccans consider an unattended flame an invitation for awful luck

Day 88

Imbolc: Clearing Space with Water

Learn today how to clear your home with the element of water. Water techniques are aimed at clearing away any stagnant emotional energies in your sacred space. Water is a natural and familiar choice for cleaning a sacred space; after all, you use water to cleanse objects in the physical world.

How to Cleanse with Water

Fill a bowl with pure, clear water and stand at the front door of your house. Move clockwise through the building, sprinkling the water with your fingertips in each of the rooms of your home. As you walk through your building, imagine that the energy of the droplets is rinsing away all stagnant energies. When you return to the front door, sprinkle a few drops there as well. Stand with your eyes closed and breathe deeply. With each exhalation, imagine that you emit a deep blue light that fills the entire house. Once you have completed this visualization, open your eyes.

How does the house feel to you with cleansing by the element of water?

Other Water Cleansing Techniques

- Fill a small, clear bottle or glass with water; set the glass on a windowsill so that the water is exposed to the light of either the sun or the moon; after the water is "charged" with either sun or moonlight, sprinkle this around your house
- Place a small fountain in each room that you sense needs a touch of water energy
- Use a humidifier in rooms that feel especially dry
- Fill a clean, empty spray bottle with water and a few drops of apple, rose, or gardenia essential oil (use only one essential oil for this clearing technique); shake up the bottle, and use this to mist the air in rooms that need a quick cleansing with the element of water

Day 89

Imbolc: Clearing Space with Earth

Today you learn how to clear your home with the element of earth. Earth techniques have a grounding, solidifying effect in the home. The Earth is your spiritual mother and she offers a solid conduction of elemental energy. When you introduce earth to your home, you evoke the most solid, nurturing aspects of the goddess.

How to Cleanse with Earth

Fill a small bowl with kosher salt[21] and stand at the front door of your house. Move clockwise through the building, sprinkling the salt around the rooms of your home. As you walk through your building, imagine that the grains of salt absorb all stagnant energies. When you return to the front door, sprinkle a bit of salt there. Stand with your eyes closed and breathe deeply. With each exhalation, imagine that you emit a green light that fills the entire house. Once you have completed this visualization, open your eyes.

How does the house feel to you with cleansing by the element of earth?

Other Earth Cleansing Techniques

- Place small bowls of kosher salt in each room of your home to absorb stagnant energies
- Place at least one river rock on each windowsill to absorb harmful vibes
- Make a rock garden, using small dark stones and sand in a box that you prominently place in your home
- Place quartz crystals in the rooms of your home to facilitate the movement of spiritual energy

Day 90

Imbolc: Incense and Oil

Imbolc Incense

Burn this incense at your Imbolc ritual, or at any time that you want to bring about the energies and insights of Imbolc.

What You'll Need:

- A handful of powdered sandalwood
- 1 teaspoon dry bay laurel
- 3 teaspoons myrrh powder or crushed resin
- 1 teaspoon dried coltsfoot (leaf or flower)
- Vegetable glycerin
- 6 drops myrrh essential oil
- 3 drops basil essential oil
- 2 drops bay essential oil

In a medium-sized bowl, place your powdered sandalwood. Stir in about two tablespoons of vegetable glycerin. Add the tablespoons one at a time and then mix with a metal whisk or a fork. You simply want to create a soft, fluffy compound. Do not add the second tablespoon of glycerin if it feels like it would be too much, causing the incense to be too "wet."

Now add your essential oils and whisk. Add your myrrh, coltsfoot, and bay laurel. Mix thoroughly. Wait for at least a day for the compound to settle before you sprinkle it on hot coals.

Imbolc Oil

Use this oil to anoint attendees of your Imbolc ritual. You can also use this oil any time that you want to awaken the insights and mysteries of Imbolc. This oil awakens the magical energies of healing, creativity, and action.

What You'll Need:

- Vegetable glycerin (or a carrier oil such as grape seed oil)
- 6 drops myrrh essential oil
- 3 drops basil essential oil
- 2 drops bay essential oil
- Pinch of coltsfoot or myrrh "tears"

Find a one-ounce bottle and fill the bottle half way with vegetable glycerin. Add plain water until the bottle is three-quarters full. Add your essential oils and your pine needles. Add dry ingredients, close the lid and shake the bottle. When you are finished making this oil, anoint yourself and contemplate any changes you might feel after application.

Days 91-120

Magical Items to Gather

You will need the following items during the next month of your training:

Day 91

- A 5–6 inch light-blue taper candle

Day 96

- Several hard-boiled eggs
- A white crayon

Day 97

- Two 5–6 inch taper candles, one black, one white

Day 102

- A small planter/pot
- A silvery coin
- A sunflower seed
- Potting soil
- A 4 x 4 inch square of green paper
- A red ink pen

Day 104

- A fresh white egg

Day 105

- ¼ ounce powdered sandalwood
- 2 teaspoons dry cinquefoil
- 1 teaspoon dried rose petals
- Vegetable glycerin
- Honeysuckle, rose, and jasmine essential oils
- Dried iris, rose, or dandelion

Day 106

- A flower (such as a rose) with many petals that you can strip from the plant and strew about. Or a variety of fresh greenery.
- A 5–6 inch red taper candle
- Another fresh flower, intact

Day 107

- ¼ ounce powdered sandalwood
- ¼ ounce cedar wood
- ¼ ounce dried juniper

Day 108

- One pint spring water
- One ounce fresh rose petals
- A few drops rose essential oil

Day 109

- Rose water
- An apple

Day 110

- A branch of freshly cut wood (from any tree) at least 12 inches in length
- A bunch of small flowers (a favorite of the Old Europeans was rosebuds)
- About 12 inches of florist's wire (obtainable at any florist's shop)

Day 112

- Several handfuls of yellow flower petals

Day 114

- Rose, apple, jasmine, and lavender essential oils

Day 115

- 4 black and 4 white candles of any length (this day has varying ritual forms; the items you will need depend on the ritual form you select)

Day 117

- Several lengths (at least 6 to 8 feet in length) of brightly colored ribbon

Day 120

- Four stones

Day 91

Contemplative Day: Going Beyond Dreams

Meditative Question: What lies beyond the realm of dream?

Symbolic Color: Blue

Symbolic Direction: West

When we go to sleep each night, each of us enters the realm of dreams. But what is it that lies just beyond dreaming? What have we become once we enter this realm? Are we exactly as we know ourselves? Or are we something else? When you venture into today's contemplative question, you will begin your path toward unraveling a great mystery.

To begin working with this contemplative question, find a comfortable, meditative sitting position in a quiet space facing the west. Light a blue candle and sit approximately two feet away from the flame.

Next, cast your gaze upon the flickering candle and hold the question firmly in your abdominal area. Breathe normally and maintain focus on the question for 20 to 30 minutes.

You may not arrive at a magically satisfactory conclusion in one sitting alone. To manifest a greater depth of answer, it will be important to see this question as it actualizes in each of your daily activities. Allow your body, mind, and spirit to become this question as you eat, sleep, work, and play. Remember not to apply logic to the question. Over time, a shift in your perception will take place and you will realize your own answer.

Day 92

Devotional Day: Honoring Demeter

Table of Correspondences: Demeter

Symbols: Grain and the scythe

Tools: The sickle, the boline, white-handled knife

Magical Essences/Herbs: Cypress, honeysuckle, oakmoss, civet, and myrrh

Direction: Demeter is aligned with the west

She Rules: Tides, rhythms, maternal influence, universal love

Animal Symbols: Lion

Sacred Foods: All ripe fruits and grains

Magical Stones: Star sapphire, cat's eye

Demeter (pronounced: *DEH-meh-ter*) is a Greek goddess who is an archetype of motherly magic, fecundity, and abundance. Her name means "earth-goddess-mother." The ancient Greeks associated her magic with the harvest, with wheat and barley. Demeter's myth intertwines with that of her mythic daughter Persephone. In the myth, Hades, lord of the underworld, abducts Persephone. One Homeric hymn to Demeter says this about the abduction of Persephone: "No one is to blame but Zeus who gave her to Hades, to be called his wife. And Hades seized her and took her loudly crying in his chariot down to his realm of mist and gloom."

Demeter then searched the worlds for her lost daughter, weeping all the while. Because of her grief, she caused the earth to become barren. It was then that Zeus sent the gods of Mount Olympus to persuade Demeter to return to her home and restore the earth's bounty, but Demeter refused to go. She avowed never to let the earth bear fruit until she was reunited with Persephone.

Wiccans most associate Demeter with the mother aspect of the feminine divine. Demeter rules all cycles and the passage of seasons, since she is the personification of all of nature. When you tap into the archetypal energies of Demeter, you also evoke your ability to work within the framework of natural cycles. Through her, you come to see that all things have their season and their time. Demeter reminds each of us that we are a manifestation of the bounty of nature—we have but to recognize the bounty of our lives. Demeter is aligned with the west, with tides, rhythms, and dusk. Her sacred colors are green and amber.

Demeter Practice

Assemble an altar in Demeter's honor today. When you have completed this task, face the altar and intone her name, one syllable at a time, until you sense her presence surrounding you. Once she has arrived, spend some time contemplating what it might mean to serve this aspect of deity. Take time to ask Demeter what it would mean to live life through her energy and listen for her answer.

Spend the day honoring this goddess by celebrating the diversity and bounty of your own existence. It does exist. Look for it!

Day 93

Day of Silence and Review

As you observe silence for the entirety of the day, focus your attention on your emotions. Do not attempt to limit your emotional reactions to events of your day, simply observe your emotional activity. When the day is complete, answer these questions:

- Was there one emotional theme to the day or did emotions fluctuate? Why?
- Are my emotions important to me? Why?
- Am I usually aware of my feelings? Why?
- Did I have times when emotional activity increased or decreased?
- How might knowing what I feel help me to develop spiritually?

Review

For today's practice, take time to ask yourself the following:

- Of the information I have learned up to now, what stands out most as vital?
- What information seems least relevant to my spiritual development?
- Which of the practices seemed to move me spiritually, and which had little impact?
- Of the information I have learned so far, what would be best to review? (Take time to review it now.)

DAY 94

Spring Equinox

The fourth of the Witches' sabbats is the Spring Equinox. The Spring or Vernal Equinox occurs when the sun enters the astronomical sign of Aries between March 19 and 23. Aries is the astrological sign that signifies action, movement, and initiation, which are the very themes that infuse this celebration of the first day of spring.

A Word to the Wise: The word "equinox" itself refers to the distribution of daylight and nighttime hours, which are in equal proportions at this festival.

Although the equinox notes this equality, Witches place a slight emphasis on the theme of "the growth of light."[22] Now, even more so than at Imbolc, the days have become warmer and the seasons of proliferation and abundance are well underway.

In temperate regions, flowers are already blooming. In rural Old Europe, one might see the birth of new herd animals and the seeding of fields in preparation for the future seasons of growth and harvest. This is the season of the budding tree, and in some regions, the full fragrant bloom.

In the classical worlds of ancient Greece and Rome, the Spring Equinox marked the beginning of the new year. The same was true for the Persians, who held a new year celebration at the time of the equinox. It is easy to see why folk from ancient cultures associated this day with "beginnings"; the seasonal wheel turned anew at the equinox, releasing the world from winter's icy grip to reveal nature's freshness, energy, rebirth, joy, and lightness.

When most of us think of spring, we immediately bring to mind the spring symbols promulgated through our dominant culture and its religions. Some of the more popular symbolic customs include decorating eggs, eating eggs and fresh green sprigs, and receiving candy and gifts from the "Easter Bunny."

Although these are symbols we commonly associate with our monotheistic belief systems, scholars trace their origins back to pre-monotheistic pagan practices. To begin, the word "Easter" itself may be a derivative from an ancient Scandinavian Spring goddess Ostara, whose symbol was the great cosmic egg. In fact, a derivative name of this goddess appears in early Christian works as *Eostre*,[23] which was likely based on a Saxon goddess of the same name.[24] Also closely related is the Greek goddess Astarte. One old pagan spring custom that predated Easter was the exchanging of brightly colored eggs, which are symbols of potential and new birth. The egg customs perhaps arose from myths of Hathor-Astarte that tell of her laying a golden egg that transformed into the sun.[25] The popularity of the egg customs continued through time, despite changes in religious affiliation, and never lost their pagan symbolic meaning. One example of the integration of pagan egg customs into the Christian faith is found in old Russia, when women used to lay out Easter eggs on graves as a resurrection charm.[26] The symbolic forms of all three Spring goddesses—Ostara, Eostre, and Astarte—include the fertile hare, flowers, and eggs.

Practice: Cosmic-Egg Colors

In the world of Witches, eggs symbolize potential. When you color eggs, you infuse them with the magical, vibrational qualities of the color you have chosen. In a couple of days you will be coloring eggs with natural dyes, but before you engage in this activity, take time today to contemplate which colors and energies you wish to promote in your life. Below are the colors we will use, as well as their magical, spiritual properties.

Red: Energy, lust, passion, drive, ambition, action, movement, decision

Pink: Love, friendship, peace, harmony, togetherness, tenderness, sentimentality

Blue: Emotions, flow, psychic awareness, freedom, peace, calmness, tranquility

Lavender: Spiritual understanding, spiritual awakening, spiritual mastery

Yellow: Communication, knowledge, speech, learning, the arts, inspiration

Gold: Health, wealth, joy, prosperity, abundance

Brown: Solidity, groundedness, practicality, clarification, work

Green: Financial gain, prosperity, health, growth, nurturing

Questions

- Which colors seem best suited to your life right now?
- Which colors would you like to represent your life?
- Which colors do you not want? Why not?
- Which colors will you select to represent what you want?

Day 95

Spring Equinox: Spring Symbols

To begin this guided imagery meditation, select one color for dying your Ostara eggs. Then close your eyes and imagine that you see this color in front of you.

Reader:
Imagine that the color transforms into a sun, shining this color brightly on the eastern horizon. As you gaze at this sun, you notice that it does not hurt your eyes. It seems pleasant and inviting.

(Reader: pause for a moment.)

Imagine that from the center of this sun a symbol made of light emerges. The symbol then lands in your hands. Look at this symbol and remember it.

(Reader: pause for a moment.)

When you feel you can remember the symbol, hold your spirit hands up and allow the symbol to fly upward. It becomes even brighter and then blends with the color of the eastern sun. Once this occurs, the scene will fade and you will open your eyes. Take a moment to draw the symbol from your vision. You will use this in tomorrow's magical practice.

Day 96

Spring Equinox: Coloring with Natural Dyes

What You'll Need:

- Your dye colors (see below)
- Hard boiled eggs
- A white crayon

Once you have several hard-boiled eggs, use a white crayon to draw the symbol from your vision onto the egg. This symbol will intensify the vibrational color of the egg, drawing its influences into your life. After you have marked the egg with your symbol, place it in the appropriate dye-color that corresponds to your vision.

Red: Soak the eggs in beet juice for 30 minutes; you can also use red cabbage juice for the same effect

Pink: Soak your hard-boiled eggs in cranberry juice for 20–30 minutes

Blue: Infuse hot water with violet blossoms; soak your eggs in the violet water overnight; alternatively, soak the eggs in blueberry juice

Lavender: Soak your hardboiled eggs in grape juice

Yellow: To a cup of hot water, add 1 to 1½ teaspoons turmeric and ½ teaspoon vinegar;. wait for the water to cool before soaking the eggs, or try the same method with saffron strands instead of turmeric

Golden: Save the skins from yellow onions; add them to the water when you hard-boil the eggs; draw your magical symbols with a felt-tipped pen after the eggs have cooled

Brown: Soak the eggs in strong coffee or espresso (whew, what a rush!)

Green: Add ¼ teaspoon baking soda to a bowl of the water from the Blue recipe before soaking your eggs; you can also try dipping the eggs in liquid chlorophyll, which you can find at pet stores and drugstores

When you have finished dyeing your magical Ostara eggs, set them aside for tomorrow's working. It is best to place them in the refrigerator so they will not spoil overnight.

Day 97

Spring Equinox: Egg Ceremony

What You'll Need:

- Your colored and symbol-marked eggs
- Two 5–6 inch candles, one black and one white

Set the eggs in a basket on a table that is on an east-facing wall of your house. Set the candles on either side of the egg basket, placing the white candle in a holder on the right and the black candle in a holder on the left. These two candles represent the balance between night and day. Light the candles and hold your hands over the eggs, imagining your wishes (related to the egg color) coming true. When the candles have burned almost completely out, extinguish them. Then bury the wax and at least one of the eggs in the ground near your home. Peel and eat the other eggs you've blessed so that you assimilate their magical virtues.

Day 98

The Meaning of Spring Equinox

Whenever I enter the spring tide, I remember my childhood and my mother's deep spring-cleaning. Every year she would turn the house upside down and shake out all of the inset dust. In many ways, spring opens us up to our own spiritual cleansing. It is a time to start over, to start fresh. The earth is renewing itself, becoming greener, more temperate, and in comparison to the previous dreary winter months, it is much livelier. It is a time for resetting our lives, just as we might press the "clear" button on a calculator. Spring is a time to set the balance of things at zero. Our important task at the equinox is to erase the polar concepts that we continually balance in our lives, such as "right," "wrong," "good," "bad," "winning," or "losing." What is winning or losing, good or bad? These are only mental abstractions, props that we use to support and define our realities. What does "right" look like, anyway? How do you show "right?" Can you pull it out from a pocket? These terms are simply limiting qualifiers that do not deserve the attention we give them.

Another way we might clarify this issue of limiting and qualifying words is in asking, "Which of the trees outside is winning or losing?" Or, "Which of the oceans is wrong or right?" When we penetrate the shell of our conceptualizations about life, we always arrive at understanding that concepts have nothing to do with actual authentic living. This is when we truly arrive at the balance, the consciousness of the Spring Equinox.

We *are* just as we are right now; there is nothing special or significant about it. The equinox is a time to reevaluate how we might have tipped the scales, and slipped from the balance point, the zero point in our lives in either one direction or another.

Reevaluation of our lives is the first stage of equinox spiritual work. The second stage has to do with correcting the imbalances we note.

Practice: Noting Imbalances

There are several ways that we might fall out of balance and thus lose spiritual empowerment. The usual ways that we lose balance are in our thinking, in our actions, in our emotions, and in our spiritual life. We shall explore each of these potential points of imbalance over the next several days. For today's work, let us examine how an imbalance in thinking might manifest in our everyday lives.

Thinking

What is an imbalance in thinking? One might define it as "too much thinking." "How could this be?" we ask ourselves, "don't we need thinking to manage our lives?" Of course thinking is necessary. However, when we rely on thinking for every aspect of our lives we have fallen out of balance. Is it possible to think your way through a relationship? Is thinking required for satisfactory eating, sleeping, toileting, loving, experiencing? It cannot be. Life is multifaceted, nonlinear and simultaneous. The critical mind works in one-at-a-time words and concepts. *Overanalysis* is the imbalance caused by reliance on the critical faculties.

Another way that we might slip from balance is when we become spacy, unfocused, and unable to maintain attention to the people and tasks of our lives. This is imbalance in the direction of pure experiencing, or nonthinking.

- In reviewing your thoughts, do you find that you are out of balance in your thinking?
- In which direction do you tip the scales? In overanalysis or in nonthinking?

Balancing the Thinking Scales: Overanalysis

If you find that you have an overly active critical mind, take time today to practice experiencing. For example, while eating, focus on emptying your mind. Simply maintain awareness of the sensations in your mouth. Try this with your other senses. Quiet the critical mind and focus on what it is you see, hear, smell, or touch.

Nonthinking

If you find that you have difficulty in focusing, take out a candle, light it, and focus your attention on the flame. Do not allow your cognitive processes to interfere with your concentration on the light of the flame. Also, whenever someone speaks to you, make direct eye contact and do not allow the wandering mind to drift away from the speaker.

Day 99

Spring Equinox: Balancing Action

When you are imbalanced in action, you might be either overly active or at the other extreme, listless. Do you find that you are always on the go? Do you feel wound up, impatient, and eager to accomplish tasks? While there is nothing wrong with getting things done, one should consider if activity is balanced with sufficient periods of rest. In looking at over-activity, ask yourself, "What am I trying to accomplish?" and "How important is this activity when I consider my life as a whole?" You might also consider if you are active to the exclusion of developing healthy relationships, or to the exclusion of restful sleep. When we are overly active, often we are masking some level of anxiety, sadness, or fear. When you keep yourself from experiencing these suppressed states you also keep magical empowerment blocked and stagnant.

The flip side of overactivity is listlessness. This can take many forms, such as procrastination, sleepiness, and feeling run-down. Listlessness can also be a form of avoidance; it may be avoidance of task completion, or of being competent (and all of the ramifications that may go with that). It may be avoidance of having other people rely on you. When you do not complete whatever it is that needs doing, you leave holes in your psyche and gaps in your true spiritual abilities.

- In reviewing your activity levels, do you find that you are out of balance in your action?
- In which direction do you tip the scales? In overactivity or in listlessness?

Balancing the Action Scales: Overactivity

If you find that you tip the scales in the direction of overactivity, take planned break times from your usual routines today. If you have ten activities or tasks planned, only complete eight of them. When you break from your routine, monitor your feelings. What happens inside of you when you are still? Allow whatever sensations you have to emerge fully, so that they flush up and out.

Listlessness

If you tip the scales in the direction of listlessness, it is time to make a plan of action. Make a list of tasks that need completion and that you have been avoiding up to now. Vow to complete at least two of the tasks today. Whenever you sense that you are resisting action, take note of your bodily sensations. Where are you gripping, tightening up? Allow the body to relax from the gripping sensations and continue on with task completion.

Day 100

Spring Equinox: Balancing Emotion

It is common for many of us to become caught up in emotional reactions to the circumstances of our lives. Even if we do not outwardly express our emotional reactions to things, we still feel them. Many of us live without awareness of how our reactions stir us into unempowered action. An imbalance in emotions causes us to act out, to speak in harmful ways, and it causes us to dip right back into the thinking mode. Reliance on thinking and emotional reactions go hand in hand. If you've noticed an imbalance in one of these areas, it is best to explore possible imbalances in the other. When we emote and react to each circumstance, we start an internal monologue of complaints. "I don't like the way she makes me feel." "He's stingy." "Why does she always criticize me?" Meanwhile, we miss out on what is actually happening. We miss the sound of the wind, the sensations of our bodies, the taste of our food, the things we see and feel. We miss out on the world,which is the realm of Deity or power.

The opposite energy of emoting is blocking emotion. Most of us have experienced painful situations as a simple matter of living life. As a result, some of us choose a strategy to block out the pain of our circumstances. We make ourselves tough; we ignore our hurts. We work at developing our insensitivity, hoping that this is the answer to a life where pain is a natural part of the process. But this doesn't work. It only results in numbing ourselves from the whole of life, so we miss out on both the pleasure and the pain.

- In reviewing your emotions, do you find that you are out of balance?
- In which direction do you tip the scales? In over-emotionality or in emotional blocking?

Balancing the Emotion Scales: Over-Emotionality

If you find that you tip the scales in the direction of over-emotionality, take emotional checks at regular intervals during the day. Emotional reacting is easy to spot. It results in hurt, anger, or sadness. It also results in extensive internal monologues. Once you recognize emotional reacting, take time to dig beneath the thoughts, the monologues that surround the reaction. What is it that lies beneath the reaction? When you shine the light of awareness on it, you will notice that the energy shifts and neutralizes in a relatively short time.

Emotional Blocking

If you tip the scales in the direction of emotional blocking, begin by drawing a circle on a piece of blank paper. Pick five crayon (or marker) colors that will symbolize the following emotions: anger, sadness, happiness, fear, and neutrality. Of course, human emotions manifest in a spectacular array of tones and attitudes, but roughly they can be categorized by these five states. Using your crayons and the circle you have already drawn, create a pie chart graph that represents how much you felt each of these emotional states during the day. After you have represented each of the emotional states, review how much of your day you spent in each. Try this exercise for the next several days, so that you can begin to notice emotions much more regularly.

Day 101

Spring Equinox: Balancing Spirit

Do you use the Tarot cards to decide whether or not to use the bathroom? Do you feel spiritually incomplete without gluten-free foods, tofu, and dietary supplements? Are you tongue-tied by rigid insistence on political correctness? Do you find yourself searching for a spiritual explanation or meaning in every aspect of your life? Do you take action (or not) based on your perception of the action's spiritual or karmic merit? Do you find yourself incessantly contemplating spirituality? It is likely that you are suffering from an imbalance in spirit. An imbalance in the realm of spirit occurs when you rely on spirituality to fill the gaps in your life. In reality, spirit does not *fill* any gaps of your life; it is your life, just as it is, plain and simple. People who are imbalanced in spirit don't want to believe this. They have ethereal, all-encompassing (and often bizarre) concepts of life that add dramatic impact and flair. Someone who is imbalanced in this way is what I call *spiritually obsessed.*

Just like Linda Blair in *The Exorcist*, spiritually obsessed people need to have their demons of excessive spirituality cast out. They need to eat a good old-fashioned cheeseburger and french fries. They need to play a game of poker and bet it all. They would be much happier if they would lighten up and learn a few good jokes. Be gone, demon! I cast thee out.

The important lesson for someone suffering from spiritual obsession is to see that all of life is an expression of spirit. One does not need to search for it, add explanations to it, develop theories about it, or ruminate incessantly about minutiae that are irrelevant to authentic spiritual expression. It is important to see that going to the bathroom is just as important to spiritual development as chanting, celebrating a seasonal passage, or working a spell. An authentic and genuinely magical life is one infused with the essence of one's spiritual practice, but it does not focus on the external artifacts of one's spirituality. Tarot cards, candles, incense, charms, incantations, etc., have their place in the Witch's world as aspects of an authentic spiritual life, but care should be taken that they do not become crutches or objects of obsessive fascination.

The opposite energy of spiritual obsession is dismissive rationality. This occurs when one focuses the attention on practical matters in an attempt to (either consciously or unconsciously) exclude spirit. The rational-dismissive individual does not see beyond the gross physical form of life and becomes mired in the density of form, the tasks of daily life, and the stimulation of the physical senses. Often, an individual who lives in this way experiences periods of feeling isolated, depressed, and intensely disconnected.

- In reviewing your spiritual state, do you find that you are out of balance?
- In which direction do you tip the scales? In spiritual emersion or in grounded practicality?

Balancing the Spiritual Scales: Spiritual Obsession

If you find that you tip the scales in the direction of spiritual obsession, take time to be silly and frivolous. There is nothing about which you need to be serious. Eat foods, wear colors, listen to music, and talk with people you generally avoid because they reputedly "stunt" your spiritual growth. Notice if you are able to find spirit in these activities. If not, why not?

Grounded Practicality

Most readers of this book will not likely fall into this category, but you may know of someone in your life who does. If you know someone who tips the scales in the direction of grounded practicality, recommend that the individual take time to explore something mysterious. Explore the meaning of existence. Why are we here? Exactly who and what are we at our core? What about exploring Stonehenge? The pyramids? How does premonition work? What about ley lines, crop circles, the Nasca figures, Atlantis, or the possibilities of extraterrestrial life?

If these topics are too metaphysical, perhaps the individual can simply contemplate why the divine does not play a part in his or her life. How did he or she arrive at a life that excluded the possibility of a divine force? Another strategy might be viewing movies or documentaries that explore nonrational or spiritual topics. The more time this individual spends offsetting the overly grounded mindset, the more fluid and flexible he or she will become over time.

Finally, the rational-dismissive individual should explore the feelings, the emotions that underlie this defensive position. Are there feelings of fear? Anger? Frustration? Sadness? This individual would benefit from examining those feelings thoroughly and placing them into perspective. This practice may leave the individual with a feeling of internal spaciousness and an ability to accommodate a personal spiritual search.

Day 102

Spring Equinox: Sowing Seeds Rite

What You'll Need:

- A small planter/pot
- A silver coin
- A sunflower seed
- Potting soil
- A 4 x 4 inch square of green paper
- A red ink pen

Using a red ink pen, write on your 4 x 4 inch square of paper a wish that you'd like to see begin sprouting and growing during the spring season. You can grow anything you'd like in your magical-wish garden; for example your finances, your love life, your intuition, or your empathy. Whatever your wish, place it at the bottom of the planter or clay pot.

Next, place the silver coin on top of the paper. For purposes of this working, the coin does not need to be made of solid silver, but simply silver colored. As you place the coin in the bottom of the pot, say:

> ***Silver moon inside this dish***
> ***Wax and wane, but grant my wish!***

Now, cover the coin and the wish with the potting soil. Hold the sunflower seed between the palms of your hands. Close your eyes and imagine your wish coming true. Bring into your imaginary senses every sight, sound, taste, touch, and smell associated with your wish coming true. Once you have a strong mental image, begin to exhale thrice upon the seed in your hands. Quickly plant the seed just an inch or so from the top of the soil. Cover it over and water it. Keep the pot in a warm, sunny spot. Tend to the sunflower seed daily so that it can grow. Know that as the seed sprouts and unfolds, so will your wish!

Day 103

Spring Equinox: A Day of Unknowing

Spring is the season that represents newness, freshness, and beginnings. The freshness of Spring can also suggest newness of mind and spirit. To assume the energies of Spring in your consciousness, it is important to take the attitude of *not-knowing*. By not-knowing, I am not referring to a lack of knowledge; it does not mean that you don't know to look down at your hands when you chop vegetables, or you don't know that electricity can be dangerous. Instead, not-knowing refers to curtailing the activity of the "discursive mind" and the incessant internal chatter that goes on between the ears. Not-knowing is the process of opening up to the full experience of life without mental analysis.

The discursive, critical mind analyzes, intellectualizes, categorizes, and labels the fluid and often indefinable experiences of your life. Most everyone engages in this sort of critical thinking continuously throughout the day. It is actually quite amazing when you pay attention to your thoughts. When you do, you will discover (as everyone eventually does) how often you live in the stories you have created about your life. In the process of living your life through mental stories, you miss what is actually happening in the moment. The key point in Wicca is to align with nature and to discover your own nature. When you grasp on to the myriad of stories you generate in your head, you lose touch with the natural world as it is manifesting around you and through you, right now.

It is natural for the brain to secrete thoughts, just as the gallbladder secretes bile and the stomach secretes acids. It is an ordinary function of the brain. However, it is when we buy into the secretions of the brain that we lose track of our own nature.[27] That is when you may start to believe that whatever is in your head must be reality. Although it offers a sense of comfort and control to live in the world of our thoughts, it is also immeasurably limiting. Spiritual development is choked off by an over-reliance on the critical faculties.

In today's practice you will learn to identify these "knowing" patterns in your mind, and in the process you will open up the energy of not-knowing, entering into an authentic, powerful alliance with the ground of your being, namely, the world. It is through not-knowing that Witches engage with the energies of life with an unspoiled vision and a clear sense of wonder. This mental position opens any obstructions to the flow of life-energy and then empowers the Witch.

Practice: Not Knowing

Begin the day by greeting the dawn. As you watch the sunrise, make a vow to yourself that you will live without judgments, categories, or critiques. Whenever you catch yourself relying heavily on classifications, say the word "stop" aloud (or to yourself when appropriate). After saying the word, take a deep breath. Inhale and expand your lungs and belly. Place your focus on these sensations and expansion. Allow your breath to flow out naturally. Try this three or four times, then go on with your day—practicing this technique whenever necessary.

Day 104

Spring Equinox: Cosmic-Egg Cleansing

Spring Equinox is the perfect time to shake out the dusty, musty, old spiritual vibrations that might have collected in your home during the winter months when your home might be shut tight against the elements. Try the following vibe-cleansing technique in your home today. This technique reputedly enlists the aid of the egg to absorb the negative and stagnant energies of your home.

What You'll Need:

- A fresh egg (you may color it with a natural dye that suggests spiritual cleansing to you)

Take a fresh egg and rub it across all doors and windows. Once you have completed this, tap a hole into the smaller, tip-end of the egg using a pin. Then make another hole at the opposite end of the egg. Take the egg outside of your home, dig a hole in the earth, and then blow the egg's contents into the hole. Close the hole and leave the site, never to return. Keep the hollowed eggshell as a charm against future negative vibrations.

Day 105

Spring Equinox: Incense and Oil

Spring Incense

Burn this incense at your Spring Equinox ritual, or at any time that you want to bring about the energies and insights of Spring Equinox.

What You'll Need:

- A handful of powdered sandalwood
- 2 teaspoons dry cinquefoil
- 1 teaspoon dried rose petals
- Vegetable glycerin
- 4 drops honeysuckle essential oil
- 3 drops rose essential oil
- 2 drops jasmine essential oil

In a medium-sized bowl, place your powdered sandalwood. Stir in about two tablespoons of vegetable glycerin. Add the tablespoons one at a time and then mix with a metal whisk or a fork. You simply want to create a soft, fluffy, compound. Do not add the second tablespoon of glycerin if it feels like it would be too much, causing the incense to be too wet.

Now add your essential oils and whisk. Add your other dried herbs and mix thoroughly. Wait for at least a day for the compound to settle before you sprinkle it on hot coals.

Spring Oil

Use this oil to anoint attendees of your Spring Equinox ritual. You can also use this oil any time that you want to awaken the insights and mysteries of Spring. This oil activates the magical energies of psychic awareness, love, and spiritual mastery.

What You'll Need:

- Vegetable glycerin (or a carrier oil such as grape seed oil)

- 4 drops honeysuckle essential oil
- 3 drops rose essential oil
- 2 drops jasmine essential oil
- Pinch of dried iris, rose, or dandelion

Find a one-ounce bottle. Fill the bottle halfway with vegetable glycerin. Add in plain water until the bottle is three-quarters full. Add in your essential oils. Add in dry ingredients, close the lid, and shake the bottle. You can use this magical oil immediately.

A Word to the Wise: Vegetable glycerin can sometimes be a tricky item to procure, although well-stocked health food stores should carry it. One mail-order supplier of this item is Star West Botanicals in Rancho Cordova, California. See the resource guide in the back of the book for more details and suggestions on obtaining this invaluable ingredient.

Day 106

Beltane

There are two high sabbats within the annual cycle of Witches' celebrations. The first occurs at Samhain, on October 31. The sobering and solemn rites of death and return mark that occasion. Directly on the other side of the year, halfway through the wheel of seasonal celebrations, you arrive at the festival of Beltane, which occurs on May 1. Beltane is a complimentary celebration to that of Samhain; it is the sweet yang to Hallows' grim yin. Beltane is a joyous, open-hearted celebration of life, as might be suggested by its balancing counterplacement in the wheel cycle to that of Samhain. When you keep in mind that Wicca is a fertility religion, this knowledge may buffer any surprise you may have in learning that Beltane focuses on the principle of life as generated through the energies of physical, sexual union.[28]

The word "Beltane" is the anglicized version of the Irish Gaelic word *Bealtaine*, which is the name of the month of May. It is also related to the Scottish *Bealtuinn*, which means "May Day."[29] The original word was derived from the "Bel fire," which was the fire lit on the first day of May in honor of the Celtic god Bel (who was a sun or light god also known as Beli and Balor). In order to symbolically announce the return of light and life to the world, the ancient Celts lit Bel fires with wood found in local oak groves. In some accounts of ancient Druid rites, the festival would sometimes culminate in the ritual sacrifice of a man who signified the Oak God. The priests offered the sacrifice to renew the "blood of the earth."

One such Celtic rite involved the burning of criminals and prisoners who were offered in sacrifice in the Bel fires. In ancient accounts from invading Romans, the Druid priests would supervise entire villages in the construction of large human figures fashioned from oak branches and pitch. Captives were then locked inside of the tall wooden figurines, which the celebrants would subsequently set aflame.

In other, less dramatic ancient Beltane rites, celebrants would cut "branches of May," which consisted of budded hawthorn limbs. They would then bring the branch of May into their homes as a sign of the goddess' return. Celebrants might also cart the branches around the village from one door to the next as a gesture of blessing.[30] The Irish believed that tying a green bough of a tree (another form of the branch of May) to a stable would cause a cow to produce an abundance of milk.[31] A lover might also place a green bush in the front yard of his beloved's house on May Day eve, believing that the fertilizing power of the nature-spirit contained in the shrub would bless their union.[32]

Another old May Day custom consisted of hunting wild hares. Contemporary occultists note that the hare has both strong lunar and fertility associations and believe that it was for these symbolic reasons the ancients held the sacred hare hunts on Beltane. Old lore of the sacred hare hunt stated that if one captured a hare on May Day, he or she would be assured of blessings for the home and family.

The maypole is another sacred object tied to the rites of Beltane, May Day, and *Walpurgisnacht.* The maypole graphically represented the King's phallus, and it was planted deep in the earth to initiate the new season of growth and fertility.[33] Celebrants would decorate the pole with ribbons, bells, and flower garlands. Later, they would dance around the pole to invigorate the earth. Maypole rites were so popular throughout Europe that the church, indignant at the sight of such open popular affection for pagan practices, had difficulty in stamping them out. The church's early attempts to eradicate these practices included efforts to incorporate them in their own "Priapus" rituals. In one account a parish priest tells of a church-sponsored Priapus procession in which villagers carried a pole that was representative of the male reproductive organs.[34]

In contemporary May Day celebrations, Wiccans embrace a liberated and direct expression of their sexuality. If this might be too daring for you just yet, perhaps Beltane can be a time for you to openly examine your sexual views, your taboos, obsessions, and practices. Sex is a part of living and in order to embrace life fully, Witches embrace all of life's components.

A Word to the Wise: Wicca is a decentralized, grass-roots spiritual endeavor, so "official perspectives" on any subject matter do not exist. However, most practitioners understand that sexuality is a personal expression. It should be an uninhibited expression of pleasure between *consenting adults.* Whether you are homosexual, bisexual, or heterosexual, any form of sexual repression, inhibition, or disregard for one's own (or someone else's) sexual orientation is not in keeping with the spirit of the Craft. If you have puritanical views on sexuality, it sounds like someone needs therapy!

For Witches, sexual energy represents the merging of individual consciousness into a collective consciousness. Through sexual union, both literally and symbolically, two become one. It is representative of the process through which an individual merges with the divine force. Because Witches expand their sexual views to include this more symbolic, sacred understanding, the sexuality of Beltane moves them beyond culturally stereotyped and often repressive overlays. In the pagan view, sexuality should be uninhibited and spontaneous, a direct manifestation of one's sexual expression.

Practice: A May Eve Incantation

What You'll Need:

- A flower (such as a rose) with many petals that you can strip from the plant and strew about, or a variety of fresh greenery
- A 5–6 inch red taper candle
- Another fresh flower, intact

Traditionally, Witches recite various chants on Beltane Eve. Tonight at midnight, mark out a nine-foot diameter circle on the floor using flower petals or greenery. Light a red candle. Hold the candle in your right hand and hold a flower, a well-budded branch of greenery, or other fresh plant in the left hand. Hold both candle and vegetation to the sky. Stand in the east of your circle of flowers and begin walking clockwise. Then recite the following chant three times.[35] Make sure, likewise, that you circumambulate the perimeter of the flower-circle three times while chanting.

O, do not tell the priest of our arts
For they would call it a sin,
But we will be in the wood all night,
A-conjuring summer in!
And we bring good news by word of mouth,
For women, cattle and corn,
For the sun is rising up from the south,
With oak, ash, and thorn.[35]

Day 107

The Meaning of Beltane

The sexual act, in and of itself, is not the final word when it comes to Beltane. As it is with all of the Witches' ritual actions, sexual union carries a deeper metaphorical and spiritual message. It conveys the principles of both universal love and of union with nature and the divine.

Love is the guiding force during this high holy day in the Witches' year. Although love means many things and you might have numerous associations to the word, when we first think of love, most of us immediately call to mind images and sensations of our romantic life. Passion can certainly be one facet of love. As we think further along the spectrum of love, we might also include the commitment, attachment, and devotion we feel toward family members, partners, children, and friends. While there are many forms of love, Beltane celebrates a universal, worldly, and unconditional form. The love at Beltane, as expressed through the principle of sexual union, is the love of life itself. It is an unemotional, detached form of love. That is not to say the love expressed at Beltane is cold and unfeeling. The opposite is true, since the love principle expressed at Beltane is not attached to anything or anyone, it is directed outward to all. It gushes forth, like water flooding a land that lies below a broken dam. It is the unstoppable principle of union as a direct expression of life's zeal and vitality. It is the unconditional benevolence of the gods that flows forward though the love expressed at Beltane.

At Beltane, one of the primary symbolic spiritual acts is that of the sacred marriage, known in world mythology as the *heiros gamos*.[36] Myths portray this principle through stories that feature a hero who marries a goddess, or when love triumphs over evil. The symbolic union between the physical polar opposites of male and female bodies represents the merging of universally opposite elements. Likewise, light and dark, hot and cold, center and periphery are all oppositional points that find their central balance in Beltane's ritual symbolic sexual activity. As the great world myths tell us, it is through the meeting of these opposite forces that life renews itself. Barren fields, once seeded, open to blossom and fruit. Life becomes possible through the universal principle of union.

The heiros gamos is not just a charming mythic theme that we can memorialize only once a year on May Day. It is a living, breathing principle that exists within your own spirit. The heiros gamos is a state of consciousness that is present whenever we become awakened by touch or sensuality. It begins with the blending of two souls in love and acts of pleasure. It ends with the outpouring of divine love for all in a consciousness of compassion.

Practice: The Beltane Fire

Make a fire today, if you can, in an open natural setting. Take every precaution that the fire will be well contained and that it has little or no chance of endangering the surrounding flora. If possible, it is best to build the base of this fire using oak branches. Be sure to build the base fire with small branches or dried twigs. Once this base fire is well underway, toss in the following ingredients, which comprise the recipe for the legendary "Fire of Azrael."[37]

What You'll Need:

- A handful of sandalwood
- A handful of cedar wood
- A handful of dried juniper

As you watch the fire burn, contemplate the theme of union. Notice that a fire cannot be without the successful union of heat, fuel, and air. When all three are in union, fire can exist. Be sure to jump over the bonfire and to make "Beltane wishes" while you vault the flames. Better yet, leap over the flames with a sexual partner to strengthen your bond and to ignite passion.

When the fire is burned out and only embers remain, take time to gaze into the embers for portents of the future.

Safety Guidelines

When building fires in open, outdoor spaces, please first consider these safety guidelines.

- Always have a bucket of water, sand, or even a shovel on hand before you build the fire; you can use these to douse the fire when you are finished with the ritual, or in an emergency
- Dig a small pit away from overhanging branches
- Circle the pit with rocks or insert a metal fire ring
- Clear a five-foot area around the pit down to the soil
- Don't use flammable liquids to start the fire or anywhere near the fire
- Once the fire is lit, stay with it at all times
- Keep your campfire safe from children and pets
- Never build a campfire on a windy day. Sparks can travel for long distances
- To extinguish the fire, pour lots of water on it and drown it out completely; then cover the ashes with sand or dirt; don't leave a fire until it's "out cold"
- Never walk away from smoldering embers

Day 108

Beltane: Magical Rose Wash

A floral wash is one of Beltane's joyous, sensual pleasures. The essence of fresh rose in water invites the magical energies of both sensuality and of universal love into your life—no matter if you are male or female.

An ewer full of rose-scented washing water was once the ultimate luxury item for bathing. One might use the scented water instead of soap to cleanse the skin and to rejuvenate the spirit. Because floral washes were once quite rare, many legends of their magical properties arose. For example, rose-scented water was believed to impart beauty and halt the aging process.

Your practice today will involve making rose-scented washing water. The process is simple and the magical waters can last in a sealed bottle for up to three weeks at a time.

What You'll Need:

- 1 pint spring water
- 1 ounce fresh rose petals
- A few drops rose essential oil

Place the water and the herbs together in a pan and bring them to a gentle boil. Turn off the heat once the water reaches boiling, cover the pot, and allow the decoction to sit undisturbed for 30 minutes. Pour the scented water into a closeable bottle, straining out the rose petals. For added rose scent, you can add a drop or two of rose essential oil to the bottle.

After making this magical floral water, store it for use in tomorrow's practice.

Day 109

Beltane: An Attraction Rite

It is important on Beltane to be attractive to one another. Here is an adaptation of an old custom that magical folk would use to make themselves attractive at Beltane.

What You'll Need:

- Rose water
- An apple

Pour a small amount of the rose water into a large bowl or basin. Chop the apple into pieces and place them into the bowl as well. Now fill the bowl to the top with fresh water. Allow the apple to steep in the basin of rose water for a few minutes. Scoop the water up with both of your hands and apply it to your face. Close your eyes, and say:

> ***Awaken beauty; hold it fast,***
> ***Bind the mists to make it last!***
> ***Raggiol*** *(rag-e-ol)!*
> ***Eytpa*** *(yit-pah)!*
> ***Lacaza*** *(la-caw-za)!*
> ***Azcall*** *(az-call)!*[38]

Day 110

Beltane: The Priapic Wand

The wand is a phallic symbol. Many old customs surround the making and using of priapic wands to encourage fertility and abundance. Today you will learn an old method for making the priapic wand, which you will use in tomorrow's practice.

What You'll Need:

- A branch of freshly cut wood (from any tree) at least 12 inches in length[39]
- A bunch of small flowers (a favorite of the Old Europeans was rosebuds)
- About 12 inches of florist's wire (obtainable at any florist or crafts shop)

Cut a 12-inch length of a tree branch, using proper, standard gardening techniques and tools.

Take the branch to a worktable and set it aside for the moment. Bunch together a number of your flowers. Arrange the stems of the flowers along one tip of the branch so that the buds are at the tip of the wand/branch. Once you have arranged the flowers, tie them to the branch using the florist's wire. When you are finished, you should have a branch that appears to be budding with a number of flowers at one end. For a more pleasing esthetic, you can even cover the florist's wire with raffia or a beautiful satin ribbon.

When you have made the wand, place it in your refrigerator to maintain freshness. If possible, plunge the wand in a deep water-filled vase so that the flower stems rest within reach of the water. That way, the flowers will remain fresh until tomorrow's practice.

A Word to the Wise: The proper tools to use for pruning a branch from a tree include: shears, loppers, and a pruning saw (all of which are available at your local gardening shop). Your first cut in the branch should be just outside the branch collar to allow the wound to seal more quickly. Make the first cut on the underside of the branch, about 5 inches from the trunk. Cut one-third of the way through the branch. Move the saw out 5 inches and cut the branch now from the top portion. (The first cut prevents the bark from tearing away later on.) After cutting through, remove the remaining stub by cutting just beyond the branch collar (about ¼ inch away from the trunk). Salve the tree where you have severed the limb to assure the health of the tree.

If you don't have access to a tree, you can purchase a 12-inch wood dowel from your local hardware or lumber store, and decorate it just as you would the fresh tree branch.

Day 111

Beltane: Blessing with the Priaptic Wand

What You'll Need:

- Rose wash in a medium bowl
- The priapic wand

Stand outside of your home with the rose wash in a bowl, placed in your left hand. Hold the wand, flowers upright, in your right hand. Face the front door of your home (or apartment building). Dip the flowered end of the wand into the rose wash and then flick the wand toward the door, sprinkling it with the rose wash.

Begin walking clockwise around your home, continuing to sprinkle the rose wash with the tip of the priapus. The proper technique for sprinkling the rose wash is to begin sprinkling to your right, and then to your left. Continue alternating, right and then left, until you have circumambulated the entire building. Once you reach the front door, place the wand at the threshold, flowered tip pointing out, toward the street. Close the door and do not open it until sunrise tomorrow. Then, take the wand apart and bury all of the pieces near your home.

Day 112

Beltane: Traditional Flower Charm

This flower charm is based on the old European pagan practice of strewing petals in order to assure fecundity and a prosperous harvest.[40] Use this charm to assure blessings and prosperity in your own life.

What You'll Need:

- Several handfuls of yellow flower petals (any variety)
- A local bush, or shrub

Stand over a bush or shrub that is close to either your home or place of business. Begin strewing the flower petals over the shrub, using your right hand. As you do so, say:

> ***Gracious goddess, mighty god,***
> ***Unite the cauldron and the rod,***
> ***You who rule the changing world,***
> ***Be your power in me unfurled.***[41]

Now close your eyes and imagine some desired outcome in your life or in the life of someone close to you. Leave the bush now. The charm is complete.

Day 113

Beltane: Sexuality and Spirit

In many ways, your year and a day training is about broadening and heightening awareness. One area of human living that many of us hide in shadows is our sexuality. Beltane is a good time not only to shine the light of awareness on this issue, but to examine our own sexual practices, views, and attitudes.

Without you ever really having full conscious awareness of it, culture has shaped your sexual views.[42] One of the most pervasive views on sexuality in the western world is the Abrahamic-religious notion that sex is a procreative activity only.[43] This view has proved devaluing and inhibiting of a full range of sexual expression. It also has reinforced stereotyped gender roles and sexual expression (e.g., males are aggressors, females are responders; heterosexuality is desirable while homosexuality is not, etc.).[44]

But from where do we get these views? And how relevant are they to our lives today? In the ancient world, childbearing held enormous value. The ancient Hebrews, whose views form the basis of the contemporary Bible, were subjected to slavery and persecution. Childbearing was almost impossible in those impoverished conditions. It is therefore no mere fluke that Yahweh commanded his people (as he did in Genesis) to "be fruitful and multiply."

The early teachings of the Catholic church were possibly the most influential in solidifying these ancient procreative views and in forging practical links to current social views, policy, politics, and practice. By the first century BCE, the Roman Empire had reached its height, and along with it came many sexually permissive activities. The Bacchanalia was one Roman festival that not only permitted free sexual expression, but evidently enforced it. The Bacchanalia rites became so offensive and debasing (especially to young males who were often forced into sexual intercourse) that the Roman Senate eventually banned them.

Later, Paul of Tarsus, a pivotal and vocal personality in the Christian church, reacted to these rites and emphasized the importance of overcoming the desires of the flesh. He also encouraged sexual celibacy and abstinence as superior spiritual practices. Other church fathers expanded on Paul's views in the following centuries. The more respected church authorities reforming sexual views over time included St. Augustine, Thomas Aquinas, Martin Luther, and John Calvin.

The legacy of the church, of the Reformation and its rigid stance against sexual behavior for any other purpose than procreation has lingered in the popular mind. Many of these views continue intact, while some have fallen since the sexual revolution of the 1960s and '70s. Nonetheless, sexual issues continue to present each of us with complex conflicts that pit social tradition against personal pleasure.

The early development of contemporary Wicca took place over the second half of the twentieth century. Because of its placement in history and because of the voices who have contributed to the reemergence of this path, the Craft is infused with many contemporary views on sexuality. These alternative perspectives often flout conventional socially upheld sexual views. To be precise, Wiccans believe that sexuality is a sacred, empowering, and pleasurable act that is a gift from the goddess.

Practice: Sexual Views

Take time today to explore your own sexual views by reviewing the following questions and then committing your answers to paper:

- In what ways do you find social views on sexuality to be personally inhibiting?
- In what ways are these views beneficial or comforting?
- What sexual norms would you implement in society?
- How might you behave sexually if there were no learned sexual "norms"?

Day 114

Beltane: Attracting Love

The following is a recipe for love oil. This is a blend of essential oils that are reputed to emit a vibration that attracts love into one's life. Create the oil today, because you will use it in tomorrow's practice.

Love Oil Recipe

Mix into one ounce of vegetable glycerin the following essential oils.

- 4 drops rose essential oil
- 3 drops apple essential oil
- 2 drops jasmine essential oil
- 1 drop lavender essential oil

Apply the finished oil blend to your heart chakra and to the chakra area just above the genitals in order to attract love.

Day 115

Beltane: The Great Rite

In Wiccan terminology, the Great Rite is symbolic, ritual sexual union. In traditional rites, this union was between consenting male and female magical partners. However, to genderize the Great Rite is to miss the spiritual point of the practice. The Great Rite is about the principle of union, becoming *one* with both the internal and external world. Sexual union is only a representational means to transmit or teach the principle. The Great Rite, therefore, is open to all. In reframing the rite, we can easily see that any two consenting adult magical practitioners, regardless of gender or sexual orientation, can practice it. There are three versions of the Great Rite presented here. The first is the rite in *actuality*, meaning through it you engage in the ritual sexual act. The second version is the *symbolic* Great Rite, which can be performed by two individuals who do not (or should not) engage in ritualized sexual activity. Decide which version best applies to you. If you are a solitary Witch, the third version is the "Great Rite for One."

What You'll Need:

- 4 black and 4 white candles
- Love oil

Version I: The Great Rite (in actuality)

If you already have a regular sexual partner who is willing to try this rite with you today, wonderful!

Set four black and four white candles (alternating their colors—one black and one white, etc.) in a circle on the floor. Turn off the lights. Each sexual partner should undress outside of the circle. Face each other and look into each other's eyes, establishing a spiritual connection. When ready, say in unison:

> ***Lord and Lady, Dark and Light***
> ***Be with us here this sacred night!***

Both magical/sexual partners enter the circle of black and white candles and join hands. They then recite the following, with each partner alternating reading individual lines.

Assist me to build
As the Mighty Ones willed,
The altar of praise,
From the beginning of days,
Thus doth it lie,
'Twixt the earth and sky,
For so it was placed,
When the Old Ones embraced.

Use the love oil to draw a double spiral design, which symbolizes the joining of opposites. Dab your finger with the oil and draw one spiral at the center of your partner's chest (at the level of the heart chakra). After you spiral out with three concentric rings from the center point at the chest, connect this to the second spiral that spirals inward to a central point just above the genital area. Once you both have done this, continue reciting the following, each taking turns with the lines:

'O secret of secrets,
That art which is hidden,
Not thee do we love,
For that is not bidden,
For that which loveth is also thou.
And thou art myself from heel to brow.

Both partners kiss now.

I am the flame that burns in the heart,
And at the core of every star.
I am life, which gives life its start.
But know ye that death is never afar.
I am alone, the unknown divine,
The Mystery of Mysteries beyond all sign.

Now take turns kissing each other in the following magical pattern:

- Kiss your partner above the pubic hair
- Kiss the right foot
- Kiss the left hand
- Kiss the right hand
- Kiss the left foot
- Kiss just above the pubic region [45]

Now, lie next to one another and read the following text, each partner taking a turn reading individual lines:

Open for me the secret way,
The pathway of intelligence
Beyond the gates of night and day,
Beyond the bounds of time and sense.

Both partners kiss. Then they should embrace, and continue reading:

Before ye stands the mystery aright;
The pentacle of love and bliss,
Here where the Lance and Grail unite,
At feet and knees and breast and kiss.

Consummate the rite.[46]

A Word to the Wise: It is *not* advisable, nor does the Craft condone that minors or individuals with sexually transmittable diseases engage in the Great Rite in actuality. If you fall into one of these categories, please use the procedures for the symbolic Great Rite or the "Great Rite for One" as outlined above. Remember: practice "safe ritual."

Version II: The Symbolic Great Rite

What You'll Need:

- The priapic wand
- Five candles: two black, two white, one gray
- A "chalice" (a fine wine glass or even a special cup) filled with wine or a red fruit juice (such as cranberry or pomegranate)

(Note: Each partner may remain dressed for this rite.)

Set four black and four white candles (alternating their colors—one black and one white, etc.) in a circle on the floor. Give each magical partner an unlit candle: one takes a black and the other takes a white one. Turn off the lights. Take a gray candle, place it at the center of the circle in a candle holder, and light it. Set the chalice and the priapic wand next to the gray candle. Step back outside of the circle. When these preparations are complete, both partners say in unison:

Lord and Lady, Dark and Light
Be with us here this sacred night!

Both magical partners enter the circle and face each other. They then recite the following, with each partner alternating reading individual lines.

Assist me to build
As the Mighty Ones willed,
The altar of praise,
From the beginning of days,
Thus doth it lie,
'Twixt the earth and sky,
For so it was placed,
When the Old Ones embraced.

Use the love oil to draw a double spiral design, which symbolizes the joining of opposites. Dab your finger with the oil and draw one spiral at the center of your partner's chest (at the level of the heart chakra). After you spiral out with three concentric rings from the center point at the chest, connect this to the second spiral which spirals inward to a central point just above the genital area. Once you both have done this, continue reciting the following, each taking turns with the lines:

'O secret of secrets,
That art which is hidden,
Not thee do we love,
For that is not bidden,
For that which loveth is also thou.
And thou art myself from heel to brow.

Both partners embrace, light their respective candles together, and then place them in holders—the white one goes in the north and the black one to the south of your circle.

I am the flame that burns in the heart,
And at the core of every star.
I am life, which gives life its start.
But know ye that death is never afar.
I am alone, the unknown divine,
The Mystery of Mysteries beyond all sign.

Now, take turns using the love oil to anoint your partner at these magical points:

- Anoint your partner above the pubic hair
- Anoint the right foot
- Anoint the left hand
- Anoint the right hand
- Anoint the left foot
- Anoint just above the pubic region[47]

Now, kneel facing each other. One partner takes the priapic wand, the other, the chalice of wine or juice. The partner holding the wand should hold it over the chalice, as though ready to plunge it into the contents. The one holding the chalice should hold it just below the bottom tip of the wand. Continue reading, taking turns reading single lines:

Open for me the secret way,
The pathway of intelligence
Beyond the gates of night and day,
Beyond the bounds of time and sense.

Before ye stands the mystery aright;
The pentacle of love and bliss,
Here where the Lance and Grail unite,
At feet and knees and breast and kiss.

The holder of the wand now plunges the bottom tip into the chalice of wine or juice. Both partners then sip from the cup until they consume the contents. When finished, extinguish all candles and put all ritual items away.

Version III: The "Great Rite for One"

What You'll Need:

- The priapic wand
- Four candles: two black, two white
- A "chalice" (a fine wine glass or even a special cup) filled with wine or a red fruit juice (such as cranberry or pomegranate)

Set four black and four white candles (alternating their colors—one black and one white, etc.) in a circle on the floor. Set the chalice and the priapic wand next to the gray candle. Step back outside of the circle. Turn off the lights and disrobe. When these preparations are complete, say:

> *Lord and Lady, Dark and Light*
> *Be with us here this sacred night!*

Enter the circle and face north. Recite the following:

> *Assist me to build*
> *As the Mighty Ones willed,*
> *The altar of praise,*
> *From the beginning of days,*
> *Thus doth it lie,*
> *'Twixt the earth and sky,*
> *For so it was placed,*
> *When the Old Ones embraced.*

Use the love oil to draw a double spiral design, which symbolizes the joining of opposites. Dab your finger with the oil and draw one spiral at the center of your chest (at the level of the heart chakra). After you spiral out with three concentric rings from the center point at the chest, connect this to the second spiral which spirals inward to a central point just above your genital area. Once you both have done this, continue reciting the following:

> *'O secret of secrets,*
> *That art which is hidden,*
> *Not thee do we love,*
> *For that is not bidden,*
> *For that which loveth is also thou.*
> *And thou art myself from heel to brow.*

Close your eyes and imagine an ideal sexual partner, standing nude within your circle. He or she appears full of sexual desire. Continue to imagine this as you say:

> *I am the flame that burns in the heart,*
> *And at the core of every star.*
> *I am life, which gives life its start.*
> *But know ye that death is never afar.*
> *I am alone, the unknown divine,*
> *The Mystery of Mysteries beyond all sign.*

Now use the love oil to anoint yourself at these magical points:

- Anoint yourself above the pubic hair
- Anoint the right foot
- Anoint the left hand
- Anoint the right hand
- Anoint the left foot
- Anoint just above the pubic region

Hold the priapic wand above the chalice of wine or juice. Continue to envision your imaginary sexual partner as he or she touches you and embraces you, full of desire and passion. Continue reading:

> *Open for me the secret way,*
> *The pathway of intelligence*
> *Beyond the gates of night and day,*
> *Beyond the bounds of time and sense.*
> *Before ye stands the mystery aright;*
> *The pentacle of love and bliss,*
> *Here where the Lance and Grail unite,*
> *At feet and knees and breast and kiss.*

Now plunge the bottom tip of the wand into the chalice of wine or juice. Close your eyes and self-stimulate while envisioning an ideal sexual encounter. After you have reached climax, consume the contents of the ritual cup. When finished, extinguish all candles and put all ritual items away.

DAY 116

Beltane: A Day of Spiritual Love

Beltane's love is also known as the *pure love of the goddess*. But what is love at its core? Is it attachment to someone special? Is it a romantic feeling? Is it a heartwarming sensation? Where do we find this experience of pure love? In Wicca, the manifestation of love at its highest level emerges from nature. It does not involve romantic ideas or feelings. There are no candlelight dinners, moonlight strolls, or sentimental words spoken. It is an *impersonal* quality that emerges from the natural expression of life. The word "impersonal," in terms of love, sounds cold and aloof, but spiritual love is an embrace of all. It is undifferentiated love. It knows no attachments to particulars or individuals. It is the love of the sun that opens a flower. It is the love of a tigress for her cubs, or of a bee gathering nectar and pollen to make honey for the hive. It is everywhere and it runs deep in our cells. It is exactly what and who we are right now beneath the layers of code learned from culture and family.

The intricate story lines we develop about our lives come from these learned codes and they inhibit our experience of the goddess' pure, natural love. To make matters worse, over time we grow to *believe* in the code world and all of the stories and plot lines we have generated around it. When this happens, we act, speak and live in code. Meanwhile, nature continually knocks at the door of our lives begging to be let in. Today's practice begins the process of cracking the codes so that we can allow the natural circulation of the goddess' love in our lives.

To begin, take a blank piece of paper and make three columns. At the top of the first column write the word "family." At the top of the second, write the word "culture," and at the top of the third, write "religion." We learn many more codes in our lives, but these are the top three that affect most of us at deep, unconscious levels. Beneath the headings, write single words or short phrases that express learned rules that have shaped your thinking, feelings, and actions. Depending on your personal experience, beneath the word "family" you might write such words as "togetherness," "exclusion," or "self-sacrifice." Beneath culture you might identify, "entitlement," "gender roles," "food choices," or whatever other codes apply to your own learned experience. If you were not raised with religion, under this heading describe how the lack of religious upbringing may have shaped your current life story line.

When finished making your lists, select one word from each column. For the remainder of the day, be aware of how these three codes influence your thoughts, actions, and feelings. At the end of the day, you should have a very good feel for each of the three codes you've chosen. Select colors that represent these codes and write those colors down, perhaps using appropriately colored crayons or markers.

Now sit in your usual meditative posture and close your eyes. Use your imagination to see one of your colors swirling around you like a thick smoke. Next, take a deep breath and imagine that, as you inhale, you absorb the colored smoke. This practice may feel counterintuitive—we naturally believe that it is important to reject our more limiting qualities. However, in this practice, it is important to accept our limits, to accept ourselves just as we are. It is through your own metaphorical embrace of these traits that they naturally find their own resolution and thus open any blocked channels of the goddess' love, so try not to make a big deal of absorbing this energy. As you take it in, imagine that it transforms into a brilliant white light. As you exhale, imagine that you send this transformed white energy around your whole body and into the world.

Sit with this for a while. Are you able to accept yourself, right now, no matter what story line runs through your life? Practice this meditation each day until you finish your list of codes. By becoming more fully aware and accepting what goes into the making of "you," you open the direct channel of goddess-love. This is the love and acceptance of life, just as it is.

Day 117

Beltane: The Maypole

Maypoles are magical phallic symbols. The ancient Celts used the Maypole as the centerpiece for dancing and fertility rites aimed at fostering fecundity in their crops and in their livestock. The earliest records of the ritual describe villagers choosing a birch tree from a local forest, trimming its branches, and then planting the trimmed pole deep in mother earth to fructify her womb. They would then attach colorful streamers and flower garlands to the pole and weave the streamers around the pole as they danced.

The Celts may have inherited this festival from the Romans, who ruled the British Isles well into the fifth century CE. At this same time of year, the ancient Romans celebrated Flora, the goddess of plants and flowers.[48]

Today, create your own Maypole with friends. The pole can be made of any wood for the purpose of this practice. You can even try a Maypole dance inside your home. Simply tie ribbons onto a pole (perhaps even a broom handle) and have an attending member hold the pole above his or her head. All other members then can grab hold of a ribbon and dance, intertwining the ribbons.

Practice this rite to ensure luck and growth in your life for the coming year.

Day 118

Beltane: Dancing

Dancing was an aspect of the Beltane rites that was abhorred by the Christian church in the fifteenth and sixteenth century. The Church officially proclaimed that "dancing was sinister."[49] The so-called "Green Garters" folk dance, documented from that period, was one such dance that caused the church fathers to get hot under their Roman collars. On Beltane eve, the village folk would dance the Green Garters in a churchyard, and then would parade through the village to the central square, where they would continue with the Maypole rites.[50] Another documented May Day dance was called the *Besant* (or *Byzant*), which the local villagers would also practice in a churchyard. Of course many of the church's buildings were erected on ground sacred to the ancient pagans, the site chosen in an ongoing campaign to stamp out the indigenous spiritual faiths. However, the old ways were hard to suppress and naturally the ancient folk would return to their holy ground to commence with the customs they learned from their mothers and grandmothers.

No matter the effort of the church, the old May Day dances continued and we still have vestiges of these practices today. One May Day dance that celebrants continue to practice is that of the Morris dancers. In Great Britain on May Day, the Morris dancers gather on hillsides with special staves made of ash or oak. In their dance, they strike the earth with their staves in order to "awaken" the earth and foster fertility.

Practice: Sacred Dancing

As a tribute to this long-standing pagan practice, take time today to dance, either to music you select or simply out of spontaneity to the moment—with or without accompaniment. The most magical dances are inspired by the natural world. If possible, plan your dance activity by going to a remote location and dancing freely upon the earth. Listen to the sounds of nature and dance in a way that represents the sound. After you dance, take time to answer the following questions.

- How did it feel to dance?
- If the experience was uncomfortable for you—what do you suppose caused your feelings of discomfort?
- Did you sense your dancing stirred any energies inside of you? How did this energy move? How is it moving right now?

A Word to the Wise: Dance Inspiration—if the weather is inclement and you are unable to venure into the wilds of nature for this exercise, try finding a sounds of nature recording. Play the recording in the comfort of your home and use the recorded nature sounds to inspire your dance.

Day 119

Beltane: Sensuality

Sensuality—getting in touch with your sense—is a central Beltane theme. It is through our senses that we experience the world. Not only that, eating, seeing, touching, smelling, and hearing are all ways that we experience the gods as they manifest through the world. In other words, what it is you taste, touch, smell, see, and hear is deity itself. Your food is the god and goddess. The smell of freshly cut grass is the god and goddess. Anything you can experience through the senses is the production of the gods, and therefore is sacred.

Today, find a delicious piece of fruit or some other appetizing food. (In our group we practiced this technique with strawberries.) Begin by simply taking time to visually regard the food. Look at its shape, size and color—all without making up a story line by thinking about the food. Simply use the eyes to behold the food item. Now use your fingers to touch the food. After that, spend time smelling it. Finally, eat the food slowly, without mental comments. Allow your tongue and taste buds to speak for themselves.

Were you able to sense the divinity within this food item? Try this exercise with sexual activity, putting on clothing, taking a shower or bath, petting the dog, or any other activity that involves bodily sensation. Leave the thinking-brain out of the mix while you engage with the body. How does doing this change your mental state? Does removing the inner, mental commentary change your way of *experiencing*? How?

Day 120

Beltane: May Eve Chant

What You'll Need:

- A priapic wand
- Four stones (I prefer river stones)

This is an adaptation of the May carols recited by pagan villagers in Old Europe on the morning of Beltane.[51] For this practice, you will first need to create a priapic wand and then gather four stones.

Find a space that will allow you to walk freely in a clockwise circle that is at least 9 feet in diameter. To assure the accuracy of your measurement, use a 9-foot length of string or cord. Lay the cord on the ground and place river stones at each end. Then lay the cord crosswise to mark out where you will place two more stones. You should have the stones mark the four cross-quarter compass points.

Hold the wand in your right hand high above your head. Begin walking slowly around the circle in a clockwise fashion, saying:

All Witches gathered 'round the ring,
And thus do we begin,
The Beltane spell to conjure spring,
And Summer Solstice in!

We have been rambling all the night,
And sometime of this day,
And now returning home aright,
We bring you a branch of May!

A garland gay, 'is strong and stout,
And at your door we stand,
'Tis not a sprout, but budded out,
The work of the goddess' hand.

The gates of Faery open on,
The path is beaten plain,
And however far ye may have gone,
Ye may return again.

Dance ye round, and let ye fall,
To conjure all this day,
Blessed be all, both great and small,
And send you a joyful May!

At the close of the chant, lay the wand in the center of the circle and gather up the stones. Bury all of this in your garden or wherever you want fertility.

Days 121-150

Magical Items to Gather

Here is a list of items you will need during the next month of training:

Day 121

- ¼ ounce powdered sandalwood (better: ¼ ounce powdered hawthorn wood)
- 1 teaspoon dry crushed almonds
- 2 teaspoons frankincense tears
- 1 teaspoon dry meadowsweet
- Vegetable glycerin
- Rose essential oil
- Rosemary essential oil

Day 122

- A 5–6 inch green taper candle

Day 125

- A bundle of dried twigs from local trees or
- A 5–6 inch red taper candle
- Cinnamon essential oil

Day 126

- A red pen
- A 12-inch ruler
- Chamomile essential oil (optional)

Day 128

- A "wreath frame" (found at a craft supply store)
- Straw or dried moss (found at a craft supply store)
- Dried flowers
- Sand/stones

Day 131

- Chamomile essential oil

Day 132

- 1¼ cup blanched almonds
- 1¼ cups sugar
- 3 large egg whites
- 2 teaspoons vanilla extract
- The zest from 1 orange

Day 134

- A small piece of topaz or a piece of gold
- A small clear-glass container

Day 136

- ¼ ounce pine (wood), either powdered or chips
- ¼ ounce powdered sandalwood
- 2 teaspoons white copal
- 1 teaspoon dried bay laurel
- 1 teaspoon hemp seed (because this item may be difficult to procure, it is listed here for traditional purposes only; it is not a required ingredient)
- Vegetable glycerin
- Cedar essential oil
- Carnation essential oil
- Cinnamon essential oil

Day 137

- A 5–6 inch brown taper candle

Day 140

- 4 dried stalks of wheat or
- 4 fresh flowers with stem and bud attached
- A cauldron or other vessel in which you can burn items safely
- Old newspaper or kindling
- A boline (the Witch term for a small sickle) or paring knife
- Several small candles or tea lights of any color

Day 146

- ¼ ounce oak (wood), either powdered or chips
- ¼ ounce powdered sandalwood

- 2 teaspoons frankincense
- 1 teaspoon dried oats (you can use the easily found rolled flakes such as that found in oatmeal)
- Vegetable glycerin
- Patchouli essential oil
- Rosemary essential oil

Day 147

- An ordinary garden sickle
- ¼ ounce black polyurethane paint
- ¼ ounce red polyurethane paint
- A thin detailing paintbrush

Day 148

- Two 5–6 inch brown taper candles

Day 149

- 2 teaspoons fenugreek seed

Day 150

- A 5–6 inch green-yellow taper candle

Day 121

Beltane: Incense and Oil

Beltane Incense

Burn this incense at your Beltane ritual, or at any time that you want to bring about the energies and insights of Beltane.

What You'll Need:

- A handful of powdered sandalwood (better: a handful of powdered hawthorn wood)
- 1 teaspoon dry, crushed almonds
- 2 teaspoons frankincense tears
- 1 teaspoon dry meadowsweet
- Vegetable glycerin
- 10 drops rose essential oil

In a medium-sized bowl, place your powdered sandalwood. Stir in about two tablespoons of vegetable glycerin. Add the tablespoons one at a time and then mix with a metal whisk or a fork. You simply want to create a soft, fluffy compound. Do not add the second tablespoon of glycerin if it feels like it would be too much, causing the incense to be too wet.

Now add your essential oils and whisk. Add your other dried herbs and mix thoroughly. Wait for at least a day for the compound to settle before you sprinkle it on hot coals.

Beltane Oil

Use this oil to anoint attendees of your Beltane ritual. You can also use this oil any time you want to awaken the insights and mysteries of Beltane. This oil activates the magical energies of sexuality, love, and union.

What You'll Need:

- Vegetable glycerin (or a carrier oil such as grape seed oil)
- 4 drops rose essential oil
- 3 drops rosemary essential oil
- Pinch of frankincense

Find a one-ounce bottle. Fill the bottle halfway with vegetable glycerin. Add plain water until the bottle is three-quarters full. Add your essential oils. Add dry ingredients, close the lid, and shake the bottle. You can use this magical oil immediately.

Day 122

Contemplative Day: Life Itself

Meditative Question: What is this life?

Symbolic Color: Green

Symbolic Direction: North

This month's contemplative question brings you toward realizing your place within the vastness of life itself. It challenges you to explore your place in the world and the purpose of your being. It opens your spiritual senses so that you come into accord with the natural world and the energies of the goddess and god. It is an important question to face as you travel along the path of Wicca.

The magical power you are able to accrue over the course of your year and a day practice is in direct proportion to your ability to align your life with that of the natural world. This contemplative question allows you to see the connection between you and life itself.

Solving this month's contemplative question will not be easy. In fact, you may choose to return to this question time and again until you reach a satisfactory understanding. Through the process of unraveling the question of the month, you will notice an increase in your wisdom and magical power. Many magical folk gain clarity in the issues of their everyday living as a result of engaging in this unique, contemplative work.

As usual, begin by finding a comfortable, meditative sitting position. This time, sit facing the north. Light a green candle, place it in front of you, and cast your gaze upon the flickering candle. As you have already learned in previous contemplative questions, be sure to sit holding the question for 20 to 30 minutes.

This month's question is one that both scholars and mystics have pursued over the course of history. Neither through intellectualization, free-association, nor even through guessing can you arrive at a satisfactory or compelling resolution and mystic realization. Don't expect to unravel the mysteries of this contemplation in one day. Instead, hold the question firmly in your mind over whatever length of time may be necessary. See the question as it manifests in each of your activities. Do not try to logically answer the question. Instead, become one with the question itself in each of your tasks. Be this question as you eat, sleep, work, and play. Over time, a shift in your perception will take place and you will realize your own answer.

Day 123

Devotional Day: Honoring Dionysus

Table of Correspondences: Dionysus

Symbols: Grapes, wine, wheat, pomegranates, and the lyre

Tools: The wand, the chalice, the thrysus (a fennel stalk)

Magical Essences/Herbs: Cedar, white oak bark, and sage

Direction: Dionysus is aligned with the west

He Rules: Insight, mystic awareness, the ability to see other dimensions, ability to commune with elemental forces

Animal Symbols: Snake, bull, goat

Sacred Foods: Wine, whole grain breads, and pomegranates

Magical Stones: Black diamond

In Greek myth, Dionysus is a complex god of vegetation, spiritual rebirth, sexuality, and ecstasy. He represents the untamed, ecstatic force behind all magic. Dionysus' title is *dithyrambos,* which means "twice born." He was first rescued from the womb of his human mother by Zeus, and then embedded for the remaining term of gestation in Zeus' thigh. Thus, Dionysus was said to be born both of mortals and gods. Because of this, he is a being that lives *between the worlds,* a concept that is sacred to all Witches.

When you evoke your spiritual center connected with Dionysus you also evoke spiritual insight, mystic awareness, the ability to see other dimensions, and the ability to commune with the elemental forces of nature. Dionysus' sacred symbols are grapes, wine, wheat, pomegranates, and the lyre. Dionysus' magical colors are maroon, deep blue, and purple. His magical essences and herbs are cedar, white oak bark, and sage. The times of the day that you can easily evoke the presence of Dionysus are at dusk and midnight. Wine, whole grain breads, and pomegranates are Dionysus' sacred foods.

Dionysus Practice

In honoring Dionysus today, make an altar that includes his sacred symbols. Light appropriately colored candles and intone the syllables of his name once and again, in sustained tones, saying "Di-o-ny-sus!" Continue to chant his name until you feel or sense his presence. Once he has arrived, spend some time contemplating what it might mean to serve this aspect of deity. Take time to contemplate the fact that you are an expression of both humanity and the gods. Honor this god today by encouraging others to step outside of the usual bounds of thinking, speaking, and action.

Day 124

Day of Silence and Review

Today, as you observe silence, focus your attention on the interplay between thoughts and emotions. Do not attempt to limit your thoughts or your emotional reactions to the events of your day; simply observe the activity and how one factor might influence another. When the day is complete, answer these questions:

- In what way did my thoughts impact my emotions?
- In what way did my emotions impact my thoughts?
- What might happen if I alter either my thought or emotional pattern?
- How do the interplay of thoughts and emotions affect my physical energy or health?
- How can understanding the interplay between emotions and thoughts help me develop spiritually?

Review

For today's practice, take time to ask yourself the following:

- Of the information I have learned up to now, what stands out most as vital?
- What information seems least relevant to my spiritual development?
- Which of the practices seemed to move me spiritually, and which had little impact?
- Of the information I have learned so far, what would be best to review? (Take time to review it now.)

Day 125

Summer Solstice

The sun is at its zenith—and paradoxically begins its decline—during the Summer Solstice, the longest day of the solar year. The Solstice usually occurs between June 19 and 23—when the sun enters the sign of Cancer. In old Europe, the Summer Solstice, or Midsummer, was an important fire festival. In some ancient accounts, villagers would set wheels made of straw or cartwheels smeared with pitch ablaze and then roll them down a hill to signify the sun's descent, or gradual darkening, which followed this longest of days.[52] Another Midsummer custom involved farmers lighting torches and then parading them around newly ripening fields. The intention of this rite was to drive out harmful dragons or spirits that might cause sickness in their communities. The rite was also aimed at preventing weakness in the harvest. Interestingly enough, the mythical dragon is a universal symbol for the element of fire, which is the primary energetic expression of Midsummer. In yet another custom, villagers would wrap a wooden pillar in a thick coat of straw and place it at the central part of town. The pillar was then set afire. The central pillar represented the phallic Maypole previously planted in the earth-womb at Beltane. Symbolically speaking, this magical act represented both the empowerment and the destruction of the phallic principle. In other words, the principle of life (as represented both by the sun and the phallus) was simultaneously at its height and in its decline at the time of the Summer Solstice. It was the realization of this principle, which includes a juxtaposition of power and energy, of height and decline, of life and death, that captured the ancient imagination. The most common Midsummer practice for the ancient Europeans was the lighting of immense bonfires at the tops of hills. The bonfires were a communal event and each of a village's family members were required to contribute firewood, straw, and twigs to the fires. Once a bonfire was extinguished, villagers would remove glowing embers and place them in the earth near their homes. They might also place them in their crop-producing fields or in the fireplace. One custom in some villages was to set the bristles of old brooms ablaze and then fling the entire broom into the air. The youngest male of a household would then preserve the remaining broom handle so that it could be stuck into the ground to protect gardens and vegetation. In other accounts, magical folks would use the extinguished, yet still smoking, broom bristles to fumigate and bless new homes.[53]

Practice: Fire Purification

What You'll Need:

- A bundle of dried twigs from local trees, or
- A red candle
- Cinnamon essential oil
- A cauldron or deep iron cooking pot filled with sand (or stones)

Fire has a purifying quality. In some ancient medical practices, doctors would use fire to cleanse and seal wounds. Fire purifies because it exhausts a source of fuel completely and cleanly. When something is burned completely, thoroughly, it is gone—cleansed from existence.

In today's practice, you will cleanse your spirit of unwanted energies, toxic forces, and in the process you will unburden your life of wasted energy. To begin, gather together some dried twigs (if you can find them; if not use a red candle). Bundle the twigs at one end with some twine and set that bundled end into a pot or cauldron filled with sand or small stones. Be sure that that the bundled end is securely wedged into the sand or small stones before you go to the next step.

Close your eyes and sense where in your body you hold dark, hot, or heavy energies. You do not need to name the energies, just sense where they are. Once you have done this, smear the twigs (or candle) with cinnamon oil. Light the bundle of twigs (or your candle) on fire now and stand back. As the bundle burns, use your hands to touch or symbolically scoop the unwanted energies away from your body and then push this energy into the fire. Imagine that the fire burns these energies completely away.

Day 126

Summer Solstice's Meaning

If you think in terms of symbolism, the Summer Solstice holds a wealth of it. Let's begin with the sun. If you change your perspective slightly to view the sun's annual passage through the heavens as a symbol that represents the passage of years in your own life, Midsummer suddenly communicates to us a vital message. Summer Solstice is the midpoint of the solar year. Symbolically speaking this represents the midpoint of a human life. Just as the sun is at its height of power at Midsummer, it also begins its decline. This is a wonderful natural metaphor for our own lives when we face the crossroads of our midlife.

But as we turn the wheel of the year to face Midsummer, how do we respond to fully facing the matter of our own mortality? This is a shamanic conundrum, an important challenge that cannot be solved through planning or strategy. Many people face the issue of their mortality for the first time during the well-known midlife crisis, a time marked with frantic activity and desperation to turn back time, or to change one's life from perceived insignificance. Behind the frenetic activity is a deep, nonverbal, unconscious fear of death. What should we do with all of this? Should we run and hide? Should we just give up?

Nature provides us with an answer, which is encoded in the sun's activity. When we think of the sun in its decline, we note that it does not scatter its power in fear and desperation. It does not attempt to turn back time or change the way things are. It simply shines fully, brightly—just as it is—fading, fading into an ever-darkening year. In our own lives, this symbolizes the practice of accepting fully our lives as they are in the moment without fear or striving for effect. It teaches us to acknowledge and surrender to a natural progression that cannot ever be changed.

The Midsummer celebration should open your consciousness to living fully in each moment, accepting your life just as it is. Tomorrow may or may not come. How does this knowledge affect you?[54]

Practice: Solar Magic House Blessing

What You'll Need:

- A page of blank white paper
- A red pen
- A ruler (to help create the solar mathematical table)
- Chamomile essential oil (optional)

Today, and on the actual Summer Solstice, bless and energize your home with the sun's "magical square," also called the *planetary kamea* by the ancient magus Cornelius Agrippa.[55] The kamea is meant to mathematically represent the spirit or energy of the sun (or of other planets or spiritual powers). By creating the solar magical square and by placing it over your doorway, you assure the strength and vitality of the sun to permeate your home and your life.

A Word to the Wise: Interestingly, if you add the numbers up in any given magic square either vertically, horizontally, or diagonally, you arrive at the same total.

To begin, take out a blank piece of paper. Magical squares are traditionally engraved on never-before-used parchment paper, but most magical practitioners agree that regular blank white paper is effective. Use a ruler or a straight edge to create an equal-sided square. Inside of this square create six rows and six columns (equally spaced), so that you have 36 smaller squares within the larger square. Fill the squares as shown here.

Cut out the square and rub the edges of the paper (rubbing clockwise around the edges) with chamomile essential oil. Hang this over the front door of your home.

6	32	3	34	35	1
7	11	27	28	8	30
19	14	16	15	23	24
18	20	22	21	17	13
25	29	10	9	26	12
36	5	33	4	2	31

Day 127

Summer Solstice: Fairy Energies

Midsummer is the perfect time to commune with the world of fairies. Belief in fairies was widespread in pagan Europe, especially in Ireland. Scholars are uncertain about the origins of the fairies. W. Y. Evan Wentz proposed three theories of the fairies in his book *The Fairy Faith in Celtic Countries*. One theory says that they are vestiges of the early Celts' rationalization about natural phenomena. The second of his theories suggests that the fairies were a race of small or pigmy people who were forced to live far from the Celtic tribes. The third theory states that the fairies were fictitious; they were folklore passed down from ancient Druids.[56]

A Word to the Wise: Fairies in Wicca are one of four orders of elemental, magical creatures. Fairies are magical creatures that reside in (and are made up of the astral energies of) the element of Air. They align with the symbolic compass direction of east. Their symbolic time is dawn. In occult lore fairies are the bringers of knowledge and they are magical teachers. As you progress through the year you will learn more about fairies, as well as the other three types of elemental beings.

Whether these creatures exist in physical form is a matter of debate. In occult lore, fairies are nature spirits of the air. Witches who tap deeply into the tides of nature feel their spiritual presence. According to myth, the favorite places where you can find these spiritual forces and tap into their energies include most untamed natural settings but especially:

- Near or beneath ferns
- Near or beneath toadstools
- Small grassy mounds (also called fairy mounds or fairy hills)
- Near or inside of wells and natural springs
- In fields of wildflowers or wild herbs
- In forests
- In deserts
- Near fireplaces and bonfires

Take time to explore a natural setting today where you sense that you might find fairies. While you are there, sit on the ground, close your eyes and silently invite the fairies into your presence. Do not make sudden moves or open your eyes. Simply sit and allow the energies to surround you. You may feel tingling or a tickling sensation on the skin or internally. This is how many folks report they first experience the elemental energies.

After a few minutes of experiencing the fairy energies, silently thank them and let them know that you will be leaving their magical plane. Open your eyes and place an offering on the ground. Then leave the spot and do not return. In Ireland, traditional offerings include bits of cheese, eggs, apples, or bread.[57]

A Word to the Wise: The spirits of fire are *Salamanders,* the spirits of water are *Undines,* the spirits of earth are *Gnomes*. You will learn more about nature spirits, their attributes and powers later in the year.

Day 128

Summer Solstice: Making the Sun Wheel

What You'll Need:

- A "wreath frame" (usually bought from a craft supply store)
- Straw or moss
- Several 4 x 4 inch squares of paper
- Dried flowers

The Sun Wheel practice is a way to honor and energize the archetypes of the sun in your life. To create the traditional "burning wheel" or "solar wheel," begin by purchasing a wreath frame from a craft supply store. If you do not have a wreath frame handy, you can simply soften a freshly cut, thin tree branch in cold water for 8–10 hours. Then tie the ends together to shape the branch into a circle. This will be your wreath frame. If you choose to make your own wreath frame, be sure to begin the project at least 1–2 days before using it for any magical purpose. The purpose of making the wreath frame ahead of time is so that it will have a chance to dry out.

Attach dried moss or dried straw to your frame. Once this is complete, take time to write down your talents, skills, or accomplishments. List one talent/skill on each 4 x 4 inch square of paper. Twist these pieces of paper, pack them into the straw and moss and attach them with florist's wire. Finish the wreath with some beautiful dried flowers. Dried sunflowers are particularly magical and evocative of the season. Set the wreath in a place of prominence to evoke the qualities of the sun in your life. You will need this wreath for tomorrow's practice.

Day 129

Summer Solstice: The Burning Wheel

What You'll Need:

- Your finished sun wheel
- Old newspaper, twigs, or other suitable kindling
- Sand and stones
- A barbecue or fire pit

Take your decorated wreath to a fire pit or other location where it can burn safely.

In this next portion of the magical working, use extreme caution when handling fire. You, your loved ones and property can be burned, damaged, or injured if you do not use standard fire safety procedures as outlined in earlier practices. If you do not wish to use fire, simply visualize the process of lighting the wheel aflame. If you do use fire, I strongly recommend keeping sand, water, and a fire extinguisher on hand for emergencies.

Set the wreath into a fire pit and place old newspaper or other kindling in and around the wreath to assure that it will properly catch fire. Light the kindling on fire using a long wooden matchstick or long-nosed lighter and quickly step away from the fire. Allow the wreath to burn completely. Have sand, water, and a fire extinguisher nearby to extinguish the fire should it pose any danger.

While the wreath burns, hold the palms of your hands toward the flames and recite this traditional Old English Summer verse:

Traditional Old English Verse

Summer is icumen in
Lhudle sing cuccu!
Groweth sed and bloweth med
and springth the wode nu.
Sing cuccu!
Awe bleteth after lomb,

lhouth after calve cu,
Bulluc sterteth, bucke uerteth_.
Murie sing cuccu!
Cuccu, cuccu,
Wel singes theu cuccu.
nu swik thu naver nu!
Sing cuccu nu, Sing cuccu!

Contemporary English Translation

Summer is a-coming in
Loudly sing cuckoo
Groweth seed and bloweth mead
and springs the wood anew
Sing cuckoo!
Ewe bleateth after lamb,
Calf loweth after cow,
The bullock jumps, the buck mounts,
Merry sing cuckoo!
Cuckoo, cuckoo!
Well singest thou cuckoo,
Nor cease thou never now!
Sing cuckoo now, Sing cuckoo!

Day 130

Summer Solstice: Sun Vigil

Today, honor the sun by watching it set. Go to a favorite natural setting where you can clearly see the sun set on the horizon. Before you do this, check in your local newspaper or almanac to know the exact time of the sunset—otherwise you may be waiting for a long time for the big event.

When you arrive at the viewing spot, lay out a comfortable blanket and sit on the ground. Close your eyes and feel the warmth of the sun on your skin. Mentally thank the sun for bringing light into your day. You can make an offering of some sweet cakes or a libation of wine on the earth at this time. Without directly looking into the sun's light, peer now and again at it as it sinks into the west. After the sun has set, take time to consider the following:

- What personal associations do you have with the sun?
- What memories do you have related to the sun (sunburn, a favorite sunny day, etc.)?
- What feelings or energies do you sense as the sun sets?
- How might the energies you have sensed be useful to you in your life?

Day 131

Summer Solstice: Solar Healing

What You'll Need:

- Chamomile essential oil

The sun has magical healing properties from which Witches and magical folk draw. Witches traditionally practice this sun-drawing technique at sunrise—or at least within the first hours of sunrise. Go to some place where you can have a full view of the rising sun. Face the sunrise, close your eyes, and feel the solar warmth on your skin.

Now imagine that the sun draws out from you any heavy, dark energies. Any illnesses or emotional difficulties you face can be eased if you allow the sun to draw them out from you now. Imagine them leaving you, floating up and out toward the sun, where they are annihilated forever.

As you stand there imagining the energies leaving you, repeat the following chant to the sun thrice:

> ***Morning sun, take my pain!***
> ***Ease my heart; illness wane.***

Conclude the rite by anointing your heart chakra (at the center of your chest) with chamomile essential oil, which aligns you with the essence of solar energy.

Day 132

Summer Solstice: Sun Cakes

During the solstices and equinoxes, many Wiccans make sun cakes, which are small, simple cakes (or more properly, cookies) that contain solar properties. Witches typically eat these during the main part of a solstice or equinox ritual. During the ritual, a facilitating Wiccan priestess or priest blesses the sun cakes by drawing the power of the sun down upon them. As celebrants eat their sun cakes they use their creative imaginative abilities to visualize the power of the sun entering them, gently warming the spirit and imbuing them with the life-giving energies of the sun.

Practice: Making Solar Cakes

What You'll Need:

- 1¾ cups blanched almonds
- 1½ cups sugar
- 3 large egg whites
- 2 teaspoons vanilla extract
- The zest from 1 orange

Put your almonds into a food processor and grind them until they are a fine powder. Use a cheese grater to remove the colorful outside part of the orange rind—its "zest." Preheat your oven to 375 degrees. Using an electric mixer, blend together the orange rind, ground almonds, egg whites, vanilla extract, and sugar. Beat this together until thick. Roll the dough into small balls and set them on a nonstick baking sheet. Flatten the balls with your fingers, making a circle. Make sure to moisten your fingers with some water before flattening the balls to avoid sticking. Use a toothpick to make a dot at the center of each circle.

This symbol of the circle with a dot at the center is the zodiacal representation (also called a "glyph") of the sun.

Day 133

Summer Solstice: Solar Cake Blessing

What You'll Need:

- Sun cakes
- Four gold taper candles

In today's practice, you will imbue the cakes you have made with the energies of the sun. Set the cakes on a windowsill during the daytime for at least an hour.

If you live in a location where there are few sunny days, or if you practice this technique on a day with no visible sun, it does not matter. What matters more than visible sun is your knowledge that the sun lies beyond the clouds. Know that its life-giving energy penetrates the earth, no matter where you are.

After the cakes have had a chance to soak up some sun energy, bring them to a table. Light four gold candles and set them in a circle around the platter of cakes. Stand in the "Provider" magical pass position, with your right hand up at shoulder height, palm facing away from the chest. The left hand is open at the hip, with the palm facing away from the hip. Modify this pose by hovering the left palm slightly above the platter of sun cakes. Close your eyes and imagine that the sun's rays enter in the space between your brows and channel down through your left hand, entering into the cakes.

While you do this, say the following incantation:

Wheel of the sun,
Great wheel of time,
Radiant scepter, shining over all!
I draw thee down,
To enter here,
Become these cakes
O shining Sphere!

When you are finished, open your eyes and place the palms of your hands together to stop the flow of solar energy. Eat one or two of the cakes. Share them with friends or with anyone who needs solar energy, blessings, or healing.

Day 134

Summer Solstice: Stone Waters

The sun at its full power is a perfect time to make magical stone waters. A stone water is plain spring water into which you drop a quartz crystal (or other gem). This then is placed in the sunlight to "steep" for several hours. In magical practice, the crystal yields its spiritual essence, like a tea bag sitting in a warm sun-tea jar. This practice comes from the early Celts who would place white or rose quartz crystals into boiling water, which was later cooled and applied to the body for healing.[58] Magical folks use stone waters for many purposes, but they use them predominantly for healing or for absorbing the magical attributes of particular stones or gems. In this case, we will make an elixir that contains the magical essence of the sun.

What You'll Need:

- A small clear-glass container
- A small piece of topaz or a piece of gold

The method is simple. Hold the small topaz or the piece of gold up to the first rays of the sun. Imagine that your mineral absorbs the sun's rays. Next, set the stone into a small clear glass container of water. Place the container with the crystal on a window ledge where the sun can shine on it all day long. At the end of the day, remove the stone and drink the water. As you do this, you will absorb the energies of the sun.

Day 135

Summer Solstice: More Stone Waters

Try making a stone water with other magical rocks. Here is a short list of stones and the properties they traditionally impart:

Amber: To enhance beauty

Amethyst: Magical dreams and visions, tranquility, spiritual awareness

Bloodstone: For success in business, courage, and healing; magical power

Jade: Luck, love, longevity, health, prosperity, wisdom

Moonstone: Moon goddess energies, psychic ability, love

Marble: Success, prosperity, solidity

Obsidian: Peace

Opal: To bring about change, magical ability, prosperity

Quartz crystal: Psychic ability, awareness, receptivity

Day 136

Summer Solstice: Incense and Oil

Summer Incense

Burn this incense at your Summer Solstice ritual, or at any time that you want to bring about the energies and insights of Summer Solstice.

What You'll Need:

- ½ handful of pine (wood), either powdered or chips
- ½ handful of powdered sandalwood
- 2 teaspoons white copal
- 1 teaspoon dried bay laurel
- 1 teaspoon hemp seed (because this item may be difficult to procure, it is listed here for traditional purposes only; it is not a required ingredient)
- Vegetable glycerin
- 5 drops cedar essential oil
- 3 drops carnation essential oil
- 3 drops cinnamon oil

In a medium-sized bowl, place your powdered sandalwood. Stir in about two tablespoons of vegetable glycerin. Add the glycerin one tablespoon at a time, mixing with a metal whisk or a fork. You simply want to create a soft, fluffy compound. Do not add the second tablespoon of glycerin if it feels like it would be too much, causing the incense to be too wet.

Now add your essential oils and whisk. Add your other dried herbs and mix thoroughly. Wait for at least a day for the compound to settle before you sprinkle it on hot coals.

Summer Oil

Use this oil to anoint attendees of your Summer Solstice ritual. You can also use this oil any time that you want to awaken the insights and mysteries of Summer Solstice. This oil activates the magical energies of joy, freedom, power, and strength.

What You'll Need:

- Vegetable glycerin (or a carrier oil such as grape seed oil)
- 5 drops cedar essential oil
- 3 drops carnation essential oil
- 3 drops cinnamon oil
- Pinch of chamomile flowers, hemp seed, white copal, or all three dried herbs!

Find a one-ounce bottle. Fill the bottle halfway with vegetable glycerin. Add plain water until the bottle is three-quarters full. Add your essential oils. Add dry ingredients, close the lid, and shake the bottle. You can use this magical oil immediately.

Day 137

Lammas

On the eve of August 1, Wiccans gather to celebrate the first of their harvest festivals, which is Lammas. The name Lammas is a derivation of "loaf-mass," or *hlaf-mas,*[59] an ancient celebration of the bread loaves that villagers would fashion from the first grains of their harvest. The gathering of grains and making of loaves marked the beginning of the harvesting season in rural Old Europe.[60] In Ireland, they call Lammas the feast of *Lughnassadh* (pronounced *Loo'-nah-sah*)—the feast of the Celtic god Lugh. Occultists draw parallels between the Celtic Lugh and the Roman Mercury,[61] since both are gods who are skilled in all arts—especially in magic. Lughnassadh was aptly named because it was a tide of great natural magic for the rural folk of Europe. The earth, their mother, was providing them once more with fruits and grain so that they might live. They watched seed become sprout, bud, leaf, and then flower. To the ancient mind—and still to us today—this was a feat of stupendous natural magic.

The theme of sacrifice was an important aspect of the ancient celebrations of Lughnassadh. This sacred harvest represented the sacrifice of the horned god, as he manifests through the grain, to sustain human lives. This archetypal theme of altruistic sacrificial offering (in this case through death) is the same found around the globe in various guises, but which remains a familiar centerpiece of the Christian mythos. In the Celtic mythic cycle of the *Mabinogian*, Lugh represented the European manifestation of the sacrificed god archetype.[62] Other names of the Old European sacrificed god were John Barleycorn and the Green Man. Pagan folk of Old Europe would actualize this theme of the sacrificed god through the reaping of their first crops, which represented the god sacrifice.[63]

Celebrants might mark the feast day with circular dances aimed at regenerating the earth and building the community. They might also offer newly harvested crops as sacrifices to the old gods. Celtic pagan priests would invoke the gods Lugh and Danu to protect the harvest. Villagers might then play at games that represented the winnowing of grain.[64]

Practice: Harvest Luck and House Protection

What You'll Need:

- Fresh produce of your choosing (favorites among pagans are corn and squash)
- A brown taper candle about 5–6 inches in length

One magical Lughnassadh custom was bringing the prized and highly magical first sheaf of corn across the front door threshold of one's home. The villagers would offer this honor to the person who obtained the first sheaf of corn, and the custom would ensure luck and protection from illness and poverty for the coming year. In your practice today, go to the grocery store and select a produce (or grain) item that has symbolic attributes that represent a quality you would like to bring into your life. For example, you may select a bunch of carrots because their orange color seems to represent the warmth of the sun. Or you may select a red pepper because you want to bring zest and vitality into the home. An apple might appeal to you because it represents soothing feminine energy. Be creative in your own selection process, make your own symbolic associations.

Bring the produce or grain to your home, but before you bring it inside, light a brown taper candle (a color that represents the earth and harvest) and hold it in your left hand. Stand before the front door of your house, hold the food item above the lit candle flame, and say:

O Holy Lugh, Lord of the Harvest,
Bring [state your desire] into my home,
With this harvested fruit of the land.

Step over the threshold of your front door. Place the food item somewhere near the door through which you just entered and set the candle close by. Allow the candle to burn completely out. After the candle extinguishes, prepare and eat a portion of the food item in silence.

Day 138

The Meaning of Lammas

The central symbol of Lammas is the sacrifice. But what exactly is the nature of sacrifice? A typical sacrifice involves something (or someone) giving of itself for the sake of others. In this broad definition, sacrifice involves one form of energy giving itself up so that it can transform into something else. From this perspective we can see that soil, for example, offers itself in sacrifice in order to nourish seeds. The seed's sprouts then offer themselves in sacrifice to become plants. Food sacrifices its energy so that it can become our bodies. It is this mystery of sacrifice, of selfless offering, that lies at the core of Lughnassadh.

The fact of existence is that life feeds on life. When one ponders this state of survival, naturally thoughts can lead to questioning the purpose of living itself. What is this life that feeds on itself? Perhaps it is comforting to know that you are not alone when facing this daunting reality. Since the beginning of time, human beings have struggled to reconcile human consciousness with this mystery of life feeding on itself. [65]

One well-known Wiccan principle that seems to stand in stark contrast to the reality of Lammas is that of "harming none." This is a central tenet of *The Wiccan Rede,* which is a rule of thumb that guides Witchcraft magic and practice. In the Rede, Witches are bade to "harm none, and do as ye will." However, the question remains: how can we survive without "harming?" Life survives by killing and eating other life. There is no other way.

There are two principal views to be considered: the *deity perspective* and the *mundane perspective.* The deity perspective encompasses the mystical view of existence and the sacrifice inherent to being alive. In this view, there are no distinctions between life and death, light and dark, here and there. Life is one functioning whole unit. From this detached (perhaps indifferent) universal perspective, there is nothing personal about life feeding upon itself. There is no harm caused to anything or anyone because nothing lives independent from anything else. In the deity perspective, there is no one to harm and no one doing the harm. When we view this same natural cycle from a mundane perspective, we label it "killing and eating," but from the deity perspective the label is removed—it is merely one of the myriad functions of existence.

However, there is also the matter of the practical mundane perspective, which does recognize differences and can see the difference between killing and not killing. It is in this realm that we live on a daily basis. From this perspective, we notice "harm." So, in one perspective there is no harm, and simultaneously, there is harm. It is a difficult quandary for each of us to consider, and the celebration of Lughnassadh calls our attention to this mystery and invites us to face it head on.

In considering these mysteries, Lughnassadh awakens in us a sense of conscious living. It calls for each of us to adopt the frame of reference of the great whole as we live our daily lives and consume. When we realize that we owe our lives to the plants and animals that we consume, we open our consciousness to an enduring sense of gratitude.

Practice: Pagan Grace

Today, before each meal, consider the substances that are about to sacrifice themselves so that they can become your own body, your own life force. Instead of thanking some notion of a divinity (as you might do in mainstream religious practices), thank the animal or plant that has given its life so that it can become you. With each mouthful, open your heart in thanksgiving.

- Did this practice change anything internally for you? If so, what changed?
- Is thanking the animal or plant that gives its life any different than thanking a god or goddess? How?

Day 139

Lammas: Breaking Bread

Breaking bread is a central Lughnassadh custom. In this ritual, members of a spiritual community gather, and each attendee bestows personal thanks and good wishes into a central loaf of bread. One member of the group then holds the bread before the community and breaks it. Each member then consumes a small portion of the loaf in order to assume its virtues and blessings. This will be our practice today.

What You'll Need:

- A whole loaf of bread, unsliced
- Several 4 x 4 inch squares of blank paper
- A red ink pen
- A cauldron or other burning vessel

Gather together a group of magical practitioners (or try this on your own). Have participants use the red pen to write down a wish or a blessing for the coming year. Place the papers in a heavy cauldron or other deep metal container. Light the wishes on fire. Hold the loaf above the flames and imagine that the energy of these wishes enters from the flames into the loaf of bread. While this happens, say:

> ***Hoof and horn, hoof and horn,***
> ***All that dies shall be reborn!***
> ***Corn and grain, corn and grain,***
> ***All that falls shall rise again!***
> ***We all come from the goddess,***
> ***And to her we shall return;***
> ***Like a drop of rain,***
> ***Flowing to the ocean!***

Break the loaf in half just as the flames begin to die out. Pass pieces of bread to the participants, saying:

May we never hunger.

If you are alone in this practice, say:

May I never hunger.

As you eat a piece of the bread yourself, imagine that you become filled with its virtues.

Day 140

Lammas: Harvesting Rite

What You'll Need:

- 4 dried stalks of wheat, or
- 4 fresh flowers with stem and bud attached
- A cauldron or other burning vessel
- Old newspaper or kindling
- A boline or paring knife
- Cutting board
- Several small candles or tea lights

At dusk, create a magical ritual space by lighting small candles (or tea lights) and placing them in a 9-foot circle on the ground. If your home or magical practice space does not allow a nine-foot circle, create a 6-foot (or in tight spaces, a 3-foot diameter circle). Set up a table to be your altar at the center of this magical space. Set all of the required ritual items on this table, along with a few more candles so that you can see. Use a compass to designate in your circle the four quarters: east, south, west, and north. At each compass direction, inside of your candle circle, place one of the wheat stalks (or flowers).

Boline is the Witches' term for a small sickle.

Begin by placing one wheat stalk on the ground in the east of your circle, saying:

I reap with knowledge.

Place one on the ground in the south of your circle, saying:

I reap with action.

Place one on the ground in the west of your circle, saying:

I reap with sensation.

Place one wheat stalk on the ground in the north of your circle, saying:

I reap in silence.

Then return to the east and hold your hands up high, saying:

All must end; this is the way.
What doth rise, but not decay?
Lugh has come, the Barleycorn,
I raise the scythe and now 'tis shorn!

Now collect the wheat (or flower) in the east, south, west, and north. Hold them together in a bunch and place them on the cutting board. Using your stronger hand, cut the buds from the stems with one firm stroke. Light the kindling in the cauldron and then ritually place the buds into the fire. Watch them burn in silence, meditating on the principle of sacrifice. When you are finished, extinguish all of your candles and bury any remaining ashes or buds.

Day 141

Lammas: Meditation

Have someone read this guided imagery to you while you meditate with eyes closed, or tape record it in your own voice for later playback.

Reader:
Close your eyes and take several deep breaths. Imagine that you become weightless. You drift in the air and soon you feel your spirit body moving through time and space. Vague images and colors flash past you as you move speedily.

Soon the movement stops and you find yourself in a field of ripening wheat. You stand in the field with the waving golden crowns brushing against your body. Begin to breathe deeply and you will notice with each exhalation, your body dissolves and becomes part of this wheat field. Imagine yourself, your energy, and your consciousness spread now across the entire wheat field. Feel your wheat-body flow and shudder in the rushing wind.

Soon you notice that farmers come with sickles and they begin to harvest your body. There is no pain in this experience—there is only the giving of your body freely, as nature always does. Do not hold back; imagine that you give of your wheat-body freely to those who reap. After some time has gone by, imagine that the wheat that made up your body is now being threshed and stored in great heaps. Imagine now the women of the village coming to you and taking of your body to make bread. Give of yourself wholly. Allow yourself to be one with the grain and one with the giving.

When you are ready, your consciousness collects and solidifies. Your spirit body now travels back through time and space quite rapidly. You are returning to the place where you began this journey. Once you feel yourself back fully to your physical body, wiggle your toes and fingers to awaken your full presence.

When you have completed the exercise, open your eyes and take time to journal about this experience.

- What was it like to dissolve and become the wheat field?
- What was it like to give so fully of your spirit-body?
- How can you use the insights you have learned in this meditation in your daily life?

Day 142

Lammas: Natural Giving

One of the main spiritual points within Wicca is for the practitioner to become unified with nature. Nature gives of itself freely. The grass grows no matter how many times you mow it. Trees annually come to blossom and offer their fruit, never giving thought to who eats. This natural selflessness, then, is the most powerful position in which you can place yourself for Lughnassadh. In magical practice, this is called *natural giving.* Selfless action is a vivid reflection of nature; it yields a positive flow of spiritual energy for yourself and for others.

Selflessness does not mean allowing yourself to be abused or to be taken advantage of by other people. It means not resisting when things need to be done. It means releasing into the flow of your own life without hesitation. It means engaging fully with nature and the universe. It means being life itself, which gives unquestioningly.

Practice: Giving by Listening

Choose an hour when you will listen deeply to someone else without commenting about your own life or interests. Simply listen with full attention to the details of the speaker's words. Repeat back in your own words the information you have heard to demonstrate to the speaker that you have heard what he or she had to say.

Day 143

Lammas: Giving of Time

For one hour today, donate your time to some charitable cause. You can donate your time to AIDS awareness, to children in foster care, or to volunteering at a local homeless shelter. Choose an activity that allows you to offer your best efforts. As you prepare to engage in the activity and while carrying it out, note any resistance or internal commentary that may be going on.

A Word to the Wise: It is natural to resist the process of giving of your time, especially since our Western culture insists that time is a commodity that can be wasted. When you deeply consider the arrangements of this existence, what else do we truly have in each moment except time and each other?

- What was your internal process as you prepared to volunteer your time?
- What happened when you carried through with giving of your time?
- How did you feel following the activity?
- Did you notice any changes in your energy levels?
- Did you notice any changes in your awareness?

Day 144

Lammas: Giving of Energy

For one hour today, put your full energies into some task that does not benefit you personally. Perhaps you can prepare some food that someone else enjoys. Perhaps you can complete someone else's dreaded tasks. Maybe you can offer one of the healing techniques you have learned to someone who needs help. As you prepare to engage in the activity and while carrying it out, note any resistance or internal commentary that may be going on. At the close of the exercise, take time to consider the following questions:

- What was your internal process as you prepared to give away your energies?
- What happened when you carried through with giving of your energies?
- How did you feel following the activity?
- Did you notice any changes in your energy levels?
- Did you notice any changes in your awareness?

Day 145

Lammas: The Garden of Pomegranates

One law of magic that you will learn in detail later in your training tells Witches that whenever they expend energy, it is always returned multiplied. This holds true for the magical practices of natural giving. As you connect with the natural state of offering and allow it to guide you, you will also notice that the world responds in kind. In other words, you will begin to notice that the gifts of the universe, the necessities of your life, will magically always be on hand. Life and all of its bounty flows freely when you link to this magical tide.

The Garden of Pomegranates is a *waking imagery* that you can use to keep the energies of natural giving flowing in your life. Waking imagery is a term that I use to refer to a spiritual image that you keep in the foreground of your awareness so that it can guide your activities, speech, thought and effort. The Garden of Pomegranates is an image of divine, natural giving. To begin you will practice a guided imagery. You can either have a friend read it to you while you follow along, eyes closed. Or you can tape record it in your own voice for playback later on.

Reader:
Close your eyes and take several deep breaths. Relax your body completely.

(Reader: pause for a moment.)

Imagine that you are walking through a garden of lush foliage. As you wander you notice that you are following along a soft red-clay path beneath your feet. As you follow the path, you'll notice that it appears to continually curve to your right. This is because the path is spiraling into the center of this beautiful garden.

(Reader: pause for a moment.)

After you follow the path for a while, you will arrive at an open, vine-covered, red-adobe arch. The archway opens to the most beautiful part of the garden filled with fruited pomegranate trees. Follow this path that leads to a clearing at the center of this pomegranate garden. At the central spot, you will notice a place of freshly dug earth. Squish your toes into the soft rich soil and immediately you will notice that your feet become rooted to the spot. The roots develop and swell beneath you. Your legs bind together and become a trunk and your arms become leafy branches that bear pomegranate fruit. Your limbs offer this succulent fruit to anyone in need of nourishment. Keep this image and the feel of becoming the offering tree in your mind's eye.

(Reader: pause for a moment.)

Whenever you are ready, open your eyes. You can flash your awareness at any time back to the garden, your tree, and your fruiting boughs.

Your task today is to engage in your daily activities with this image in mind. You should give freely as the pomegranate tree.

Day 146

Lammas: Incense and Oil

Lammas Incense

Burn this incense at your Lammas ritual, or at any time that you want to bring about the energies and insights of Lammas.

What You'll Need:

- ½ handful of oak (wood), either powdered or chips
- ½ handful of powdered sandalwood
- 2 teaspoons frankincense
- 1 teaspoon dried oats (such as rolled oats for oatmeal)
- Vegetable glycerin
- 5 drops patchouli essential oil
- 2 drops rosemary essential oil

In a medium-sized bowl, place your powdered sandalwood. Stir in about two tablespoons of vegetable glycerin. Add the glycerin one tablespoon at a time and then mix with a metal whisk or a fork. You simply want to create a soft, fluffy compound. Do not add the second tablespoon of glycerin if it feels like it would be too much, causing the incense to be too wet.

Now add your essential oils and whisk. Add your other dried herbs and mix thoroughly. Wait for at least a day for the compound to settle before you sprinkle it on hot coals.

Lammas Oil

Use this oil to anoint attendees of your Lammas ritual. You can also use this oil any time that you want to awaken the insights and mysteries of Lammas. This oil activates the magical energies of giving, prosperity, abundance, and riches.

What You'll Need:

- 5 drops patchouli essential oil
- 2 drops rosemary essential oil
- Pinch of dried oak (powdered or chipped wood) or dried oats (such as rolled oats for oatmeal)

Find a one-ounce bottle. Fill the bottle halfway with vegetable glycerin. Add plain water until the bottle is three-quarters full. Add your essential oils. Add dry ingredients, close the lid, and shake the bottle. You can use this magical oil immediately.

Day 147

Lammas: Making a Ritual Sickle

The ritual sickle is one that you can use to bless your own garden, to consecrate your harvest bounty, or use in your Lammas rituals.

What You'll Need:

- An ordinary sickle
- ½ ounce black polyurethane paint
- ½ ounce red polyurethane paint
- A thin detailing paintbrush

For this magical tool, it is best for you to purchase a new sickle from a hardware and gardening store. Magical sickles cannot have been used for any purpose other than symbolic. If you happen to have a sickle in storage that has gone unused, then that will do as well. Use any type of sickle, either the short hand-held or the long harvesting variety.

Sharpen the blade of the sickle using a sharpening stone. When the blade is highly sharpened, paint it with the black paint, front and back. Paint the handle as well. When painting the blade, be sure to leave a thin ¼-inch margin of the sharpened silver blade edge unpainted. This margin represents the moon and the power of the goddess, who not only sows, buds, and blossoms, but who also reaps.

Wait for this to dry. Once dry, use the red paint and the thin detailing brush to apply the magical design below in a line across the entire blade. The design is based on the old Greek water-wave design below. Apply the design to both sides of the blade, then set the project aside to dry for the remainder of the day. Magically charge the blade by leaving it near a window so that the moon can shine down upon it.

Ritual Sickle Design.

Day 148

Lammas: Consecrating the Ritual Sickle

What You'll Need:

- Lammas incense
- A burning vessel (such as a deep cast-iron pot or an iron cauldron)
- Self-lighting charcoal
- Lammas oil
- Two brown taper candles
- The ritual sickle

On a table at twilight, set out the ritual objects: the sickle, the incense, oil, incense burner, and charcoal. Place the sickle between the two brown candles. Light the charcoal and when it begins to turn ash-white, sprinkle some of the incense on it. Hold the sickle blade over the smoke and say:

> ***I consecrate thee, O harvest hand!***
> ***Do the Mother's work,***
> ***And scythe the land!***

Next, place the sickle back between the candles. Take out the oil and anoint the exposed silver edge of the blade with the oil, saying the incantation once again:

> ***I consecrate thee, O harvest hand!***
> ***Do the Mother's work,***
> ***And scythe the land!***

Allow the sickle to rest between the two candles again. Sprinkle a dash of the incense on the coals once more and then allow the sickle to remain on the table until the candles burn completely out.

DAY 149

Lammas: A Harvest Blessing

No matter the time of year, try this technique. Even if the ground is covered with ice and snow, the rite brings forth the energies of the Mother's bounty.

What You'll Need:

- Your ritual sickle
- Hot water
- 2 teaspoons fenugreek seed
- A clear, recloseable jar

Heat the water until it is just about boiling. Place the fenugreek seed into the small recloseable jar and pour the hot water over it. Allow this to steep and cool on its own, roughly 15 minutes.

Go to a garden with your sickle—and bring your fenugreek infusion as well. Within the garden, pound the handle of the sickle on the ground three times, hold it in both hands above your head and say:

> *Mother of all,*
> *Of vine and grain,*
> *Bring forth thy bounty*
> *In the Mighty Ones' names!*
> *By all thy love,*
> *Do thou descend,*
> *Offer thy fruits*
> *Without end!*

Pantomime gestures of harvesting, using the sickle while waving it over the field in all directions. Then dip the tip of the blade in the fenugreek infusion and fling it toward the field, so that the fenugreek infusion sprinkles out to bless the soil.

When you are done, close the fenugreek infusion in the jar and return to your home. Strain out the infusion, allowing the seeds to remain in the jar. Close the jar back up and place it somewhere where you can see it regularly. This bottle is reputed to attract bounty, especially in the form of money. The next time you receive money, empty the jar immediately and bury the seed.

Day 150

Contemplative Day: Finding Who You Are

Meditative Question: Who am I?

Symbolic Color: Green-yellow

Symbolic Direction: Northeast

What is it that makes up this entity called "you?" Are you the body? Are you the mind, feelings, memories, or your history? As you explore this month's contemplative question, you also explore a core spiritual realization. Through it you come to see what forces underlie your existence.

To begin working with this question, assume your usual meditative sitting position in a quiet space while facing the northeast. Light a green-yellow candle, place it before you and gaze upon the flickering candle. Hold the question firmly, internally, for 20 to 30 minutes. The resolution of this question may require you to sit with it more than once. If so, simply add it to your spiritual routine until you arrive at a magically satisfactory insight. Over time, a shift in your perception will take place and you will know just who you are.

Days 151-180

Magical Items to Gather

Here is a list of items you will need during the next month of training:

Day 153

- A handful of dried corn kernels (popcorn)
- Corn husks, fresh or dried, about 6–8 pieces
- 4 cotton balls
- Twine

Day 154

- 4 tea light candles
- Dried corn kernels (popcorn)

Day 155

- 5 smooth sticks or small branches (about ¼ inch in diameter and 8 inches in length)
- A black felt-tipped pen (indelible usually works best) or a small, sharp knife
- Twine (or raffia)

Day 156

- 5 lengths of white ribbon (at least 6 inches in length, at least 1 inch in width)

Day 158

- 1 teaspoon dried blessed thistle
- A small jar of dried corn
- 1 teaspoon dried mandrake root

Day 160

- A cup of red wine (or a red fruit juice such as cranberry)
- A baked good (such as cake or bread)
- A wooden or silver platter

Day 161

- Powdered sandalwood
- ½ handful of crushed, dried white sage
- 2 tablespoons myrrh
- 1 tablespoon patchouli
- 2 teaspoons benzoin
- Vegetable glycerin
- 2 drops patchouli essential oil
- 5 drops patchouli essential oil
- 6 drops sage essential oil
- 3 drops myrrh essential oil
- 2 drops rose essential oil

Day 169

- 2 tablespoons star anise, crushed
- 2 tablespoons dried eucalyptus leaves
- 10 drops lavender oil
- Vegetable glycerin
- Bergamot essential oil
- Eucalyptus essential oil

Day 170

- Air oil (both incense and oil are made from ingredients from Day 169)
- Air incense

Day 172

- A 5–6 inch red taper candle

Day 176

- One handful of powdered sandalwood
- 2 tablespoons myrrh
- 2 tablespoons dried angelica leaves
- 2 tablespoons dried bay leaves
- Bay leaf essential oil
- 5 drops cinnamon essential oil
- Vegetable glycerin
- Clove essential oil
- Pinch of dried clove or cinnamon

Day 177

- Several red taper candles or
- A fire pit filled with branches and other kindling
- Fire oil (Incense and oil are made from ingredients from Day 176)
- Fire incense

Day 179

- Jasmine essential oil

Day 180

- A 5–6 inch orange taper candle

Day 151

Devotional Day: Honoring Ra

Table of Correspondences: Ra

Symbols: Sun, the scarab beetle, spheres, and eggs

Tools: The wand, the candle, sacred fires, incense

Magical Essences/Herbs: Sandalwood, myrrh, and cinnamon

Direction: Ra is aligned with the east

He Rules: Vitality, strength of mind and spirit, potency, and immortality

Animal Symbols: Hawk, lion

Sacred Foods: Eggs, oranges, and red apples

Magical Stones: Topaz, tiger's eye

In ancient myth, Ra was a sun god, creator god, and chief of all Egyptian gods and goddesses. Mythology tells us that Ra emerged from primordial chaos at the beginning of time. Ra was represented in Egyptian art with a human body and a hawk's head. Often hovering above the hawk's head was a solar disk. Egyptian legend sometimes refers to Ra as *Amun-Ra*. The word "Amun" is linked with the Egyptian word for the solar-disk. Ra's depiction with the solar disk was meant to symbolize his qualities of endless vitality and enduring strength. Ra's name is also linked with the word *phrah*, which later became translated as *Pharaoh*. In fact, each Pharaoh called himself a "son of Ra." Whenever the queen became pregnant, she and the court believed it was Ra and not the king who impregnated her.

The energies Ra brings to you are vitality, strength of mind and spirit, potency in all affairs, and physical/spiritual immortality. Ra's sacred symbols are the sun, the scarab beetle, spheres, and eggs. Ra's magical colors of are gold, yellow, red, and orange. His magical essences and herbs are sandalwood, myrrh, and cinnamon. The times of the day that you can easily evoke the presence of Ra are dawn and dusk. Eggs, oranges, and red apples are Ra's sacred foods.

Ra Practice

In honoring Ra today, make an altar that includes his sacred symbols. Light appropriately colored candles and intone the single syllable of his name once and again, in sustained tones ("Raaaah . . . Raaaaah"). Continue to chant his name until you sense his presence around you. Once he has arrived, spend some time contemplating what it might mean to serve this aspect of deity. Ask Ra what it means to live life through his energy. Contemplate how you might live your life if you were an expression of the sun.

Spend the day honoring this god by acting from the knowledge of your immortality.

Day 152

Day of Silence and Review

As you observe silence today, focus your attention on your sense of sight. This may be difficult to do for extended periods of time, so throughout your day, find 10–20 minute intervals during which you will be able to focus your attention on what it is you see. During and in between intervals, remain silent. When the day is complete, answer these questions:

- What was it like to focus my attention on my sense of sight?
- In what way did my visual focus impact my thoughts, emotions, actions, or spirit?
- How does what I see affect my physical energy?
- Did my visual acuity increase or decrease with my focused attention? Why might that be?

Review

For today's practice, take time to ask yourself the following:

- Of the information I have learned up to now, what stands out most as vital?
- What information seems least relevant to my spiritual development?
- Which of the practices seemed to move me spiritually, and which had little impact?
- Of the information I have learned so far, what would be best to review? (Take time to review it now.)

Day 153

Fall Equinox

When the sun enters into the astronomical sign of Libra (between September 19 and 23), you have officially entered Autumn. Just as at the time of the Spring Equinox, day and night, light and dark are in a state of equilibrium at the start of Autumn. Interestingly enough, the astrological symbol for the sign of Libra is the scales, depicting a state of perfect balance. The Autumnal Equinox marks the beginning of shorter days and longer nights. The indigenous folk of Old Europe knew that Winter's chill was about to set in and the night would once again rule supreme. Fall Equinox is an important magical tide, from the Witch's point of view, since it is a season that hangs somewhere "between the worlds." It is neither day nor night, neither light nor dark. It occurs between a season of bounty and that of coming dearth. It is a time between lush foliage and stark barrenness.

Because this celebration lies between these two extremes, spirit is highly active. In fact, paranormal experts document that hauntings occur in cyclical peaks during the equinoxes and believe that these are times of psychic stress.[66] The Fall Equinox is a psychic tide of great magical power that centers on the mysteries of the final harvest.

In the northern countries, the coming of autumn marks the end of the harvesting season. The air begins to take on a chill, especially in the evenings and mornings. The change of temperature and of sunlight prompts the leaves of the summer shade trees to take on warm, rich colors—iridescent reds, opulent shades of gold, and leathery browns. In response, the energies of trees begin to move inward; they draw up the sap that once nourished their branches and store it in their sturdy, woody trunks.

In the old European agricultural cycle, this was the time of Harvest Home, a tide that marked the end of one year's toil. It also marked the time of respite before farmers and their families would have to return to the fields once more.[67] In some locales, masters would treat their farm laborers to a feast, during which laborers were also allowed to speak their minds to the master without regard for rank. Folks living in farming communities would observe customs surrounding the "Corn Mother," who, interestingly enough, needed to be driven out of the fields by the time of the final harvest. Some old customs held that the spirit of the Corn Mother was contained in the last ear of corn on the final cornstalk. In some parts of Europe, the final cornstalk might be harvested when all reapers would throw their sickles at it to bring it down. Lore had it that whoever cut the final stalk would find good marriage within the year.

Once someone harvested the final corn sheaf, he or she would strip the kernels from the cobs, and then ritually burn them in a communal fire. Alternatively, villagers might drench the entire final corn sheaf with water and then hang it in a place of prominence as a charm to ensure plentiful rain. Or the oldest married woman in the village would dry the husks of the final sheaf and would weave them into a wreath. She would then present this wreath to the prettiest maiden of the village, or she might hang it in a barn as a charm to guard against vermin. Similar rural rituals from territories throughout agrarian Europe refer to the Corn Mother alternatively as the Rye Mother, Oats Mother, Barley Mother, or Wheat Mother.[68]

Practice: Making Corn Husk Dollies

Throughout rural Old Europe, pagan folk would practice harvest customs that often included making corn dollies. The dollies were often made of an entire sheaf of corn, dressed in woman's clothing, representing the Corn Mother. In other customs, folks would remove the corn's husks, dry them, and then fashion these into a figurine. [Directions for making a corn dolly follow, and you may refer to the diagrams on page 148.]

In today's practice, you will make your own corn dolly to use as a representation of the magical energies of the mother goddess at harvest time.

What You'll Need:

- Corn husks, fresh or dried, about 6-–8 pieces.
- 4 cotton balls
- Twine
- Scraps of cloth, yarn, buttons, and dried twigs (optional)

To begin, choose the kind of husks you would like to use in this magical practice. If you use fresh corn husks, begin by taking a strip of husk and placing a few cotton balls in the middle. Twist and tie it with string to make a head (step 1). If you choose to use dried husks (which you can find in most grocery stores), soak the husks in a pail of fresh water for at least 2–4 hours before attempting the project. Once the husks have been soaked and are pliable, try making the head using the cotton balls and twine.

Next, you can make the doll's arms by folding another husk and tying it near each end to make hands (step 2).

Slip the arms between the husks that extend under the head. Tie with string below the inserted arms to form the doll's waist (step 3). Next, arrange enough husks around the figure's waist so that they overlap slightly, and then tie them in place with string. Fold these husks down carefully so that you do not see the string beneath (step 4). This then forms the skirt of the dolly.

You can leave this figure as is (which is my preference), or you can give it a face, hair, or even some magical-looking clothing (step 5). Use buttons to form eyes, use fabric scraps (maybe even fabric scraps from your own mother's clothing) and yarn to fashion the doll's clothing. For greater stability of the figure, you can make a staff, broom, or cane with twigs, which can help the figure stand upright.

Set this figure aside for tomorrow's magical work.

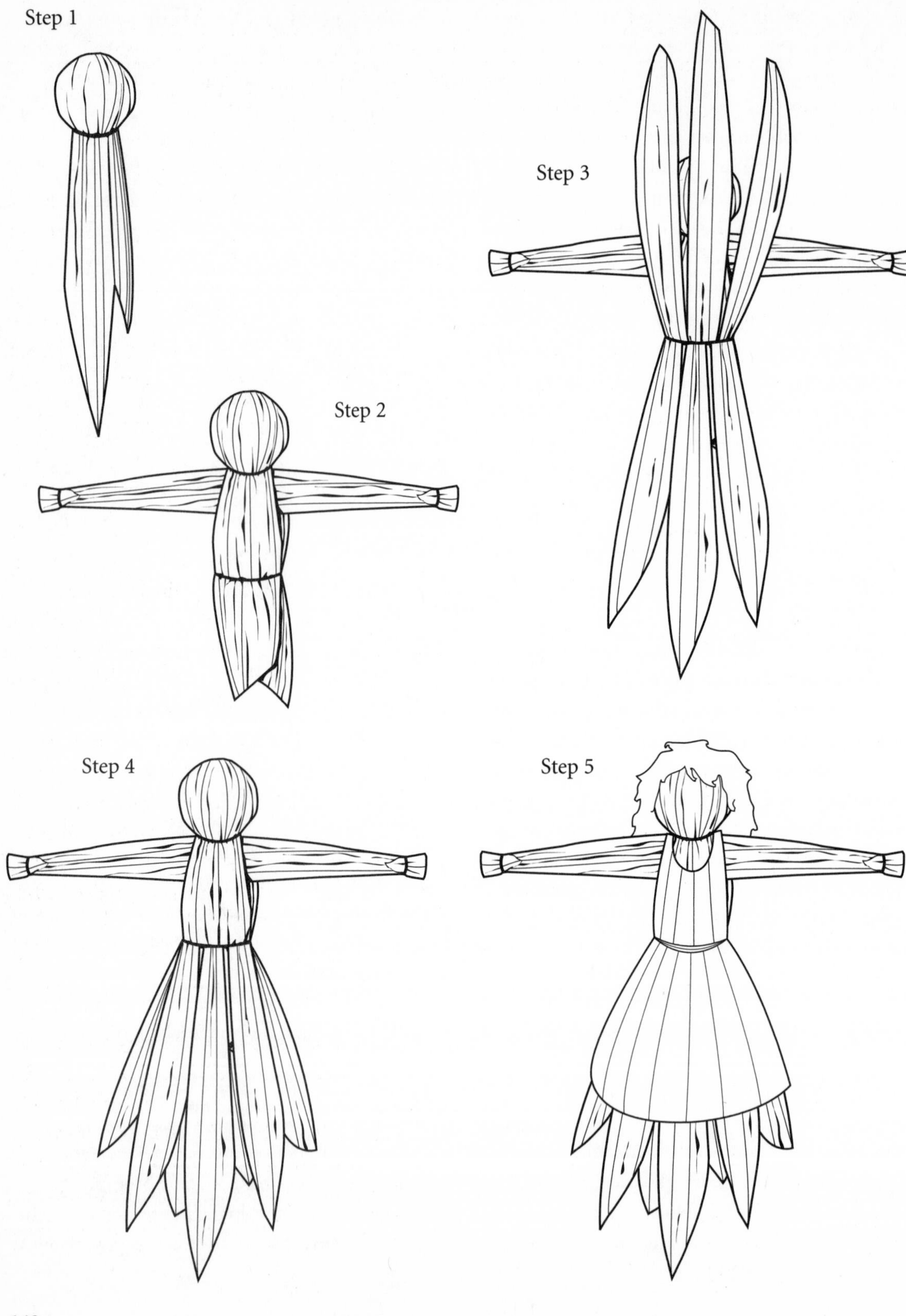
Step 1
Step 2
Step 3
Step 4
Step 5

Day 154

Fall Equinox: Corn Dolly Blessing

What You'll Need:

- 4 tea light candles
- Your corn dolly
- Dried corn kernels (popcorn)

Form a 5–6 inch diameter circle with your handful of dried corn kernels. Place each tea light just outside of the circle at the four compass points: east, south, west, and north. Hold your hands, palms down, over the circle and say the following incantation:

Mystic dame of Harvest Home
Lend the spirit of the gnome,
In this circle of the corn,
May your blessings thus be born!

Once you are done, set the dolly within the corn circle, allowing it to stand upright. Light the four candles. Silently regard this small ritual for a few moments, then extinguish the candles. Whisk the corn kernels into a glass jar and store them away for use in a magical practice that you will do on another day.

Finally, if you place the dolly near your hearth or in your kitchen you will invite the blessings of the Earth Mother and all kindly spirits and energies of bounty.

Day 155

The Meaning of Fall Equinox

In the Spring and Summer we saw the world of vegetation sprout and blossom in a magical feat of external, visible, productive movement. Fall signals the natural cycles of inward, silent movement. We see this phenomenon most vividly in the vegetation cycle. Trees draw up their sap and store it in their trunks. The tree's annual growth cycle has peaked and now it turns from outward to inward movement. The movement and vitality of nature that we once experienced as the blossoming and fruiting of the limb now becomes the mysterious inward movement of the sap.

At the time of Fall Equinox, Witches follow the example of the natural world and refocus outward-directed attention toward the inner processes. In the Witch's view, autumn is not a time to initiate new projects or to start new ventures. Instead, it is a period of deep reflection when you retract goal-directed efforts in order to explore the depths of your interior. The Fall Equinox signals our need to explore internalized ideas, paradigms, and world-views that ultimately shape our experiences. It is an occasion to find out just what makes you tick—what motivates you, what repels you. This kind of self-knowledge allows you to take powerful action based on insight and reflection.

Like the Spring Equinox, Fall is a time of balanced light. There are equal durations of night and day during the Equinoxes, but the accent of each celebration differs slightly. The Spring Equinox focuses our attention toward the growth of light, beginnings, and fecundity, while the Fall Equinox honors the diminishing light, endings, and the cycles of return. Fall Equinox aligns with the compass direction of west, since west is the natural symbolic direction of endings (day ends when the sun sets).

Fall symbolizes the twilight time of your own life cycle. It celebrates the human passage to elderhood as well as the knowledge, cunning, and wisdom that accompanies such a passage. If this particular life-cycle does not correspond with your own, you can use the spiritual tide of the Fall to explore and develop your own wisdom.

Another symbol that pervades the rites and energies of autumn is that of *reaping*. Fall Equinox is an auspicious tide to regard the circumstances of your life and to consider the ways you have contributed to your conditions—for better or worse. This is often a difficult task for us to undertake because our lives often don't measure up to our expectations. Like most of us, you might not want to face your contribution to an undesirable circumstance and you might be tempted to assign blame for this elsewhere. It is much easier for us to attribute bad luck, negative vibes, chance, or other people for our messes than it is to face our actions squarely, unflinchingly. Who wants to face their shadowy aspects—their inadequacies, jealousies, anger, manipulation, greed, or laziness? And yet this is exactly the activity that can produce the perfect wisdom and spiritual clarity called for during the Fall.

We have to laugh, since we are often quick to see how we might have contributed to agreeable circumstances. Neither looking outside of ourselves for blame nor claiming the entirety of a congratulation works. We don't live in a vacuum, and in all respects our lives are a vast and indescribable network of circumstances and conditions that have come together in this moment.

Instead of looking for blame or self-congratulation, the most important spiritual stance is one that allows for simple observation without the need for judgment. It is important during this season to consider your life without allowing personal commentary and opinions to take over. Our lives are simply what they are in this moment, whether we find the circumstances agreeable or not. This is the most natural and magically powerful view we can take. It was Robert Ingersol who said, "In nature there are neither rewards or punishments; there are consequences."

When you observe your life conditions in this way, your participation in how things have evolved becomes transparent. This then gives you the opportunity to make realistic and feasible plans for change in order to cultivate future "harvests."

When we consider the symbolic meaning of the harvest, of reaping what we have sown, it becomes clear that Wiccans honor the concept of *karma* in their spiritual path. Karma is a word that Witches conveniently use, since it is one that has entered the popular vernacular. However, the concept of karma (which means "action" in Sanskrit) is one that was common to the ancient Celtic peoples. The Celts believed in past and future lives, all of which were predicated on one's action. Classical writers have attested to the fact that the most basic belief of the ancient Celtic world was reincarnation. The Celtic folk so widely held the belief of reincarnation that arrangements were sometimes made for debts to be paid in another lifetime.[69] As did our ancestors, Witches observe action and result as a central theme during the time of the Fall Equinox.

Practice: Action and Reaction

Witches believe that action results in the current state of one's life. That is not to say that Witches have control over the universe and that their actions are the only factor in determining the outcomes of their lives. Accidents happen. Fate intervenes. Circumstances often arise that are outside your immediate ability to control. A car might crash into your rear fender. You might win the lottery or develop illness. What is important in a Witch's lifetime is what she does, the action she takes, in response to life's circumstances.

During the Fall Equinox, Witches are challenged to square off with the actions they have taken during the course of the year. Today you will touch on this process and begin taking steps toward opening to a greater awareness of action and reaction.

What You'll Need:

- 5 smooth sticks or small branches (about ¼ inch in diameter and 8 inches in length)
- A blank piece of white paper
- A black felt-tipped pen (indelible usually works best) or a small, sharp knife
- Twine (or raffia, if you prefer its looks to twine)

Lay the five sticks before you. Think of five important actions you have taken over the course of the year. These should be actions that led to some important growth, change, or perhaps a spiritual insight. Now think of one word that summarizes each of your actions. Write each word in a column on the blank piece of paper.

Next to each word, create a small symbol that represents each action. Try to create simple shapes to represent your actions. Using your felt-tipped pen, draw one symbol on each of the five sticks. If you prefer, use a small whittling knife to carve the simple designs into each of the sticks. When you are finished, lay the sticks out so that they form a five-pointed star (or pentagram). Use your twine or raffia to tie the ends of each "point" in the pentagram together. When you are finished, you should have a pentagram with symbols drawn or etched onto each stick. Hang the pentagram in a place of prominence to remind you of the actions that you have taken over the course of the year.

Day 156

Fall Equinox: Alternate Action

What You'll Need:

- 5 lengths of white ribbon (at least 6 inches long and at least 1 inch wide)
- A felt-tipped pen

Consider the five actions you have taken over the course of the year. How might you have done things differently? For each action, consider what alternative action you might have taken. Use the felt-tipped marker to write your alternative actions, one on each ribbon. Tie the corresponding alternative-action ribbons to each of the action sticks. As you attach each ribbon, consider how the alternative action might have affected the outcome. What might your life be today if you had taken any one of these alternative actions?

DAY 157

Fall Equinox: The Mythic Chain

The *Mythic Chain* is a spiritual practice that can facilitate your understanding of karma. The Mythic Chain is the chain of practical circumstances in your own life through which one event connects to another. Just as in mythology, the hero's actions link one to the next and finally result in found riches, powers, or in recovering something valuable. In this exercise, you will learn about your own hero or heroine's journey, and in the process discover the interconnectedness of people, places, and events.

To begin, think of a person with whom you have a friendship or close relationship. Take a blank piece of paper and at the top write down your relationship to this person. Next, draw a short vertical line directly below your first statement. This line represents a link in the mythic chain. Below this link line, write down the circumstances through which you met this person. Draw another link line below this statement. Beneath this link line, write down the circumstances that led to the situation through which you met this person. Continue with this chain for as long as you can.

Here is an example of a mythic chain:

My good friend is Varda Ninna.

|

I met Varda through my initiation with Oruborus et Ova.

|

I became associated with O.E.O. because I put a flyer up at a bookstore hoping to form a Wiccan study group.

|

I put up the flyer because I was working with a magical friend, Tentangle, and we wanted to expand the group.

|

I met the Tentangle at a Halloween street festival in Los Angeles.

|

I was at the Halloween street festival because a fellow writer had invited me.

You will find that the mythic chain can trace backward in time indefinitely, sometimes beyond your own birth. This exercise demonstrates the magical and spiritual significance of each encounter in your life and how each person or event shapes what will happen next.

When you have completed this exercise, commit your answers to the following questions to paper:

- How did reviewing this chain of causality affect the understanding of your life?
- What does this chain say about the circumstances of your life as they exist right now?
- Would your life circumstances be the same had one link in the chain been broken or altered?

Day 158

Fall Equinox: Corn Blessing

What You'll Need:

- A small jar of dried corn
- Purified water
- 1 teaspoon dried blessed thistle
- 1 teaspoon dried mandrake root

Use the corn kernels that you saved in a jar several days ago. Add to the jar your dried herbs. Begin with the mandrake root. As you add the root, say:

Mandrake to preserve and bless all life.

Then add the blessed thistle, saying:

Thistle to protect and guard against strife!

Cover the corn and herbs with purified water and seal the jar with a tight-fitting lid. Allow this to sit on a windowsill at nighttime for one complete lunar cycle. Put the jar away each morning and set it back out each night for 28 days. When the lunation is complete, drain the liquid from the jar. You can use this holy water to bless and protect your home, your family, and yourself.

Day 159

Fall Equinox Meditation: Past-Life Regression

This practice is meant as a simple introduction to past-life exploration. It is by no means the final authority on the subject. Its purpose is to align your awareness with the grand mythic chain, which is also called the *Chain of Causality.* The Chain of Causality explores the conditions of past lives that help bring clarification to your current life circumstances.

The understanding of past lives depends greatly on balance. Witches do take responsibility for their actions and note how their very presence (let alone intention and behavior) affects the world, either directly or indirectly. However, there are activities in the world, in the galaxy, in the universe, over which we have no direct control. We cannot stop the seasons, prevent the setting of the sun, or delay a wave crashing to the shore. Likewise, we cannot change the conditions of our birth, our childhood, or anything from the past. Through years of practice and magical endeavors, Witches come to understand—in their bones—that they are only a "strand" in the web of life, as Chief Seattle eloquently stated.[70]

Past-life regression can help Witches understand how the strand of their own current life-webs intermingles with the webs of the past. Through this process, Witches can learn how to unblock the karma of the past and create a powerful new future.

To begin, spend some time considering what you consider to be the unexplainable circumstances of your own life. Take time to sense how these circumstances make you feel. Where do you sense the feelings in your body? Everyone senses feelings in different body zones, so there is no one correct answer to this. It is a highly personal process. Follow the guided imagery outlined below. You can either have a magical partner read it to you or you can record it for later playback.

Reader:

Find a comfortable position, preferably lying down on the floor, and close your eyes. Once again, sense the body feeling that your life circumstances produce. Mentally follow the feeling in your body and imagine that you travel within until you reach the place where the feeling resides. Give the feeling a color and a shape.

Project yourself into the color-shape and you will sense that you are traveling very rapidly through the color-shape. It forms into a tunnel that transports you back through time. It takes you back to a time before you were born. It takes you to a time when you had this same bodily feeling. Soon you arrive at a shining doorway. Pass through the doorway and observe your surroundings. Where are you? Who are you? What are the circumstances of this lifetime?

(Reader: pause for a few minutes.)

It is now time to return to your physical body and its current time and place. From where you are in this vision, take one step backward. When you do this, you will see that you have stepped back through the shining doorway. You begin speeding through the tunnel once again, heading back to the place where your physical body rests comfortably. You now find yourself back in your body at the place where you held the color-shape. When you are ready, you can open your eyes, stretch, and awaken from this vision.

Once you are back, take time to journal about your experience.

- How did your past life circumstance relate to your present conditions?
- What of this exercise surprised you?
- What did not surprise you?

DAY 160

Fall Equinox: Libations

Libation is a pagan spiritual practice based on the concept of karma: action and reaction. A libation is a return of food or drink to the earth. It represents a poetic full circle of action. A food offering to the earth represents the principle that beginnings and endings are one in the same. Food and drink originate from the earth and it is to the earth that they return. Libations are highly personal and they link directly to your own sense of taste. You can use any food that you consider delicious as a libation. Those foods that you would avoid consuming you should also avoid offering as a libation.

What You'll Need:

- A cup of red wine (or a red fruit juice such as cranberry)
- A piece of a baked good (such as cake or bread)
- A wooden or silver platter (optional)

Take your wine and baked good to a secluded natural setting. Place the cup of wine and the baked good on the platter and set it beneath a suitable tree. Hold your arms out to shoulder level, palms facing up, saying:

Great Mother and Horned Lord
Accept this offering of food and drink!

Take only a sip of the drink and then pour the remaining contents near the roots of the tree. Next, take a bite of the baked good and crumble the remains along the tree roots, saying:

From east to west, from south to north,
Ancient ones, I call thee forth!

Quickly gather your belongings and leave this sacred spot. Come back to this location at least once annually and repeat this libation ceremony.

Day 161

Fall Equinox: Incense and Oil

Fall Incense

Burn this incense at your Fall Equinox ritual, or at any time that you want to bring about the energies and insights of Fall Equinox.

What You'll Need:

- A handful of powdered sandalwood
- ½ handful of crushed, dried white sage
- 2 tablespoons myrrh
- 1 tablespoon patchouli
- 2 teaspoons benzoin
- Vegetable glycerin
- 2 drops patchouli essential oil

In a medium-sized bowl, place your powdered sandalwood. Stir in about two tablespoons of vegetable glycerin. Add the tablespoons one at a time and then mix with a metal whisk or a fork. You simply want to create a soft, fluffy compound. Do not add the second tablespoon of glycerin if it feels like it would be too much, causing the incense to be too wet.

Now add your essential oils and whisk. Add your other dried herbs and mix thoroughly. Wait for at least a day for the compound to settle before you sprinkle it on hot coals.

Fall Oil

Use this oil to anoint attendees of your Fall Equinox ritual. You can also use this oil any time that you want to awaken the insights and mysteries of Fall Equinox. This oil activates the magical energies of giving, prosperity, abundance, and riches.

What You'll Need:

- 5 drops patchouli essential oil
- 6 drops sage essential oil
- 3 drops myrrh essential oil
- 2 drops rose essential oil
- Pinch of dried or fresh white sage.

Fill a one-ounce bottle halfway with vegetable glycerin. Add plain water until the bottle is three-quarters full. Add your essential oils. Add dry ingredients, close the lid, and shake the bottle. You can use this magical oil immediately.

Day 162

Learning about the Elements

Witches believe that life itself is sacred, so it stands to reason that they also deem anything that *sustains* life to be holy. The four basic elements that sustain our lives are air, fire, water, and earth. Wiccans believe that life begins when all four elements meet and combine. There is literal truth in this. We need air to breathe, water to drink, the earth beneath our feet, and the warmth of fire in order to exist.

But as in all Witchy matters, Wiccans look beyond the gross physical manifestations of life in order to sense the symbolic, energetic, and mysterious (sometimes referred to as "occult") traits of the elements. Symbolically, air represents our thoughts and our communication. The occult power of air is in *knowing*. Fire represents our passions and drives. Fire's occult power is in *willing*. Water symbolizes our dreams, emotions, and visions. The occult energy of water is that of *daring*. Our abilities to be pragmatic, realistic and practical are our earthy qualities. The earth's occult quality is the wisdom of *silence*.

Practice: Knowing the Elements

Below is a chart that describes each of the Witches' elements and their traditional symbolic associations. Over the course of the next several weeks you will be exploring each of the elements in depth. It is important, therefore, that you take time today to commit to memory the basic information about the elements given in the table.

Day 163

The Elements of Your Life

Take time to review the elemental chart from yesterday's exercise. While you review the information, think about which of the elements seems most to represent you. For example, if you are someone who spends a great deal of time communicating, then the element of air might best represent you. If you are an energetic, active person, then fire might best represent your essence. If you are emotional and sensitive, perhaps you more naturally align with water. If you are silent, stoic, and practical, you most likely align naturally with earth.

Once you have determined the element to which you closely align, see which of the elements represents the people who are closest to you. Take time to explore these questions:

- Which elements represent the sort of people who interest you?
- Which represent the kinds of people who turn you off?
- Which element best represents your job?
- Which element represents your style of relating to people?
- What elemental colors are you wearing today?
- How do those elemental colors affect you?
- What element symbolizes your relationship with a partner, friend, or loved one?
- Which of the elemental colors do you have painted on your house (inside and out)? How do these colors affect you in your home?

Contemplate which of the elements seem to be most prevalent and which seem to be lacking in your life.

Day 164

The Element of Air

In the spiritual, symbolic language of magical practice, air broadly represents the category of communication. Practically speaking, without air we could not produce sound from our throats, nor could the vibrations that comprise sound travel through space without the conductive properties of air. Air is also the "breath of life," both literally and symbolically. Many Witches believe—as do shamans across the globe—that human life begins with your first breath. Our ancestors understood air to be an invisible realm that magically supported the visible realm. One can find evidence and echoes of this notion throughout both ancient and contemporary magical practices. Throughout the ancient world, air was strongly connected with the spirit world. In fact, in older occult lore, spirits were said to move invisibly through the air. In Old European lore, the howling wind represented spiritual voices. In the native cultures of both North America and Australia, initiatory rites began with use of a "bull-roarer," which was a flat piece of wood tied to twine and swung through the air to produce the "voices of the gods."[71]

Additionally, throughout the history of global magical practice, shamans employed their healing methods through the techniques of "sucking" and "blowing" air on and around patients.[72] In the East, the control of one's personal flow of air is a central practice in the disciplines of yoga and tantric magic.

Elemental Table of Correspondences

Element	Air	Fire	Water	Earth
Color	Yellow, white	Red	Blue	Green, brown, black
Direction	East	South	West	North
Time of Day	Dawn	Noon	Dusk	Midnight
Phase of Life	Birth/childhood	Youth	Adulthood	Old age/death
Season	Spring	Summer	Fall	Winter
Governs	Thought, communication, knowledge	Passions, physical energy, action	Dreams, visions, emotions	Practicality, stillness, contemplation
Traditional Witch Power	The Power to Know	The Power to Will	The Power to Dare	The Power to Be Silent

Symbolically speaking, air connects your past with your present; the same air that gave life to our ancestors gives life to us right now. It connects us with all living, breathing beings. We all live within this vast ocean of air and we depend upon it for our lives. Because of this, air can represent a force that binds us into a human community.

◐ In ancient Latin, the term *spiritus* means the animating vapor, which, of course, is air.

Take time today to familiarize yourself with the following table of correspondences for air. You will learn more about each of these as you progress through the coming week.

Table of Correspondences: Air

Alchemical Symbol: 🜁

Air Governs: Thought, mental acuity, the arts, communication, verbal expression, knowledge, television, film, radio, writing, speaking, performing, analysis, and learning

Magical Tool: The wand

Color: Yellow

Alternate Colors: Clear, white, pastels

Fragrances: Bergamot, lavender, marjoram, sage, peppermint

Elemental Beings: Fairies

Elemental King: Paralda

Tarot Card Suit: Wands (in some magical systems, swords)

Magical Stone: Quartz crystal

Outward Expression: The Power to Know: knowledge, linear-cognitive information, judgment, practical sense

Inward Expression: The Power to Wonder: not-knowing, mental openness, non-judging, non-sense, nonlinear thought

Day 165

The Breath of Life

Find a quiet place and a comfortable sitting position. Close your eyes and breathe naturally. Focus on your breath. Use a timer and allow yourself five minutes of contemplation time with each of the questions below as you following your breath.

- How does your breath feel as it enters your body?
- Where do you feel air enter?
- What energies do you sense the air imparting to you (knowing or wondering)?
- Where do you feel those energies entering your body?
- Where does your body store those energies—or are they not stored?
- What does your breath feel like as it leaves you?
- What is it like to focus on your breathing?

When you are finished with your contemplations, jot down your insights. For periods throughout the rest of the day, continue to come back to a focused attention on your breath. Review your initial insights prior to going to bed. How would you revise your initial answers at this point? Save your answers to review later in the week.

DAY 166

Air: The Power to Know

As with all in Wicca, the elements express themselves in a balance of light and dark, yin and yang, active and passive. In Wicca, we say that each of the elements has two basic expressions: an outward and an inward expression. The outward expression of an element is the visible, active expression of unseen, subtle, elemental forces. The inward expression is the nonvisible, receptive, internal process and manifestation of the element's subtle forces.

In its outward, active expression, the element of air governs *the power to know*. In magical parlance, knowing represents the acquisition of rational understanding of the world around you. The areas of knowledge, communication, education, learning, thinking, and speaking are all ruled by air. The energies of air manifest in individuals who feel drawn to work in theater, film, television, acting, writing, producing, publishing, philosophy, psychology, and education.

When this active expression takes control and an individual loses the delicate balance between the active and passive air energies, an individual might appear flighty, talkative, overly analytical, hypercognitive, exclusively rational, and only able to experience the world through mental understanding.

Commit to paper your own relationship to the energies of knowing:

- In what ways do you feel you are connected to the power to know?
- In what ways do you feel disconnected from the power to know?
- Has knowledge been an important part of your life? Your culture? Your upbringing?
- What part does knowledge play in your life today?

Practice: Rebalancing Knowing

When you notice that you are overanalyzing and too caught up in knowing, take time to practice this grounding exercise. Stand outside in a breeze, or if there is none, stand in front of a fan. Whether you are outside or indoors, stand facing the breeze directly. Open your arms and welcome this energy into your being. Close your eyes. Imagine that you have become transparent, and allow the breeze to pass directly through you, blowing away your thoughts. Imagine that this leaves you empty and clean. Stay with this visualization for at least ten minutes. When you are finished, jot down notes about your experience.

Day 167

Air: The Power to Wonder

In its inward expression, air governs *the power to wonder.* Wondering is the polar opposite of knowing. Because it lies at the other end of the spectrum from knowing, wondering has to do with the relinquishment of knowledge. Wondering is about unlearning your life and your relationships to everything and everyone. Wondering is experiencing the wisdom that emerges when you release opinions or judgments about life. What is there to know? Life is fluid and movable. Fixing your opinion, knowing a fact, and then sticking to that knowledge only creates rigidity and powerlessness. Without the power to wonder, how would we have ever understood that the world is round, or that we could invent a way to fly? It is through this wondering frame of mind that Witches are able to see beyond the limitations that knowing works hard to establish. The power to wonder allows Witches to discover truth as it reveals itself in each moment without resorting to fixing perceptions, cognitive understanding, or mental anticipation.

When this receptive expression takes control of a Witch's life, there is a loss of the delicate balance between the passive and active air energies. When this happens, an individual might appear inattentive, spacy, sleepy, distractable, dense, and dull-witted.

Commit to paper your own relationship to the energies of wondering:

- In what ways do you feel you are connected to the power to wonder?
- In what ways do you feel disconnected from the power to wonder?
- What are the dangers of not knowing?
- Would not knowing have any benefits in your life?

Practice: Rebalancing Wondering

When you notice that you are imbalanced in wondering, take time to practice this grounding exercise called "adjusting the breath." Sit in a comfortable chair and align your head and spine. Instead of beginning your usual breath by inhaling, begin a breath by exhaling and voiding the lungs completely. Allow your solar plexus region to contract inward, toward the spine, as far as it can. What is important here is that you get all of the air out of your lungs. Once you reach your own limit of inward contraction (and please don't do this to the point of discomfort), release your hold and allow the lungs to fill naturally. Do not try to compensate for the voiding of your lungs by deeply refilling with a large breath of air. Instead, simply allow the lungs to release from the contraction and fill naturally, of their own accord. Repeat this process three more times. Finally, allow the breath to settle into its own natural rhythm of inhalation and exhalation. Following this exercise, your mind should be refocused and clear. If not, repeat the process as needed.

DAY 168

Air: Contemplation

Today you will work with the spiritual (also called *subtle*) invisible energies of air through guided imagery. When you have finished the meditation, spend time journaling about your experience.

To begin, sit in a comfortable position, either on a meditation cushion or on a straight-backed chair. You can either commit the words and images of this guided journey to your memory before you begin or you can have someone read it to you while you take the journey.

Reader:
Close your eyes and take three deep, slow breaths. Allow your breathing to become deep and rhythmic. After a few moments, imagine that a twisting white mist begins to form in a ring around your feet. You notice that with each inhalation, the ring of mist grows, expands and climbs your legs. Continue to visualize that with each inhaled breath the mist climbs your body until it covers you completely.

Once you feel the mist covering you completely, you begin to feel it lift you up. Your body becomes as light as the mist that surrounds it. Soon you are hovering over the place where you were sitting. Imagine that the mist now begins to move you across a colorless, imageless void. It is moving you through time and space. It is taking you to a sacred place of magic and power. Soon the movement stops and the mist dissipates. The swirling mist vanishes to reveal a grassy meadow at dawn. As you inhale deeply, you smell the scent of weeds and wild herbs, blossoms and morning dew. Face the dawn and raise your arms. In moments, you notice that a soft wind begins to blow from the east. The wind picks up some force; it is warm and strong, but it does not threaten. Begin to take deep, slow breaths. With each inhalation, you take in the clean, clear power of air. Notice how this energy feels as it enters your body.

As you continue to inhale and absorb this element, you notice that the wind dies down. Look now at your own spirit body and you'll notice that you've taken on a golden aura. You are filled with the element and powers of air.

(Reader: pause for a few moments.)

It is now time to return to the place where you began your journey. Look down at your spirit feet and you'll notice that the glowing white mist has already begun to encircle your body like a cocoon of magic. Once it covers you completely, it lifts you and swiftly carries you back to the place where you began. When you are ready, open your eyes and stretch. Take note of how different you may feel now that you've taken on the qualities of air.

Day 169

Air: Incense and Oil

Burn air incense any time you want to bring about the energies of the element of air, which include thought, mental acuity, the arts, communication, verbal and written expression, and knowledge.

What You'll Need:

- One handful of powdered sandalwood
- 2 tablespoons star anise, crushed
- 2 tablespoons dried eucalyptus leaves
- 10 drops lavender oil
- Vegetable glycerin

In a medium-sized bowl, place your powdered sandalwood. Stir in about two tablespoons of vegetable glycerin. Add the tablespoons one at a time and then mix with a metal whisk or a fork. You simply want to create a soft, fluffy compound. Do not add the second tablespoon of glycerin, if it feels like it would be too much, causing the incense to be too wet.

Now add your essential oils and whisk. Add your other dried herbs and mix thoroughly. Wait for at least a day for the compound to settle before you sprinkle it on hot coals.

Air Oil

Anoint yourself or other people with this oil to activate the magical energies of air.

What You'll Need:

- Vegetable glycerin
- 10 drops lavender
- 3 drops bergamot
- 2 drops eucalyptus
- Pinch of dried sage or lavender

Fill a one-ounce bottle halfway with vegetable glycerin. Add plain water until the bottle is three-quarters full. Add your essential oils. Add your dry ingredient, close the lid, and shake the bottle. You can use this magical oil immediately.

Day 170

Becoming Air

It is important work to learn how to transform into each of the elements in order for you to gain complete mastery of the elemental world. Transformation is tricky and deep magical work. Pay close attention to the process and spend time eliminating any internal hindrances that you may note. In order for a transformation to be complete, you must have the ability to focus your attention for an extended period of time.

Some practitioners feel a bit jittery in respect to transformation, since it involves an absolute surrender of body and mind. Those folks who are fearful of the process dread losing the self, but what is this *self* that we fear losing? If you have these concerns, spend time contemplating the source of your trepidation before you continue with this practice. Where did this fear begin? Is this fear legitimate? Quietly, gently probe your heart and mind until you feel ready to continue.

Surrender of body and mind is a liberating experience. It is a direct shamanic experiential practice that can help you surpass the usual obstacles and boundaries of your life. So just let go. To what can you cling? We are all falling freely, without end, through time and space. Exercises that encourage a sense of surrendering allow you to vividly experience this truth.

As you gain training in each of the elements—air, fire, water, and earth—you will encounter an exercise for transformation. Today's magical working takes you into the essence of air, where you will learn to become one with it and experience this element as a part of your own being.

What You'll Need:

- Air oil
- Air incense

To begin, light the Air incense and sit down facing the east. Place the bowl of lit incense in front of you. With your middle finger, dab a drop of air oil approximately at the center of your brow. Gather some of the wafting incense into your hands and bring your hands toward your face.

Witches believe that this process blesses and cleanses the practitioner with the element. Repeat this cleansing process twice more.

Assume a meditative sitting posture, your spine straight and aligned. Now, focus your attention on the gentle, curling tendrils of incense. Allow your breathing to become deep and rhythmic. Continue to focus intently upon the smoke, barring all other thoughts. If you should have a thought unrelated to the smoke, simply observe it and allow it to pass through you. Do not allow it to disturb you. Most importantly, do not allow it to take your focus.

Imagine that with each inhalation, your mind becomes the smoky incense that surrounds you. Feel your body become the smoke; it should feel light and expansive. Feel the place where you sit becoming the smoke and all objects around you becoming the incense. Focus intently so that nothing exists but the incense smoke. Stay focused, preferably for 20–30 minutes.

When you are done, take time to close your eyes and imagine that your smoke-body solidifies and becomes stable once again. Get down on your hands and knees and place your forehead to the floor to ground and center your personal energy.

When you are ready, open your eyes and stretch. Take time to journal about your experience or to discuss it with a friend.

Day 171

The Element of Fire

In magical practice, the physical element of fire broadly represents energy, and it also symbolizes warmth, passion, strength, and action. Fire is the energy of our bodies; it is the life-force within each of us. Because of its dynamic nature, Witches consider fire a masculine, active energy form. In Hermetic philosophy, fire is the first element that emerges from pure spirit. In other words, it is the purest elemental form, following spirit. Again in this philosophy, fire has a warming, expanding, and extending influence.

It seems that fire has always had ancient, sacred connotations, since it is one of the oldest representations of deity. Fire has always been a part of magical practices throughout the world; even in the mainstream spiritual paths, fire always seems to represent a "higher source" or a presence of the divine in a visible, physical form.

Fire is basic to life. Without warmth and light, life could not exist. Besides this, fire has a transformative quality to it. When you apply fire to other substances, they never remain the same. Fire releases the pure energy, warmth, and light that lie latent in objects. Likewise, the *symbolic* essential fire inside each of us is transformative. It propels us into interactions with the world. It moves us, and like the great mother, whatever it is we touch we change forever.

Take time today to familiarize yourself with the following table of correspondences for Fire. You will learn more about each of these as you progress through the coming week.

◐ Hermeticism is a branch of occult studies reputedly founded by the ancient Egyptian philosopher Hermes Trismegistus. The myth of Trismegistus is that he allegedly lived when the race of humans was still young. Hermeticism focuses on the magical workings of nature as it manifests through seven spiritual principles: mentalism, correspondence, vibration, polarity, rhythm, cause and effect, and gender.

The principle of mentalism holds that everything is a manifestation of mind, and that the universe is essentially mental in nature. The principle of correspondence notes the interconnection between the visible and the invisible planes of nature (e.g., "as above so below; as below so above"). The principle of vibration notes that everything is continually in motion. This principle asserts that nothing rests, everything moves, everything vibrates. The principle of polarity holds that everything in the natural world is dual. Everything has a polar quality (e.g., yin and yang). The principle of rhythm teaches that everything in the universe has its rhythm, its rise and fall. In Hermeticism, rhythm is a compensatory magical action. The principle of cause and effect is essentially the principle of karma. The principle of gender notes that gender manifests on all planes—seen and unseen.

Table of Correspondences: Fire

Alchemical Symbol: △

Fire Governs: Action, movement, passion, anger, strength, sexuality, achievement, mastery, power, transformation

Magical Tool: The athame

Color: Red

Alternate Colors: Orange, gold, and vibrant colors

Fragrances: Basil, clove, cinnamon, hyssop, rosemary

Elemental Beings: Salamanders

Elemental King: Djin

Tarot Card Suit: Swords (in some magical paths, wands)

Magical Stone: Fire opal, iron

Outward Expression: The Power to Will: Mastery, exercising the individual will, movement

Inward Expression: The Power to Surrender: opening to the universal will, group achievement, nonstriving

DAY 172

Gathering Fire

What You'll Need:

- A 5–6 inch red taper candle

Find a quiet, dark environment and then take a comfortable sitting position. Light a red candle and set it on a table in front of you. Block out as many other light sources as possible so that you can focus solely on the candle flame. As you sit, breathe normally and gaze into the flickering candle light. Imagine that, with each inhalation, you absorb the energy of the flame. Imagine that this energy flows down to your feet and builds up, layer by layer until it fills you completely. Hold the energy in tightly, and feel as though you are compressing it in your body. After a minute of this, release the energy. With an audible sigh, imagine that you release all of the energy into the atmosphere around you. Keep only that amount of energy that your body needs.

- How does the energy of fire feel as it enters your body?
- Where in your body did you seem to hold on to the fire energies after you consciously released them?
- What does your body feel like as this fire energy leaves you?
- What is it like to gather the energies of fire into your body?

When you are finished with your contemplations, jot down your insights. Review your initial insights prior to going to bed. How would you revise your initial answers at this point? Save your answers to review later in the week.

Day 173

Fire: The Power to Will

Just as you learned with the element of air, fire has two basic magical expressions; one is an active, outward expression, and the other is passive and internalized. Fire's outward expression is *the power to will*. For Witches, the term "willing" means actualizing one's personal desire. The active expression of fire centers around movement, action, passion, directness, attentiveness, strength, and assertion. People who naturally align with fire energy work best in jobs that require leadership, quick action, or physical strength. Fire people are often quick and agile. They can also be passionate, sexual, assertive, athletic, goal-oriented, and a bit sharp-tongued.

When this active expression takes control of a Witch's life, there is a loss of the delicate balance between the passive and dynamic fire energies. When this happens, an individual might appear hostile, angry, rageful, aggressive, destructive, hypersexual, nervous, over-assertive, impatient, demanding, backbiting, competitive, or vengeful. It may also result in only being able to relate to the world through action and achievement.

Take time to commit to paper an exploration of your own relationship to willing:

- In what ways do you feel you are connected to the power to will?
- In what ways do you feel disconnected from the power to will?
- Have the outward qualities of fire been an important part of your life? Your culture? Your upbringing?
- What part does willing play in your life today?

Practice: Rebalancing Willing

When you notice that you are too focused on striving for outward achievement, take time to practice this grounding exercise. Light a fire in a fireplace or in a fire pit. Alternatively, light four or more red candles. Stand directly in front of the fire. Open your arms, breathe deeply, and mentally invite this energy into your being. Close your eyes. Imagine that you become transparent and you allow the heat and flames to pass directly through you. Stay with this exercise for at least ten minutes. When finished, jot down notes about your experience.

Day 174

Fire: The Power to Surrender

In its receptive expression, fire governs *the power to surrender.* Surrendering is the polar expression of willing and, at first blush, this hardly seems to be a power at all. In the popular mind, surrendering means giving up. We think that giving up might be a way of courting harm to ourselves or to others. We wonder how we might survive if we surrender by giving up.

In the magical world, surrendering is about aligning your personal will with the universal or the divine will. It is an attitude of not striving; it is about not insisting on the energies of your life flowing in some preconceived way. When you surrender you live in harmony with the flow of life energy; you live in accord with whatever circumstance arises. Surrendering comes from a deep understanding that life energy does not need to flow in one way or another, since that energy is what you are already.

Surrendering is also about letting go. And this sense of release manifests differently in each of our lives. It may mean releasing your physical stress and tension, it may mean letting go your emotional tension. It may mean releasing your grip, your insistence on getting your own way. It might mean leaving a job that pays you more but causes you misery. It may mean releasing your hold on a relationship that no longer functions.

The power to surrender is a revelation of nature's greatest power; it is the power of the wave that surrenders its hold on the shore and recedes back to the sea. Magical surrendering is not an action; it is a *being* statement. Witches can tap this power by mirroring nature's non-striving in their own lives. Through mirroring nature, Witches actually unify with nature and the divine.

There is a loss of the delicate balance between the passive and active fire energies when the receptive expression of surrendering takes control of a Witch's life. When this happens, an individual might appear lazy, depressed, dependent, inactive, idle, indirect, and perhaps dangerously passive or unable to act.

Take time to commit to paper your own relationship to this power of surrendering:

- In what ways do you feel you are connected to the power to surrender?
- In what ways do you feel disconnected from the power to surrender?
- What are the dangers of surrendering?
- Would surrendering have any benefits in your life?

Practice: Rebalancing Surrendering

When you notice that you have become lazy, depressed, or unable to take decisive action, take time to engage in rigorous physical activity. Go to the gym. Take a hike along a mountain path. Go running. Whatever it is you choose to do, make a commitment to do it regularly for several days. Keep your mind clear while engaging in the activity. Once you complete your activity, stop and allow yourself time to feel the vibration of the energy you raised in your own body. Feel the hum of blood as it courses through you. Feel your aliveness. Now take action in your life as needed.

Day 175

Fire: Contemplation

In order to experience the spiritual energies of fire, you will take an inward journey to your own sacred fire source. To begin, sit in a comfortable position while also assuring that your spine is straight and aligned. You can first read through this journey and commit it to memory before you begin or you can have someone read it to you. You can also record it for later playback.

Reader:
Close your eyes and take three deep, slow breaths. Now, allow your breathing to become rhythmic and natural. After a few moments, imagine that a twisting white mist begins to form a in a ring around your feet. You notice that with each inhalation, the ring of mist grows, expands and climbs your legs. Continue to visualize that with each inhaled breath the mist climbs your body until it covers you completely.

Suddenly you feel the sensation of lifting. Your body feels as light as the mist that surrounds you. Soon you discover that you are hovering over the place where you were once sitting. Imagine that the mist now begins to move you across a colorless, imageless void. It is moving you through time and space. It is taking you to a sacred place of magic and power.

Soon the mist dissipates and the movement stops. You find yourself at the base of a sand dune in the center of a vast, blazing desert. It is high noon and the sun shines above you with a bright gold luminescence. As you peer around, you notice the flicker of fire at the top of the sand dune. Moved by curiosity, you begin to climb the immense mountain of sand.

Once you reach the top, you find a bonfire surrounded by a ring of flat, smooth desert stones. The fire glows with a red aura and as you approach it, and the closer you come to the fire the more you notice that the red aura begins to surround and warm your body. Begin breathing deeply. With each inhalation, imagine that you absorb this red aura. Feel this power of fire fill your spirit. Feel it energize you and allow it to awaken your passions and drives.

As you continue to inhale and connect to this element, you notice that the aura and the fire within the ring of stones eventually dissipates and vanishes before you. You are filled with the element and powers of fire, aglow with this fiery red aura.

(Reader: pause for a moment.)

It is now time to return to the place where you began your journey. Look down at your spirit feet and you'll notice the glowing white mist beginning to encircle your body. Once it covers you completely, it lifts you and swiftly carries you back to the place where you began. When you are ready, open your eyes and stretch. Take note of how different you may feel now that you've taken on the qualities of fire.

Day 176

Fire: Incense and Oil

Fire Incense

Burn fire incense any time that you want to bring about the energies of the element of fire, which include: action, movement, passion, anger, strength, sexuality, achievement, mastery, power, and transformation.

What You'll Need:

- One handful of powdered sandalwood
- 2 tablespoons myrrh
- 2 tablespoons dried angelica leaves
- 2 tablespoons dried bay leaves
- 5 drops bay leaf essential oil
- 5 drops cinnamon essential oil
- Vegetable glycerin

In a medium-sized bowl, place your powdered sandalwood. Stir in about two tablespoons of vegetable glycerin. Add the glycerin, one tablespoon at a time, and then mix with a metal whisk or a fork. You simply want to create a soft, fluffy compound. Do not add the second tablespoon of glycerin if it feels like it would be too much, causing the incense to be too wet.

Now add your essential oils and whisk. Add your other dried herbs and mix thoroughly. Wait for at least a day for the compound to settle before you sprinkle it on hot coals.

Fire Oil

Anoint yourself or other people with this oil to activate the magical energies of fire.

What You'll Need:

- Vegetable glycerin
- 5 drops cinnamon essential oil
- 5 drops clove essential oil
- 3 drops bay leaf essential oil
- Pinch of dried clove or cinnamon

Fill a one-ounce bottle halfway with vegetable glycerin. Add plain water until the bottle is three-quarters full. Add your essential oils. Add your dry ingredient, close the lid and shake the bottle. You can use this magical oil immediately.

Day 177

Becoming Fire

What You'll Need:

- Several red taper candles or
- A fire pit filled with branches and other kindling
- Fire oil
- Fire incense

To begin, create a bonfire in a safe area, if possible. If this does not fit your circumstances, light several red candles and then sit facing south, with the candles in front of you. (If you are working with a bonfire, light the branches aflame and sit while simultaneously facing the fire and south.) Using your middle finger, dab a drop of fire oil approximately two inches below your navel, at the level of the solar plexus chakra. Light fire incense and gather some of the wafting smoke into your hands and bring your hands toward your face. Repeat this elemental cleansing with fire twice more.

Focus your attention on the flickering, dancing flames before you. Allow your breathing to become deep and rhythmic. Continue to focus intently upon the flame, barring all other thoughts. Allow your mind to become the flame. Feel your body become the flame. Feel the place where you sit to become the flame. Focus intently so that nothing exists but fire. Stay focused, preferably for 20 to 30 minutes.

When you are done, take time to close your eyes and imagine that your fire body solidifies and becomes stable once again. Get down on your hands and knees and place your forehead to the floor to ground and center your personal energy.

When you are ready, open your eyes and stretch. Take time to journal about your experience or to discuss it with a friend.

Day 178

The Element of Water

Water is an elemental force that represents the origins of the world in many of the primal mythologies found across the globe. The most common water myths involve the theme of life springing forth from the chaotic or churning, dark waters of the "abyss." In the case of water, mythic images and real-life facts support one another. Life on earth almost certainly emerged (and evolved) from organisms that thrived in a watery, swampy environment. So once we moved out of the swamps, we learned how to take the water with us. Water is our embryonic habitat; each of us germinated in the waters of our mother's womb. And have you ever tried to go for long without a drink of this element? Eighty percent or more of the human body consists of water and our lives quickly come to a halt without regular H_2O refills.

Symbolically speaking, water represents intuition, dreams, and visions. It represents the depths of the unconscious mind, the cycles of nature and women's mysteries. For Witches, water represents the flow of energy, the movement of the seasons and of life. Water represents the limitlessness of all things. Water teaches us that existence is cyclical, tidal. Water sits in the west of your circle, and Witches associate the west with such themes as endings, transition, and death. Water represents these themes too.

Take time today to familiarize yourself with the following table of correspondences for the element of water. You will learn more about each of these as you progress through the coming week.

Table of Correspondences: Water

Alchemical Symbol: ▽

Water Governs: Intuition, dreams, visions, peace, compassion, understanding, women's mysteries, cycles, spirituality, psychic ability, love, music, illusion, fantasy, and flow

Magical Tool: The chalice

Color: Blue

Alternate Colors: Various shades of blue: navy, blue-green, turquoise, etc. In some traditions of Wicca, the color is green (the color of the sea)

Fragrances: Mugwort, chamomile, geranium, gardenia, sandalwood, rose, jasmine

Elemental beings: Undines, Mer-people

Elemental King: Necksa

Tarot Card Suit: Cups

Magical stone: Moonstone, lapis lazuli

Outward Expression: The Power to Dare: the ability to go beyond the known boundaries.

Inward Expression: The Power to Accept: to recognize the boundaries

Day 179

Absorbing Water

What You'll Need:

- Jasmine essential oil

Try this exercise in either a bathtub filled with cool water or under a cool shower. I prefer to use cool water for this exercise since one of water's basic alchemical/symbolic characteristics is coolness.

For bath-takers: Once the bath water is drawn, place a few drops of jasmine essential oil into the tub. Ease yourself into the cool water and soak for a few moments.

For shower-takers: As you stand under the cool water, allow the water to cascade down you and stay with the sensations of the water. Apply a few drops of jasmine essential oil to your heart chakra center after you complete the shower and you dry yourself.

A Word to the Wise: *Jasmine officinale* is a plant that is native to northern India and Persia. In these countries, Jasmine is known as "queen of the night." Jasmine has very strong magical links to the element of water. It is a good conductor of psychic energy as well. If you live in a climate that supports the growth of jasmine, plant some around your home. It will come in handy during sabbat moon rituals. It also elevates the psychic energies of wherever it is planted.

For both bath and shower-takers: Fully focus on the experience of the water as it wets your skin. How does water cause you to physically and emotionally feel? After some time in the water, begin to breathe and to imagine that, with each inhalation, you absorb the energy of the water that surrounds you. Imagine that this energy flows down to your feet and builds up, layer by layer, until it fills you completely. Hold the energy in tightly, compacting it in your body. After a minute of this, release the energy with an audible sigh. Retain some of this energy that you intuit your body may need.

- How does the energy of water feel as it enters your body?
- What energies do you sense water imparting to you (daring or accepting)?
- Where in your body did you seem to hold on to the water energies after you consciously released them?
- What does your body feel like as this water energy leaves you?
- What is it like to absorb the energies of water into your body?

DAY 180

Contemplative Day: Words of Power

Meditative Question: What are words of power?

Candle: Orange

Direction: Southeast

Witches often make use of "words of power" in their magical practices. Words of power are utterances that make change both internally and externally. The vibration of sound penetrates the various layers of existence and it causes change in the physical and spiritual worlds. But from where do these utterances come? Where do they go? What are words of power for *you*?

To begin working with this contemplative question, find a comfortable meditative sitting position in a quiet space while facing the southeast. Light an orange candle and sit approximately two feet away from the flame. Cast your gaze upon the flickering candle and hold the question firmly for 20 to 30 minutes.

You may not arrive at a magically satisfactory conclusion in one sitting alone, so to manifest a greater depth of answer, it will be important to see this question as it actualizes in each of your activities. Over time, a shift in your perception will take place and you will realize your own answer.

Days 181-210

Magical Items to Gather:

Here are the items you will need for your next month of training.

Day 186

- One handful of powdered sandalwood
- 4 tablespoons myrrh (preferably powder)
- ½ teaspoon lemon zest
- ½ teaspoon poppyseed
- Jasmine essential oil
- Vegetable glycerin
- Cucumber essential oil

Day 187

- A 5–6 inch blue taper candle
- Water oil
- Water incense

Note: incense and oil made from ingredients of Day 186.

Day 193

- 1 handful of powdered sandalwood
- ½ handful of dried patchouli
- 2 teaspoons mandrake
- 2 teaspoons storax
- Lilac essential oil
- Patchouli essential oil
- Vegetable glycerin
- Pine essential oil

Day 194

- A 5–6 inch green taper candle
- Earth oil
- Earth incense

Note: incense and oil made from ingredients of Day 193.

Day 196

- A cup of red wine (or a red fruit juice such as cranberry)
- A baked good (such as cake or bread)

Note: you will need the same items that you used today for Days 199, 202, and 205.

Day 210

- Pruning shears or saw
- 12 inches of red ribbon
- Dried white sage
- A thurible (a small iron pot in which you can safely burn small ritual items, such as herbs)
- A small pouch made of cheesecloth or muslin in which you place two teaspoons of dried hyssop and lavender.

Day 181

Devotional Day: Honoring Pan

Table of Correspondences: Pan

Symbols: Acorns, oak leaves, pan pipes, seashells and twigs

Tools: The phallus, the wand

Magical Essences/Herbs: Musk, false unicorn, saw palmetto, patchouli, and myrrh

Direction: Pan is aligned with the center.

He Rules: Ecstasy, connection with nature, happiness, sexuality, grounding, life, and health

Animal Symbols: Goat

Sacred Foods: Wine, meats, and grapes

Magical Stones: Obsidian, carnelian, sunstone

Pan is an ancient Greek god of nature. The ancients described Pan as a god of the woods, of animal husbandry, and of fertility. Scholarship divides as to the meaning and origin of his name. Some scholars say Pan means "all," suggesting his embodiment of the universe. Others argue that his name was derived from the Greek *paeon*, meaning "pasturer," a word that connects Pan to the earthly seasons.

Ancient artists depicted Pan as a goat-footed god playing a flute-like musical instrument. Scholars connect Pan's worship with the earlier cults of Dionysus. Pan is present in your life whenever you feel sexual urges, playfulness, or a sense of inner joy. He is there in the eyes of any lover, or in the heart of an individual who embraces life no matter what it might present. Pan's magical energies are those of ecstasy, connection with nature, happiness, sexuality, and grounding. Symbols sacred to this god are acorns, oak leaves, pan pipes, seashells, and twigs. The magical colors of Pan include forest green, amber, and deep, earthy brown tones. Wine, meats, and grapes are foods sacred to Pan. Magical essences and herbs sacred to Pan include patchouli and myrrh. You can most readily evoke Pan's energies at midday.

Pan Practice

Make an altar honoring Pan that includes his symbols. Light candles of an appropriate color on his altar and intone his name slowly, fully. Since Pan is a one-syllable word, you can resonate it loudly and clearly. Intone his name until you feel or sense his presence. Once he has arrived, spend some time contemplating what it might mean to serve this aspect of deity. Ask Pan what it would mean to live life through his energy. Contemplate how you would live each day as a manifestation of this one unified, immense *All*, rejecting nothing and embracing the whole.

Spend the day honoring this god by recognizing that which is wild and natural in each person you encounter.

Day 182

Day of Silence and Review

As you observe silence, focus your attention on whatever it is you hear. How attuned are you to the sounds of your immediate environment? Do they all seem to run together and disrupt your thinking? Or do you hardly recognize environmental sounds? How closely do you listen to the ones you love? How openly do you listen to the voices of the planet? When the day is complete, answer these questions:

- What was it like to focus my attention on my sense of hearing?
- In what way did my hearing impact my thoughts, emotions, or spirit?
- How does what I hear affect my physical energy or my attention?
- Did my capacity to listen to other people either increase or decrease with my focused attention? Why might that be?

Review

Take time to ask yourself the following:

- Of the information I have learned up to now, what stands out most as vital?
- What information seems least relevant to my spiritual development?
- Which of the practices seemed to move me spiritually, and which had little impact?
- Of the information I have learned so far, what would be best to review? (take time to review it now)

Day 183

Water: The Power to Dare

The power to dare is water's active, outward expression. In this dynamic expression, water brings forth a power of fearlessness. Water does not recognize formal boundaries. The ocean does not distinguish one drop of water from the next, nor does it discriminate. It accepts all forms of water. If you observe any large body of water, you can easily note that it moves in its own way, based only on the laws of nature. Similarly, water's power to dare encourages you to go beyond human-constructed, socially accepted and institutionalized boundaries. If you dare, then just as naturally as water, you glide across that artificial line drawn in the sand by culture, gender, ethnicity, family, or by any other arbitrarily assigned conventions.

The areas of dreams, visions, empathy, compassion, understanding, cycles, and lunar mysteries are all ruled by water in this active expression. The energies of water manifest in those who are best suited for work in counseling, film, storytelling, psychotherapy, social work, the medical field, and professional psychism. People whose personalities are filled with water energies are naturally empathetic, dreamy, compassionate, loving, and emotional.

When the power to dare takes control in an individual, causing an imbalance in the delicate natural interplay between light and dark water energies, it can cause an individual to appear weepy, sad, depressed, fixed on the past, brooding, secretive, emotionally reactive, and inappropriately empathetic.

Take time to commit to paper an exploration of your own relationship to daring:

- In what ways do you feel you are connected to the power to dare?
- In what ways do you feel disconnected from the power to dare?

- Have the outward qualities of water been an important part of your life? Your culture? Your upbringing?
- What part does daring play in your life today?

Practice: Rebalancing Daring

When you notice that you are too emotional, dreamy, and lacking in boundaries, take time to practice this grounding exercise. Go to a place in nature where you can find water. If this is impossible, fill up the bathtub or the sink with water. Place your hands lightly on the surface of the water. As you do this, exhale onto the water. Close your eyes and imagine that a blue field of energy leaves your body through your hands and out through your breath. Now imagine that it enters the water on which your hands are placed. Continue with this process until you feel calm and emotionally centered.

Day 184

Water: The Power to Accept

In its receptive expression, water governs *the power to accept.* Since water's natural expression is a free flow in any direction, the complementary, "reversed" aspect of water focuses more on the container of water rather than upon the water itself. Therefore, the heart of magical *accepting* is defining and honoring the boundaries. It is the power of the cup, the chalice, the cauldron that holds and gives shape to water. In practical terms, accepting is about grounding yourself in the circumstances of your body, your environment, family, friends, work, life, etc. It is fully knowing where you are right now and determining how to get where you'd like to go.

When it is raining, you get wet. In the summer, it's hot. There is a simple, clean reality involved in accepting life as it is. There is power in acknowledging the whole truth of your life, pleasant and unpleasant alike. How honestly can you assess your advantages and limitations? Although discomfort may be involved in such a prospect, accepting is a golden doorway of opportunity. It invites you to take effective action in your life that can lead to significant change. It may begin with becoming aware that you are overdrawn at the bank, or with recognizing that you are angry or sad. It may mean acknowledging a secret desire, a hidden passion, or a repressed urge, but once you define the parameters of your existence, you can take meaningful steps in any direction you would like. Without accepting, you become dangerously paralyzed and ineffective; you do not see that you are soaked by rainwater or baked by the summer sun.

When the receptive aspect of water takes control in an individual, causing an imbalance in the delicate natural interplay between light and dark water energies, it can cause an individual to appear rigid, hyper-alert, self-deprecating, demanding of boundaries, needy of high structure and order, or only able to relate to what can be defined.

Take time to commit to paper your own relationship to acceptance:

- In what ways do you feel you are connected to the power to accept?
- In what ways do you feel disconnected from the power to accept?
- What are the dangers of accepting?
- Would accepting have any benefits in your life?

Practice: Rebalancing Accepting

Engage in this magical activity whenever you notice that you are feeling rigid, hyper-alert, or self-deprecating. Go to water in a natural setting, such as at a lake, a stream, or the ocean. If you do not live near a natural source of water, fill a large pot or cauldron with fresh clear water. Stand directly in front of the water. Open your arms and welcome this energy into your being. Close your eyes. Imagine that you become transparent and you allow the cool, slow, watery flow to pass directly through you. Stay with this exercise for at least ten minutes.

Day 185

Contemplating Water

Sit in a comfortable meditative position that assures spinal alignment. Read through this guided imagery and commit it to memory before you begin or have someone read it to you. You can also record it for later playback.

Reader:

Close your eyes and take three deep, slow breaths. Now allow your breathing to become rhythmic and natural. After a few moments, imagine that a twisting white mist begins to form a in a ring around your feet. You notice that with each inhalation, the ring of mist grows, expands and climbs your legs. Continue to visualize that with each inhaled breath the mist climbs your body, until it covers you completely.

Suddenly you feel the sensation of lifting. Your body feels as light as the mist that surrounds you. Soon you discover that you are hovering over the place where you were once sitting. Imagine that the mist now begins to move you across a colorless, imageless void. It is moving you through time and space. It is taking you to a sacred place of magic and power.

Soon the mist dissipates and the movement stops. You find yourself standing along sea cliffs that overlook a vast ocean. It is dusk and the sun is nearly set. It hovers half-hidden as it sinks slowly below the blue-green horizon.

Begin breathing deeply. With each inhalation, imagine that the ocean begins to churn and large waves crash up against the cliff below your feet. Each wave throws a magical, sparkling, blue-green mist into the air around you. Feel the cool energy of this mystical sea spray as it comes in contact with your skin. This cool energy now penetrates your skin and begins to fill the entirety of your body. It is a tingling, soft energy. If you look at your spirit body, you'll notice that you glow with this blue-green aura. You are filled with the element and powers of water. Stand with this energy and simply allow it to penetrate to the very depths of your spirit. Become one with the power of water.

(Reader: pause for a few moments.)

It is now time to return to the place where you began your journey. Look down at your spirit feet and you'll notice the glowing white mist beginning to encircle your body. Once it covers you completely, it lifts you and swiftly carries you back to the place where you began. When you are ready, open your eyes and stretch. Take note of how different you may feel now that you've taken on the qualities of water.

Live the rest of your day through the magical energies of water.

Day 186

Water: Incense and Oil

Water Incense

Burn this incense any time that you want to bring about the energies of the element of water, which include: intuition, dreams, visions, cycles, peace, compassion, understanding, spirituality, and women's mysteries.

What You'll Need:

- One handful of powdered sandalwood
- 4 tablespoons myrrh (preferably powder)
- ½ teaspoon lemon zest
- ½ teaspoon poppyseed
- 10 drops jasmine essential oil
- Vegetable glycerin

Place your powdered sandalwood in a medium-sized bowl. Stir in about two tablespoons of vegetable glycerin, adding one tablespoon at a time and then mixing with a metal whisk or a fork. As you have done before, create a soft, fluffy compound. Do not add the second tablespoon of glycerin if it feels like it would be too much, causing the incense to be too moist.

Now add your essential oil and whisk. Add your other dried herbs and mix thoroughly. Wait for at least a day for the compound to settle before you sprinkle it on hot coals.

Water Oil

Anoint yourself or other people with this oil to activate the magical energies of water.

What You'll Need:

- Vegetable glycerin
- 10 drops jasmine essential oil
- 5 drops cucumber essential oil
- Pinch of dried lemon zest or willow bark

Fill a one-ounce bottle halfway with vegetable glycerin. Add plain water until the bottle is three-quarters full. Add your essential oils. Add your dry ingredient, close the lid, and shake the bottle. You can use this magical oil immediately.

Day 187

Becoming Water

What You'll Need:

- A 5–6 inch blue taper candle
- Water oil
- Water incense
- Bowl of water

To begin, light a blue candle and sit down facing the west. Place the bowl of water in front of you and the lighted blue candle behind that. With your middle finger, dab a drop of water oil at approximately the center of your chest, at the level of the heart chakra. Light the water incense and gather some of the wafting smoke into your hands and bring your hands toward your face. Repeat this elemental cleansing with water energies twice more.

Now, focus your attention on the water in the bowl before you. Allow your breathing to become deep and rhythmic. Allow your mind to become the water. Feel your body become fluid. Imagine that the place where you sit flows and undulates like the tides. Focus intently so that nothing exists but water. Stay focused, preferably for 20 to 30 minutes.

When you are done, take time to close your eyes and imagine that your water-body solidifies and becomes stable once again. Get down on your hands and knees and place your forehead to the floor to ground and center your personal energy.

When you are ready, open your eyes and stretch. Take time to journal about your experience or to discuss it with a friend.

Day 188

The Element of Earth

Earth is an elemental energy that represents the diversity of forms and shapes, the physical expressions of our existence. In magical terms, earth is a feminine element; after all the earth itself gives birth to life forms and then nourishes those forms, just as women give birth to and then suckle their young. There is a spiritual symbolic link between woman and earth, between these spheres of microcosm and macrocosm. Our ancient ancestors had a clear understanding of the link between women and the earth as well. Consider the hundreds of ancient artifacts archaeologists have unearthed in the past century from the "Old Europe" communities of Hacilar and Catal Huyuk, most of which have been goddess and vulva figures formed of mud and clay.[73]

This theme of the earth as a goddess is not a phenomenon peculiar only to Old Europe. Almost every ancient primal culture across the globe has included earth goddess veneration. There exists evidence for goddess veneration in the creation myths from such disparate cultures as Africa, the Near East, India, Japan, Europe, Siberia, North, Central, and South America, and Australia.[74]

In Wicca, earth is more than our home planet or a "goddess theme." It is an authentic, energetic expression of solidity, substance, form, manifestation, embodiment, and grounding. It represents the vast human web that links us with other humans, animals, plants, and minerals. For Witches, the element of earth represents the mystery dimension and the physical body itself. Earth is the "grounding" element. It is the energy that brings to us into awareness of practicality, physical pleasure, and abundance. Earth sits in the north of your circle, and this particular compass direction has cross-cultural associations with darkness, the void, and unnamed, unspoken, not-yet-formed potential.

Take time today to familiarize yourself with the following table of correspondences for earth. You will learn more about each of these as you progress through the coming week.

Table of Correspondences: Earth

Alchemical Symbol: 🜃

Earth Governs: Solidity, substance, form, manifestation, embodiment, pleasure, money, all minerals, practicality, work, reliability, seasons, and grounding

Magical Tool: The Pentacle

Color: Green

Alternate Colors: Black, brown

Fragrances: Patchouli, oak moss, lilac

Elemental Beings: Gnomes

Elemental King: Ghob

Tarot Card Suit: Pentacles ("coins" in some decks)

Magical Stone: Salt, fluorite, obsidian, jade, slate, lead

Outward Expression—The Power to Be Silent: The ability to keep one's counsel; silence as a manifestation of who we are in our essence; darkness, the void, and the unnamed, unspoken, not-yet-formed potential

Inward Expression—The Power to Resonate: The ability to speak with the voice of the Gods and of nature, the ability to become "one" with the world; potential that has taken form

Day 189

Holding Earth

Go out into a natural setting where you will be able to lie down on the earth undisturbed. (If this is not possible, find a spot in your home where you will be able to lie down on a solid floor.) Once you identify the location where you will practice this exercise, form a simple earth-circle by sprinkling sea salt (or kosher salt) approximately nine feet in diameter. You can also place crystals or stones at each of the circle's four compass points for added enhancement. Using the moonwalking technique you learned earlier in the year, start in the east of your circle and walk the perimeter thrice while focusing your attention on maintaining your own silence.

A Word to the Wise: Moonwalking is slow, half-steps that you take while maintaining mindfulness on the sensations of your walking—the pressure on your feet, your weight, balance, etc.

Once you have moonwalked around your circle three times, enter it from the northernmost point. Lie down in the center of this salt-circle so that the top of your head aligns with the north. While you are lying down, simply experience the effect of the earth (or the firm floor) as it comes in contact with your back. How does it feel physically? What feeling or mood does it bring up in you? After some time to breathe intentionally, establish a rhythm and imagine that with each inhalation, you absorb the energy of the earth that lies beneath you. Imagine that this energy flows up through the points where your body makes contact with the earth and that it fills you completely. Hold the energy tightly in your body. After a minute of this, release the energy with an audible sigh. Retain whatever energy you feel your body may need.

- How does the energy of earth feel as it enters your body?
- What energies do you sense earth imparting to you (silence or resonance)?
- Where in your body did you seem to hold on to the earth energies after you consciously released them?
- What does your body feel like as this earth energy leaves you?
- What is it like to hold the energies of earth in your body?

Day 190

Earth: The Power to Be Silent

Witches say that *the power to be silent* is earth's outwardly expressed, dynamic energy. The earth is, after all, a silent presence; it is only natural that its active power reflects this wordless, unspeakable reality. In another way, this might seem puzzling, because in Western cultures we equate outward or dynamic expression with observable movement or noticeably directed energy. But here in the element of earth, we arrive at a peculiar magical fulcrum point, and in it we discover that earth is an energetic expression of paradoxes and surprises.

Silence is what Westerners normally consider a receptive trait, and in many ways it is. Silence is an energy of stillness and rest. Through this energy, the body, mind, and spirit find a sense of opening, broadening, and deepening. However, the stillness of silence also represents the void. This void is, as the yogis of India called it, *shunyata*, the original emptiness of all things. Paradoxically, the energy of emptiness is also one of potential; the void is eternally ready to manifest as new forms—trees, birds, streets, people. In a sense, then, emptiness is also fullness. The usually receptive energy of stillness is also the active energy of readiness, and of unlimited potential.

A Word to the Wise: In Wiccan practice, silence serves many functions. It the ancient past, silence was a measure of safety for adherents of the old ways who wanted to avoid Witch hunters, the gallows, and death by burning. Out of respect for folk who died keeping their pagan faith, Wiccans observe periods of regular silence—especially at the time of Samhain. Aside from its mundane practical value, silence is a skill that is imperative to successful magical workings. Witches believe that maintaining silence about their rites and magics assures their success. A basic premise of occult practice is that one risks weakening spells and rituals by speaking of them to anyone—including to other magical folk.

In its active expression, the element of earth rules material gain, wealth, prosperity, riches, work, service, strength, fortitude, honesty, practicality, pleasure, comfort, music, and art. Earthy people enjoy the simple pleasures of life such as good food, good sex, and a nice place to live. They are grounded and practical in their approach to what some people consider to be complex issues. If you naturally align with the outward expression of earth energies, you are best suited for work in real estate, banking, investing, engineering, farming, mineralogy, archaeology, building, architecture, dentistry, or medicine.

When the this active element of earth is out of balance in an individual it can cause one to appear rigid, stubborn, pessimistic, conventional, cruel, worrisome, inactive, possessive, stupid, slothful, greedy, or covetous.

Practice: Rebalancing Silence

When you notice that you are out of balance in the active energy of earth, take time to practice this freeing exercise. Go to a place in nature where you can touch the bare earth. (If this is impossible, fill a bowl with salt, which is the magical representative of earth.) Place your hands lightly on the surface of the earth (or the salt). As you do this, exhale onto the earth. Close your eyes and imagine that a green field of energy leaves your body through your hands and out through your breath. Now imagine that it enters the earth. Continue with this process until the green energy field feels rebalanced and you feel whole and serene.

Day 191

Earth: The Power to Resonate

The element of earth governs *the power to resonate* in its inward, more passive expression. Again we can note the paradoxical nature of earth here, since most of us would not consider resonation a passive trait. The power to resonate sounds vibrant and active. In magical terms, resonance is the energy that emerges from silence. Resonance represents the interconnectedness of all reality. It is an energy that widens your perspective to understand that there is no division between you and anything else. The receptive energy of earth connects you to the undulating pulse of the universe, the spiritual vibrations that underlie all of existence. Sometimes, in moments of silence, we can naturally connect to this energy and we feel the pulse of life throbbing all around us. Through this power, Witches gain access to experiencing the divine as it manifests in the world. It places our concepts, our academic terms of "god" and "goddess," into a palpable experiential form.

Often, when Witches tap into the power to resonate, they make spontaneous utterances. In Wiccan lore these utterances are presumably the voice of the gods; they are the sounds and the words of life itself. Not only that, but when you tap into resonance, the denseness of earth renders itself luminous, weightless and effortless. When you strongly align with this power to resonate, spontaneity guides your actions; the energies of life itself guide you.

When this receptive element of earth falls out of balance, it can cause an individual to appear lightheaded, detached, disoriented, and out of touch with one's surroundings/reality.

Practice: Rebalancing Resonance

When you notice the signs of resonance imbalances, take time to practice this grounding exercise. Begin by heating seven small river stones under hot running tap water. Do not allow the stones to heat so much that you cannot handle them. Then, take off your clothing and lie flat on your back. Use table salt to form a line down the center of your body from the base of your throat to the pubic area. Place one heated stone each at the center of your brow, at the base of your throat, at the center of your chest, about two inches above the navel, and just above the genitals. Place one stone in the palm of each hand and lie so that your palms face upward. As you lie on the ground, imagine that you absorb the earth energies both beneath you and from the stones.

Day 192

Contemplating Earth

In order to experience the spiritual energies of earth, you will take an inward journey to your own sacred earth source. To begin, sit in a comfortable position while also assuring that your spine is straight and aligned. You can first read through this journey and commit it to memory before you begin, or you can have someone read it to you. You can also record it for later play back.

Reader:
Close your eyes and take three deep, slow breaths. Now allow your breathing to become rhythmic and natural. After a few moments, imagine that a twisting white mist begins to form in a ring around your feet. You notice that with each inhalation, the ring of mist grows, expands, and climbs your legs. Continue to visualize that with each inhaled breath the mist climbs your body until it covers you completely.

Notice that not only does the mist surround you, it penetrates you. With each breath, your body becomes one with the mist. You can feel your body shift from its usual weight and density; it now glows and becomes light and buoyant. Soon your body lifts and you find that you are suspended above the place where you were sitting. In an instant, the energy of the mist transports you to a colorless, soundless, imageless void. In that void, you feel as though you are moving through time and space to a sacred place of magic and power.

Soon the movement stops and you find yourself standing just outside a labyrinth with spiraling passages that are dug out from the earth. It is midnight and as you look to the stars, you notice that there is no moon in the sky. Some distance from you, you notice a glow that emanates from the center point of the labyrinth.

Enter the labyrinth, knowing that you will soon arrive at the center point that contains the brilliant, shining light. As you walk the labyrinth, notice that the trench becomes deeper and deeper with each step. Along the way you can see old roots, mushrooms, and mossy growth sprouting all along the sides of the labyrinth. Touch them with your hands. Soon the walls of the labyrinth are slightly taller than you. You are no longer able to see the shining light of the central point. But you can feel its presence and it continues to guide you.

As you continue to walk, feel the cool, heavy energy of the earth surrounding you. Inhale the rich, earthy scent that fills the pathway. As you breathe in this scent, allow it to fill you completely.

(Reader: pause for a few moments.)

Once you reach the center of the labyrinth, you find a glowing crystal suspended in midair. Look directly above the crystal and you will see that its source of power is the north star, which it reflects and magnifies. As you stand before the crystal, raise your spirit arms and welcome the power of earth. In an instant, the crystal emanates a beam of light that strikes you at the center of your brow. Feel the power of earth fill you and energize you.

(Reader: pause for a few moments.)

It is now time to return to the place where you began your journey. Look down at your spirit feet and you'll notice the glowing white mist beginning to encircle your body. Once it covers you completely, it lifts you and swiftly carries you back to the place where you began. When you are ready, open your eyes and stretch. Take note of how different you may feel now that you've taken on the qualities of earth.

DAY 193

Earth: Incense and Oil

Earth Incense

Burn earth incense any time that you want to bring about the energies of the element of earth, which include: stability, practicality, reliability, grounding, material gain, wealth, prosperity, and riches.

What You'll Need:

- One handful of powdered sandalwood
- ¼ handful of dried patchouli
- 2 teaspoons mandrake
- 2 teaspoons storax
- 6 drops lilac essential oil
- 4 drops patchouli essential oil
- Vegetable glycerin

Place your powdered sandalwood in a medium-sized bowl. Stir in about two tablespoons of vegetable glycerin. Add the tablespoons of glycerin one at a time and then mix with a metal whisk or a fork. As you have already learned, create a soft, fluffy compound. Do not add the second tablespoon of glycerin if it feels like it would be too much, causing the incense to be too moist.

Now add your essential oil and whisk. Add your other dried herbs and mix thoroughly. Wait for at least a day for the compound to settle before you sprinkle it on hot coals.

Earth Oil

Anoint yourself or other people with this oil to activate the magical energies of earth.

What You'll Need:

- Vegetable glycerin
- 5 drops lilac essential oil
- 3 drops patchouli essential oil
- 3 drops pine essential oil
- Pinch of dried patchouli

Fill a one-ounce bottle halfway with vegetable glycerin. Add plain water until the bottle is three-quarters full. Add your essential oils and dry ingredients, then close the lid and shake the bottle. You can use this magical oil immediately.

Day 194

Becoming Earth

What You'll Need:

- A 5–6 inch green taper candle
- Earth oil
- Earth incense
- Bowl of earth

To begin, light a green taper candle and sit down facing the north. Place the bowl of earth in front of you and the candle behind that. With your middle finger, dab a drop of earth oil at the base of your spine and at the crown of your head, at the levels of the root and crown chakras. Light the earth incense and gather some of the wafting smoke into your hands and bring your hands toward your face. Repeat this cleansing with earth energies twice more.

Focus your attention on the soil in the bowl before you. Allow your breathing to become deep and rhythmic. Continue to focus intently upon the earth, barring all other thoughts. Allow your mind to become the earth. Feel your body become the earth; it feels cold, moist, and heavy. Imagine that the place where you are sitting also becomes soil. Focus intently so that nothing exists but earth, clay, mud, stone, or however you experience the energies of earth. Stay focused, preferably for 20 to 30 minutes.

When you are done, take time to close your eyes and imagine that your earth-body becomes your usual natural self once again. Get down on your hands and knees and place your forehead to the floor to ground and center your personal energy.

When you are ready, open your eyes and stretch. Take time to journal about your experience or to discuss it with a friend.

Day 195

The Elemental Spirits: Sylphs and Fairies

Elementals are the spiritual creatures that reside in each of the four elements. Francesco Maria Guazzo was the first to write about elementals in the *Compendium Malificarum*, the second of two works adopted by the Catholic church to curb the believed spread of witchcraft in the Renaissance period. Guazzo's volume was consulted by church clerics and legal professionals to reveal the operations of suspected witches against humanity and the supposed remedies that thwarted their evil practices.[75] Throughout the work, Guazzo cites his varied sources of information, including the hermetic philosophy of Marsilio Ficino. Craft historians suspect that it is from the Ficino material that information about elementals emerged. Later occult lore elaborated on the *Compendium* and named the four types of elemental beings: the elementals of air were called *sylphs*, the elementals of fire were *salamanders,* the elements of water were *undines,* and the elementals of earth were *gnomes*.

Our study of these magical creatures begins with air and sylphs. Traditional occultists claim that sylphs live within the *etheric* dimensions of the element air.[76]

A Word to the Wise: In Theosophical and occult lore, the etheric realm is reputedly an energetic force invisible to the eyes, but which shapes and moves the natural phenomena of the earth. You can observe etheric forces at work in magnets and you can experience them in natural earth-energy "power spots" such as at Stonehenge, in the power vortexes of Sedona, Arizona, in Machu Picchu, etc.

The name "sylph" reputedly comes from the Greek *silphe*, which is a butterfly. In traditional Wiccan lore, sylphs are beautiful tiny winged creatures, similar in appearance to butterflies. Another mythic tiny winged creature associated with air is the fairy. In occult lore, Paralda is the king of the sylphs. In myth and lore fairies have a queen who has no name, but whose title is Queen of the Elphame.

As with each of the elemental creatures, sylphs are spiritual helpers. They impart the spiritual powers and energies of air: clear thought, imagination, creativity, communicative skills, listening skills, intellectual capacity. Reputedly, sylphs can diminish these skills and abilities as well. When that happens, one can become "air-headed," confused, unable to communicate or understand ideas. Witches work with sylphs (and fairies) when they want to rebalance their own air energies, or when they work with the magic of air. They also call upon sylphs to guard and protect the eastern quarter of the ritual circle.

Practice: Meeting the Sylphs

What You'll Need:

- Air incense
- Air oil

To begin, light some air incense and dab the air oil at all seven body-energy centers: base of the spine, pubic region, solar plexus, heart, throat, center of the brow, crown of the head. Next you will engage in a guided imagery. As always, you can read it and memorize the imagery sequence now, have a friend read it to you with your eyes closed, or tape record it for later playback.

Reader:

Find a comfortable lying-down position and close your eyes. Take several deep breaths and allow your body to become relaxed. Slowly allow the earth to hold you completely. Surrender your body weight to the planet, where it belongs.

Imagine that you stand on the cliff overlooking a vast grassy plain. The cliff faces the east. You hold your spirit hands up and flex the palms of your hands so that they face outward toward the grassy plain. Feel the energy of the land circulate through you completely until you feel that you are one with the energy. Then imagine that you cast this energy out through your hands and it appears as an electric-yellow power that crackles and sizzles. Imagine that you turn your spirit body in a clockwise direction, casting a circle of protection and containment with this energy that bursts forth from your hands. When you face the east again, the energy stops emanating from your hands.

You are now completely surrounded by this field of energy, yet you are able to clearly see through it, out across the grassy plain. Raise your hands to the sky and mentally summon forth the sylphs, the spirits of air. Soon the wind begins to blow and little by little they appear. They surround your magic circle. Take time to observe them carefully. As they surround you, your circle takes on a sparkling golden hue. Ask the sylphs where you can find them near your home. Remember what they tell you.

When you have heard their answer, bid them farewell and request that they return to their magical realm. Little by little, you observe them fly away, leaving only the golden aura that surrounds you and your magic circle. This aura left behind is the balancing force of air. Feel it balance you, center you, and cause you to become whole.

(Reader: pause for a few moments.)

When you feel you have absorbed enough of the elementals' powers, it is time to banish the circle you created. Hold your hands up again to the east, begin to turn your spirit-body in a clockwise direction. This time as you turn, imagine that you draw the energies of the circle back into your body. Allow the energy to return to the earth below your feet, grounding it completely.

(Reader: pause for a few moments.)

Once you have finished, it is time to open your eyes. Get down on your hands and knees and place your forehead to the floor, grounding and solidifying all of the energy you raised.

Take time to journal about your experiences, to draw a picture of the sylphs, and to write down where you can find them near your home.

A Word to the Wise: Never invoke or summon the elemental spirits into your home without first casting the magic circle (which you will learn how to construct in future days). The circle acts as a buffer that transforms raw, wild elemental energy into something magically usable. Some witches believe that the elementals can act like naughty children who require high structure and a specific purpose. Otherwise they can run amok and cause unfortunate events.

Day 196

Elementals: Sylph Offerings

In yesterday's vision, the sylphs indicated where near your home they reside. Today you will go to this place and make an offering to them. The offering is a libation (based on the practice you learned earlier in the year) which assures that the sylphs will become good magical partners in future spiritual endeavors.

What You'll Need:

- A cup of red wine (or a red fruit juice such as cranberry)
- A piece of a baked good (such as cake or bread)

When you first arrive at the place of the sylphs, sit on the ground and close your eyes. Imagine the sylphs gathering behind plants, stones, trees, or buildings. Open your eyes and pour out a cup of wine. Grasp the filled cup and baked good in your hands. Hold your arms out, to shoulder level, offering the food to the spirits. Cast your gaze to the ground (a respectful gesture), saying:

> ***Sylphs of the air, Lord Paralda,***
> ***Accept this offering of food and drink!***
> ***May the magic that I do be aided by your powers,***
> ***The powers of life that were, that are, and that shall be,***
> ***So Mote It Be!***

Leave the baked good on the ground and pour the wine over it, saying:

> ***From east to west, from south to north,***
> ***Ancient ones, I call thee forth!***

Quickly gather your belongings and leave this enchanted spot. Return only when you wish to contemplate the sylphs or if you wish to invoke their magical energies for some purpose.

Day 197

Elementals: King Paralda

Today, you will meet the sylph king, Paralda, (pronounced *pah-RAL-dah*) and you will learn what energies the sylphs offer to your life and magical practice. You will also learn which of your energies they limit.

What You'll Need:

- Air incense
- Air oil

A Word to the Wise: The word "intone" means to vocally sustain a particular sound or word. When intoning a sound (or word) first select a comfortable tone of voice. Next, draw a deep breath and then sustain the selected sound on a single vocal tone until the breath runs out.

It is best to try this practice in the location near your home where the sylphs reside. Light the air incense and allow it to waft over your body. Dab some of the air oil on all seven body-energy centers: base of the spine, pubic region, solar plexus, heart, throat, center of the brow, and crown of the head.

Find a comfortable sitting position and close your eyes. Take several deep breaths and allow your body to become relaxed. With your eyes still closed begin to intone King Paralda's name, one syllable at a time for each exhaled breath:

Inhale slowly. Exhale, intoning the sound: ***Pa.***

Inhale slowly. Exhale, intoning the sound: ***Ral.***

Inhale slowly. Exhale, intoning the sound: ***Da.***

Repeat these intonations twice more and then practice the following guided imagery. You can read it and memorize the imagery sequence now, have a friend read it to you with your eyes closed, or tape record it for later playback.

Reader:

Imagine that you stand once again on the cliff overlooking the vast grassy plain that you visited before when you first met the sylphs.

Hold your spirit hands up and flex the palms of your hands so that they face outward toward the grassy plain, and again draw up the energies of this place and cast them in a circle of light that surrounds you.

You are now completely surrounded by this field of energy. Raise your hands to the sky and mentally summon forth King Paralda. Soon the wind begins to blow and he arrives, standing just outside of your magic circle. Do not waste Paralda's time—get right to the point and ask him what powers he offers to your life and what powers he diminishes in your life.

(Reader: pause for a moment.)

When you have heard his answer, bid him farewell and watch him fly away. When he has vanished, it is time to banish the circle you created. Hold your hands up again to the east and begin to turn your spirit-body in a clockwise direction. This time as you turn, imagine that you draw the energies of the circle back into your body. Allow the energy to return to the earth below your feet, grounding it completely.

Once you have finished, it is time to open your eyes. Get down on your hands and knees and place your forehead to the floor, grounding and solidifying all of the energy you raised.

Take time to journal about your experiences, to draw a picture of Paralda and write down what powers he offers and diminishes in your life.

Day 198

Elementals: Salamanders

Salamanders are the elementals of fire. The name salamander reputedly comes from the Greek *salambre*, which means fireplace. In traditional Wiccan lore, salamanders are small, lizard-like creatures (some say they are dragon-like) that live within the etheric forces of fire. If you have innate mystic vision, perhaps you can discern their movements among the embers of bonfires and in fireplaces. In occult lore, the salamanders are ruled by their king, Djin.

Salamanders bestow the powers of the element fire, such as passion, inspiration, sexuality, drive, ambition, energy, movement, and linear direction. Salamanders also have the power to invert these traits and abilities. When that happens, they can create hot-headedness, force, aggression, anger, rage, or intimidation. Witches work with salamanders when they want to rebalance their own fire energies or work magic that connects to fire. They also call upon salamanders as guardians and protectors of the magic circle's southern quarter.

Today's work centers on meeting the salamanders and on learning where they reside near to your home.

Practice: Meeting Salamanders

What You'll Need:

- Fire incense
- Fire oil

To begin, light the fire incense and allow it to waft over your body, infusing you with its energies. Place a dab of the fire oil at all seven chakra centers: base of the spine, pubic region, solar plexus, heart, throat, center of the brow, and crown of the head. Next you will engage in a guided imagery. As always, you can read it and memorize the imagery sequence now, have a friend read it to you with your eyes closed, or tape record it for later playback.

Reader:
Find a comfortable sitting or lying-down position and close your eyes. Take several deep breaths and allow your body to become relaxed. Slowly allow the earth to hold you completely; surrender your body weight to the planet, where it belongs.

Imagine that you stand facing the south atop a sand dune that dominates a vast white-hot sand desert. No matter where you cast your gaze, all you can see is this burning white sand that seems to stretch into infinity. Hold your spirit hands up toward the south. Feel the heated energy of the land as it circulates completely through you until you feel that you are unified with the energy.

Next imagine that you are casting this energy out through your hands and it appears as an electric-red power that crackles and sizzles. Turn your spirit body in a clockwise direction, casting a circle of protection and containment with this energy that bursts forth from your hands. When you face the south again, the energy that once emanated from your hands subsides.

You are now completely surrounded by this field of energy, yet you are able to clearly see through it, out across the dunes. Imagine that you raise your hands to the sky and summon forth the salamanders, the spirits of fire. Soon you see small flickers of fire sprout up from the desert floor. Hundreds, perhaps thousands of these little flames appear and they begin to move toward you and your circle. As they surround your magic circle, you have a chance to observe them carefully. You can see a fiery-red lizard (or miniature dragon) contained within each of the flames. As they surround you, your circle takes on a sparkling rosy hue. Ask the salamanders where near to your home you can find them. Remember what they tell you.

(Reader: pause for a moment.)

When you have heard their answer, bid them farewell and firmly request that they return to their magical realm. Little by little, you observe the salamanders pop back below the white sands, leaving only the sparkling rosy aura that surrounds you and your magic circle. This aura left behind is the balancing force of fire. Feel it balance you, center you, and cause you to become whole.

(Reader: pause for a moment.)

When you feel you have absorbed enough of the elementals' powers, it is time to close the circle that you have created. Imagine that you hold your hands up to the south, begin to turn your spirit-body in a clockwise direction. This time as you turn, imagine that you draw the energies of the circle back into your body. Then allow the energy to pass through your body and return to the earth below your feet, grounding it completely.

Once you have finished, it is time to open your eyes. Get down on your hands and knees and place your forehead to the floor, grounding and solidifying all of the energy you raised.

Take time to journal about your experiences, to draw a picture of the salamanders, and to write down where you can find them near to your home.

Day 199

Elementals: Salamander Offerings

In today's practice, you will go to the place where the salamanders indicated that they reside and you will make an offering of food and wine to them. As you learned with the sylphs, the offering influences the salamanders to become good magical partners in future magical endeavors.

What You'll Need:

- A cup of red wine (or a red fruit juice such as cranberry)
- A piece of a baked good (such as cake or bread)

When you first arrive at the place of the salamanders, sit on the ground and close your eyes. Close your eyes and imagine the salamanders gathering, popping up from the ground as small flames, watching you. Open your eyes and pour out a cup of wine. Grasp the filled cup and baked good in your hands. Hold your arms out to shoulder level, offering the food to the spirits. Cast your gaze to the ground (a respectful gesture), saying:

Salamanders of flame, Lord Djin,
Accept this offering of food and drink!
May the magic that I do be aided by your powers,
The powers of life that were, that are, and that shall be,
So mote it be!

Leave the baked good on the ground and pour the wine over it, saying:

From east to west, from south to north,
Ancient ones, I call thee forth!

Quickly gather your belongings and leave this sacred spot. Return only when you wish to contemplate the salamanders or are in need of their magical energies.

Day 200

Elementals: King Djin

Today, you will meet the salamander king, Djin, (pronounced *JIN*) and you will learn what energies the salamanders offer to your life. You will also learn which of your energies they limit.

What You'll Need:

- Fire incense
- Fire oil

It is best to try this practice in the location near your home where the salamanders reside. Light the fire incense and allow it waft over your body. Dab some of the fire oil on all seven body-energy centers: base of the spine, pubic region, solar plexus, heart, throat, center of the brow, crown of the head.

Find a comfortable sitting position and close your eyes. Take several deep breaths and allow your body to become relaxed. With your eyes still closed begin to intone King Djin's name on each exhaled breath.

Inhale slowly. Exhale, intoning the sound Djin.

Repeat this intonation twice more and then practice the following guided imagery. You can read it and memorize the imagery sequence now, have a friend read it to you with your eyes closed, or tape record it for later playback.

Reader:

Imagine that you stand once again atop the sand dune overlooking the vast white-hot sand desert. This is where you first met the salamanders.

Hold your spirit hands up so that they face outward toward the sands, and again draw up the energies of this place and cast them in a circle of brilliant red light that surrounds you.

You are now completely surrounded by this field of energy. Raise your hands to the south and mentally summon forth King Djin. Soon a large bonfire springs up from the sands just outside of your magic circle. Without wasting time, ask Djin what powers he offers to your life and what powers he diminishes in your life.

(Reader: pause for a moment.)

When you have heard his answer, bid him farewell and watch him vanish back into the white- hot sands. When he has left, it is time to close the circle you created. Hold your hands up again to the south and begin to turn your spirit-body in a clockwise direction. This time as you turn, imagine that you draw the energies of the circle back into your body. Allow the energy to return to the earth below your feet, where it is completely grounded.

Once you have finished, it is time to open your eyes. Get down on your hands and knees and place your forehead to the floor, grounding and solidifying all of the energy you raised.

Take time to journal about your experiences, to draw a picture of Djin and write down what powers he offers and diminishes in your life.

Day 201

Elementals: Undines

Undines and mermaids are the watery elemental spirits. Although the origins of the word "undine" are not clearly known, some occultists believe that it originated from the Latin word *unda*, which means wave. Undines are indeed creatures of the waves. But they are also everywhere: they are the thrust of whitewater rivers, the soothing undulations of serene mountain lakes, and the gentle splash of your swimming pool. In traditional Wiccan lore, undines are gilled, finned, and able to live in the depths of the seas—although occult lore says that their favorite dwelling places are wells, springs, and small streams. Undines are ruled by their king, Necksa (sometimes written and pronounced *Niksa*).

Undines bestow the spiritual powers of water, including intuition, dreams, insight, compassion, spirituality, flexibility, understanding, love, and tenderness. Undines can also impishly invert these desirable qualities. When that happens, they can create foggy-headedness, weepiness, hypersensitivity, crabbiness, weakness, emotional instability, depression, and self-pitying. Witches work with undines to rebalance their own water energies or work magic that connects to water. They also call upon undines as guardians and protectors of the magic circle's western quarter.

Today's work centers on meeting the undines and on learning where they reside near to your home.

Practice: Meeting Undines

What You'll Need:

- Water incense
- Water oil

To begin, light the water incense and allow it to waft over your body, infusing you with its energies. Place a dab the water oil at all seven chakra centers: base of the spine, pubic region, solar plexus, heart, throat, center of the brow, and crown of the head. Next you will engage in a guided imagery. As always, you can read it and memorize the imagery sequence now, have a friend read it to you with your eyes closed, or tape record it for later playback.

Reader:

Find a comfortable sitting or lying-down position and close your eyes. Take several deep breaths and allow your body to become relaxed. Slowly allow the earth to hold you completely; surrender your body weight to the planet, where it belongs.

Imagine that you stand at the western edge of a large freshwater spring. The spring is set within a lush, green forest and you cannot see beyond the surrounding greenery. Hold your spirit hands up toward the west. Feel the cool, fresh energy of the spring water circulate through you completely until you feel that you are one with it. Then imagine that you cast this energy out through your hands and it appears as an electric-blue power that forms a protective shield around you. Turn your spirit body in a clockwise direction, casting this circle of protection and containment with the energy that bursts forth from your hands. When you face the west again, the energy that once emanated from your hands subsides.

You are now completely surrounded by this blue field of energy, yet you are able to clearly see through it. Imagine that you raise your hands to the sky and summon forth the undines—the spirits of this magical spring. Soon you see finned, human-like figures emerge from the depths of the spring. When the undines appear, you notice that your circle takes on a sparkling cobalt hue. Ask the undines where near to your home you can find them. Remember what they tell you.

(Reader: pause for a moment.)

When you have heard their answer, bid them farewell and firmly request that they return to their magical realm. Watch them as they glide back below the surface of the spring, leaving only the sparkling cobalt aura that surrounds you and your magic circle. This aura left behind is the balancing force of Fire. Feel it balance you, center you, and cause you to become whole.

(Reader: pause for a moment.)

When you feel you have absorbed enough of the undine's powers, it is time to close the circle that you have created. Imagine that you hold your hands up to the west and begin to turn your spirit-body in a clockwise direction. This time, as you turn, imagine that you draw the energies of the circle back into your body. Then allow the energy to pass through your body and return to the spring, grounding it completely.

Once you have finished, it is time to open your eyes. Get down on your hands and knees and place your forehead to the floor, grounding and solidifying all of the energy you raised.

Take time to journal about your experiences, to draw a picture of the undines, and to write down where you can find them near to your home.

Day 202

Elementals: Undine Offerings

In today's practice, you will go to the place where the undines indicated that they reside and you will make an offering of food and wine to them. As you learned with the sylphs and salamanders, the offering influences the undines to become good magical partners in future magical endeavors.

What You'll Need:

- A cup of red wine (or a fruit juice such as cranberry)
- A piece of a baked good (such as cake or bread)

When you first arrive at the place of the salamanders, sit on the ground and close your eyes. Close your eyes and imagine the undines gathering, watching you. Open your eyes and pour out a cup of wine. Grasp the filled cup and baked good in your hands. Hold your arms out to shoulder level, offering the food to the spirits. Cast your gaze to the ground (a respectful gesture), saying:

Undines of the deep, Lord Necksa,
Accept this offering of food and drink!
May the magic that I do be aided by your powers,
The powers of life that were, that are, and that shall be,
So Mote It Be!

Leave the baked good on the ground and pour the wine over it, saying:

From east to west, from south to north,
Ancient ones, I call thee forth!

Quickly gather your belongings and leave this sacred spot. Return only when you wish to contemplate the undines or are in need of their magical energies.

DAY 203

Elementals: King Necksa

Today, you will meet the undine king, Necksa, (pronounced *NECK-suh*) and you will learn what energies the undines offer to your life. You will also learn which of your energies they limit.

What You'll Need:

- Water incense
- Water oil

It is best to try this practice in the location near your home where the undines reside. Light the water incense and allow it to waft over your body. Dab some of the water oil on all seven body-energy centers: base of the spine, pubic region, solar plexus, heart, throat, center of the brow, crown of the head.

Find a comfortable sitting position and close your eyes. Take several deep breaths and allow your body to become relaxed. With your eyes still closed begin to intone King Necksa's name, saying one syllable on each exhaled breath.

Inhale slowly. Exhale, intoning the sound: ***Neck.***

Inhale slowly. Exhale, intoning the sound: ***Sa.***

Repeat this intonation twice more and then practice the following guided imagery. You can read it and memorize the imagery sequence now, have a friend read it to you with your eyes closed, or tape record it for later playback.

Reader:
Imagine that you stand once again near the spring in the forest where you first met the undines.

Hold your spirit hands up so that they face outward toward the west, and again draw up the energies of this place and cast them in a circle of brilliant blue light that surrounds you.

You are now completely surrounded by this field of energy. Raise your hands to the west and mentally summon forth King Necksa. Soon a radiant, magnificent merman emerges from the spring, outside of your magic circle. Without wasting time, ask Necksa what powers he offers to your life and what powers he diminishes in your life.

(Reader: pause for a moment.)

When you have heard his answer, bid him farewell and watch him vanish back into the dark depths of the pool. When he has left, it is time to close the circle you created. Hold your hands up again to the west and begin to turn your spirit-body in a clockwise direction. This time, as you turn, imagine that you draw the energies of the circle back into your body. Allow the energy to return to the earth below your feet, where it is completely grounded.

Once you have finished, it is time to open your eyes. Get down on your hands and knees and place your forehead to the floor, grounding and solidifying all of the energy you raised.

Take time to journal about your experiences, to draw a picture of Necksa and write down what powers he offers and diminishes in your life.

Day 204

Elementals: Gnomes

Okay, so you've got the cheap plastic garden gnomes in wheelbarrowing or pickaxing poses on your front lawn. That's nice. But these are not the magical creatures you will encounter in the coming days. Gnomes are spiritual beings that live in the etheric realm of earth. The word "gnome" seems to be related to the Greek *gnoma*, which means knowledge. So what do they know? They can tell you a lot about the earth, since they are guardians all of her mysteries. Traditionally, Wiccans envision the gnomes as small, stout creatures who live in small hills or mountains. According to legend, gnomes maintain vast stores of treasure—gold and jewels—in their under-earth dwellings and in caves. Humans who are lucky enough to gain their countenance stand to inherit these treasures. Gnomes are ruled by their king, Ghob (whose name may well be related to the term goblin).

Gnomes bestow the spiritual powers of earth, such as stability, growth, material gain, mastery of the physical body, sensuality, pleasure, money, riches, and stamina, but when gnomes invert these qualities they can cause thick-headedness, tiredness, heaviness, dullness, insensitivity, gluttony, greed, or stinginess. Witches work with gnomes when they want to rebalance their own earthy qualities or when they want to work with magical energies related to the element of earth. In ritual, Witches call upon undines as guardians and protectors of the magic circle's western quarter.

Today's work centers on meeting the gnomes (assuming they won't be insulted by those tacky statuettes of yours) and on learning where they reside near to your home.

Practice: Meeting Gnomes
What You'll Need:

- Earth incense
- Earth oil

To begin, light the earth incense and allow it to waft over your body, infusing you with its energies. Place a dab of the earth oil at all seven chakra centers: base of the spine, pubic region, solar plexus, heart, throat, center of the brow, and crown of the head. Next you will engage in a guided imagery. As always, you can read it and memorize the imagery sequence now, have a friend read it to you with your eyes closed, or tape record it for later playback.

Reader:
Find a comfortable sitting or lying-down position and close your eyes. Take several deep breaths and allow your body to become relaxed. Slowly allow the earth to hold you completely; surrender your body weight to the planet, where it belongs.

Imagine that you stand at the northern edge of a large, freshly ploughed field. A musky, heavy earth scent fills the air and you welcome it. Hold your spirit hands up so that they face outward toward the north. Feel the cool, weighty energy of the ploughed earth circulate through you completely until you feel that you are one with it. Then imagine that you cast this energy out through your hands and it appears as an electric-green power that forms a protective shield around you. Turn your spirit body in a clockwise direction, casting the energy that bursts forth from your hands into a circle of protection and containment. When you face the north again, the energy that once emanated from your hands subsides.

You are now completely surrounded by this field of energy, yet you are able to clearly see through it. Imagine that you raise your hands to the sky and summon forth the gnomes—the spirits of this earthy realm. Soon you see figures crawl out from their holes beneath the neatly ploughed rows. The gnomes approach your circle and surround it. As they do, your circle takes on a sparkling emerald hue. Ask the gnomes who have joined you where they reside near to your home.

(Reader: pause for a moment.)

When you have heard their answer, bid these magical creatures farewell and firmly request that they return to their magical realms. You watch as the gnomes depart and crawl back beneath the earth's surface. All that is left behind is the green aura that surrounds you and your magic circle. This aura left behind is the balancing force of earth. Feel it penetrate you. This force centers you, and causes you to become whole.

(Reader: pause for a moment.)

When you feel you have absorbed enough of the elementals' powers, it is time to close the circle you have created. Imagine that you hold your hands up to the north and begin to turn your spirit-body in a clockwise direction. This time, as you turn, imagine that you draw the energies of the circle back into your body. Then allow the energy to pass through your body and return to the earth below your feet, grounding it completely.

Once you have finished, it is time to open your eyes. Get down on your hands and knees and place your forehead to the floor, grounding and solidifying all of the energy you raised.

Take time to journal about your experiences, to draw a picture of the gnomes and write down you can find them near to your home.

Day 205

Elementals: Gnome Offerings

In today's practice, you will go to the place where the gnomes indicated that they reside and you will make an offering to them. Again, the offering is a libation to assure that the gnomes will become good magical partners.

What You'll Need:

- A cup of red wine (or a fruit juice such as cranberry)
- A piece of a baked good (such as cake or bread)

When you first arrive at the place of the gnomes, sit on the ground and close your eyes. Close your eyes and imagine the gnomes gathering, rising out from their underground dwellings and watching you. Open your eyes and pour out a cup of wine. Grasp the filled cup and baked good in your hands. Hold your arms out to shoulder level, offering the food to the spirits. Cast your gaze to the ground (a respectful gesture), saying:

Gnomes of the earth, Lord Ghob,
Accept this offering of food and drink!
May the magic that I do be aided by your powers,
The powers of life that were, that are, and that shall be,
So Mote It Be!

Leave the baked good on the ground and pour the wine over it, saying:

From east to west, from south to north,
Ancient ones, I call thee forth!

Quickly gather your belongings and leave this sacred spot. Return only when you wish to contemplate the gnomes or are in need of their magical assistance.

Day 206

Elementals: King Ghob

Today, you will meet the gnome king, Ghob, (pronounced *gawb*). As with each of the elemental kings, he will teach you about what energies the gnomes offer to your life and what they limit.

What You'll Need:

- Earth incense
- Earth oil

It is best to try this practice in the location near your home where the gnomes reside. Light the earth incense and allow it to waft over your body. Dab some of the earth oil on all seven body-energy centers: base of the spine, pubic region, solar plexus, heart, throat, center of the brow, and crown of the head.

Find a comfortable sitting position and close your eyes. Take several deep breaths and allow your body to become relaxed. With your eyes still closed intone King Ghob's name on each exhaled breath.

Inhale slowly. Exhale, intoning the name: *Ghob.*

Repeat this intonation twice more and then practice the following guided imagery. You can read it and memorize the imagery sequence now, have a friend read it to you with your eyes closed, or tape record it for later playback.

Reader:
Imagine that you stand once again near the freshly ploughed field. This is the spot where you first met the gnomes. Hold your spirit hands up so that they face toward the north, and again draw up the energies of this place. Cast them in a circle of brilliant green light that surrounds you.

You are now completely surrounded by this field of energy. Raise your hands to the north and mentally summon forth King Ghob. Soon a bejeweled gnome emerges from the earth, just outside of your magic circle. Immediately ask Ghob what powers he offers to your life and what powers he diminishes in your life.

(Reader: pause for a moment.)

When you have heard his answer, bid him farewell and watch him vanish back into his hole in the earth. When he has gone, it is time to close the circle you created. Hold your hands up again to the north and begin to turn your spirit body in a clockwise direction. This time as you turn, imagine that you draw the energies of the circle back into your body. Allow the energy to return to the earth below your feet, where it is completely grounded.

Once you have finished, it is time to open your eyes. Get down on your hands and knees and place your forehead to the floor, grounding and solidifying all of the energy you raised.

Take time to journal about your experiences, to draw a picture of Ghob and write down what powers he offers and diminishes in your life.

Day 207

Elements and the Witches' Tools

Witches have magical tools for just about every occasion, but there are four main tools (some traditions refer to them as "weapons") that every Witch keeps for ritual and magical purposes. Each of these tools symbolizes and evokes the energies of specific elements.

The primary Witches' tools are the *wand,* the *athame,* the *chalice,* and the *pentacle.* The wand is a length of willow or oak that represents the element of air. The athame (pronounced *ah-THAW-may*) is a double-edged, black-handled knife that represents fire. The chalice can be any cup or drinking vessel, and it represents the element of water. The pentacle is usually a flat ceramic or copper circle that has a five-pointed star (a pentagram) engraved upon it. This tool represents earth.

Elemental-Tool Correspondences

In the following discussions, the element is given first, followed by the tool associated with that element, and then the description.

Air—Wand: The wand is usually a length of wood (traditionally willow for a woman's wand and oak for a man's wand) that a Witch uses to summon spiritual energies. Witches also use the wand in lunar rituals and in rituals that involve "drawing down" the goddess or god into a priest or priestess. Witches sometimes "load" the wand by carving out a hole in the top and bottom and filling it with magical herbs and stones.

Fire—Athame: The athame is a double-edged, dark-handled knife. The athame is the essential Witches' tool, used to cast and summon magical forces. Traditionally, a Witch might magnetize the athame's steel blade using a lodestone. This practice allegedly assures the athame's appropriate "attracting" powers.

Water—Chalice: The chalice is traditionally a stemmed cup. The chalice can be of any material, however, since the chalice aligns with the energies of the goddess, Witches give preference to cups made of silver (or silver metals). Witches use the cup for blessing and fertility rites as well as for making potions and magical elixirs.

Earth—Pentacle: The pentacle is a disk that has a five-pointed star engraved upon it. The disk can be made of any earthy material. Traditionally, Witches make the pentacle from wood, wax, clay, or copper. The pentacle is a tool of fertility rites, blessing rites, and of summoning the goddess.

Each of these four magical tools represents the Witch's individual power as well as her personal connection to each of the four elements. There are also ritual tools that represent collective elemental energies—the energies of a spiritual community or Witches' coven. Witches call the collective ritual tools the *grand* tools. Review and familiarize yourself with each of the tools listed below, along with their elemental correspondences.

Table of Grand Tools

Air—the Staff: A wooden branch the length of a Witch's body—from head to toe. It represents a coven's collective link to air and their collective knowledge. The staff also represents the phallus.

Fire—the Sword: Magical swords are usually double edged. They are only used in ritual. The sword represents a coven's collective link to fire and the collective will. Tool used in summoning the god, and in casting a coven's magic circle.

Water—the Cauldron: The cauldron is usually a deep-set iron pot that Witches use in a ritual context. The cauldron represents a coven's collective link to water and their collective power to dare. It also represents the goddess' womb.

Earth—the Human Body: In certain rituals, the body itself becomes the grand pentacle, with the head, arms and legs representing the five points of the pentagram. Typically the priestess' body is the grand tool of earth; however many covens believe that the human form *of either gender* is magically effective.

Below, I have listed additional tools that you will find useful in magical practice. Many of these items are purely optional. As you develop your own spiritual practice over time, you will be able to decide which of these tools are best for you. In the meantime, review the list and commit these items to memory.

Table of Additional Witch Tools

Air—the Boline: The boline is a small knife with a sickle-shaped blade. Witches use this tool to harvest ritual/magical herbs.

Air—the Bell: The bell starts and finishes ceremonies. Witches also use the bell to summon energies and entities. They also use the bell in initiatory rites.

Fire—the Thurible: The thurible is a metallic dish or bowl that Witches use to burn incense, herbs, and other small ritual items. The thurible is usually made of iron.

Fire—the White-Handled Knife: The white-handled knife is usually a single-edged knife with a white (or light-colored) handle. Witches use the white-handled knife to chop herbs, to inscribe candles, and to serve as a tool for all mundane purposes within a magic circle.

Water—the Scourge: The scourge consists of a 12-inch length of dowel. At the top end nine (sometimes five or seven) individual lengths of leather cord are attached to a single eyehook. Usually British Traditional Wiccans are the only ones who use the scourge in initiatory rites. They use this tool to purify an initiate's chakra system by stimulating the root chakra.

Earth—the Cords: Witches use the cords to cinch their robes at the waist. They also use the cords in initiatory rites. In various traditions of Witchcraft, the cord color that a Witch wears can represent his or her level of attainment or "degree" within a system of study. Cords also symbolize the umbilical cord and therefore represent an individual Witch's connection to earth and/or to a spiritual community.

Earth—the Broom: Witches use the broom in fertility rites. The broom represents women's power and the regenerative principle.

Spirit—the Book of Shadows: A Book of Shadows is traditionally a handwritten book that contains the rituals and spellwork particular to a Wiccan tradition or coven. Each tradition has its own Book of Shadows. Some Witches develop their own. Witches call a personal (nontraditional) book of spells a ritual *grimoire.*

A Word to the Wise: The fifth element that Witches observe—Spirit, or akasha—aligns with no compass direction. It is the subtle substance that pervades all and resides everywhere. Spirit has no magical colors or correspondences, although some traditions say that spirit operates through sound and vibration. Spirit is also believed to be the magical "electrical charge" at the basis of all successful magical operations. The alchemical symbol for spirit, an eight-spoked wheel, is shown here.

Other tools that Witches use in their craft are candles, incense, essential oils, herbs, divination tools (such as a magic mirror, a scrying bowl, tarot cards, or a crystal ball), magical jewelry, robes, a moon crown, red garters (British Traditionalists only), god and goddess images, and antlers. As you learn more about each of the elements in future lessons, you will also learn more about how to make and use these magical tools.

- Which of the tools seems to be "mismatched" with an element?
- If you were to make your own correspondences, which of these tools would you match with elemental energies?

- Consider the tools of your daily life (your car, your refrigerator, your lights, your garbage disposal, etc.). How might each of these ordinary items align with elements? Take time to consider this and commit your thoughts to paper.

A Word to the Wise: Ritual robes are certainly one way for you to acquire a magical spiritual presence while preparing for a Wiccan ritual. Witches have no specific rules regarding ritual attire. However, it is best to know that one common ritual custom is that of *skyclad* magical practice. Skyclad means "without clothing." After all, Wicca is a fertility religion; should ritual nudity really come as a shock to you? Skyclad ritual is not for everyone, but practitioners who engage in skyclad rites usually observe certain protocols. For example, it is best not to insist on skyclad practice when guests are present, or when a group participant may not feel comfortable or ready for ritual nudity. If you are considering skyclad ritual alone—go for it! If you are with another person or a group, try to gain consensus among your members regarding ritual attire prior to your rites.

Day 208

The Wand

Witches typically make their own wands from wood branches, although some contemporary practitioners use a variety of other materials for wand construction. Some of these additional materials include elongated or phallic-shaped quartz crystals, bone, copper or silver, antlers, and feathers. The type of wood a Witch uses to make a wand varies from one magical tradition to another—although choosing oak for a male's wand and willow for a female's wand is an old magical custom. When considering what type of wood you might use to construct your own wand, begin by considering your current spiritual goals and your personal spiritual expression. Then look at the chart on page 202 that describes various types of woods and their magical associations. Match up your own spiritual qualities and goals with the magical qualities of specific types of wood.

Nine of the traditional Celtic wand-making woods include: apple, ash, cedar, hazel, holly, juniper, oak, pine, and poplar.

A Word to the Wise: In many Wiccan traditions the wand symbolizes the element of air. Other traditions say the wand symbolizes the element of fire. It is easy to see how both the air and the fire associations evolved. Seeing that wood was good fuel for fires, our ancient ancestors believed that wood naturally contained fire within it, and the fire only needed to be coaxed out of the wood. This gave rise to the wand and fire correspondences.

On the other hand, because branches "grasp" the passing wind, it is likely that our ancestors believed that branches were infused with gusts and flurries. Thus, over time, the wand and air became linked in occult lore. In our year and a day practice, we will focus on the wand as representative of the element of air.

Magical Wood Correspondences

In the following chart, the magical wood is followed by planetary ruler, elemental influence, and magical influences.

Apple—Venus—Water: Divine female principle, flowing of the four elements, mystic visions

Ash—Sun—Fire: Insight, divination, illumination, spiritual justice, equilibrium, balance

Cedar—Sun—Fire: Rebirth, purity, consecration, longevity, success

Hazel—Mercury—Air: Knowledge, divination, control of the weather

Holly—Saturn—Earth: The eternal principle, spiritual healing, happiness

Juniper—Saturn—Earth: Fertility, protection, strength, spiritual rebirth, material growth.

Oak—Sun—Fire: Solar energy, divine male principle, horned god, strength, power

Pine—Mars—Air: Compassion, magical protection, healing, movement, enlivenment

Poplar—Moon—Water: Moon mysteries, lunar energies, cycles, intuition, moon goddess

Some other magical woods that Witches use in the making of wands include:

Alder—Blending male/female principles, links to fairies, mysteries revealed, offerings to gods

Birch—Goddess energies, beginnings, change, transition, purification

Willow—Moon magic, underworld journeys, link to the gods

If none of these woods are available to you locally, where do you live? Not to worry—as was the custom among our ancient ancestors, you can create the wand from any wood that comes from local plant sources. Discover the energies of your local plant life for yourself!

Day 209

Making a Wand: Preparation

In the best of circumstances, a Witch collects her wand from a living tree at midnight on Midsummer. Wiccan lore says that the Witch should cut the wand from a living tree branch. This practice ensures that the wand retains the tree's spiritual essence. The branch should be no more than one inch in diameter (in old measurements, the wand was to be no thicker than your thumb) and it should be equal to the measurement from the tip of your middle finger to the crook of your elbow. To assure the wand's magical vitality, cut the branch with a single blade stroke.

Wand Symbolism and Lore

Witchcraft workings often involve planetary influences that aid in spiritual endeavors. The wand links closely with the planet Mercury,[77] a planet that is a melting pot of spiritual energies and symbolism. In Roman mythology, Mercury was the messenger of the gods. He moved between the worlds of humanity and divinity, so he was thought to be composed of both spiritual and earthly energies.

Interestingly enough, Wiccan lore says that the wand is best harvested at midnight on Midsummer, a magical time that vividly represents the shifting, polar qualities of Mercury: the depth of night at the height of the sun's power. Witches harvested their wands at this tide of contrasting energies to infuse them with Mercury's archetypes.

Important to your own wand harvesting is keeping in mind the symbolism behind these contrasting spiritual forces. This means that it is important to harvest your wand in a spiritual frame of mind that is "between the worlds," where all polar energies collide.

Practice: 'Twixt the Earth and Sky

Today's practice involves centering yourself between the contrasting forces of earth and sky. This technique aligns you to the wand's Mercurial nature. It is preferable to practice this technique when you can feel the warming energies of the sun directly on your skin.

To begin, turn to face the north. Raise your right arm, making sure that the palm of your right hand faces the sky—toward the sun. Close your eyes. Imagine that the energy of the sun begins to concentrate and focus into a beam that enters your raised palm. Breathe deeply. With each inhalation, imagine that the power of the sun draws down into your body, filling it. Continue to draw the sun's energy until you feel completely flooded with solar light.

Hold your left arm at your side and flex your left hand at the wrist so that your left palm is parallel with the surface of the earth. Continue to keep your eyes closed. Imagine that a cool green energy radiates from the earth and focuses into a beam that merges with the palm of your left hand. With each inhalation, the power of the earth enters your body and fills it. Continue to draw the energies of the earth into your body in this way until you feel it blend with the energies of the sun.

When you are finished, open your eyes and place both palms flat against each other, in "prayer hands." Hold them in this way, pressing them together until you sense that the intensity of these two energies subsides. When you are finished with this practice, place both of your hands under cold running water or flat on the ground for a few minutes to restore your own natural energy patterns.

DAY 210

Wand Harvest Ceremony

What You'll Need:

- Air oil
- Pruning shears or saw
- Salt and water in separate bowls
- 12 inch length of red ribbon
- Dried white sage
- A thurible (or other similar burning vessel)
- A bundle of hyssop, or lavender, or small tinkling bells

Go to the tree from which you will harvest your magic wand. Select an appropriate branch to harvest. At the point that you intend to cut the branch, adorn the tree with a red ribbon. From this ribbon, you may tie bells or small bundles of healing herbs, such as hyssop or lavender.

Practice the earth and sky visualization that you learned yesterday. When you have finished the visualization, grasp the selected tree branch in both of your hands and say aloud:

> ***Strong creature from before time of my own,***
> ***You without flesh, you without bone,***
> ***You without vein, you without blood,***
> ***You without head, but who opens to bud,***
> ***You who are as wide as the earth,***
> ***But who were never born,***
> ***Lend me now your magic,***
> ***From the Amalthean Horn!***

Combine three scoops of salt into a bowl of water. Mix the elements together and then rub the salted water on the tree branch, saying:

> ***I welcome thee with water and earth.***

Blow on the branch and then say:

> ***I welcome thee with the air of my body.***

Hold the branch between the palms of your hands and visualize energy leaving you and joining the limb. While you do this, say:

I welcome thee with the fire of life.

Rub the branch with a small amount of the air oil. Then, with your pruning shears (or saw), cut the branch swiftly with one snip. If you are using a saw, cut the branch as quickly as you can from the limb of the tree. Place the harvested branch at the foot of the tree and stand before the cut limb and the tree. Light the white sage and walk the perimeter of the tree with the smoldering herb, saying three times:

The tops of the trees
Will sprout of late.
They'll change and renew
From their withered state!

Rub a small amount of air oil on the spot where you removed the limb. Collect your new wand and take leave from the tree without looking back. Set your wand in a special place in your home for the remainder of the day.

Days 211-240

Magical Items to Gather

Here are the items you will need for the next month of your training.

Day 211

- A 5–6 inch purple taper candle

Day 214

- Your wand
- Two yellow candles

Day 218

- An athame (a black-handled knife with sharpened double edges; for further explanation, see Days 207 and 217)

Day 219

- Two red candles
- Fire oil
- Fire incense

Day 223

- Two blue taper candles, any length
- Water incense
- Water oil

Day 226

(optional activity)

- Craft paper
- Clay
- Large empty coffee can
- Rolling pin

Day 227

- Two green taper candles, any length

- Earth incense
- Earth oil
- Ceramic paint or enamel paint (black is traditional)

Day 233

- Fire oil
- A 5–6 inch red candle

Day 234

- Air incense, or
- Dried white sage (also called desert sage), or
- Loose, dried sandalwood powder
- Air oil
- A 5–6 inch red taper candle

Day 235

- Four candles; one yellow, one red, one blue and one green.
- Self-igniting charcoal
- A 5–6 inch red taper candle
- Air incense

Note: you will need these basic items for the next several days.

Day 236

- A thurible (a container in which you burn the incense or other magical objects)

A Word to the Wise: By the end of this month's practice, it will be necessary for you to gather the four Witches' tools: the athame, the wand, the chalice, and the pentacle. For descriptions of these items please see the appropriately marked days. You can potentially make two of the four magical tools; however, if you would like to purchase these items well ahead of time, please check the Resources Guide in the back of the book.

Day 211

Contemplative Day: The Power of Magic

Meditative Question: What is the power that drives magic?

Symbolic Color: Purple

Symbolic Direction: Southwest

Contemplating the power that is behind magic is the same as becoming one with this mysterious source. In our year's training we have not yet discussed magic indepth. Because of this, you might wonder how to contemplate magic without prior knowledge of the subject matter. It is important to keep in mind that knowledge appeals only to the linear, unidirectional mind. Magic (and contemplation) begins with letting go of what we know, getting into our bodies, becoming acquainted with our emotions, our physical energy patterns, and the world around us in an experiential way. Academic knowledge of magic is as useful to a spiritual practice as is academic knowledge of the color red, or of a symphony. You can't adequately explain these things in words; they are experiences that transcend verbal explanation. Today's contemplation should take you to the bottom of any assumptions, ideas, or information you have.

To begin, find a comfortable meditative sitting position in a quiet space while facing the southwest. Light a purple candle and sit approximately two feet away from the flame. Next cast your gaze upon the flickering candle and hold the question firmly for 20 to 30 minutes.

You may not arrive at a magically satisfactory conclusion in one sitting alone, so to manifest a greater depth of answer, it will be important to see this question as it actualizes in each of your activities. Become one with it in each of your tasks. Allow your body, mind, and spirit to become this question as you eat, sleep, work, and play. Over time, a shift in your perception will take place and you will realize your own answer.

Day 212

Devotional Day: Honoring Hecate

Table of Correspondences: Hecate

Symbols: Nighttime sky, crossroads, the broom, and the cauldron

Tools: The cauldron, the magic mirror, divination tools

Magical Essences/Herbs: Camphor, water lily, and jasmine

Direction: Inward

She Rules: Hidden mysteries, old age, wisdom, secrets, death, the underworld, birth, midwifery, herbalism, divination

Animal Symbols: Owl, horse, boar, and dog

Sacred Foods: Pomegranate and apple

Magical Stones: Mother of pearl, amethyst

Who is Hecate? Hecate is the Greek goddess of crossroads, of the underworld, of magic and the moon. Wiccans most associate her with the dark aspect of the feminine divine, although she is historically a triple goddess of birth, fertility, and maturity. As an underworld figure, Hecate rules the mysteries that dwell in our minds and hearts just beneath the surface of our immediate knowing and feeling. In myth, Hecate was said to take her place in the underworld next to Thanatos (a deity of death), Hypnos (a deity of sleep), and Morpheus (a deity of dreams). Hecate's sphere of influence was the nighttime sky. She was well regarded by the ancient world as a patroness of Witches, and her reputation as such continues today.

When you tap into the archetypal energies of Hecate, you evoke your own ability to create magic, and to reverse the "evil eye." Hecate reminds us that we are all multifaceted beings, and that we should honor each of our "faces," both the strong and the less-than-stalwart. Her sacred symbols are crossroads, the broom, and the cauldron. Her totem spirits are the owl, horse, boar, and dog. Her magical essences and herbs are camphor, water lily, and jasmine. Hecate is aligned with the north, with silence, and with midnight. Her sacred colors are black, midnight blue, and white (to symbolize the moon). Hecate's sacred foods include pomegranate and apple.

Hecate Practice

In honoring Hecate today, honor an old Roman custom by going to a crossroads at midnight and leaving an offering of a single apple and a black candle. Walk away from the offering without looking back. As you walk, intone her sacred name one syllable at a time (pronounced *Heh-KAH-tay*) until you feel her presence surrounding you. Once she has arrived, spend time contemplating how you might serve this deity. Take time to ask Hecate what it would mean to live life through her energy, and listen for her answer.

Spend the day honoring this goddess by considering the mystery behind each aspect of your daily routine and every person you encounter.

A Word to the Wise: You cannot know it all, so why misplace your efforts? There is an old story of a Native American medicine man who was sworn in to testify in a court of law. "Do you swear to tell the whole truth and nothing but the truth?" he was asked by the bailiff. "No," said the medicine man, "I do not know the whole truth."

Day 213

Day of Silence and Review

Today, as you observe silence, focus your attention on your sense of touch. Throughout your day, perhaps in intervals, direct your attention on what it is you physically feel. What is the sensation of clothing on your body? How does it feel to have someone touch you? Do you feel the wind on your face or in your hair? How does it feel to stand or sit? When the day is complete, answer these questions:

- What was it like to focus my attention on my sense of touch?
- Am I a person who reacts strongly to physical touch?
- In what way did my sense of touch impact my thoughts, emotions, or spirit?
- How does what I touch affect my physical energy?
- Did my capacity to touch meaningfully either increase or decrease with my focused attention? Why might that be?

Review

Take time to ask yourself the following:

- Of the information I have learned up to now, what stands out most as vital?
- What information seems least relevant to my spiritual development?
- Which of the practices seemed to move me spiritually, and which had little impact?
- Of the information I have learned so far, what would be best to review? (Take time to review it now.)

Day 214

The Wand: Inscriptions

What You'll Need:

- Your wand
- Two yellow candles
- Air oil
- Air incense

There are two kinds of magical markings you will want to inscribe upon your wand. The first are the traditional Witch markings (also called *sigils*). The supposedly traditional sigils first appeared on the Witch scene in the 1930s through Gerald Gardner. Gardner maintained that his initiators revealed to him the sigils and implied that they were of ancient "witch" origins. Curiously enough, the sigils appear to be derived from a variety of occult sources, not the least of which is Francis Barrett's occult classic *The Magus.* In this work, originally published in 1801, Barrett pieced together never-before translated Kabalistic occult manuscripts from the sixteenth century.[78] Another source for the sigils may be *The Key of Solomon*, another Kabalistic manuscript based on sixteenth-century occult knowledge.

The second kind of marking for your wand is the personal power symbol. This symbol represents your personal link to the divine as it manifests in the element of air.

In today's working you will inscribe the wand with the traditional markings found below:

Wand Sigils

Begin by inscribing each of the yellow candles lengthwise with the wand sigils. Set the candles in holders on either side of you and light them. Ignite air incense and dab yourself with air oil at the center of your brow. Begin the wand-inscribing process. You can either inscribe the wand by painting the sigils on the surface of the branch with yellow paint, by carving them into the wood or by magical infusion. As you inscribe the sigils, follow your breath and try not to allow the mind to wander away from the task at hand. Note: if you don't want to mar the natural beauty of the wood by carving it or painting on it, you can magically infuse the wand with your power symbols.

Magical Infusion for the Wand

What You'll Need:

- Self-igniting charcoal
- A 7–10 inch circle of yellow paper
- A black pen
- Air incense

Inscribe the wand sigils in black ink, bisecting the center of the yellow circle. Sprinkle air incense into the center of this yellow circle on which you have drawn your sigils. Twist the paper closed with the incense inside of it. Light a charcoal and set the incense bundle on the hot coal. Place your hands just above the bundle and imagine that the incense becomes infused with the sigils. Hold the wand above the bundle as it smolders and smokes. While you do this, chant:

> ***By the blessed thirteen moons***
> ***Sealed are ye by sacred runes!***

When this is completed, lay the wand between the two inscribed yellow candles and allow it to remain there until each of the wand sigils has melted away.

Day 215

The Wand: Personal Symbol of Power

When you inscribe the wand with your personal symbol of power, it is like placing your spiritual signature on it. It is a way of linking your individual energies with the grand archetypal flow of the element.

In today's magical working, you will first discover your personal symbol of power for the element of air and then inscribe it on your wand. You can also use the air personal-power symbol for any later magical workings that involve the element of air, so be sure to not only inscribe it upon your wand, but to mark it in a journal or some other special place for later reference.

In order to find the power symbol, you will first engage in a guided imagery meditation. As you have already learned, you may read this and memorize the imagery, have a friend read it to you while you meditate, or record it for later playback. To begin, hold the wand in your hands and assume a comfortably seated meditation position.

Reader:

Close your eyes and take several deep breaths. Scan your body from head to toe and note wherever it is you seem to hold physical tension. As you note tension, breathe through the body part and release the tension. Continue relaxing each part of your body until you feel wholly still and internally silent.

(Reader: pause for a moment.)

Although your eyes are closed, imagine that you can see the wand you hold in your hands. Imagine now that you hold the wand up to the eastern sky and say: "I summon thee, O symbol of power!" Suddenly, a warm breeze blows and it carries a multitude of tiny glowing golden symbols—all of them are alike. The symbols float and dance like fairies in the air around the wand. Within moments, the wand blazes with a golden energy. You peer at it and discover that it is engraved with the power symbol you saw floating nearby just moments ago. Remember the symbol that you see, as well as where it is engraved upon the wand.

Once you have seen your air power symbol, allow the vision of the magical meadow to fade and then open your eyes when you feel you are ready. Record the symbol on a blank piece of paper and transfer this to the wand by painting it, engraving it, or magically infusing it (see Day 214 for details).

When you have finished setting the personal power symbols on the wand, place it in a visually prominent location for the remainder of the day.

Day 216

Storing Magical Tools

You might be wondering by now how and where to store the wand and your other magical tools. In magical lore, the tools should be hidden from view when not in ritual use, especially from the view of non-Witches. Many practitioners dedicate a special storage case, chest, or closet to hold their magical tools. Occultists from days gone by recommended wrapping each tool in silk after use in order to preserve the tool's magical power. Here are the traditional silk colors for the various tools:

Air tools: Yellow silk

Fire tools: Red silk

Water tools: Blue silk

Earth tools: Green or black silk

Please note that you can use black silk to wrap all magical tools, since this earth color contains all colors. Finding and procuring enough various colored silks is a costly venture. Not only that, but its value may be overrated since one should always bear in mind that it is the Witch and not the tools that generates magical power. Wrapping tools is really a method that assures cleanliness and avoids accidental damage to the tools. With this in mind, wrap your tools in any cloth you would like prior to storing them. Decorate your storage cloths with your personal power symbol or the traditional Witch sigils of each tool if you'd like. Be creative!

A Word to the Wise: Non-witches are called cowens by Witches.

Wrapping and storing tools can be a ritual unto itself. Because silk easily slips off tools, many practitioners use lengths of appropriately colored cords to bind the silk around the tool. As you wrap each tool in cloth, say this simple incantation, either aloud or to yourself:

Power be bound,
Truth be found!
Now I wrap thee
Thrice around!

Take the length of cord, if you are using it, and wrap it three times around the cloth-bound tool.

Day 217

The Athame

The Athame (pronounced: *ah-THAW-may*) is a double-edged dagger with a black hilt. The oldest of the Wiccan traditions link the athame with the element of fire for the simple reason that it is forged in extreme heat and it is phallic in shape. Some pagan paths assert that the athame symbolizes air because of the way one typically brandishes the tool, as though slicing through the air, during spell-casting and other magical activities.

The athame represents the Witch's individual will and Witches use it to direct the flow of magical energy in their rituals and spellwork. In some traditions, the athame is considered to be the *only* tool essential for Witchcraft, in order to create magic and to direct energy.

The athame is, without a doubt, the most aggressive looking of the magical tools. Because of its visibly warlike associations, the athame has a strong affinity with the energies of Mars, the Roman god of battles, and of all generally pointy male things.

The athame is typically 10 to 12 inches in length from base to tip, and it is made of any type of metal (although Witches prefer high grades of steel). Upon occasion, one might stumble across a blade that is solid silver or silver-plated. Silver blades hold additional value, since this metal links symbolically to the moon and the goddess. A silver blade has a dual-polar quality, since it simultaneously represents both the goddess and god energies.

Practitioners who are averse to using this tool for political or personal reasons find suitable athame alternatives. Some of the substitutes that I have seen include:

Quartz crystal	Feather
Letter opener	Butter knife
Outstretched hand	Wand
Red dowel	Lighted candle

Wicca is not a system that relies on standard forms, central authority, or doctrine. It encourages a do-it-yourself sensibility that allows for a certain amount of mix and match within a specific ritual framework. Keeping this in mind, it is important to know that some students and practitioners believe that the athame is a symbol of male dominance, warfare, and aggression (as are all weapons). They further assert that such a symbol may not be a useful representation in a matrifocal spiritual discipline. Wiccans who have a feminist focus might not appreciate the athame's overt male symbolism and these individuals might choose an alternative tool that holds less of a negative psychological charge for them. While there is nothing wrong per se with using an athame alternative, the reader should be advised that using such a replacement is not customary to Wiccan practice.

Contemplate the benefits and the drawbacks of using either an athame or an alternative tool, then answer the following questions:

- Why might the athame be difficult for some magical practitioners to use in a ritual setting?
- What are my own feelings about using a knife in a spiritual tradition?
- What might be the benefits of using the athame in ritual? What might be the drawbacks?

Day 218

Obtaining an Athame

Do you have a hammer and an anvil handy? Making an athame is an art in itself that requires knowledge of metallurgy, blacksmithery, and even astrology. The athame aligns with the element of fire, which is also closely associated with the planet Mars and all of its martial vibrations. Ideally, a pagan who has blacksmith experience will forge an athame during a full moon. Also, it is magically desirable to forge an athame on a day and an hour that spiritually aligns with the energies of Mars.[79] Even more ideally, one should forge the athame at a full moon closest to either the Summer or Winter Solstice, at an hour that spiritually aligns with Mars.

Here is a listing of various magical metals that might be included in your athame. Each metal has its own planetary and spiritual associations:

Silver—Moon: Psychic forces, intuition, flow, women's mysteries, the goddess, the collective will

Copper—Venus: Peace, tranquility, harmony, happiness, material world, beauty, opulence

Tin—Jupiter: Prosperity, expansion, growth, fruition, success, development

Iron—Mars: Energy, movement, change, direction, the individual will, force, power, men's mysteries, the god

Gold—Sun: Success, achievement, ultimate attainment, unity, the divine, universal mysteries

Lead —Saturn: Karma, destiny, wisdom, reality, knowledge, final outcome, realization, work, practicality, weight (as in either physical or mental weight); note: lead is not an ideal metal for the athame because of its toxicity and malleability; it is listed here for your reference only

Most contemporary Witches purchase an athame, since making one is often impractical. Most professional metalsmiths blend several of the sacred metals listed here when they make an athame. It is useful if you can find out which of the magical metals went into making a blade before you purchase it.

Take time today to review the list of metals and their magical associations. Commit them to memory and then decide which metals you would like to have in your own athame blade. Take a field trip to a knife shop, a sports-equipment store or go online to explore your athame options.

Today is the day! In order to proceed with our further magical lessons, it is important for you to obtain an athame (or an alternative). Before you purchase your athame, become acquainted with the following traditional Wiccan athame lore:

- Haggling over the price of the athame—or any other magical tool for that matter—reputedly taints the efficacy and quality of your magic; never haggle over the price of your athame
- The athame should be new; the blade should never before have been used for any purpose; avoid searching for an athame in antique or secondhand stores since it is important to know the history of your blade
- Your athame should never have drawn blood; Witches say that once an athame draws blood (even accidentally) it is rendered magically useless
- It is customary for the athame blade to have both of its edges and its point sharp at all times; this means that letter openers and butter knives are not traditionally appropriate choices for the athame
- The athame handle does not have to be perfectly black; it can be any dark color: dark brown, blue, or green
- The length or shape of your athame has no effect on its potency; my athame is a criss blade, meaning its edges curve from side to side before they conjoin at the knife's point
- Witches advise that one should never use the athame outside of Wiccan ritual

- Use the athame for only these purposes: to bless elements, to consecrate other magical tools, to create ritual sacred space, to direct magical energy, and to invoke spiritual forces during a ritual.
- If a Witch needs a utensil for any other cutting purpose, she or he should use the white-handled knife. A Witch can also use the boline as another cutting option. I will explain both of these ritual blades and their purposes at a later time.

Day 219

Athame: Lore & Inscriptions

What You'll Need:

- Your new athame
- Two red candles
- Fire oil
- Fire incense

Today, inscribe the athame on only one side of its blade with the traditional markings shown here:

Traditional Athame Sigils.

Begin by inscribing each of the red candles with the athame sigils. Set the candles in holders on either side of you and light them. Light the fire incense and then dab yourself with fire oil at the center of your solar plexus. Begin the athame-inscribing process. You can either inscribe the athame by painting the sigils on the blade with red paint, by etching them with an electric carving tool, or by using the magical infusion method.

While inscribing, split the focus of your attention between your work at hand and the energy of your solar plexus region. Sense the feeling of energy that runs through your body at that chakra point. If you notice that your mind drifts from the shared focus of inscribing and sensing the energy, discontinue inscribing the athame. Take three deep breaths and realign your awareness.

Finally, remember that you can use the magical infusion method for setting the runes upon the athame.

Magical Infusion for the Athame

What You'll Need:

- Another red candle
- A red piece of paper cut into an equilateral triangle
- A black ink pen
- A deep pot or cauldron

Inscribe the central red candle lengthwise with the athame sigils and then light it. As the wax burns through each inscribed sigil, pass the blade briefly through the candle flame. Each time you pass the athame through the fire, chant:

> ***By the blessed thirteen moons***
> ***Sealed are ye by sacred runes!***

Continue with this until all the sigils on the candle have been melted. When this is completed, use the black ink pen to inscribe the red triangular paper with the same sigils and then set it aflame. While it burns, drop it into a deep pot or cauldron. Take the cooled ashes into your stronger hand and rub these ashes along the athame blade.

A Word to the Wise: When painting on metal consider the paint you plan to use. The best option is metal paint that you can buy at any arts and crafts supply store. Metal paint is waterproof and nontoxic—both of which are features that make this paint ideal for ritual work. Another option you can try is acrylic paint. Acrylic works well in the short run, but over time it might chip away from the blade. One online distributor of metal paint is Cupboard Distributing at *cdwood.com*.

Day 220

The Athame: Personal Power Symbol

To magically empower your athame, it is a good practice to inscribe it with your personal magical symbol. As you learned with the wand, your personal magical symbols come from trance and inner visionary work. Your personal power symbol of fire represents your psychic link to this element.

In order to find the power symbol, you will first engage in a guided imagery meditation. As you have already learned, you may read this and memorize the imagery, have a friend read it to you while you meditate, or record it for later playback. To begin, hold the athame in your hands and assume a comfortable seated meditation position.

Reader:

Close your eyes and take several deep breaths. Scan your body from head to toe and note wherever it is you seem to hold physical tension. As you note tension, breathe through the body part and release the tension. Continue relaxing each body part until you feel wholly still and internally silent.

(Reader: pause for a moment.)

Once you are fully relaxed, imagine that you stand facing south, before a small bonfire, while holding your athame. The midday sun blazes down upon your shoulders as you stand close to the fire. Warmth radiates from both the sun and the small fire before you. Imagine now that you hold the athame over the fire and say: "I summon thee, O symbol of power!" Release the athame to the fire and you will see it slowly descend into the flames. Soon the fire takes on a bright red aura and the athame then rises from the fire. You grasp the hilt of the knife only to find that it is cool to the touch. Examine the blade and you will notice a power symbol engraved and glowing there. Remember this glowing symbol for later.

Once you have seen your fiery symbol of power, allow the vision of the bonfire to fade and then open your eyes when you feel you are ready. Record the symbol on a blank piece of paper and transfer this to the athame by either painting it, engraving it with a carving tool, or magically infusing it (see Day 219 for details).

When you have finished setting the personal power symbols on the athame, set it in a place of visual prominence for the remainder of the day. Before going to bed, wrap the athame in a special cloth, such as a red silk, and store it until it is time for the athame consecration. (For tool-wrapping guidance, see Day 216.)

Day 221

The Chalice

The cup or chalice is the magical tool that represents the element of water. It symbolizes the energetic water associations such as receptivity, intuition, flow, love, emotions, and the female principle. The chalice also symbolizes the womb principle, which is regeneration, and spiritual rebirth. In Wiccan ritual, the chalice is the receptacle for wine that is consecrated and consumed during the circle-closing ceremony of "cakes and wine" (you will learn more about this ceremony in coming days). The chalice is also a focal point in some Wiccan initiatory rites, as well as in the formulation and blessing of brews and magical elixirs.

Chalice Practice

Each time you use any type of cup today, focus your awareness on what the cup symbolizes. As you drink from any cup, imagine that you infuse your body with the chalice's receptive, flowing energies. To help you focus awareness, say this couplet whenever you drink:

Flowing, churning, waters divine,
To my lips like sacred wine.

A Word to the Wise: Cakes and wine is the name of a closing portion of a traditional ceremonial circle. During cakes and wine, participants consecrate wine and sweet cakes. Offerings of thanks to deity and the communal sharing of food concludes the rite. Eating food and drinking wine grounds one's experience in the physical body. Therefore, cakes and wine is one practical Witchcraft method for transitioning from the magical world of the ritual circle back to ordinary consciousness.

Day 222

Searching for Your Grail

When you meet other Witches in a ritual context, you will notice that the chalice is often a personal "magical signature." The chalice is a highly individualized tool, and it is the only one that you use practically. Since the chalice is so personal, and because it does not require any specific traditional characteristics, Witches exercise a great deal of imagination when it comes time to select one.

Pewter and silver goblets are favorites among Witches, but chalices made of blue glass or glazed porcelain are sometimes better, cleaner, safer choices. Further along the alternative continuum are the chalices formed of large seashells (perhaps abalone), crystal bowls, hollowed-out bulls' horns, lava rock, or coconut shells. The following are important chalice selection considerations:

- You can typically find a variety of chalices in any well-stocked magical supply shop; less expensive resources include a variety of nonmagical retail sources, such as Pier 1 Imports, Cost Plus, Pottery Barn, and Crate and Barrel
- Always consider safety when selecting a chalice; understand that you will often drink the chalice contents, so be sure to select a vessel that can be thoroughly cleaned with warm water and soap
- Stay away from brass and certain pewter chalices, since they can leach traces of carcinogens into wine
- Glass and earthenware chalices are the safest, cleanest choices, but remain aware of potential breakage, especially during ritual
- If you choose a glass or earthenware chalice, consider selecting one with a blue glaze in order to evoke the elemental force behind this tool

---

A Word to the Wise: One old Witch custom is that of adopting ordinary household objects as ritual tools. In Wiccan lore, Witches had to practice their arts secretly during the Witch hunts in Europe's late Medieval and Renaissance periods. Ordinary household objects could thus disguise a ritual use. The lore holds some truth; many reputed witches were burned or drowned simply because they possessed some object that witch-hunters construed as blasphemous. In light of this lore, perhaps you might select a special cup from your own home to serve as your chalice. Remember that Witches use ritual tools only for spiritual purposes. If you select a chalice from among your own treasures, set it in a special place to avoid using it for nonritual purposes.

Chalice Meditation

Before you select a chalice, practice the following guided imagery meditation. Read it and then follow along by yourself, record and play it back, or have a friend read it to you as you visualize.

Reader:
Close your eyes and take several deep breaths. Focus on your breathing for the next minute.

(Reader: pause for several moments.)

Imagine that you stand at the edge of a vast ocean at dusk. Direct your attention to the waves as they crash and foam on the shore. Take a deep breath, inhaling the salty sea spray.

As you stand there, a glowing object with a blue aura emerges from the waters. The object rises and hovers above the surf. It then moves toward you and settles into your hands. When it touches your hands, the blue aura fades and you can clearly see a magical chalice. How does it look? How does it feel? What are its dimensions?

When you are done observing the chalice, it will rise from your hands and descend back to the waters. When you are ready, open your eyes.

Take time to journal about what you saw. Allow this vision to influence your selection of a chalice.

Please note: *It is important that you obtain a chalice today in order to continue with tomorrow's lesson.*

Day 223

Chalice: Magical Inscriptions

What You'll Need:

- Two blue taper candles, any length
- Water incense
- Water oil

Today you will inscribe the chalice with the traditional markings found below:

Traditional Chalice Sigils

To begin, inscribe the chalice sigils into the two blue candles, set them on either side of you and light them. Then light some water incense. Anoint yourself at the heart chakra with water oil. Then begin the inscription process. You can either inscribe the chalice by painting the sigils on its surface with blue or black paint, by inscribing the sigils (on metal chalices) using an electric carving tool or with the magical infusion method. When you inscribe the chalice, allow your internal focus to settle on your heart energy center, your emotions, intuitions, and sensations. If, during the inscribing process, you notice that your attention drifts from the task at hand, stop until you are able to refocus. When finished, extinguish the candles.

Magical Infusion for the Chalice

What You'll Need:

- A deep pot filled with water
- A 10–12 inch strip of aluminum foil
- A blue indelible marker
- Water oil

Fill the pot with water and on the strip of aluminum foil write the sigils for the chalice. Submerge the sigil-inscribed foil (hold it down to the bottom of the pot with stones if necessary). Next, place a few drops of water oil into the pot. Submerge the chalice and chant:

By the blessed thirteen moons
Sealed are ye by sacred runes!

Keep the chalice submerged until the blue candles on either side have burned down past the engraved sigils.

Day 224

Chalice: Symbol of Power

As you learned with the wand and athame, it is important to inscribe the chalice with your personal magical symbols. The personal symbol for the chalice represents your psychic link to the element of water.

In order to find the power symbol, you will first engage in a guided imagery meditation. As you have already learned, you may read this and memorize the imagery, have a friend read it to you while you meditate, or record it for later playback. To begin, hold the chalice in your hands and assume a comfortably seated meditation position.

Reader:
Close your eyes and take several deep breaths. Scan your body from head to toe and note wherever it is you hold tension. As you note tension, breathe through that body part and release the tension. Continue relaxing each body part until you feel wholly still and internally silent.

(Reader: pause for a moment.)

Once you are fully relaxed, close your eyes and evoke the image of the ocean from yesterday's working. Imagine that it is dusk and you stand at the seashore, facing west. Imagine that you wade in up to your knees in the warm, inviting sea. You carry the chalice with you and ritually submerge it into the brine, saying: "I summon thee, O symbol of power!" Soon you will notice that the chalice glows with a bright blue aura. Lift it from the water, examine it, and you will see your power symbol inscribed and glowing upon the cup. Look at this symbol closely and remember it.

Once you have seen your power symbol, allow the vision of the ocean to fade. Open your eyes when you are ready. Record the symbol on a blank piece of paper and transfer this to the chalice, either painting it, engraving it (metal chalices only—try using a carving tool), or magically infusing it (see Day 223 for details).

When you have finished setting the personal power symbols on the chalice, set it in a place of visual prominence for the remainder of the day. Before going to bed, wrap the chalice in a special cloth, such as a blue silk, and store it until it is time for the chalice consecration. (For tool-wrapping guidance, see Day 216.)

Day 225

The Pentacle

Representative of the earth, the *pentacle* is a disk—usually made of ceramic, stone, wood, or metal—that has been engraved with a five-pointed star formed from interconnecting, bisecting lines. Each point of the pentagram represents one of the four elements; the fifth point represents the fifth element, which is akasha or spirit. With the pentacle upright—that is, with a single point at its top—each of the pentacle points represents in turn: akasha (top), water (right), fire (bottom right), earth (bottom left) and air (left).

The pentacle serves a great many uses in magical practice. It functions as a platform for the consecration of other magical tools, for fashioning spells, and, in some traditions of Wicca, for invoking the gods. During the ceremony of cakes and wine the pentacle is a platter upon which celebrants bless sweet cakes.

The *pentagram* is the name of the five-pointed star inscribed upon the pentacle. The name is derived from the Latin root *penta,* indicating the number five. The pentagram is loaded with symbolism, which probably explains Wiccans' penchant for wearing it (usually as a pendant). The five points of the pentagram not only represent elemental forces, but also the human body (the topmost point is the head, the side points are arms, and the bottom points are legs) and the five senses. A ring often girds the pentagram. This circle represents the eternal principle, binding together all elements, the Witch's ritual space, and the sixth sense, of psychic ability.

Word to the Wise: In magical practice, each of the five senses aligns with the elements: Air = hearing; Fire = sight; Water = taste; Earth = touch; Akasha = smell.

Pentacle Practice

Take time to consider your body as the living symbol of the pentacle and know that you are a manifestation of all elements. The following pentagram exercise helps connect you to the earth, provides grounding and centering of your energy, and provides magical protection.

Get a container of salt (preferably kosher or sea salt) and take it outside with you. Use the salt to form a 6–7 foot pentagram on the ground. As you create this pentagram, chant these words of power:

Five-fold forms the sacred birth,
Of air, fire, water, and earth.

Lie down in the center of the pentagram with your head at the top point, your arms within the side points and your legs inside of the bottom points. Close your eyes and take several deep breaths. Now imagine that a golden glow begins to form in your left hand. In your right hand, a blue glow begins to form. In the sole of your left foot you can see a red glow forming, and in your right foot a green glow takes form. Focus now on your breath. As you inhale, draw each of these glowing colors toward your chest. Once the colors meet at the center of your chest they explode into rays of blinding white. Imagine that this energy travels up your spine and out through the top of your head. This energy then links you to the universe. When you are done, open your eyes, stand up, and scatter the salt pentagram on the ground with your left foot.

DAY 226

The Pentacle: Crafting Your Own

What You'll Need:

- Craft paper
- Clay
- Rolling pin
- Access to a kiln
- Empty large coffee can

A Word to the Wise: If you do not have access to a local kiln for firing (hardening) the ceramic pentacle, you can use Sculpey® brand fast-drying modeling clay, or purchase a suitable manufactured pentacle.

Contemporary Witches often consider making the pentacle because it's a fun and relatively simple project. To begin, lay out some craft paper about 12 x 12 inches square. Use a rolling pin to flatten out a lump of clay so that it is approximately ½ inch thick and 10 inches in any direction. Find a large empty coffee can that is 7–10 inches in diameter. Press the coffee can, open top down, into the clay, and clear away the rest around the can. Gently shake the can so that a perfectly cut circle drops out.

Using a ruler, knife-edge, or other long, fine-edged tool, gently impress the clay's surface to form the five intersecting lines of the pentagram. Here is one way to get a perfectly formed pentagram. Use the craft paper to draw the outline of the coffee can, so that you have a circle that matches the size of your clay pentacle. Use a pencil to draw a pentagram inside of the circle. Cut the paper circle with the pentagram out and place it on top of your clay circle. Make small markings along the edge of the clay disk to mark the points of the pentagram. Now get out your ruler or sharp-edged tool. Using the markings on the sides of the clay disk as a guide, you can now form the intersecting lines of the pentagram.

As a last step, fire and glaze your pentacle in a kiln. If you are like most people and don't own a kiln, check with colleges, schools, or local potters to see if they can fire the pentacle for you.

If you plan to purchase a pentacle, here is a guided imagery meditation to help you in your selection process. Read it and then follow along by yourself, record and play it back, or have a partner read it to you as you visualize.

Pentacle Meditation

Reader:

Close your eyes and take several deep breaths. Focus on your breathing for the next minute.

(Reader: pause for a while.)

Imagine that you stand at midnight in the center of a stone circle. A canopy of stars shimmers overhead. As you watch the sky, you notice the stars beginning to move, slowly, almost imperceptibly at first. Then they take on a life of their own and form a shining pentacle in the black sky. The pentacle then takes on more substance and form, and it glows brightly with a green aura. It drifts down from the nighttime sky into your hands.

You reach out for the pentacle and the green aura fades. You can clearly see the pentacle in your hands. From what is it made? What is its size? What colors are prominent?

When you are done observing the pentacle, it will rise from your hands and ascend back to the heavens, where it dissolves into the black of the nighttime sky. When you are ready, open your eyes.

Take time to journal about and even sketch what you saw. Allow your vision to influence you as you select a pentacle. Note: you will need a pentacle in order to continue with tomorrow's lesson.

Word to the Wise: Medieval and Renaissance period Witches reputedly constructed pentacles from beeswax. The tool could easily be destroyed in a fireplace should someone dangerous—like Witch hunters—pay an unexpected visit. This is interesting lore, but using a wax pentacle would have disadvantages, posing some sticky ritual prospects.

Day 227

Pentacle: Magical Inscriptions

What You'll Need:

- Two green taper candles, any length
- Earth incense
- Earth oil
- Ceramic paint or enamel paint (black is traditional)

Today you will paint the pentacle with the traditional markings found below:

Pentacle with traditional symbols

To begin, inscribe the pentacle sigils lengthwise into the two green candles, set them on either side of you, and light them. Then light some earth incense. Anoint yourself at the base chakra (at the base of your spine) with earth oil. Then begin the inscription process. You can either inscribe the pentacle by painting the sigils on its surface with black enamel paint, or with the magical infusion method.

As you inscribe the pentacle, focus on the feeling of your body weight, your center of gravity. If you note that your mind wanders from the inscribing process, take three deep breaths, refocus your intent and continue inscribing. When finished, extinguish the candles.

Magical Infusion for the Pentacle

What You'll Need:

- A patch of bare earth (or, if indoors, use a large, deep baking pan filled with potting soil)
- A knife
- Salt (fine sea salt or kosher salt is recommended, but ordinary table salt is fine)

It is best to magically infuse the pentacle out of doors in the earth herself, but if this is not possible, fill a large, deep baking pan (or any other large container) with potting soil. Create a hole in the soil large enough to accommodate your pentacle. Set the pentacle in the earth and bury it. With a knife, draw a circle in the soil that girds the buried disk. Carefully pinch some salt between your fingers and sprinkle this (as one might create a sand painting) to form the pentacle sigils within the earth circle. Set the two green inscribed candles on either side of the buried pentacle and chant:

By the blessed thirteen moons
Sealed are ye by sacred runes!

Keep the pentacle buried until the green candles on either side have burned down past the engraved sigils.

Day 228

Pentacle: Symbol of Power

As with the other tools, it is important to inscribe the pentacle with your personal, magical symbols. The personal symbol for the pentacle represents your psychic link to the element of earth. In order to find the power symbol, you will first engage in a guided imagery meditation. As you have already learned, you may read this and memorize the imagery, have a friend read it to you while you meditate, or record it for later playback. To begin, hold the pentacle in your hands and assume a comfortable seated meditation position.

Reader:

Close your eyes and take several deep breaths. Scan your body from head to toe and note wherever it is you hold tension. As you note the tension, breathe through that body part and release the tension. Stay with relaxing each part of your body until you feel wholly still and internally silent.

(Reader: pause for a moment.)

Once you are fully relaxed, imagine that you are standing once again at the Witching hour within the great stone circle. You carry the pentacle with you and you hold it out to the silence, saying, "I summon thee, O symbol of power!" Soon you will notice that the pentacle glows in your hands with a bright green aura. Examine the pentacle now, and you will see your power symbol inscribed there in glowing script. Look at this symbol closely and remember it.

Once you have seen your personal power symbol, allow the vision of the stone circle to fade. Open your eyes when you are ready. Record the symbol on a blank piece of paper and transfer this to the pentacle, either painting it or magically infusing it (see Day 227 for details).

When you have finished setting the personal power symbols on the pentacle, set it in a place of visual prominence for the remainder of the day. Before going to bed, wrap the pentacle in a special cloth, such as a green silk, and store it until it is time for the pentacle consecration. (For tool-wrapping guidance, see Day 216.)

Day 229

Casting the Circle: Myths and Realities

Witches practice their spiritual activities within the sacred space of the magic circle. In pagan practice, the magic circle is a platform for the gods. It is space set aside specifically for pagan religious and magical practices such as raising and directing spiritual energy, celebrating seasonal festivals, practicing divination, invoking the gods, and engaging in rites of passage. Witches have a name for the practice of formally setting up the magic circle—it is called *casting the circle.*

Film, television, and other popular media often sensationalize the magic circle and contribute to public confusion and misinformation. In order to gain some clarity about the Witches' magic circle, let's look closely at some of the most common misunderstandings:

Circle Myth: The circle is a container for the spiritual energies that Witches raise

Circle Reality: The circle may be a focal point for your spiritual work—much like a magnifying glass, but it does not *contain* or hold power in and of itself; in fact, the circle must be spiritually "porous" for magical energies to enter and to exit

Circle Myth: The circle is a barrier that keeps out unwanted spirits

Circle Reality: The circle is a permeable environment that does not avert unwanted spiritual forces

Circle Myth: Being within the circle makes you more vulnerable to negative spirits and psychic energies

Circle Reality: The circle is a platform for your spiritual work, so in that sense it can heighten spiritual sensitivity; however, it does not cause vulnerability to any form of energy or spirit

Circle Myth: The perimeter of the circle can never (and should never) be crossed

Circle Reality: The perimeter of the circle may be crossed and some rituals and magical work necessitate individuals crossing the perimeter

Circle Myth: Only a very powerful person can correctly cast a magic circle

Circle Reality: Anyone, no matter the level of ability or spiritual advancement, can cast a circle

Circle Myth: Only an initiated Witch can cast a circle

Circle Reality: Casting a magic circle is technology and anyone can do it

Circle Myth: The dimensions of the magic circle must be perfectly circular

Circle Reality: No; magic circles come in all sorts of odd shapes; most commonly, Witches need to adapt the shape of the circle to the space in which they practice their rituals; life occurs in many shapes, and in this way the magic circle reflects life in all of its complexity

Circle Myth: The magic circle must be nine feet in diameter

Circle Reality: This is a British traditional practice that is not a requirement; nine is a magical number that represents spiritual attainment; it is the sum of three multiplied by itself (the number three is sacred because of the triple goddess); incorporating numerology into your sacred space is fine, as long as it does not become a point of obsession or a requirement; remember not to get sidetracked into minutiae that will only distract you from genuine spiritual work

Circle Myth: The circle is the only place where one practices Wicca

Circle Reality: Hopefully not; Wicca is a way of life, a philosophical construct, and a spiritual practice that should inform each moment of your life both within and outside of the magic circle

Practice: Looking at Beliefs

Today, ask yourself the following questions:

- What expectations or ideas do I have about the magic circle?
- What do I know about it from books, movies or television?
- What expectations do I have for myself regarding my ability to cast a circle?
- How might my expectations and beliefs impact my approach to the practice of circle casting?

Day 230

Casting the Circle: The Order

Casting the circle has its own order and rhythm. Many new Craft practitioners (and even seasoned practitioners) wrestle with the question of why a circle casting should have any particular sequence. Who determined the order of the circle anyway? And why should we believe that the order of the circle casting is useful or effective for Witchcraft, or any form of spiritual development? The debate over circle casting divides Witches down sharp lines.

In one camp are the free-spirited, unstructured types. For these Wiccans, ritual is an individual (or collective) expression of the divine. Unstructured Wiccans typically stress the older, shamanic qualities of the Craft. In their view, the spontaneity that emerges from a direct connection to the divine will likely result in a transcendence of rules and strictures imposed by limited, ordinary human consciousness. Pagan ritual is all about personal expression and individual exploration of the mysteries of the gods for these magical folk. In this view, ritual and magic can occur any time, anywhere, with or without a recognizable form.

Then there are the structured types. These folks assert that ritual has a distinct order that reflects an archetypal mythological pattern. In this perspective, the components and the order of Wiccan rituals, while not direct descendants of ancient rites, are based on the insights and practices of millennia of custom and magical observation. The order of the circle casting, as it exists today, evolved from a mystic understanding of the spiritual order of nature. In this view, each component of circle casting contains symbolic meaning that forms a direct link between the individual human consciousness and universal or nature-consciousness.

There is also a third perspective on ritual and order. It is not a truly unique perspective, but rather a combination of the first and second views. For the moderate magical folk who follow this third path, the circle has a recognizable order, but this order may take on innovative expressions and dimensions. It can be expanded or contracted according to a Witch's or a coven's magical needs.

Whichever approach toward circle casting you might eventually adopt, it is a good magical practice and a solid discipline to learn the basics of traditional circle casting and the customary pattern of Wiccan ritual. But from where does this order derive?

Most pagans agree that Gerald Gardner and his *Book of Shadows* heavily influenced the form of many Wiccan practices—including the magic circle. However, some research suggests that Gardner's association with Freemansonry and ceremonial magic was the prime inspiration for the magic circle format. Based on Gardner's ritual formula, here are the basic circle-casting components and their suggested order:

- Blessing of the elements
- Cleansing of the ritual space with elements
- Cleansing of participants with elements
- Formally casting the circle
- Calling the quarters (which means summoning the elemental energies of each compass direction)
- Summoning deity
- The ritual core celebration (which could be a sabbat, esbat, magical working, or divination)
- Cakes and wine
- Dismissing deity and dismissing the quarters
- Formally banishing the circle

Practice: What Type Am I?

Explore the type of ritual format for which you might best be suited:

You might prefer the nonstructured circle casting if:

- You are generally easy-going
- You prefer relaxation to activity
- Spontaneity does not cause you anxiety
- You believe that life has no pattern or design
- You believe that people create their own meanings
- You prefer to cook by making things up as you go along
- You believe that rules are constricting
- You like a level of unpredictability in your life
- You like to allow spirit to speak through you spontaneously
- You are highly creative
- You worry that other people are putting words into your mouth

You might prefer the structured circle casting if:

- You are generally structured in your life
- You prefer planned activities during relaxation time
- You prefer routine in your daily life
- You can see a distinct pattern or design to life
- You believe in destiny
- You believe in a grand design
- You can see how archetypes are meaningful to your life
- You prefer predictability
- You prefer to cook using recipes
- You like to read the words of other people and draw insight from them
- You feel that making things up is just plain wrong

Questions for the Practitioner

- Which type of ritual practitioner do you think you might be: a spontaneous one or a structured one? Or are you a blend of the two?
- Why do you think your choice of ritual style may be useful to you?
- Do you believe that there might be correct and incorrect ways to cast a circle? Why?
- What do you believe could happen if you cast a circle incorrectly?

Day 231

Starting the Circle: Water Blessings

Water is the first element that a priestess or priest blesses in a traditional circle casting. Water is an archetypal symbol of chaos; it represents the unformed, the potential, and the shifting, fluctuating nature of reality. Nothing is ever set in stone as a permanent condition, and even if it is, stone wears away. All things are tidal—they come and they go, they rise and they fall. Many world myths express this theme of existence emerging from water. To mirror this mythic archetype, one of the first tasks of circle casting is introducing the element of water to the sacred space. In the magic circle, your first task is to bless the water. In blessing water, you are beginning the process of focusing the fluid energies of the life force into a structured space.

What You'll Need:

- A small bowl
- Water

Fill a bowl halfway with water. Hold your hands over the water bowl and focus on your breathing. Imagine you draw in a blue light of energy with each inhalation. With each exhalation, you send that blue energy into the water. Once you visualize the water filled with this energy, say the following words:

> ***I consecrate thee, O creature of water,***
> ***In the names of the Great Mother and the Horned Lord.***

Dab your forefinger and middle finger together into the water bowl and then touch water droplets to your heart (and to any other body part that could benefit from blessing by water). While doing so, say:

> ***I am consecrated with the element of water.***

Imagine that you internally fill with a blue radiance. If you want to bless someone within your circle, dab some of your blessed water onto his or her heart, saying:

> ***I consecrate thee with the element of water.***

When you have completed this exercise, you must properly dispose of the consecrated water. Wiccan lore says that you should release it into some form of running water. For those of us living in cities, this usually means a sink or toilet. If you live in a rural area, dispose of the blessed water in a stream or river. If you live near the ocean, dispose of the blessed water there.

Day 232

Elemental Consecrations: Earth

Earth is the second element blessed in the circle casting. In hermetic lore, earth is the first concretization of the chaotic matter of water. Hermetics say that when the etheric, chaotic matter of water becomes dense, it transforms into earth. Earth is the first manifestation of the unformed energies of the universe.[80] In blessing earth, you are symbolically solidifying unformed energies into the form of the magic circle.

What You'll Need:

- A bowl
- Salt

Fill the bottom of a small bowl with salt. Although any salt will suffice, I prefer Kosher salt because it has an artful, aesthetic appeal. Hold your hands over the bowl and focus on your breathing. Imagine you draw in a green light of energy with each inhalation. With each exhalation, you send that green energy into the salt. Once you visualize the salt filled with this energy, say the following words:

I consecrate thee, O creature of earth,
In the names of the Great Mother and the Horned Lord.

Dab your forefinger and middle finger together into the salt. Touch the salt to your root chakra center at the base of the spine. Also sprinkle salt on the crown of your head, and then apply it to any other body part that you sense might benefit from blessing by earth. While doing so, say:

I am consecrated with the element of earth.

Imagine that a green radiance fills you. If you want to bless someone within your circle, dab some of your blessed salt onto the appropriate energy centers, saying:

I consecrate thee with the element of earth.

When you have completed this exercise, you must properly dispose of the consecrated salt. Wiccan lore says that you should release it into running water. Again, city Witches call a sink or toilet "running water," and so can you.

Day 233

Elemental Consecrations: Fire

Fire is the third element that a priestess or priest blesses in the cycle of casting the magic circle. In hermetic mysticism, the element of earth needs the life spark of fire in order to move it into action. Fire is energy (both physical and spiritual), without which earth would be barren and immobile. Keep in mind that as you bless fire, you are symbolically enlivening the solid earth energies of your circle.

What You'll Need:

- A 5–6 inch red candle (when used in a ritual context and placed on your altar, this object is known as the *fire candle*)
- Fire oil

Anoint the candle shaft with fire oil, light it, and set it firmly in a holder. Carefully cup the flame with your hands (without burning yourself or catching your sleeve in the flame), holding them about 3–5 inches from the fire. Focus on your breathing. Imagine you draw in a red light of energy with each inhalation. With each exhalation, you send that red energy into the flame. Once you visualize the flame filled with this energy, say the following words:

> ***I consecrate thee, O creature of fire,***
> ***In the names of the Great Mother and the***
> ***Horned Lord.***

Next, bless yourself with the fire by holding the candle's flame 3–5 inches away from your forehead. Pass it vertically down along the center line of your body—all the way down to your genitals. For additional blessing of specific body areas, you may also hold the candle flame 3–5 inches near the body part that could benefit from fire energy. While doing so, say:

> ***I am consecrated with the element of fire.***

Imagine that you are filled with a red radiance. If you want to bless someone within your circle, hold the candle 3–5 inches from his or her forehead and pass it vertically down along the center line of the body, saying:

> ***I consecrate thee with the element of fire.***

Extinguish the candle *with your fingertips* and set it aside for tomorrow's practice.

A Word to the Wise: In traditional Wiccan practice, one does not blow out candles. Some magical practitioners believe that blowing the candle out is pitting one element against another. Pinching out the candle flame *denies* the flame of oxygen, which is different from using one element to finish off another.

Day 234

Elemental Consecrations: Air

Air is the fourth element that a priestess or priest blesses in the magic circle. It is the finest and least dense of the four elements. Hermetics assert that air spiritually encourages the life spark of fire. In blessing air, you are symbolically fanning the flames, feeding the fires of life that you have invited into your magic circle.

What You'll Need:

- Air incense, or
- Dried white sage (also called desert sage), or
- Loose, dried sandalwood powder
- Air oil
- Your Fire candle
- Self-igniting charcoal

If you are using dried white sage or sandalwood blend it with a few drops of air oil. Light your fire candle (from yesterday) and use this flame to ignite the charcoal for your incense. Once the coal is hot enough, sprinkle it with incense. As the incense smolders, cup your hands around the smoke. Inhale deeply and imagine that with each inhalation, you draw in a yellow light of energy. With each exhalation, you send that yellow energy into the smoke that fills your sacred space. Once you imagine that the incense is filled with the spiritual energy of air, say the following words:

I consecrate thee, O creature of air,
In the names of the Great Mother and the
Horned Lord.

Bless yourself with air by gently fanning the smoke toward your body. Draw the smoke first toward your forehead and then continue fanning downward along the vertical center line of your body, down to your genitals. You may also hold the incense anywhere near to a body part that could benefit from additional blessing by air. While doing so, say:

I am consecrated with the element of air.

If you want to bless someone within your circle, hold the incense toward his or her forehead and use your hand to fan it along the center line of the body, down to the genital area, saying:

I consecrate thee with the element of air.

Allow the incense to extinguish on its own. Once it stops smoking, you can dispose of this in running water.

A Word to the Wise: Use a sturdy 10–12 inch feather (or a group of them bound together with a leather cord) to ritually fan the incense toward yourself and others. For added ritual interest, dress the feather's stem with beads, leather, bells, or charms.

Day 235

Casting the Circle: The First Layer

Casting the circle means setting up the energetic, spiritual essence of the ritual space. When you demarcate the ritual space's perimeter, you have cast the circle. It involves energetically sealing the perimeter of your sacred space with the five elements. (Yes, I did say *five*. Don't forget that the fifth element is spirit.) The energies of water and earth combine to form the circle's first layer.

What You'll Need:

- Your dish of salt
- Your bowl of water
- Fire candle
- Air incense
- Four "quarter candles" (these can be any variety or shape of candle, but one must be yellow, one red, one blue, and one green)
- Your unconsecrated athame, wand, chalice, and pentacle

To Begin:

- Set up a table that will serve as an altar that you will place at the center of your ritual space
- Set out all of your unconsecrated magical tools in ritual positions: wand in the east of the altar, athame in the south, cup in the west, and pentacle in the north of the altar
- Set the bowl of water and the dish of salt on your altar

Use a compass to accurately locate the four directions and then lay out your four quarter candles at the proposed edges of your ritual space. In the east of your space place a yellow candle; in the south place a red candle; in the west place a blue candle; in the north place a green candle. Light each of the candles, saying:

Fire, flame in the Old One's name

A Word to the Wise: You might use colored votive candles for the four quarters. Votive candles usually come in a glass jar. The glass is a safety feature that comes in handy should your quarter candles tip over. Cleaning wax off the floor or carpet is another story altogether.

Next, complete the circle-casting steps you've learned so far:

- Consecrate each of the four elements (water, earth, fire and air) on your central altar (see Days 231–234)
- Consecrate yourself and anyone else present with each of the elements

Once you have completed these steps, you are ready to cast the first layer of the circle. Begin by using your index and middle finger to brush three "scoops" of the salt into your bowl of water. Hold your hands over the bowl of water and salt and say:

Water and earth I cast thee 'round,
By thy essence, life be bound.
Flowing vision, holy birth,
Blessed be by water and earth.

Stir the water and salt together. Take the saltwater mixture to the eastern quarter of your sacred space. Dip your fingers into the saltwater and sprinkle this along the edge of your sacred space. Do this while silently walking clockwise around the inside perimeter of your circle. Imagine that you seal the sacred space with a blue and green light. Continue with this silently until you walk the entirety of the circle, returning to the east where you began.

A Word to the Wise: Clockwise in magical parlance is *deosil*. Sometimes Witches call this clockwise movement sunwise. A counterclockwise movement is called moonwise or *widdershins*.

Avoid obsessing on technical perfection and minutiae such as size of your circle, or where the water and salt drops are falling as you cast them. Precision is not mandatory, but your intent, your focus and clarity, *are.*

When you are finished, sit within the sacred space you have created so far. How does it feel?

Closing Your Space

To close this layer of the circle, stand again in the east and face the outer edge. Hold your hands outward toward the east. Silently circumambulate the space in a counterclockwise direction. Continue to hold your hands out toward the edge of the circle as you walk. Imagine that the energies you've raised begin to subside and sink into the earth where they are reabsorbed and neutralized. Once you reach the easternmost point again, pause to sense the difference in energy now that you have banished the circle.

It is always a good magical practice to store away all of your ritual items immediately following your rites. Be sure to flush the ritual water, salt, and burned incense into running water.

Day 236

Casting the Circle: The Second Layer

Fire and air compose the second layer of your magic circle. One point to bear in mind while casting the fire/air layer is that a burning piece of charcoal represents the element of fire. When you place incense upon the burning coals, it symbolizes the synthesis of both fire and air. You could, if you prefer, cast each of these elements separately. That is to say, you could first circumambulate the perimeter of the magic circle with incense and then with your fire candle (instead of the lighted charcoal). For that matter, you could do the same with water and earth. However, the most traditional practice is that of combining the two elements and then casting the perimeter with the elemental combination.

What You'll Need:

- Your dish of salt
- Your bowl of water
- Fire candle
- Air incense
- Four quarter candles
- Self-lighting charcoal
- A thurible (a container in which you burn the incense or other magical objects)
- Your unconsecrated athame, wand, chalice, and pentacle

To Begin:

- Complete the circle-casting steps you've learned so far:
- Set up your main altar at the center of your ritual space and arrange your magical tools on it in their ritual positions (see Day 235)
- Set out the four quarter candles and light them, saying,

Fire flame in the Old One's name.

- Light your charcoal and set it in the thurible
- Consecrate each of the four elements (water, earth, fire, and air) on your central altar (see Days 231, 232, 233, and 234)
- Consecrate yourself and anyone else present with each of the elements
- Cast the first layer of the circle with water and earth, as you learned yesterday (see Day 235)

Once you have completed these steps, sprinkle some of the air incense on the charcoal and allow it to smolder. While it does, hold your hands over the smoke and say aloud:

Fire and air I cast thee 'round,
By thy essence, life be bound.
Knowledge of thy true desire,
Blessed be by air and fire.

Carry the incense in the burner to the eastern quarter of your sacred space and begin to walk deosil along the perimeter. As you walk, silently hold out the incense so that it imparts its magical essence. Imagine that you seal the sacred space with a red and yellow aura as you cast this layer of your circle. Continue until you return to the east where you began.

When you are finished, sit within the sacred space you have developed so far. How does it feel?

Closing Your Space

To close the first two layers of the circle, stand again in the east and face the outer edge. Hold your hands outward toward the east. Silently circumambulate the space, going widdershins. Continue to hold your hands out toward the edge of the circle as you walk. Imagine that the energies you've raised begin to subside and sink into the earth where they are reabsorbed and neutralized. Once you reach the easternmost point again, pause to sense the difference in energy now that you have banished the circle.

Store all ritual items immediately following your rites. Flush the water, incense, and salt in running water.

A Word to the Wise: Witches always use their ritual tools during any ceremony. By simply having them present on the altar, the tools are the magical representatives of each element. No matter what ritual you perform, it is important to set out all of your ritual tools.

Day 237

Casting the Circle: The Third Layer

Spirit is the third layer of your magic circle. In this layer, you formally seal the circle with divine energies, the energies of the goddess and god. Sealing the final circle layer requires use of the athame. When two or more Witches gather, the final layer of the circle is cast with the sword.

So now we come to the Witches' paradox. Wiccans believe that unconsecrated magical tools are ineffective in ritual use. Tools can only be consecrated within the magic circle. So how can you cast a circle without consecrated tools? Many Witches consecrate their tools in a magic circle that was cast for them by an initiated and properly prepared (meaning formally initiated) Witch.

When this is not possible, or when formal tools are unavailable you can use the natural tools. Since your body comprises these tools, they are *always* consecrated. Here they are:

Wand—Extended arm; index and middle fingers (only) extended to the first knuckle

Cup—Both hands cupped together

Athame—Extended arm; index and middle fingers (only) extended

Pentacle—The entire body, standing in the "pentacle position," which is arms outstretched to the sides and legs spread to shoulder width; in this position your head, arms, and legs form the five points of the pentacle

What You'll Need:

- Your dish of salt
- Your bowl of water
- Fire candle
- Air incense
- Four quarter candles
- Self-lighting charcoal
- A thurible
- Your unconsecrated athame, wand, chalice, and pentacle

To Begin:
Complete the circle-casting steps you've learned so far:

- Set up your altar at the center of your ritual space
- Set out all of your magical tools in their compass positions upon the central altar
- Set out the four quarter candles and light them, saying,

  Fire flame in the Old One's name.

- Light your charcoal and set it in the thurible
- Consecrate each of the four elements (water, earth, fire, and air) on your central altar
- Consecrate yourself and anyone else present with each of the elements (see Days, 231, 232, 233 and 234)
- Cast the first layer of the circle with water and earth (see Day 235)
- Cast the second layer with fire and air, as you learned yesterday (see Day 236)

Once you have completed these steps, return to the east of your circle. Extend your right arm, pointing only your index and middle fingers. Plant your feet solidly beneath your body and feel your weight. Close your eyes. Take several deep breaths. Imagine that a magical root extends from the base of your spine into the ground. Allow the psychic taproot to continue to plunge deeper into the earth until it meets with the planet's white-hot core. Once you envision it there, imagine that you draw up this core energy through the root. Draw up energy with each inhalation. As you draw it up, feel the energy fill your body. Once the energy reaches the top of your head, imagine that you send the energy through your arms and out through the tip of the extended two fingers.

Circumambulate the perimeter of the circle, moving deosil, casting out this energy and saying:

I summon the Circle, the Circle I summon.
Power, peace, and protection will come in
And bind to the womb of our spiritual birth,
Through Air, Fire, Water, and Earth!

If you finish the words before you have completed walking the perimeter of the circle, simply walk the remainder in silence.

When you are finished, sit within the sacred space you have developed so far. How does it feel?

Closing Your Space

To close the three layers of the circle you have cast today, stand again in the east and face the outer edge. Hold your hands outward toward the east. Silently circumambulate the space going widdershins. Continue to hold your hands out toward the edge of the circle as you walk. Imagine that the energies you've raised begin to subside and sink into the earth where they are reabsorbed and neutralized. This time (and every time hereafter), as you walk, say:

Earth will crumble my circle,
Water will cause it to fall,
Fire will burn what's left in the urn,
And the winds will scatter them all!

If you finish the words before you walk the entirety of the circle, simply continue walking in silence until you reach the east once more.

When you arrive in the east, face outward toward the eastern quarter, and say:

The circle is open, but unbroken!
Merry meet, merry part, and merry meet again!

Once you reach the easternmost point again, pause to sense the difference in energy now that you have banished the circle.

Store your ritual items and flush water, salt, and incense in running water.

DAY 238

Calling the Quarters: East

Calling the quarters involves ritually gesturing with your arms or magical tools at each of the four compass directions in order to summon the elemental forces. The elemental spirits are summoned to witness your rites, to guard, and to energize your magical space. You will typically use your athame for calling the quarters and forming the ritual gestures that summon the elemental forces. Today, however, you will use your natural athame.

A Word to the Wise: There are variations to using the athame for quarter-calling. Some Wiccans use the tool that represents the specific element they are summoning. For example, when calling the western quarter, a Witch might use her chalice to invoke the undines and the powers of water—or when invoking the gnomes of the north, the Witch might use her pentacle.

To begin calling the quarters, you will first need to practice drawing what are known as the *invoking* and *banishing* pentagrams.

Invoking Air **Banishing Air**

Each element has a specific pentagram that invokes and banishes its elemental energy. There are a couple of rules about invoking and banishing elemental pentagrams with which you should become acquainted prior to beginning this practice.

Traditionally, Witches only use invoking pentagrams while they are standing within the magic circle. This is an important point to consider. The elemental forces that you summon during calling the quarters are high-voltage energies. The circle itself, once cast, acts as a buffer to these raw, wild energies. It is never a good practice to call quarters when you do not have all three layers of your circle cast.

Banishing pentagrams can be done at any time. In fact, Witches often use banishing pentagrams to dismiss imbalanced energies that they sense in their immediate vicinity.

Folks who are new to either banishing or invoking pentagrams should practice within the magic circle until they become familiar with the process.

Here are the invoking and banishing pentagrams for air.

What You'll Need:

- Your dish of salt
- Your bowl of water
- Fire candle
- Air incense
- Four quarter candles
- Self-lighting charcoal
- A thurible (container in which you safely burn items)
- Your unconsecrated athame, wand, chalice, and pentacle

To Begin:

Complete the circle-casting steps you've learned so far:

- Set up your main altar at the center of your ritual space
- Set all of your magical tools on the altar
- Set out the four quarter candles and light them saying,

Fire flame in the Old One's name.

- Light your charcoal and set it in the thurible
- Consecrate each of the four elements (water, earth, fire, and air) on your central altar
- Consecrate yourself and anyone else present with each of the elements
- Cast the first layer of the circle with water and earth
- Cast the second layer with fire and air
- Cast the circle with your natural athame, drawing the final spiritual perimeter of the circle

---

A Word to the Wise: Remember, the natural athame is your right arm extended, along with only your index and middle finger. The blade of the athame is your outstretched index and middle fingers.

Once you have completed these steps, walk to the east of your circle and face outward. With your right arm outstretched in the natural athame position, draw the invoking-air pentagram in the air.

Start at the farthest right point and draw the blade horizontally to the left. Draw the blade down to the bottommost right point. Then draw the blade up toward the topmost point. Draw the blade to the bottommost left point and then draw it back to the point where you began.

As you draw the pentagram, imagine that you leave a golden yellow aura suspended in midair. As you draw the pentagram, say:

I summon, stir and call thee up,
Mighty Ones of the East, Powers of Air,
To witness my (our) rites and to seal this circle!

After you have summoned the powers of the east, sense the elemental energies you have summoned. Imagine them sealing the eastern quarter of your magical space. After you have sensed how this feels, banish the elemental forces of air. Again, face the east. This time, draw the banishing-air pentagram with your natural athame.

Start at the leftmost horizontal point of the pentagram and draw the blade horizontally to the right. Then draw the blade down to the bottommost left point. Draw the blade upward to the topmost point, then draw it down to the bottommost right point. Then draw the blade back to the point where you began.

As you banish, imagine the golden aura fading away. As you banish the eastern powers, say:

Hail ye mighty ones of the East,
We thank thee for attending.
Before ye depart for your lovely realms,
We say hail and farewell!

Kiss the athame blade (in this case, your index and middle fingers), and point once again toward the east.

Steps to Banish the Circle You Have So Far:
Close the three layers of the circle you have cast. Stand in the east and hold your hands outward. Walk widdershins around the perimeter of the circle, imagining the energies subsiding. As you walk, say:

Earth will crumble my circle,
Water will cause it to fall,
Fire will burn what's left in the urn,
And the winds will scatter them all!

When you arrive in the east, face outward, toward the eastern quarter, and say:

The circle is open, but unbroken!
Merry meet, merry part, and merry meet again!

Day 239

Calling the Quarters: South

As we continue with our practice of building the magic circle, we call the southern quarter, the dwelling place of the salamanders and the element of fire.

First take time to practice drawing the invoking and banishing pentagrams for fire:

Invoking Fire

Banishing Fire

What You'll Need:

- Your dish of salt
- Your bowl of water
- Fire candle
- Air incense
- Four quarter candles
- Self-lighting charcoal
- A thurible
- Your unconsecrated athame, wand, chalice and pentacle

To Begin:

- Complete the circle-casting steps you've learned so far:
- Set up your altar at the center of your ritual space
- Set all of your magical tools in their ritual positions on the altar
- Set out the four quarter candles and light them, saying,

Fire flame in the Old One's name

- Light your charcoal and set it in the thurible
- Consecrate each of the four elements (water, earth, fire, and air) on your central altar
- Consecrate yourself and anyone else present with each of the elements
- Cast the first layer of the circle with water and earth
- Cast the second layer with fire and air
- Cast the circle with your natural athame, drawing the final perimeter of the circle
- Draw the invoking pentagram for air

Once you have completed these steps, walk to the southern edge of your circle. Outstretch your natural athame and draw the invoking Fire pentagram in the air before you.

Start at the topmost right point and draw the blade downward and to the bottommost right point. Draw the blade up to the left horizontal point. Then draw across the horizontal line to the right horizontal point. Continue drawing the blade back toward the bottommost left point. Finish the pentagram by drawing the line back up to the topmost point, where you began.

As you draw the pentagram, imagine that you leave a fiery red aura suspended in midair. While invoking, say:

I summon, stir, and call thee up,
Mighty Ones of the South, Powers of Fire,
To witness my (our) rites and to seal this circle!

Stand and sense the fiery energies you have summoned. Close your eyes and imagine this fire energy sealing the southern quarter of your magical space and simultaneously linking with the elemental energies of the eastern quarter.

After a few moments, banish the elemental forces of fire. Again, face the south and draw the banishing pentagram in the air with your natural athame. This time, start at the bottommost right point and draw the blade up to the top. Draw the blade down to the bottommost left point. Then draw the blade up toward the right horizontal point. Draw the blade across the horizontal line to the left horizontal point. Then continue drawing the blade back to the bottommost right point, where you began.

As you banish, imagine the fiery aura fading away. As you banish the southern powers, say:

Hail, ye mighty ones of the South,
We thank thee for attending.
Before ye depart for your lovely realms,
We say hail and farewell!

Now, kiss the athame blade (your index and middle fingers) and point it toward the south.

Steps to Banish the Circle You Have So Far:

- Stand in the east and draw the banishing pentagram for the powers of air.
- Close the three layers of the circle you have cast. Stand in the east, hold your hands outward. Walk widdershins around the perimeter of the circle, imagining the energies subsiding. As you walk, say:

Earth will crumble my circle,
Water will cause it to fall,
Fire will burn what's left in the urn,
And the winds will scatter them all!

When you arrive in the east, face outward, toward the eastern quarter, and say:

The circle is open, but unbroken!
Merry meet, merry part, and merry meet again!

Day 240

Calling the Quarters: West

As you continue with building the magic circle, you will call the western quarter, the dwelling place of the undines and the element of water.

First, practice drawing the invoking and banishing pentagrams for water:

Invoking Water

Banishing Water

What You'll Need:

- Your dish of salt
- Your bowl of water
- Fire candle
- Air incense
- Four quarter candles
- Self-lighting charcoal
- A thurible
- Your unconsecrated athame, wand, chalice, and pentacle

To Begin:
Complete the circle-casting steps you've learned so far:

- Set up your main altar at the center of your ritual space
- Set all of your magical tools in their ritual positions on the altar
- Set out the four quarter candles and light them, saying,

  Fire flame in the Old One's name

- Light your charcoal and set it within the thurible
- Consecrate each of the four elements (water, earth, fire, and air) on your central altar
- Consecrate yourself and anyone else present with each of the elements
- Cast the first layer of the circle with water and earth
- Cast the second layer with fire and air
- Cast the circle with your natural athame, drawing the final perimeter of the circle
- Draw the invoking pentagram for the powers of air
- Draw the invoking pentagram for the powers of fire

Once you have completed these steps, walk to the western edge of your circle. Outstretch your natural athame and draw the invoking water pentagram before you. Start at the leftmost horizontal point of your pentagram and draw the blade across the horizontal line to the right. Draw the blade down to the bottommost left point. Then draw it upward to the topmost point. Continue drawing the blade back down toward the bottommost right point. Finish the pentagram by drawing the line back up to the leftmost horizontal point, where you began.

As you draw the pentagram, imagine that you leave a shimmering blue aura suspended in midair. As you invoke the element of water, say:

> ***I summon, stir, and call thee up,***
> ***Mighty Ones of the West, Powers of Water,***
> ***To witness my (our) rites and to seal this circle!***

Stand and sense the watery energies you have summoned. Close your eyes and imagine this water energy sealing the western quarter of your magical space and simultaneously linking with the elemental energies of the southern quarter. Imagine too, the southern energies linking with the eastern energies.

After a few moments, banish the elemental forces of water. Again, face the west and draw the banishing pentagram in the air with your natural athame. This time, start at the rightmost horizontal point and draw the blade across to the left. Draw the blade down to the bottommost right point. Then draw the blade up toward the top. Draw the blade back down to the bottom left point. Then continue drawing the blade back to the right horizontal point, where you began.

As you banish, imagine the shimmering blue aura fading away. As you banish the western powers, say:

> *Hail ye mighty ones of the West,*
> *We thank thee for attending.*
> *Before ye depart for your lovely realms,*
> *We say hail and farewell!*

Now, kiss the athame blade (your index and middle fingers) and point it toward the west.

Steps to Banish the Circle You Have So Far:

- Stand in the south and draw the banishing pentagram for the powers of fire
- Stand in the east and draw the banishing pentagram for the powers of air
- Close the three layers of the circle you have cast. stand in the east, hold your hands outward; walk widdershins around the perimeter of the circle, imagining the energies subsiding; as you walk, say:

> *Earth will crumble my circle,*
> *Water will cause it to fall,*
> *Fire will burn what's left in the urn,*
> *And the winds will scatter them all!*

When you arrive in the east, face outward toward the eastern quarter, and say:

> *The circle is open, but unbroken!*
> *Merry meet, merry part, and merry meet again!*

Days 241-270

Magical Items to Gather:

Here are the items you will need during the next month of your training.

Day 243

- Simple sweet cakes, such as muffins, scones, or sweetbreads
- Wine (alternative: juice or fruit nectar)

Day 244

- A bowl of hot water in which you infuse dried hyssop
- An *asperges* (a ritual device Witches use to sprinkle a mixture of salt and water; the asperges is usually a bundle of either fresh or dried herbs; the best herb choice is rosemary)
- Lavender, rosemary, or hyssop essential oil

Day 245

- A 5–6 inch blue-green taper candle

Day 248

- Fire incense (of if you do not have that prepared, use frankincense)
- Fire oil (or one of the following essential oils: cinnamon, bergamot, clove, orange, or pennyroyal)

Day 249

- Air incense (if you do not have that prepared, use frankincense or white copal)
- Air oil (or one of the following essential oils: bergamot, sage, star anise, or lemon

Day 250

- Water incense (if you do not have that prepared, use frankincense or sandalwood)
- Water oil (or one of the following essential oils: apple, jasmine, rose, or water lily)

Day 251

- Earth incense (or if you do not have that prepared, use frankincense or oak)
- Earth oil (or one of the following essential oils: patchouli, honeysuckle, tulip, or lilac)

Day 261

- Percussive music

Day 265

- A quartz crystal with at least one terminal (or pointed, beveled end)

Day 267

- Dragon's blood ink (most new age/magical shops carry dragon's blood red ink) or
- A red ink pen
- Rosemary essential oil

Day 268

- A round mirror (at least 5 inches in diameter)
- A bowl of water steeped with the herb hyssop
- A dark blue candle of any size/shape (this color is good for dispelling evil)

Day 269

- Cheesecloth
- A sprig of fresh rosemary and at least a teaspoon of dried rosemary
- 12 inches of red cord
- A 5–6 inch red taper candle
- Red thread and a needle

Day 270

- An empty, clear-glass jar
- Old razors, rusty nails, pins, needles, and tacks (enough to fill the jar)
- Vinegar
- Dried white sage (also called desert sage) or
- A self-igniting charcoal
- Dragon's blood resin

Day 241

Calling the Quarters: North

As you continue with building the magic circle, you will call the northern quarter, the dwelling place of the gnomes and the element of water.

First, practice drawing the invoking and banishing pentagrams for earth:

Invoking Earth **Banishing Earth**

What You'll Need:

- Your dish of salt and bowl of water
- Fire candle
- Air incense
- Four quarter candles
- Self-lighting charcoal
- A thurible
- Your unconsecrated athame, wand, chalice, and pentacle

To Begin:

Complete the circle-casting steps you've learned so far:

- Set up your main altar at the center of your ritual space
- Set all of your magical tools in their ritual positions on the altar
- Set out the four quarter candles and light them, saying,

> ***Fire flame in the Old One's name***

- Light your charcoal and set it in the thurible
- Consecrate each of the four elements (water, earth, fire, and air) on your central altar
- Consecrate yourself and anyone else present with each of the elements
- Cast the first layer of the circle with water and earth
- Cast the second layer with fire and air
- Cast the circle with your natural athame, drawing the final perimeter of the circle
- Draw the invoking pentagram for the powers of air
- Draw the invoking pentagram for the powers of fire
- Draw the invoking pentagram for the powers of water

Once you have completed these steps, walk to the northern edge of your circle. Outstretch your natural athame and draw the invoking earth pentagram before you. Start at the topmost point of your pentagram and draw the blade down to the bottommost left point. Draw the blade up to the rightmost horizontal point. Then draw across the horizontal line to the leftmost horizontal point. Continue drawing the blade back down toward the bottommost right point. Finish the pentagram by drawing the line back up to the topmost point, where you began. As you draw the pentagram, imagine that you leave a bright green aura suspended in midair. As you draw the pentagram, say:

> ***I summon, stir, and call thee up,***
> ***Mighty Ones of the North, Powers of Earth,***
> ***To witness my (our) rites and to seal this circle!***

Stand and sense the earthy energies you have summoned. Close your eyes and imagine this earth energy sealing the northern quarter of your magical space and simultaneously linking with the elemental energies of the western quarter. Imagine, too, the western energies linking with the southern energies and the south joining to the east. Now imagine that the eastern energies link with the north, completing the energetic chain. Each element now links with its neighboring elemental energy.

After a few moments, it is time to banish the elemental forces. Again, face the north and draw the banishing pentagram with your natural athame. This time, start at the bottommost left point and draw the blade up to the top. Draw the blade back down to the bottommost right point. Then draw the blade up to the leftmost horizontal point. Draw the blade across the horizontal line to the rightmost point. Then continue drawing the blade back to the bottommost left point, where you began.

As you banish the northern powers, imagine the iridescent green aura fading away, and say:

> ***Hail ye mighty ones of the North,***
> ***We thank thee for attending.***
> ***Before ye depart for your lovely realms,***
> ***We say hail and farewell!***

Now, kiss the athame blade (your index and middle fingers) and point it toward the north.

Steps to Banish the Circle You Have So Far:

- Stand in the west and draw the banishing pentagram for the powers of water.
- Stand in the south and draw the banishing pentagram for the powers of fire.
- Stand in the east and draw the banishing pentagram for the powers of air.
- Close the three layers of the circle you have cast; stand in the east, hold your hands outward; walk widdershins around the perimeter of the circle, imagining the energies subsiding; as you walk, and say:

> ***Earth will crumble my circle,***
> ***Water will cause it to fall,***
> ***Fire will burn what's left in the urn,***
> ***And the winds will scatter them all!***

When you arrive in the east, face outward, toward the eastern quarter, and say:

> ***The circle is open, but unbroken!***
> ***Merry meet, merry part, and merry meet again!***

Day 242

Summoning the Gods

The final step in erecting the magic circle is inviting the gods into your sacred space. Summoning the gods involves traditional hand gestures that Wiccans call the *triangles of manifestation.*

What You'll Need:

- Your dish of salt
- Your bowl of water
- Fire candle
- Air incense
- Four quarter candles
- Self-lighting charcoal
- A thurible
- Your unconsecrated athame, wand, chalice, and pentacle

To Begin:
Complete the circle-casting steps you've learned so far:

- Set up your main altar at the center of your circle
- Set all of your magical tools in their ritual positions on the altar
- Set out the four quarter candles and light them saying,

  Fire Flame in the Old One's name.

- Light your charcoal and set it in the thurible
- Consecrate each of the four elements (water, earth, fire, and air) on your central altar
- Consecrate yourself and anyone else present with each of the elements
- Cast the first layer of the circle with water and earth
- Cast the second layer with fire and air
- Cast the circle with your natural athame, drawing the final perimeter of the circle
- Draw the invoking pentagram for the powers of air
- Draw the invoking pentagram for the powers of fire
- Draw the invoking pentagram for the powers of water
- Draw the invoking pentagram for the powers of earth

Once you have completed these steps, stand at your altar in the center of your magic circle and face the south. Allow your arms to hang at your sides naturally. Open your hands so that the fingers all point down. Open the thumbs away from the fingers so that they create a 90-degree angle. Bring your hands together now at your pelvic level so that the

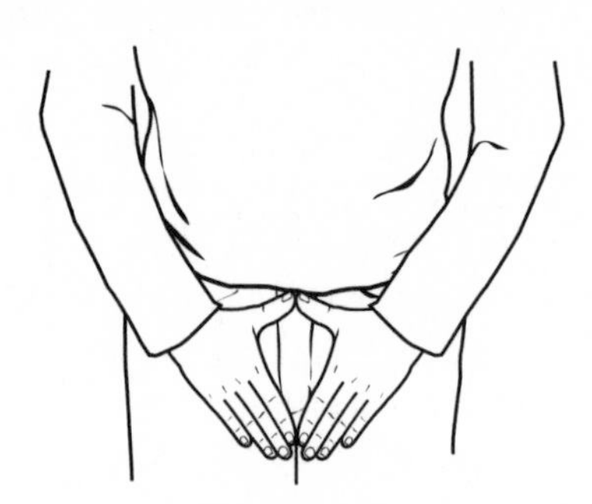

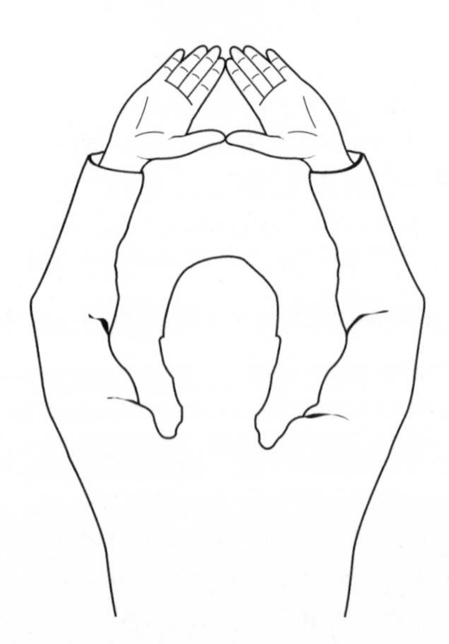

The Triangle of Manifestation.

tips of your thumbs meet and the tips of your index fingers meet. This should form a triangle with the point down. The palms of your hands should be facing your pelvis.

Take several slow, deep breaths. Imagine sacred energies from the earth climbing your legs and filling your body. When you sense this energy, separate your hands and slowly bring them up in an arc along the sides of your body so that they meet above your head to form a second triangle—thumbs and tips of index fingers touching. This time, the point of the triangle is up, and the palms of your hands are facing away from you. Now imagine a white-hot energy penetrating the crown of your head, filling you with divine energy. Imagine this energy mingling with the energies of the earth.

A Word to the Wise: The triangle with the point facing down represents the alchemical sigil for earth. The triangle with the point facing up represents the element of air. In essence you are bringing the spheres of earth and sky together. These two sigils combined create the hexagram or "Star of David," which represents perfect union and the magical axiom of "As above, so below."

Tilt the top point of the triangle away from you and point it down, bringing the triangle back to the place where you began, in front of your pelvis. Imagine the energies of earth and sky meeting within you. Now say:

You who have been from beginning to end,
Our rites and mysteries now attend.
Most ancient of Maidens, Mothers, and
Crones,
Lord of the Hoof, of antlers and bones,
Where fire meets earth, and wind meets sea,
Harken our call; so mote it be!

You have successfully cast a complete circle! Take some time to sit in the center and feel its energies. If you have some magical rite to perform, such as that of the full moon, a sabbat, or a divination, now is the time for you to engage in the core of your ritual working. Since there is no core magical working beyond the circle casting itself, take a few moments to rest and then it is time to dismiss the circle.

At the close of each circle you must thank the gods for attending and dismiss them from the circle. To do this, stand at the center of your circle and say:

Witches all, our rites conclude
In merriment, the earth renewed.
The cock doth crow the end of night,
We thank the gods who've joined our rite.

(Pause in silence, thanking the gods for attending and bidding them farewell.)

To all I charge thee lock away,
Our magics and our mystery play.
Then raise a toast, a hearty draught,
To bid the gods preserve the Craft!

Now it is time to close the circle. You have so far been learning how to dismiss the quarters/elements in the same order that you summoned them. However, this was only for the sake of practice, to keep things simple. It is important to know that the dismissal of the quarters occurs in the same order as their summoning. That is to say, in both the summoning of the quarters and in their banishing, you always begin with the east, then go to the south, west and north.

Here are the steps to banish the circle:

- Stand in the east and draw the banishing pentagram for the powers of air
- Stand in the south and draw the banishing pentagram for the powers of fire
- Stand in the west and draw the banishing pentagram for the powers of water
- Stand in the north and draw the banishing pentagram for the powers of earth

- Close the three layers of the circle you have cast. Stand in the east and hold your hands outward; walk widdershins around the perimeter of the circle, imagining the energies subsiding; as you walk, say:

Earth will crumble my circle,
Water will cause it to fall,
Fire will burn what's left in the urn,
And the winds will scatter them all!

When you arrive in the east, face outward toward the eastern quarter and say:

The circle is open, but unbroken!
Merry meet, merry part, and merry meet again!

Day 243

Cakes and Wine

After the central working of any ritual, just prior to ending the rites, Witches engage in the custom of *cakes and wine.* (Some traditions within Wicca call this custom *cakes and ale.*) In this practice, the officiating priest/ess blesses sweet cakes and wine, ale, or some other sweet fruit drink. The attendees then share the food and drink. This rite may appear simple, but it contains layers of symbolism.

Cakes are a link to the earth through grain, which is a symbol for the fruition and bounty of the harvest. In pagan theology, the earth itself is the mother; grain is her offspring. How can we not recognize that although earth and grain appear as separate manifestations, they are unified, as are a mother and her child?

Wine is an old-world symbol for the earth's life essence. In ancient Europe, the spirit of the grapevine was wine. Through cakes and wine Witches can recognize a vast, interconnected network of sun, moon, rain, sky, circling planets, seasons, and human beings. The purpose of consuming cakes and wine is to cultivate an appreciation for this interconnectedness of life, to develop a deep reverence for nature and for each other.

While circle participants consume cakes and wine, it is traditional for them to discuss their experiences during the body of the ritual. It is a time to explore what worked and what didn't. This process of eating and talking assists Witches in restoring their mundane sensory functions in order to transition from the magical mind to everyday consciousness.

Today's practice can be done outside of the magic circle. Later you will incorporate this rite as part of your usual circle format.

What You'll Need:

- Simple sweet cakes (muffins, scones, sweet breads)

- Wine (as an alternative, use juice)
- An empty bowl (for libations)

To begin, pour some wine into your chalice and set it on the altar. Hold your natural athame with the blade pointed to the sky and say:

Now we'll feast in the Old Ones' names,
Then fetch thy besom and hie thee hame.
To north, to west,
To south, to east,
Blessed be the sacred feast!

Now turn the point of the natural athame down, hold it just above the wine-filled chalice, and say:

Gracious goddess, lend thy hand,
Gentle lady of the land,
From seed to leaf, from bud to vine,
Mystic Mother, bless this wine.

Dip the blade of your natural athame into the cup and say:

Blade and vessel so combined,
The lovers' limbs are thus entwined.
Blend and merge divine duet,
Where the blade and cup have met!

Next, place the cakes upon your pentacle and touch the tip of the natural athame to each, saying:

Lord of living, lord of dead,
King of field and grain and bread,
Of this life we must partake,
Horned Hunter, bless this cake.

Pass cakes to each group member, saying:

May you never hunger.

Pass the chalice around for each member to drink, or fill each participant's chalice with wine, saying:

May you never thirst.

You will now libate (offer) a portion of whatever it is you have eaten or drank into the empty libation bowl. When the circle is opened, empty the libation bowl upon the bare earth.

DAY 244

Casting the Circle: Putting It All Together

Today's practice consists of completely casting the circle, conducting the cakes and wine rite, and then banishing the magic circle. The entire circle-casting/banishing script that is contained on the following pages is the one that you will use whenever you hold an esbat or sabbat, do a divination, or cast a spell.

A Word to the Wise: An *Esbat* is a coven meeting other than one of the eight seasonal sabbats. Typically Witches hold esbats on nights of the full moon, but they can take place at any time between sabbat celebrations. Esbats are often times when Witches raise and direct magical energy to attain their goals.

Circle Casting/Banishing

Although the order of putting the circle together is similar to that which you've learned over the past days, you will notice some differences in the completely integrated circle.

What You'll Need:

- A bowl of hot water in which you infuse dried hyssop
- Your dish of salt
- Your bowl of water
- Fire candle
- Air incense
- Four quarter candles
- Self-lighting charcoal
- A thurible

- Your unconsecrated athame, wand, chalice, and pentacle
- An asperges—a ritual device Witches use to sprinkle a mixture of salt and water; the asperges is usually a bundle of either fresh or dried herbs; the best herb choice is rosemary
- Anointing oil (which can be any essential oil you choose, but for best magical effect try lavender, rosemary, or hyssop essential oil)
- Simple sweet cakes (muffins, scones, sweet breads)
- Wine (or as an alternative, fruit juice)
- A libation bowl

Prior to beginning a full circle casting ritual, heat a cup of water. In the hot water, steep two teaspoons of dried hyssop. Sprinkle this infusion all over your body to cleanse it magically prior to the ritual. Another method of magical body cleansing is to bathe in an entire bathtub full of the hyssop infusion.

A Word to the Wise: Hyssop is the traditional herb that Witches use to spiritually cleanse their bodily energies prior to a ritual. You can also anoint yourself with hyssop essential oil as an alternative to the infusion.

When you are finished with ritual cleansing, wear your robe or other magical clothing. You may also choose to engage in this rite skyclad—which means ritually disrobed.

Set all of your magical tools on the central altar. Lay out the quarter candles at each of the four compass points and light them.

Begin the circle casting by standing in the eastern quarter of your circle. Face the circle's perimeter, hold out your arms and say:

I awaken the Power to Know!

Repeat this at the southern edge of your circle, saying:

I awaken the Power to Will!

Repeat this in the west, saying:

I awaken the Power to Dare!

Repeat this in the north, saying:

I awaken the Power to Be Silent!

Return to the central altar and say:

The Powers of the Elements have been summoned, and the circle binds them as one.

Bless the elements of water and earth. Hold your natural athame over your bowl of water and say:

I consecrate thee, O creature of water,
In the names of the Great Mother and the
Horned Lord.

Hold your natural athame over the dish of salt, saying:

I consecrate thee, O creature of earth,
In the names of the Great Mother and the
Horned Lord.

Use your natural athame to place three scoops of the salt into the water and say:

Water and earth I cast thee 'round,
By thy essence, life be bound.
Flowing vision, holy birth,
Blessed be by water and earth.

Take the bundle of herbs (your asperges) and your bowl of water to the eastern perimeter of your circle. Walk the perimeter deosil, using the herb bundle to sprinkle your salt/water mixture. When you return to the east, bless yourself with the water and salt mixture. While doing so, say:

I am blessed with the elements of water and earth.

If you want to bless someone within your circle, dab some of your water and salt onto their heart, saying:

You are blessed with the elements of water and earth.

Bless the elements of fire and air. Hold your natural athame above the lighted red candle, saying:

I consecrate thee, O creature of fire,
In the names of the Great Mother and the Horned Lord.

Hold your natural athame above the incense, saying:

I consecrate thee, O creature of air,
In the names of the Great Mother and the Horned Lord.

Sprinkle some of the loose incense over the lit charcoal. Once it begins to smolder, say:

Fire and air, I cast thee 'round,
By thy essence, life be bound.
Knowledge of thy true desire,
Blessed be by air and fire.

Take the incense to the eastern edge of the circle. Hold up the incense burner in an offering gesture and walk deosil around the perimeter. Once you return to the east, bless yourself with fire and air (use the incense burner with incense in it, since the lighted charcoal and the incense together represent the blended elements of fire and air), saying:

I am blessed with the elements of fire and air.

If you want to bless someone within your circle, fan some of the incense across the person's heart, saying:

You are blessed with the elements of fire and air.

Bless yourself in the names of the god and goddess with the anointing oil (such as lavender, rosemary, or hyssop essential oil). In this part of the ritual, you can feel free to insert the names of specific deities where I have written "great mother" and "horned lord." If you are not working with specific deity names, simply recite the text below.

Dab a bit of your blessing oil onto your forehead or your heart with your middle finger, drawing a small earth-invoking pentagram. While doing so, say:

I am consecrated in the names of (the great mother) and (the horned lord).

Bless other attendees of your circle similarly.

Go to the eastern edge of your circle, point your natural athame outward, walk deosil, and say:

I summon the Circle, the Circle I summon.
Power, peace, and protection will come in
And bind to the womb of our spiritual birth,
Through air, fire, water, and earth!

Return to the east. Draw the invoking air pentagram, saying:

I summon, stir, and call thee up,
Mighty Ones of the East, Powers of air,
To witness my (our) rites and to seal this circle!

Continue to the southern quarter. Draw the invoking-fire pentagram and say:

I summon, stir, and call thee up,
Mighty Ones of the South, Powers of fire,
To witness my (our) rites and to seal this circle!

Continue to the western quarter. Draw the invoking-water pentagram and say:

I summon, stir, and call thee up,
Mighty Ones of the West, Powers of water,
To witness my (our) rites and to seal this circle!

Continue to the northern quarter. Draw the invoking-earth pentagram and say:

I summon, stir, and call thee up,
Mighty Ones of the North, Powers of earth,
To witness my (our) rites and to seal this circle!

Stand at your central altar, facing the south. Hold your hands in the triangles of manifestation positions, then say:

You who have been from beginning to end,
My (our) rites and mysteries now attend.

Most ancient of Maidens, Mothers, and
Crones,
Lord of the Hoof, of Antlers and Bones.
Where earth meets sun, and wind meets sea,
I (we) summon you forth, so mote it be!

If you have a magical working or a sabbat/esbat celebration, this is where you would practice it. At the conclusion of your magic or celebration, you would proceed to the circle closing. For today, sit for a few moments in silence within the circle you have cast and regard this sacred space as an extension of your own life. When you feel ready, proceed to closing the circle, which begins with cakes and wine.

To begin, pour some wine into your chalice and set it on the altar. Hold your natural athame with the blade pointed to the sky and say:

Now we'll feast in the Old Ones' names,
Then fetch thy besom and hie thee hame.
To the north, to the west,
To the south, to the east,
Blessed Be the sacred feast!

Now turn the point of the athame down, hold it just above the wine-filled chalice, and say:

Gracious goddess, lend thy hand,
Gentle lady of the land,
From seed to leaf, from bud to vine,
Mystic mother, bless this wine.

Dip the blade of the athame into the cup and say:

Blade and vessel so combined,
The lovers' limbs are thus entwined.
Blend and merge divine duet,
Where the blade and cup have met!

Next, place the cakes upon your pentacle and touch the tip of the athame to each, saying:

Lord of living, lord of dead,
King of field and grain and bread,
Of this life we must partake,
Horned Hunter bless this cake.

Pass cakes to each group member, saying:

May you never hunger.

Pass the chalice around for each member to drink, or fill each participant's chalice with wine, saying:

May you never thirst.

Place a small portion of your food and drink into the libation bowl as an offering to the deities present. After you have eaten, stand at the center of the circle facing south and say:

Witches all, our rites conclude
In merriment, the earth renewed.
The cock doth crow the end of night,
We thank the gods who've joined our rite.

Pause in silence, thanking the gods for attending and bidding them farewell.

To all I charge thee lock away,
Our magics and our mystery play.
Then raise a toast, a hearty draught,
To bid the gods preserve the Craft!

Take your athame to the eastern perimeter of the circle and face outward. Draw a banishing-air pentagram, saying:

Hail, ye Mighty Ones of the East!
We thank thee for attending,
And 'ere ye depart for your lovely realms,
I (we) say hail and farewell!

Take your athame to the southern perimeter of the circle and face outward. Draw a banishing-fire pentagram, saying:

Hail ye Mighty Ones of the South!
We thank thee for attending,
And 'ere ye depart for your lovely realms,
I (we) say hail and farewell!

Take your athame to the western perimeter of the circle and face outward. Draw a banishing-water pentagram, saying:

Hail, ye Mighty Ones of the West!
We thank thee for attending,
And 'ere ye depart for your lovely realms,
I (we) say hail and farewell!

Take your athame to the northern perimeter of the circle and face outward. Draw a banishing-earth pentagram, saying:

Hail, ye Mighty Ones of the North!
We thank thee for attending,
And 'ere ye depart for your lovely realms,
I (we) say hail and farewell!

Return to face the east. Hold your athame out and begin to walk widdershins around the perimeter of the circle, saying:

Earth will crumble our circle,
Water will cause it to fall,
Fire will burn what's left in the urn,
And the winds will scatter them all!

Return to the east and face inward toward the altar, and say:

The circle is open, but unbroken.
Merry meet, merry part, and
merry meet again!

This concludes the ritual. Quickly and silently store away all ritual tools and artifacts. Flush ritual salt, water, and used incense in running water. Empty the libation bowl on the bare earth.

Day 245

Contemplative Day: Sacred Balance

Meditative Question: Where do you find sacred balance?

Candle: Blue-green

Direction: Northwest

Looking for balance is not easy. Many of us search for it in our daily lives. Do we find balance at our work? How about at home? Is it in the sacred life or in secular activities? Moreover, what is balanced and what isn't? The spiritual search for balance can produce deep insights.

To begin, find a comfortable meditative sitting position in a quiet space while facing the southwest. Light a blue-green candle and sit approximately two feet away from the flame. Next, cast your gaze upon the flickering candle and hold the question firmly for 20 to 30 minutes.

You may not arrive at a magically satisfactory conclusion in one sitting alone, so to manifest a greater depth of answer, it will be important to see this question as it actualizes in each of your activities. Become one with it in each of your tasks. Allow your body, mind, and spirit to become this question as you eat, sleep, work, and play. Over time, a shift in your perception will take place and you will realize your own answer.

Day 246

Devotional Day: Honoring Cernunnos

Table of Correspondences: Cernunnos

Symbols: Antlers, animal figures, animal pelts, serpents, pine cones, fire, the erect phallus, the sun

Tools: The athame, the sword

Magical Essences/Herbs: Musk, benzoin, and frankincense

Direction: South

He Rules: Strength, agility, assertiveness, decisiveness, wild animals, sexuality, and knowledge of all earthly things

Animal Symbols: Stag

Sacred Foods: Wild meats and whole-grain breads

Magical Stones: Amber, tiger-eye

Cernunnos (pronounced *ker-NOO-nos*) is a Celtic god who is the archetype of pure, active male energy. He is the male divinity that Witches most commonly invoke in their rites. Scholars first identified his name when they discovered it inscribed on various shrines and altars found throughout excavations of Old European sacred sites. Cernunnos is the horned god of the animals and his name appears to be closely related to the Italian word *corno*, which is related to *horns.* There also appears to be a link between the gods Cernunnos and Herne. Celtic artists depicted Herne/Cernunnos on the Gundestrup cauldron, sitting in a meditative position and surrounded by animals. It is from this image that contemporary mythologists derive his association with the animal world. Cernunnos traditionally governs animals and the wild hunt; he is the archetype of men in their full strength.

The energies that Cernunnos brings to you are physical agility, assertiveness, decisiveness, the powers of wild animals, and knowledge of all earthly things. Cernunnos' sacred symbols are antlers, animal figures (especially horned or antlered ones), animal pelts, serpents, pinecones, fire, and the sun. Cernunnos' magical colors are brown, black, woad-blue (navy), and gold. His magical essences and herbs are musk, benzoin, and frankincense. The time of the day that you can easily evoke the presence of Cernunnos is noon. Wild meats and harvest-grain breads are Cernunnos' sacred foods.

Cernunnos Practice

Make an altar honoring Cernunnos that includes his sacred symbols. Light appropriately colored candles and intone his name slowly, one syllable at a time (pronounced: *ker-NOO-nos*) until you feel his presence surrounding you. Once he has arrived, spend time contemplating how you might serve this deity. Take time to ask Cernunnos what it would mean to live life through his energy, and listen for his answer. Contemplate how you might live your life if you were an expression of unfettered wildness.

Spend the day honoring this god by attending to your wild instincts.

Day 247

Day of Silence and Review

As you observe silence today, focus your attention on your sense of smell. This may be difficult to do for extended periods of time, so throughout your day, find 10 to 20 minute intervals during which you will be able to focus your attention on what it is you smell in your immediate environment. Do you smell your body? Do you smell other people? Do you savor the smell of your food? When the day is complete, answer these questions:

- What was it like to focus my attention on my sense of smell?
- Am I a person who reacts strongly to environmental smells?
- In what way did my sense of smell impact my thoughts, emotions, or spirit?
- How does what I smell affect my physical energy?

Review

- For today's practice, take time to ask yourself the following:
- Of the information I have learned up to now, what stands out most as vital?
- What information seems least relevant to my spiritual development?
- Which of the practices seemed to move me spiritually, and which had little impact?
- Of the information I have learned so far, what would be best to review? (Take time to review it now.)

Day 248

Consecrating Your Athame

Now that you have learned how to cast the circle, it is time to consecrate each of your magical tools. Consecration involves both blessing the tool and dedicating it to the gods. If you were trained with an established coven or an initiated priest/ess, most likely you would have consecrated your tools under their direction immediately after you obtained or made them. However, since this book supposes that you are learning on your own, your tool consecration is occurring after you have learned how to forge your own circle.

The athame is always the first tool that the Witch consecrates.

What You'll Need:

- Your usual circle-casting tools and sacred object
- Fire incense (or use frankincense)
- Fire oil (or one of the following essential oils: cinnamon, bergamot, clove, orange, or pennyroyal)
- A deep bowl of earth

A Word to the Wise: Frankincense is a useful, all-purpose incense. If you have no other incense blend prepared, use it alone.

To begin, prepare a small altar at the southernmost point of your sacred space. Cast your magic circle (see Day 244). Once the circle is cast, transfer your pentacle, incense burner, incense, fire candle, essential oil, and water, and salt bowls from the central main altar to the altar you have prepared in the south of your circle. Set the athame on your pentacle, kneel before the altar with your arms open to the sky, and say:

Lady and lord, god and goddess,
I bring before you this athame, ready to
Receive your blessing, that it may ever
Be guided by your hands—in the ways of
nature.

Sprinkle water on the athame from hilt to blade-point and say:

Consecrated are you with the element of water.

Take a small portion of salt in your hand and rub it onto the hilt and blade, saying:

Consecrated are you with the element of earth.

Place a small amount of the fire incense onto the hot coals of your censer. Hold the athame over the smoke and say:

Consecrated are you with the element of air.

Hold the tip of the athame in the flame of the fire candle for 10–15 seconds. While it is there say:

From fire, fire is made. Consecrated are you
with the element of fire, your brother.

Plunge the tip of the athame into the bowl of water and hold it there until the blade is completely cooled.

Finally, hold the athame between the palms of your hands and imagine that you fill it with your own life energy.

Rub the blade with fire oil, saying:

Consecrated are you in the art magical.

Your athame is now consecrated. Plunge the blade into the deep bowl of earth and allow it to stay there for twenty-four hours. Close your circle as usual, and use the athame in your ritual work from now on.

A Word to the Wise: One other traditional way of "charging" the athame is by rubbing it with a magnetic lodestone. This practice reputedly increases the athame's ability to attract whatever the holder desires.

Day 249

Wand Consecration

What You'll Need:

- Your usual circle-casting tools and sacred objects
- Air incense (or if you do not have that prepared, use frankincense or white copal)
- Air oil (or one of the following essential oils: bergamot, sage, star anise, or lemon verbena)

To begin, prepare a small altar at the easternmost point of your sacred space. Cast your circle as usual. *This time use your newly consecrated athame to cast the circle.* Once the circle is cast, transfer your pentacle, incense burner, fire candle, incense, essential oil, water, and salt bowls to the altar placed in the east of your circle. Set the wand on your pentacle, kneel before the altar with your arms open to the sky, and say:

Lady and lord, god and goddess,
I bring before you this wand, ready to
Receive your blessing, that it may ever
Be guided by your hands—in the ways of
nature.

Sprinkle water on the wand and say:

Consecrated are you with the element of water.

Take a small portion of salt in your hand and rub it onto the wand, saying:

Consecrated are you with the element of earth.

Place a small amount of the air incense onto the hot coals of your censure. Hold the wand over the smoke and say:

From air, air is made. Consecrated are you
with the element of air, your brother.

Hold the wand above the flame of the fire candle. While it is there, say:

Consecrated are you with the element of fire.

Finally, hold the wand between the palms of your hands. Close your eyes and imagine that the energies of your body, mind, and spirit channel through your hands and enter into the wand. Rub the wand with air oil, then hold the tip of the athame blade to the wand and say:

Consecrated are you in the art magical.

Your wand is now consecrated. Close your circle as usual.

Day 250

Chalice Consecration

What You'll Need:

- Your usual circle-casting tools and sacred objects
- Water incense (if you do not have that prepared, use frankincense or sandalwood)
- Water oil (or one of the following essential oils: apple, jasmine, rose, or water lily)

To begin, prepare a small altar at the westernmost point of your sacred space. Cast your circle as usual. Once the circle is cast, transfer your pentacle, incense burner, fire candle, incense, essential oil, and water and salt bowls to the altar in the west of your circle. Set the chalice on your pentacle, kneel before the altar with your arms open to the sky, and say:

Lady and lord, god and goddess,
I bring before you this chalice, ready to
Receive your blessing, that it may ever
Be guided by your hands—in the ways of
nature.

Sprinkle water on the chalice and say:

From water, water is made.
Consecrated are you with the element
of water, your sister.

Take a small portion of salt in your hand and rub it onto the cup, saying:

Consecrated are you with the element of earth.

Place a small amount of the water incense onto the hot coals of your censer. Hold the chalice over the smoke and say:

Consecrated are you with the element of air.

Hold the cup above the flame of the fire candle. While it is there, say:

Consecrated are you with the element of fire.

Finally, hold the chalice between the palms of your hands. Close your eyes and imagine that the energies of your body, mind, and spirit flow through your hands and enter into the cup.

Rub the chalice with water oil. Hold the tip of the athame to the cup and say:

> ***Consecrated are you in the art magical.***

Your chalice is now consecrated. Close your circle as usual.

Day 251

Pentacle Consecration

What You'll Need:

- Your usual circle casting tools and sacred objects.
- earth incense (or if you do not have that prepared, use frankincense or oak)
- Earth oil (or one of the following essential oils: patchouli, honeysuckle, tulip, or lilac)

To begin, prepare a small altar at the northernmost point of your sacred space. Cast your circle as usual. Once the circle is cast, transfer your pentacle, incense burner, fire candle, incense, essential oil, water and salt bowls to the north altar. Set the pentacle in front of you, kneel before the altar with your arms open to the sky, and say:

> ***Lady and lord, god and goddess,***
> ***I bring before you this pentacle, ready to***
> ***Receive your blessing, that it may ever***
> ***Be guided by your hands—in the ways of***
> ***nature.***

Sprinkle water on the pentacle and say:

> ***Consecrated are you with the element of water.***

Take a small portion of salt in your hand and rub it onto the pentacle, saying:

> ***From earth, earth is made. Consecrated are***
> ***you with the element of earth, your sister.***

Place a small amount of the earth incense onto the hot coals of your censer. Hold the pentacle over the smoke and say:

> ***Consecrated are you with the element of air.***

Hold the pentacle above the flame of the fire candle. While it is there, say:

> ***Consecrated are you with the element of fire.***

Finally, hold the pentacle between the palms of your hands. Close your eyes and imagine that the energies of your body, mind, and spirit flow through your hands and enter into the pentacle.

Rub the pentacle with earth oil. Touch the tip of the athame to the pentacle, saying:

Consecrated are you in the art magical.

Your pentacle is now consecrated. Close your circle as usual.

Day 252

Magic

The early twentieth-century mystic Dion Fortune stated that magic was "the ability to change consciousness at will." This definition contains a central Wiccan axiom, that of *changing consciousness*—or changing your mind. That definition represents a big shift in awareness for many readers who are new to the magical arts, and who may believe some of the more popularized notions of the magical arts. In the popular mind, magic is a practice aimed at getting the things that you want from the world, and while magic may start for many newcomers as a practice through which they can focus on and achieve their personal goals, it is ultimately a process through which they align with the whole of nature. When one aligns with nature, the whole of life, nature yields its bounty. When the Witch shifts consciousness from the personal mind to the universal mind, the infinitesimal thing that the Witch focused on attaining fades quickly into the background. What comes to the fore is the understanding that people and things are not separate; that all is interconnected. The thing you want is already a part of you and there is nothing that impedes your attainment.

The most appropriate term that defines Wiccan magic is *transformation.* Magic transforms your position to the world through altering the mind. In other words, once you change your mind, you transform how you interact with the world. If you have an angry mind, you will interact with the world in one way. If you have a grasping mind, you will interact in another way. If you have thoughts of loneliness, you act in yet another way altogether. When you change your position to the world, then the world, your environment, changes how it interacts with you.

Wiccan magic is not grandiose, sparkling, and flamboyant. It is not about miraculous quick fixes in your life. Instead, Wiccan magic is a modest, measured, quiet, and natural practice. Wiccan magic works as subtly as the sun rising and setting. It is difficult to know when exactly the shadow of a tree shifted from east to west during the course of a day. The sun's progress is natural, smooth, and understated—just as it may be difficult to know when exactly a plant bud becomes a leaf and then a flower. In nature, in magic, and in your own life, the final outcome is not as important as the process. Magic is the process that shifts your consciousness and then shifts the circumstances of your life.

Witches engage the powers of magic through spells. A spell is an act that symbolizes a Witch's desired change. Symbolism is key to Wiccan magic. Symbols bridge the worlds of the conscious and unconscious minds. The conscious mind is the part of you that knows language and is able to think in linear, sensible ways. It knows and respects the learned rules and traditions of a culture. The unconscious is the deeper, more powerful realm of the mind. Dreams, nonlinear and nonverbal thought, and creativity spring forth from the unconscious. The unconscious knows only the rules of the cosmos, the rules of unfettered nature. Magic takes root here in the fertile ground of the unconscious mind. Because the unconscious mind is nonverbal, spells rely on symbols. Because this realm of mind is nonlinear, the most powerful spells are those that a practitioner improvises using symbolic objects and tools that come into hand at any given moment.

In preparing for a spell, a Witch collects symbols that she feels confident will harness the energies of her mind, body, earth, and spirit. Many Witches create their own magical symbols for their spells; however, there is a great body of magical lore surrounding traditional symbolic correspondences. These correspondences include stones, fragrances, potions, colors, numbers, plants, times of day, and special images. As you learn about many of these traditional correspondences, keep in mind that a magical symbol is anything that holds meaning for you. It needs to speak to and open the contents of *your* deep, unconscious mind. Your magical symbols should help you feel connected in some way to your desire.

The next step of Wiccan magic is when the Witch directs spiritual energy through her collected symbols. Finally, the Witch should take practical action in order to obtain her goals. Magic is not about lighting candles and mumbling a chant, hoping that these symbolic acts will in and of themselves cause change. They won't. You must act practically in order to produce discernible change.

The three components of Wiccan magic that you will learn over the next days include:

1. Gathering symbols that will attract a desired goal
2. Timing the spell to coincide with influential planetary and lunar tides
3. Raising and directing spiritual energy

It is important for you to know that there are entire books devoted exclusively to the subject of magic, and ours is only a brief introduction to the topic. The magical arts are a discipline in and of themselves. They take years of training, contemplation, and steady practice before one masters the art fully.

It is common for first-year Witches to expect dramatic change, and to experience something else altogether. When your magic appears not to have taken effect, keep reminding yourself that magic is equivalent to the changing of seasons; it is slow and organic. First comes the planting of seeds, then tiny roots form, tender shoots appear, and gradually blossoms appear. For today's practice, contemplate the following questions:

- Is magic what you thought it would be?
- What were you hoping you would be able to do with magic?
- What influences do you think might have shaped your ideas about magic?

Day 253

The Law of Threefold Return & The Wiccan Rede

Did you know that magic has its own law? It most certainly does. The law of magic emerges from the principle of *karma*. For readers new to this term, karma is a principle that emerges from the mystic practices of India. The principle of karma is old enough to predate Buddhism and one can find its roots in the earliest of yogic practices, in the religion of the Jains and in the *Upanishads*. Karma is a Sanskrit word meaning "action." The law of karma is plain and pragmatic: for each action there is a reaction. Nothing could be simpler.

A Word to the Wise: Wicca is not an ancient practice that evolved from solely Western occult sources. It is a reconstructed path. It is likely that Gerald Gardner, one of the principal founding figures of contemporary Wicca, was involved with Aleister Crowley, another dominant figure in Edwardian England's occult scene. Both Gardner and Crowley appear to have been influenced by the writings and teachings of Theosophy (a system founded by Madam Blavatsky), a forerunner of today's New Age movement, which included many Eastern principles. It is likely that Gardner and other shapers of contemporary Wicca included the concept of karma in Wicca to serve as a non-Abrahamic model for guiding practitioners in positive magical practice. The Eastern origins of the term karma are irrelevant to our contemporary practice, as Wiccans adapt and adopt truth from many disparate paths. The truth of this principle is that whatever you do has an effect, and that effect returns to you.

Since the rebirth of Witchcraft in the 1950s, contemporary Witches have adopted the principle of karma and they have incorporated it into magical practice. Not only that, but Witches take the concept of karma a step further than originally intended and believe in the *Law of Threefold Return.* This spiritual law holds that whatever forces one magically sets in motion will return to its original source threefold. Naturally, Witches direct magic toward positive ends. Healing, blessing, bringing about positive change are all *workings* of the Witch. These same energies return to the Witch and empower her life. Witches avoid harmful practices because they know that harmful magic harms everyone. Harmful magic usually centers around controlling people in some way, or forcing nature to comply with the individual will.

Some decades ago, due to popularized versions of Witchcraft, it was fashionable to classify the forms of magic by color. In Wicca's earliest days, Witches called constructive forms of magic "white magic" and they called the destructive forms "black magic." The hierarchies implied by these terms (racial and otherwise) have caused people to abandon their use.

A Word to the Wise: Witches commonly refer to magic in terms of "spells" or "workings."

There also exists a third category of magic that is neither constructive nor destructive. Witches call these more neutral workings "bindings" and they practice this form of magic in order to stop people from harming themselves, other people, animals, or the environment.

The Wiccan Rede

The Wiccan Rede is the Witches' code for both living life and for working magic. The Rede states, "An it harm none, do as ye will." The Rede, although only a few short words, presents Witches with complex issues that require careful consideration. The central issue that stirs the Witches' cauldron of questions concerns the sentiment of "harming none." At first blush, the statement seems simple enough. We are bade to work magic and to live without creating harm. However, as we consider the rede deeply, it becomes a puzzle. How, in fact, do we live without harming? As we had learned at Lammas, one of the central mysteries of living is that life feeds upon itself. But is our life condition itself a state of perpetual harm? Is it possible for us to live without causing harm to anything or anyone else? At its most basic level, we can see that life consumes itself at every turn. The key to unlocking this riddle is in our conceptualization of harm. When we consider the ultimate reality—that we are all part of the same unit, we are "one"—harm is impossible. Nothing ever lives and nothing ever dies ultimately, simply because there never was anything "individual" or separate that could live or die. Yet even as we keep this one rather "ultimate" aspect of reality in mind, we also find that we live in a temporal reality where life and death do exist. The Rede reminds us to bear in mind both aspects of reality, and to therefore be mindful of our intentions, our words and our actions as we live our lives in each moment.

- Describe a time when you *wished* for something either positive or negative and your wish came true. What were the results on your life?
- An old Gypsy saying warns, "Be careful of what you wish for; it may come true." Why might this saying be important for us to consider?
- Spend time today considering a positive spell you would like to cast. Consider all of the possibilities and outcomes of this spell. Is this spell truly positive for all concerned? Is there an element of "controlling" in this spell? How might this spell advance you spiritually?
- Can you think of a time where a negative magical working would be necessary? Why? What would it be? What might be the result?
- How might you rework the negative spell in a positive way?
- Do ethics belong in magic? Why?

Practice: Theban Alphabet

Witches often inscribe candles and parchment paper for spiritual work using magical alphabets. The Theban alphabet is one channeled by Honorious in the sixteenth century. The alphabet was then transcribed by Francis Barrett in his work *The Magus*.[81] For today's practice, learn the alphabet and use a red pen to inscribe your name. Inscribe words for the things you would like in your life or in the world, such as love, peace, prosperity, etc.

A	H	O	V
B	I	P	W
C	J	Q	X
D	K	R	Y
E	L	S	Z
F	M	T	
G	N	U	

Day 254

The Moon and Magic

As you have learned so far in your year and a day's study, timing is an important part of Wiccan practice. Witches pay heed to the seasons, the time of day, and the position of the sun and moon, since these directly affect their calendar of spiritual celebrations and rituals. In magical work, this is no less true. The moon plays a significant role in the timing of magical operations. Not only does the phase of the moon carry a symbolic quality that influences magical operations, but it exerts tangible energetic influences on our bodies and upon the earth itself. Because the moon affects the body, it also affects human consciousness. Whatever ripples one feels in consciousness are also sent like waves into the field of magical energy.

But how does the moon affect magic? Each phase of the moon holds specific symbolic and energetic influences that can aid in the success of your spells. Here are the important lunar phases and their magical significance.

Waxing Moon

The period from a dark moon (no visible moon in the sky) to a full moon is best for spells concerning birth, beginnings, foundation, increase, gain, construction, creation, accomplishment, progress, development, commencement, growth, improvement, expansion, and flourishing.

Full Moon

Although almanac listings state only one night of the full moon, Witches believe that there are three full moon nights. These three nights include the day prior and the day following the actual almanac listing. The full moon is suited for spells concerning achievement, triumph, victory, success, conquest, realization, command, control, influence, authority, attainment, fulfillment, power, strength, psychic ability, and magical prowess.

Waning Moon

The period from when the moon is full to when it is no longer visible is the waning cycle. The waning moon is the tide for spells concerning ending, concluding, inhibiting, hindrance, transformation, holding, returning, stopping, internalizing, loss, defeat, failure, blocking, interrupting, dwindling, diminishing, collecting, altering, and replenishment.

If you own a computer with a modem and know a bit about accessing the Internet, the following is a web page where you can find the current lunar phase, as well as the time of sun and moon-rise for any day of the year: http://skyandtelescope.com/observing/almanac/. If you prefer, check the almanac section of your local newspaper.

- This evening, go outside to observe the moon. Lie on your back and gaze into the sky. Allow the lunar light and energy to pour down upon you. What effect does it seem to have on you?
- What is the moon's current phase?
- What kinds of magic could you do on a night like tonight?

Day 255

The Ingredients of Magic

"Like attracts like" is one of the key axioms of Witch magic, meaning that if you can symbolize your desire, you *personify* its essence. Magical theory says once you have personified the essence of your desire, you can attract the desirable situation itself.

The key to success in magical operations is in gathering together the symbols that subtly, vibrationally attract your desire. There are many traditional symbols (and items) that correlate to specific magical outcomes. Many of these symbolic items include stones, herbs, colors, and herbal essences. Gathering together just the right symbols can make or break a spell and Witches take great care to choose their symbols wisely. Our task over the next days is to learn the traditional

The Colors of Magic

Color	*Traditional Correlations*	*Planetary Influence*
White	Purity, spirituality, honesty, spiritual cleansing, virtue, goodness, perfection, unity	All Planets
Yellow	Knowledge, communication, the arts, mental acuity, charm, confidence—	Mercury
Orange	Happiness: joy, stimulation, adaptability, resilience, tolerance	Jupiter
Red	Physical energy, passion, strength, vitality, motivation, sexuality, movement, men's power, men's mysteries, anger, intensity, drive, ambition, achievement	Mars
Pink	Friendship, love, warmth, kindness, morality, forgiveness, affection, the heart, tenderness, intimacy, marriage, relationships	Venus
Purple	Psychic power, attainment, divinity, worldly power, influence, accomplishment, fulfillment—	Uranus, Pluto
Blue	Peace, tranquility, soothing, cycles, moods, emotions, balancing, healing, comfort, sleep-inducing, calming	Neptune
Green	Growth, fertility, money, finances, prosperity, healing, hope, women's power, women's concerns, birth, midwifery, sharing, bonding, the earth	Earth, Venus
Black	Binding, holding, returning, stopping, ending, internalizing, loss, blocking, interrupting, dwindling, collecting, changing, renewing, transforming	Saturn
Brown	Solidity, manifestation, grounding, business, work, strength, stability, honor, endurance	Earth, Saturn
Gray	Neutralizing, counterbalancing, canceling, confusing	All planets in retrograde (or reversed movement)
Gold	Solar power, success, power, generosity, material wealth, the god	Sun
Silver	Lunar power, money, psychic ability, magic, change, spirituality, the goddess	Moon

symbols of magical practice and to commit them to memory.

The Colors of Magic

The chart on page 262 contains a list of magical colors that Witches commonly believe to possess both symbolic and occult, vibrational power. Through the correct color selection of candles, robes, room lighting, and so forth, Witches can highly influence their magical operations. Along with each color, I have noted traditional magical correlations. Again, your task today is to review this list and commit it to memory.

Choosing Colors for a Purpose

- Think of a specific magical working you would like to do. Which color would be most appropriate for the working?
- What planetary association goes with that color?
- Wear a specific color today for its magical effect. Did the color affect anything?

Ways to Use Color in a Spell

- Choose a candle of the color that represents your goal
- Write your goal in an ink of a corresponding color
- Wear clothing of the color that represents your goal
- Write your goal on paper of the color that represents your goal
- Visualize yourself surrounded by an energy field of the color that represents your goal

DAY 256

Days of the Week and Magic

An important element for you to consider in your magical timing is the day of the week. Each day of the week corresponds with a planetary influence. Each planetary influence carries attributes that can help with specific magical outcomes. On page 264 is a chart of the days of the week that describes how they correspond with the planetary influences and the types of magical work that would be successful on each day.

A Word to the Wise: A glyph is a symbol that represents or embodies certain spiritual or magical principles.

- What day of the week is it today? Considering only the day of the week, determine what kinds of magical workings would be successful if employed today.
- Think of a magical effect you would like to have. Now consider: 1) Which day of the week would best suit the magic? 2) Which phase of the moon would best suit the magic? 3) Which color would best suit the magic? Research when the moon phase coincides with a day of the week that can aid in your magic.
- Create flash cards to help you commit the weekdays and planetary glyphs to memory. (A glyph is a symbol that represents or embodies certain spiritual or magical principles.

Ways to Use Planetary Glyphs in a Spell

- Inscribe a candle of the color that represents your goal with its corresponding planetary glyph.
- Draw a planetary glyph that represents your goal on paper and carry it with you.
- Visualize the planetary glyph glowing inside of you or someone else.

Day 257

Magical Stones

Witches believe that certain precious stones possess specific magical powers. Hermeticists of the Middle Ages believed that stones were conduits of planetary energies. Ancient alchemists worked with these influences in a highly specialized manner in order to obtain the Philosopher's Stone. This was a key substance that was alleged to enable alchemists to spiritually transform one material into another (such as turning lead into gold). The practitioners of these arts developed elaborate tables of correspondence that classified stones by their occult powers. It is from these traditions that contemporary Witches trace their magical practices with stones. In Wiccan magic, a Witch can incorporate stones in specific spells, or she can carry them for their vibrational influences, set them into jewelry, ritual tools, or altar decorations.

Below is a list of the stones that Witches use most commonly in their spells. There are many other stones with magical influences. Your task today is to review this list and commit as much of it to memory as possible.

Adamant: Brings joy in all things

Agate: Protects against venomous bites, improves vigor, calms storms

Amber: Soothes the disposition, prevents disease, improves sight

Magical Correspondences to Days of the Week

Day of the Week	*Planetary Alignment*	*Planetary Glyph (or symbol)*	*Magical Workings*
Monday	Moon	☾	Purity, spirituality, honesty, spiritual cleansing, virtue, goodness, perfection, unity, lunar power, money, psychic ability, magic, change, spirituality, invoking the goddess' aid, childbirth
Tuesday	Mars	♂	Physical energy, passion, strength, vitality, motivation, sexuality, movement, men's power, men's mysteries, anger, intensity, drive, ambition, achievement
Wednesday	Mercury	☿	Knowledge, communication, the arts, mental acuity, charm, confidence, change, adaptability, acceptance
Thursday	Jupiter	♃	Luck, expansion, growth, honor, attainment, worldly power, influence, accomplishment, fulfillment
Friday	Venus and Earth	♀	Fertility, money, prosperity, healing, hope, women's power, women's mysteries, sharing, bonding, the arts, grace, charm, appeal, goodness
Saturday	Saturn	♄	The law, limitations, binding, holding, returning, stopping, ending, internalizing, dwindling, blocking, interrupting, loss, collecting, changing, renewing, transforming
Sunday	Sun	☉	Solar power, success, personal empowerment, generosity, material wealth, immortality, spirituality, health, vitality, invoking the god's aid

Amethyst: Pleasant dreams, psychic powers, maintains chastity or celibacy

Aquamarine: Courage, nimble mind and actions, stops procrastination

Azurite: Meditation, divination

Bloodstone: Wisdom, recognition, long life, place under pillow for prophetic dreams

Carnelian: Stimulates the conscious mind, movement, stops negative energy, solar power

Chalcedony: Protects against spells, home protection, healing

Copper: Conducts/directs energy, stabilizes energy

Coral: Protection against evil, promotes true love

Diamond: Truth, loyalty, protection from spirits, helps troubled relationships, wisdom

Emerald: Channels power, fulfillment, peace, calming, exposes deceit and evil

Garnet: Love, sex, friendships

Gold: Accomplishment, wealth, achievement, immortality, attunement with the god

Jade: Gives one a "green thumb," helps with kidney ailments, aids plant growth

Jet: Banishes evil spirits and evil forces

Lodestone: Attracting desires, draws off energy that causes illness

Lapis Lazuli: Bounty, alchemy, psychic protection, protection by Mother Earth

Lead: Grounding, centering, reality

Moonstone: Dreams, psychic visions, invokes the aid of the moon goddess

Obsidian: Control over magical forces

Onyx: Neutralizes negative energy; depending on use, creates or breaks friendships

Opal: Raises magical power

Pearl: Peace, wisdom, acquired knowledge

Quartz (clear): Divination, transmits/receives energies, draws desires

Rose Quartz: Love, beauty, positive energy

Tourmaline Quartz: Astral projection

Amethyst Quartz: Directs magical power

Ruby: Health, strength, peaceful heart

Sapphire: Truthfulness in speech, spiritual attainment

Silver: Moon magic, balance of feminine energy

Topaz: Promotes physical beauty, joy, happiness

Turquoise: Protection from all harm, protection from evil magic, banishes negativity

Ways to Use Stones in a Spell

- Choose a stone that represents your goal and carry it around with you
- Paint a planetary glyph on a corresponding magical stone and place it somewhere prominent
- Wear jewelry embedded with magical stones that represent your goal
- Lying down, place the stones that represent your magical goal on each of your chakra points

---

A Word to the Wise: Many Witches discover an increase in their magical potency when they gather a number of matching magical correspondences that are related to their intended working, but quantity is never a substitute for quality. A high number of magical correspondences do not automatically guarantee a spell's success. It is the Witch's intent and focus that causes change. The symbols only aid Witches in the focusing process.

Consider a magical working you would like to do. Name the following symbols you might use for this working:

- Moon phase
- Day of the week
- Color
- Planetary glyph

- Magical stone:
- What keyword would you write in Theban on a candle or other magical object?

Exploring Magical Stones

- Have you ever experienced the magical influences of a stone? Discuss it in writing or with a friend.
- How might you use one of the stones listed here today?

In a small pouch, place one or two stones that hold a magical influence that you desire. Place the pouch on a string and wear it around your neck, or place the pouch somewhere that allows it to have close bodily contact. Monitor the effects of the stone and journal about your experiences.

A Word to the Wise: Magic is not a game. Never use magical symbols or objects to "test" their effects. This diminishes their potency in your magical practice. Passive use of magical objects and symbols often backfires on the user, resulting in an array of misfortune. The untamed natural energies inherent in magical objects and symbols require the Witch's strong directed intent in order to channel them into a proper effect.

Day 258

Magical Herbs

Herbs play an important role in magical work, as you have come to learn throughout your training. Herbs form the basis of many magical incenses, oils, and potions. Witches believe that herbs are living vibrational representations of specific magical influences. Because they are living, they carry great strength and hold their own spiritual power. From time immemorial, Witches have used herbs to heal and to create magical change. Below is a list of some traditional Wiccan herbs and their magical uses. Perhaps it was the Witch names for herbs that gave rise to the many dark fantasies of Inquisitors regarding the practices of Witches during the Witch hunts of sixteenth-century Europe.[82]

- Select an herb from the chart on page 267–268 for its magical influence. Hold it in your hands during meditation, or place it somewhere near you during the day. What effects do you note?
- What herbs do you eat in your food? Do they have any magical effect that you can note?
- Start a magical garden and plant herbs that will aid you in your magical work.

Ways to Use Herbs in a Spell

- Choose an herb that represents your goal and carry it with you in a small sachet pouch
- Steep the herb in water and bathe in the water
- Make a potion of the herb by steeping it in a cup of hot water. If the herb is not poisonous, you can drink it for the magical effect, or sprinkle the potion around your home
- Burn the herbs as "incense on hot coals to release their magical influence

Note: In the following chart I discuss only briefly the various herbs and their magical properties. In the coming days you will learn more about herbs in depth

Magical Correspondences and Uses of Herbs

Common Name	*Other Names*	*Witch Name*	*Magical Uses*
Aconite	Wolfsbane, Blue Rocket	Monkshood, Friar's Cap	Magical prowess, creates illusion, magical flight, returning, diminishing
Agrimony	———	Church Steeples	Produces sleep, deep dreaming
Angelica	Masterwort	———	Carried to market to obtain fair dealing, protection from evil
Anise	Chinese Anise	———	Preserves youthful appearance, safety, restful sleep
Basil	St. Josephswort	———	Love, romance, initiation
Bay Laurel	Bay	Daphne	Honor, visions, prophecy
Benzoin	———	———	Inner strength, visions, strong mind
Blessed Thistle	———	Holy Thistle, Witch-Thorn	Invokes Pan, sexuality, removes curses
Chamomile	Plant's Physician	Maythen	Healing, curing, invokes solar power
Cinnamon	———	———	Purification, energy, strength, awareness
Cinquefoil	Five-Finger-Grass	Five-Fingers	Used in flying ointments, enhances all spellwork
Clover	Trefoil	Hare's Foot	Luck, consecration
Comfrey	Healing Herb	Ass's Ear, Blackwort, Knitbone	Placed in shoes to assure safe journeys
Elder	———	Elder-Tree-Mother	Invokes the Mother Goddess, protection against lightning, divination
Eyebright	Euphrasia	———	Psychic balance, visions, clairvoyance
Fennel		Fenkel	Strength, virility, fertility
Ferns	———	———	Invisibility
Foxglove	Fairyglove	Bloody Fingers, Fairy-Caps	Communing with elemental spirits
Hops	Marrubium	———	Dreams, sleep
Horehound	———	———	Opens up creative channels, inspiration
Hyssop	Azob	Holy Herb	Spiritual protection, spiritual cleansing

Magical Correspondences and Uses of Herbs, Cont'd

Common Name	*Other Names*	*Witch Name*	*Magical Uses*
Ivy	Ground Ivy	Cat's Paw	Worn to prevent drunkenness
Juniper	———	———	Invites spirits, tree magic, justice
Lavender	———	———	Calms the nerve; love, honesty
Mandrake	———	Duck's Foot, Satan's Apple	Aids in all magical endeavors, brings the sight, protection
Mistletoe	———	Druid's Herb	Fertility, immortality, prophecy
Mugwort	———	———	Sleep, dreams, prophetic dreams, astral projection
Pennyroyal	Tickweed, Squawmint	Run-by-the-Ground	Consecration, brings spirits of the departed
Pomegranate	Grenadier	———	Women's mysteries, cycles
Rosemary	Incessier	———	House protection, aids memory, eternal youth
Rue	Garden Rue	Herb of Grace	Dismisses evil forces, breaks dark spells
Sage	———	Sawge	Prolongs life, common sense, wisdom, insight
Saint John's Wort	John the Conqueror	High John	Success, power, attainment
Tansy	———	Bitter Buttons	Secrets revealed, underworld journeys, meditation
Yarrow	Bloodwort	Devil's Plaything	Burned for success in tarot or other divination methods

Day 259

Magical Essential Oils

Below is a listing of essential oils that correspond with various magical goals. Commit the list to memory and anoint your clothing or your skin with one of the oils today to benefit from its magical properties. (The type of oil is followed by what it influences.)

Oils and Their Influences

Apple: Love, peace, friendship, spiritual joy

Basil: Energy, passion, physical strength

Bay: Purification, protection

Bergamot: Sleep, control, commanding

Chamomile: Sleep, dreams, prophecy, purification

Cardamom: Sex

Carnation: Magical strength, love, health, transformation

Cedar: Invokes spirits, protection by spiritual forces

Cinnamon: Compelling, drawing, changing, prosperity

Clove: Memory, protection, courage, strength

Clover: Protects animals, summons animal spirits and powers

Cypress: Healing, money, prosperity

Eucalyptus: Purification, business

Fennel: Change, magic, sexuality, communication, the arts

Frankincense: Spiritual understanding, spiritual awareness

Gardenia: Lunar power, emotional strength

Geranium: Happiness, writing, acting, singing, dancing

Honeysuckle: Stability, growth, solidity, slow steady change

Hyssop: Spiritual cleansing

Jasmine: Love, sexuality, sensuality, universal love, dreams

Juniper: Healing, protection, strengthens all magic

Lavender: Health, love, magic, insight, clarity, focus

Lemon: Happiness, energies of the crone, consecration

Myrrh: Meditation, enlightenment, healing sorrow or depression

Nutmeg: Psychic visions, spiritual aid, animal powers

Orange: Joy, energy

Patchouli: Grounding, sexuality, weight control, gain, wealth

Pennyroyal: Protection, reversal of negative energies

Peppermint: Healing, soothing, balancing

Pine: Healing, longevity, youth, strength

Rose: Love, protection from evil, attracts fairies, goddess energies

Rosemary: Improves memory, stimulates and energizes

Sage: Purification, wisdom, mental health

Sandalwood: Meditation, divination, and trance induction

Spikenard: Enables one to learn from karmic circumstances, clears karma

Thyme: Enables one to see the elementals, protection from evil and wild animals, communication with the dead

Yarrow: Banishes anger and hostility, grants one's wishes

Ways to Use Essential Oils in a Spell

- Choose an oil that represents your goal and anoint yourself with it daily, or until you obtain the goal
- Place a few drops of the essential oil in water and sprinkle this around your home
- Anoint a candle of a color that represents your goal with the oil. Then burn the candle

- Mix the essential oil into herbs that correspond to your goal and burn this to release its magical influences
- Anoint a stone or an herb sachet with the oil and carry these with you for an intensified magical effect
- Anoint your chakras with an essential oil that represents your goal
- Place a few drops of the essential oil in bathwater and then bathe in the scented water
- Using the middle finger of your dominant hand, smear the oil to form a planetary glyph or other symbol onto a candle, yourself, or another person

---

A Word to the Wise: Witches call the process of anointing a candle with an essential oil for a magical purpose *dressing* a candle. In order to appropriately dress a candle, dab some oil on your right middle finger. Starting at a point midway between the candle's tip and base, rub the oil clockwise around the candle, spiraling downward to the base. Then anoint the candle, spiraling clockwise upward from the same midway point of the candle to its tip.

DAY 260

Hours of the Day and Magic

Each hour of the day resonates with specific magical energies. In hourly intervals, the planets take turns imparting their specific virtues. Once you know the repeating sequence of planetary hours, you will find it easy to calculate the time of day that might best suit your magical purposes. The repeating pattern of planets is as follows:

Sun	☉	Health, wealth, success, joy, luck, healing
Venus	♀	Love, friendship, relationship, compassion, the arts
Mercury	☿	Magic, knowledge, communication, writing, speech
Moon	☾	Psychic ability, spirituality, goddess energy, divination
Saturn	♄	Work, stability, attention, reversals, impeding, stopping
Jupiter	♃	Luck, expansion, prosperity, money, empire
Mars	♂	Strength, vitality, health, sex, anger, passion

The first hour of each day is ruled by the planet that rules the entire day. Then the sequence of seven planets follows. For example, let's say that on Monday the sunrise will be at 6:30 AM. The planetary influence governing the first hour on Monday (from 6:30 to 7:30) is the same as the planetary ruler for that day of the week, namely the moon. The following hour from 7:30 to 8:30 AM is ruled by Saturn. The hour between 8:30 and 9:30 AM is ruled by Jupiter, and so on. On Tuesday, the hour of sunrise is governed by Mars, then the sequence continues with Sun, then Venus, Mercury, etc. The pattern of seven repeats itself again and again until the twenty-fourth hour of the day. The best source of information regarding the hour of your local sunrise is your newspaper.

Planetary Influences of the Hours

Below is a chart to help you determine the planetary influence of the hour during sunrise to sunset. The chart begins with the first hour of each day and ends with the twelfth hour.

Magical Hours 1 through 12:

Hour	Mon	Tue	Weds	Thur	Fri	Sat	Sun
1	☽	♅	☿	♃	♀	♄	☉
2	♄	☉	☽	♅	☿	♃	♀
3	♃	♀	♄	☉	☽	♅	☿
4	♅	☿	♃	♀	♄	☉	☽
5	☉	☾	♅	☿	♃	♀	♄
6	♀	♄	☉	☽	♅	☿	♃
7	☿	♃	♀	♄	☉	☽	♅
8	☽	♅	☿	♃	♀	♄	☉
9	♄	☉	☽	♅	☿	♃	♀
10	♃	♀	♄	☉	☽	♅	☿
11	♅	☿	♃	♀	♄	☉	☽
12	☉	☾	♅	☿	♃	♀	♄

Here are the hours and planetary influences from the thirteenth hour to the twenty-fourth hour of each weekday.

Magical Hours 13 through 24:

Hour	Mon	Tue	Weds	Thur	Fri	Sat	Sun
13	♀	♄	☉	☽	♅	☿	♃
14	☿	♃	♀	♄	☉	☽	♅
15	☽	♅	☿	♃	♀	♄	☉
16	♄	☉	☽	♅	☿	♃	♀
17	♃	♀	♄	☉	☽	♅	☿
18	♅	☿	♃	♀	♄	☉	☽
19	☉	☾	♅	☿	♃	♀	♄
20	♀	♄	☉	☽	♅	☿	♃
21	☿	♃	♀	♄	☉	☽	♅
22	☽	♅	☿	♃	♀	♄	☉
23	♄	☉	☽	♅	☿	♃	♀
24	♃	♀	♄	☉	☽	♅	☿

- What hour of the day, since sunrise, is it right now?
- Find out the time of sunrise from your newspaper. Consider the day of the week and calculate the magical hour you are in right now.
- What types of magic are best suited for this planetary hour?
- Check the newspaper for tomorrow's sunrise time. What is the planetary influence at this same time tomorrow?

DAY 261

Raising Power

Once you have your spell ingredients and you have selected the proper day, moon phase, and hour, it is time to raise power. You will produce only minimal (if any) magical results if you merely gather raw spell ingredients (candles, oils, incenses, etc.) and rely on magical timing. Raising power is how Witches give their spell ingredients life, energy, and movement.

Contrary to popular notions, raising power does not entail tapping into forbidden or uncontrollable forces. Witches work with nature and the spiritual essences of wind, sea, soil, sun, and moon. Witches also harness the natural energies inherent to the human mind and body.

There are many traditional methods that Witches use to raise natural magical power. However, only four of the methods are useful to readers who are just starting out in Wicca. These four methods are dance/movement, breath control, chanting, and drumming. During the next several days you will learn these methods. It is important to note that no method is better than another; each has its own merits and at least one method will resonate closely with your personality and spiritual style. Through practice, you will discover which methods are most and least effective for you.

Dance and Movement

Although all varieties of dance can facilitate the movement of magical energy, Witches use primarily shamanic forms. One shamanic technique involves the evocation of spontaneous body movement. One traditionally shamanic method that facilitates spontaneous body movement is allowing the mind to follow the metronomic effects of drums. Witches call this drum/dance technique *trance dance*. The wild, unchoreographed, and often primitive trance dance usually leads a participant into a state of consciousness that anthropologists call *ecstasy*. In this heightened state of mind, the dancer loses the sense of self and becomes one with sound and movement. Within this magical state of consciousness, Witches harness spiritual power. When transitioning back from the ecstatic to the ordinary realm of consciousness, a Witch is able to magically use her harnessed power for some desired end.

Practice: Trance Dance

What You'll Need:

- Loose clothing
- Percussive music (preferably with no vocals), or
- Someone to play a percussive instrument while you dance

Warning: *It is extremely important that you avoid trance dancing if you have heart ailments, high-blood pressure, or other restrictive bodily disorders that might result in physical injury. If you are not certain of your condition, consult your physician first.*

A Word to the Wise: Good trance-dance music is not hard to find these days. Search online for the following artists: Gabrielle Roth, Steve Roach and Byron Metcalf, and Jim McGrath.

To begin, take time to stretch your body and limber up. When you are sufficiently warmed up, stand in the center of an open space. Be sure that the floor is clear of furniture and objects over which you might trip.

Turn on some percussive music, or have a friend begin drumming for you with a steady beat. As you stand in the center of your space, begin by listening to the drumbeat. Close your eyes. Without editing your movements, allow your body parts to move to the sound of the percussion. Begin by allowing your feet to express the essence of percussive beat. Move only your feet. Then move up to your knees and move only them. Isolate each of these body parts, allowing each one to move as it will in response to the drum beat. Move up to hips/thighs, then stomach, torso, arms, hands, and head.

After isolated body parts have moved to the beat, begin to combine the parts. To do this, I recommend that you half-open your eyes. Open them just enough so that you can see your environment, to prevent injury. Begin by moving your feet. Then add your knees, your thighs, hips, stomach, torso, arms, hands, and head. When complete, you should be moving freely and wildly to the drumbeat. Continue with this dancing until you sense the energy levels within your body beginning to increase. Some practitioners say that they see lights or feel heat when they are ready to harness magical power. Once you feel you are ready, imagine that you gather power with your hands from the air around you. Actually scoop the air around you, imagining that you form large balls of energy. When you feel you have created an energy ball, place it physically within your chest. Continue the process until you sense that you have gathered enough energy for your spell.

After you have gathered enough energy, drop yourself physically to the floor. Lie on your back and feel the energy swirling around inside of you. After you have sensed this energy, allow it to flow into the ground beneath you. Close your eyes and imagine the energy melting away from your body, into the ground, where it is neutralized. To further ground this energy, turn over so that your stomach is on the floor. Now curl up into a ball, pressing the palms of your hands, your knees, and your forehead all to the floor until you feel that you are returning to your normal sense awareness.

Day 262

Raising Power: Breath Control

In earlier lessons, you learned about the importance of breathing in the magical process. Correct breathing directly affects the Witch's vitality and therefore, her magic. Another component of effective magic is one's emotional state, which is directly affected by one's breathing patterns. For example, states of anxiety and anger can be calmed through deep rhythmic breathing, or states of lethargy and depression can be altered with specific patterns of quick, forceful breaths.

In ordinary breathing, inhalations and exhalations are generally shallow, and they occur without conscious exertion. Magical breathing focuses on conscious awareness of expanding the abdomen, lungs, and rib cage on the inhalation, and full emptying of the lungs upon exhalation. Patterns are typically involved in magical breathing, such as in the technique you will learn today. Many of the patterns upon which breath control is based link to the discipline of numerology. In general, this means that the number of breaths one takes in a pattern has symbolic numerical significance.

Practice: Power Breathing

The following power-breathing technique comes from the ancient Polynesian system of magic called *Huna*. The word Huna is similar to the English word *occult*; both mean "secret." The benefits of using this technique to raise energy include:

- It is silent, so you can practice it anywhere
- It involves a completely internal process, so you don't need candles, drums, incense or anything else to aid you

To begin, find a quiet place to sit with your feet planted solidly on the ground. Close your eyes. Imagine that you hear soft, rhythmic drumming in the distance. Begin to inhale. Using the imaginary drumbeat as a metronome, inhale on an even count of four. Hold the breath for another even count of four. Exhale the breath to an even count of four. Hold in that exhaled position for another even count of four. That entire cycle of *inhalation-hold-exhalation-hold* is counted as *one* breath in this magical technique. In order to create power, you must complete forty magical breath cycles. This may take about fifteen to twenty minutes to complete.

To further enhance this technique, use the following visualizations:

- As you inhale, imagine that you breathe in pure, raw energy
- As you hold the breath, imagine that this energy transforms in color to a deep blue
- As you exhale, imagine that you aim the blue energy to the area just above your head; while you continue on with all forty cycles, imagine that the pool of blue energy increases in size

The Polynesians believe that this energy you first inhale is unrefined. They say that the human body converts this energy into a useable form. The pool of energy that gathers above your head does not dissipate; it remains intact until you use it.

When you are finished with this technique, be sure to ground and center yourself by pressing the palms of your hands, your knees, and your forehead to the ground.

Day 263

Raising Power: Chanting

Much like trance dance, chanting is a technique that helps the Witch bypass the analytical mind. Magical chanting usually involves the rhythmic repetition of phrases and couplets. This process occupies the conscious mind, thus freeing the unconscious with all its psychic power. The technique of magical chanting involves careful awareness of the pace and the pitch (or voice level) of your recitation. You should intensify both the pace and pitch as the chant progresses so that you can feel the energy of magic building up inside you.

In today's practice, begin by choosing one of the chants provided below. Take time to commit the chant to memory. As you recite the chant, visualize energy building up as you gradually increase the chanting intensity and speed. Once you have sensed the buildup of energy inside you, stop your chanting and lie with your back to the floor. Then imagine that the energy you built up projects out of you, downward into the ground, where it is neutralized.

When you are finished practicing this technique, be sure to ground and center yourself by pressing the palms of your hands, your knees, and your forehead to the ground for a few moments.

Magical Chants

The Witch's Rune

The Witch's Rune is one of the most well known and frequently used chants among contemporary Wiccans. Remember to practice building up speed and volume during the chant until you sense that you have raised energy inside you.

> *Darksome night and shining moon,*
> *Harken to the Witches' Rune,*
> *East and south, then west, to north,*
> *Here come I to call thee forth!*
> *By all the powers of land and sea,*

Be obedient unto me,
Wand and pentacle and sword,
Harken ye unto my word.
Cords and censer, scourge and knife,
Waken all ye unto life.
Powers of the Witches' blade,
Come ye as the charge is made.
Queen of Heaven, Queen of Hell,
Send your aid unto the spell,
Horned hunter of the night,
Work my spell by magic rite.
By all the powers of land and sea,
As I do say, "So mote it be."
By all the might of moon and sun,
As I do will, it shall be done.[83]

The Eko Eko Chant

This chant enlists the aid of angelic forces to assist in the magical working.

Eko, eko, Michael (pronounced mee-kai-el)
Eko, eko, Gabriel (pronounced gab-ree-el)
Eko, eko, Raphael (pronounced rahf-eye-el)
Eko, eko Samael! (pronounced sam-ay-el)

A Goddess Chant

Chant this whenever you want to tap into the energies of the divine feminine.

Isis, Astarte, Diana, Hecate,
Demeter, Kali, Innana!

A God Chant

Chant this whenever you want to tap into the energies of the divine masculine.

Janus, Cernunnos, Dumuzi, Iacchus,
Apollo, Hermes, Anubus!

An Elemental Chant

Use this chant to empower your spells through the elementals.

Sylph, Undine, Dragon, and Gnome,
Come ye forth, from where ye roam.
Build your power; lend it to me,
Bless this magic, blessed be!

Day 264

Directing Power

Raising the power you intend to use in a spell is the first portion of the magical process. Next comes directing the energy you have raised. Wiccans use several methods that direct magical energy to a desired end. Each method requires your focused attention and visualization ability. In directing energy, you first create what Witches call the *cone of power,* which is a vortex of magical energy. Using your powers of visualization, you then project the raised energy into the symbols you collected for your spell (such as your stones, scents, planetary glyphs, images, etc.).

The Cone of Power

Most Witches practice raising the cone of power within spiritual communities, although solitary practitioners use this method with great success. The technique involves a combination of raising magical energy and guided visualization. As the Witch dances, chants, or magically breathes, she visualizes energy gathering and swirling deosil around her magic circle. She continues collecting power, visualizing the energy as it gradually forms an apex, or cone shape, far above the center of the magic circle. She then releases her hold on the energy and visualizes it either leaving the sacred space to manifest her desired outcome, or projecting through her collected magical symbols (candles, glyphs, incense, etc.), to manifest her desire.

Calling the Drop

One of the key components of the cone of power is in sensing when it is time to release the energy you have collected. There is no set rule for when you should release the cone of power; however, the optimal timing coincides with the climax of your energy buildup. While you engage in raising the cone of power, it will be important for you to concentrate on your psychic *sensing*. Although the energy buildup process usually lasts between ten and twenty minutes, you will need to take note of when you *feel* the energy reaching its highest point of tension.

At the moment of this crescendo, you call *the drop*, which is the instant at which you project your magical energy toward a goal. The drop is named so because, in practice, Witches physically drop to the ground when they direct their collected energy.

Practice: Cone of Power

What You'll Need:

- Your usual circle-casting tools

Begin by casting a circle. Select one of the power-raising methods you have learned over the past several days (dancing, breath control, or chanting) and use it to generate magical energy. As you build this energy, visualize a cone of power forming within your circle. Hold your athame in your stronger hand while you build energy. In the moment you sense the highest point of magical tension, physically drop to the floor and point your athame toward the sky. Visualize the cone of power leaving the circle and dissipating in space.

Day 265

Directing Power: Crystals

Directing magical energy through a quartz crystal is another powerful technique. To begin this practice, choose a crystal that has not had its shape altered in any significant way. The crystal should look as natural as possible. Highly polished crystals or ones that artisans have shaped in some way seem to yield unpredictable results. Use quartz crystals that have at least one natural terminal or pointed (beveled) end. It is through this terminal end that you project the energy you've raised.

The size of the crystal does not ultimately matter, although many Witches who use this method choose crystals that are the length of their palm (about 3 to 4 inches, or 8 to 10 millimeters in length). What is most important is that you choose a crystal that you can hold comfortably in your stronger hand.

Witches believe that quartz crystals intensify the vibrations of anything in the vicinity and therefore they require continual grounding until their intended use. Before you use any crystal for magical work you should cleanse (or *clear*) it of any inadvertent, environmental vibrations. To clear a quartz, lay it lengthwise (on its side) in a container into which you have poured a 1-inch layer of rock salt. Once the quartz is lying on the first layer of salt, pour more rock salt over the crystal until it is completely covered. Prior to first-time use, keep the crystal in the salt for at least one hour.

Practice: Using a Quartz

What You'll Need:

- Your circle-casting tools
- A *cleared* quartz crystal with one terminal end

Begin by casting a circle. Select one of the power-raising methods you have learned over the past several days and use it to generate magical energy. As you raise magical energy, visualize a cone of power forming within your circle. Practice sensing when the cone is at its greatest power. At that moment, drop to the floor and grip the quartz crystal in your stronger hand. Extend your index finger down the length of the crystal and point it toward the sky. Once you point the crystal, use your imagination to visualize the cone of power projecting through the terminal point of the crystal toward your intention.

Depending on your intent and your magical goal, you might choose any number of directions to point the crystal. If, for example, your goal is to heal someone within the circle, you can point the crystal directly at the individual and imagine that the cone of power enters his or her body, or if you direct the energy toward someone at a distance from your circle, aim the crystal in the general direction of the person, imagining the cone of power filling the individual with energy. If you are directing energy toward some goal and not toward a person, you might choose a compass direction that best corresponds to your magical intent. For example, if you cast a spell for environmental awareness, you might point the crystal toward the north, the direction of earth. If you cast a spell for peace, you might point the crystal toward the west, the direction of water and emotions.

When you are finished with directing power, place the quartz back in rock salt.

Practice: Other Tools for Directing Power

Raise the cone of power several more times. Each time, use a different magical tool to help direct the cone up and out of the magic circle. If you are simply practicing this technique and you have no specific intent toward which you are aiming the cone of power, imagine the cone leaving the circle and dissipating in space.

For directing the cone of power, try using:

- Your wand
- Your pentacle
- Your cup
- Your hand
- What effect did each tool have? Which tool do you prefer to use in your own magical practice for sending the cone of power?

Day 266

Practice: Your First Spell

Today's working is a bit unusual since you will be starting without an intent, or magical goal. Instead, you will first consider the following:

- Today's moon phase
- The magical day of the week, the planetary associations and corresponding glyph
- The current planetary hour and glyph

Now consider what magical working you might be able to do at this time. Make a list of potential ideas and then consider what additional magical aids you might need, including:

- The candles of a color that would suit your magical goal
- The magical stones that would suit your magical goal
- The herbs that would suit your magical goal
- The essential oils that suit your goal
- The way you could raise and direct power that might be best suited for this goal

Once you gather the appropriate magical correspondences/symbols, decide which techniques you might use with each magical object (based on what you have learned in previous lessons). Once you have your plan in place, cast a magic circle, raise the cone of power, and then direct your power through the symbols you have collected. Close your circle as usual and keep any symbols that you can (such as herbal sachets or stones) with you until you have attained your goal.

A Word to the Wise: In your usual magical work, you would start with your intention or goal. Then you would consider moon phase, timing, and supplemental magical aids.

Day 267

Magical Attack and Protection

Before you learn about what Witches call *magical attack,* it is important to first understand several points about energy. Always keep in mind that energy is neutral; it is neither inherently harmful nor beneficial. How we use energy is what determines its outcome. For example, there is neither harmful nor beneficial electricity. An exposed current can cause death, but a channeled current can empower entire cities in a myriad of ways. This same tenet holds true for magical power.

Witches do not have exclusive access to magical energies; these are natural forces that form the universe and all of life. It doesn't take much for someone unskilled in the ways of magic to set psychic energies in motion.

Surprised? High emotional states are good conduits of energy, and whether or not we are trained to direct magical power we can do so when we feel intensely. Love and joy are emotions that can effectively mobilize energy patterns that result in one set of outcomes, but jealousy, hate, anger, and sadness can also marshal psychic force. Whether or not we know it, emotions can become the focal point for sending the energies of magic. When someone sends these energies in an undisciplined manner, there can be unexpected results.

Luckily, Witches have developed techniques to shield themselves from these unexpected energetic patterns, which constitute a magical attack. But before you learn any techniques, take time to study and learn some of the warning signs of attack.

Warning Signs of a Magical Attack

Yourself: Watch for signs of *inexplicable* lethargy, sadness, or anger, *unexplained* illnesses or multiple injuries in a short time span; look for *unexplained* mood swings, confusion, swift changes of heart, or a run of bad luck

Family: Watch for multiple, inexplicable arguments, estrangement, tantrums, illnesses and injuries, or romantic affairs

Home: Watch for an inexplicable sensation of heaviness or oppression in your home, a feeling of being watched, unexplained noises, odors, or images

Pets: Inexplicable, unusual behavior in pets, inexplicable illness in pets

If you sense that you might be influenced by negative spiritual vibes, it is time to use a magical protection. Today, create the SATOR charm as your first magical defense.

Practice: The SATOR Charm

What You'll Need:

- A blank piece of white paper, at least 8 x 8 inches square
- Dragon's blood ink (you can purchase this ink made from dragon's blood reed from most New Age/magical shops.) or
- A red ink pen
- Rosemary essential oil
- Your circle-casting tools

Cast a circle as you normally do. At the center point of your ritual, work this magic. On a blank piece of paper, use your red ink pen to write the following words in a square.

S A T O R
A R E P O
T E N E T
O P E R A
R O T A S

Anoint the edges of the paper with rosemary essential oil. Raise energy and then direct it into the charm, using your powers of visualization to imagine that this charm takes on a silvery glow. When you are done, close the circle as usual. Hang the SATOR charm above your front door. If you would like extra protection, create several of these charms. Charge them magically (all together) and then hang them above each door and window of your home.

Day 268

Practice: A Mirror Protection

If you've got the heebie-jeebies and the prickling hairs on the back of your neck seem like little antennas picking up unfriendly vibes, try this traditional technique to dispel the dark clouds hanging over you.

What You'll Need:

- A round mirror (at least 5 inches in diameter)
- A dark blue candle of any size/shape (this color is good for dispelling evil)
- Salt
- A bowl of water steeped with the herb *hyssop*

Cast your circle as usual. Bless the candle by holding it between the palms of your hands while saying:

> ***Blessed be this creature of magic.***
> ***May it be purified and consecrated***
> ***To bring me magical aid.***

Light the candle and set it in a holder. Set the candle and the holder on top of the reflective surface of the mirror. Dab your fingers into the bowl of hyssop water and rub this into each of your chakra points. Sprinkle the remaining hyssop water around your sacred space.

Hold the mirror in your left hand and the candle in your right. Stand at the eastern perimeter of your circle. Turn the mirror's reflective surface so that it faces the east—away from you and the circle. Hold the candle in front of the reflective surface so that the mirror reflects the light away from you. Slowly *moonwalk* deosil three times around the circle without making a sound. During your first circumambulation, imagine that the perimeter of the circle *becomes* itself a reflective surface, a mirror that deflects unwanted energies. During the second circumambulation, imagine that your body *becomes* a mirror that deflects unwanted energies. On the third lap, imagine that your home becomes a mirror that deflects unwanted energies.

Now return to your central altar and set down the candle. Pour salt over the reflective surface of the mirror until it is completely covered. Hold your hands over the salted mirror and say thrice:

> ***Creature of earth, you take away***
> ***This curs'ed evil sent my way!***

Pour the salt into an empty dish, making sure not to spill a single grain. Close your circle as usual. Take the salt far from your dwelling and bury it. The negative vibes should vanish.

Day 269

Practice: A Rosemary Protection

What You'll Need:

- Cheesecloth
- A sprig of fresh rosemary and at least a teaspoon of dried rosemary
- 12 inches of red cord
- A 5–6 inch red taper candle
- Red thread and a needle
- Your circle-casting tools
- Scissors

Wait until nearly midnight on the night of a full moon, and then gather together your ingredients. Cover all the mirrors and windows in the room in which you create this charm. Cast a magic circle, then use a pin or a white-handled knife to inscribe the red candle with the planetary glyph for Saturn (♄). Cut a 3-inch square out of the cheesecloth. Thread the needle with the red thread. Dip the sprig of fresh rosemary in the salt and then in water. Pass it briefly through the red candle flame. Sprinkle the dried rosemary over the coal and then hold the sprig of fresh rosemary over the smoke. Place the sprig in the center of the cheesecloth square, fold the fabric in half, and then sew it closed with the red thread and the needle.

Once you have this completed, hold the cheesecloth bag in between the palms of your hands. Stand in the west of your circle and moonwalk widdershins three times, chanting:

> ***Thrice I walk the edge of time,***
> ***Protection come at midnight's chime!***

After you have walked the circle thrice, stand facing the west. Hold the charm in front of you as you would a shield, and say:

To bane, to bane!
Begone! Begone!
Thrice take ye back from whence ye came!

Repeat this final incantation in the south, east, and north of your circle. Now tie the bag with the red cord so that you can wear the bag around your neck. Close the circle when you are done and wear the amulet, making sure that it comes in contact with your body.

Day 270

Quick House Protections

Here are two more techniques to try today for protection against unwanted energies.

The Witches' Bottle

What You'll Need:

- An empty clear-glass jar
- Old razors, rusty nails, pins, needles, and tacks (enough to fill the jar)
- Vinegar

You won't need to cast a circle to prepare this magical object. After dark, fill an empty, clear glass jar with razors, nails, pins, needles, tacks, and any other small, sharp, metal object. If any of the items that fill the jar are rusty, that is all the better. Now pour vinegar into the jar until nearly full. Men who prepare this bottle can add semen for additional strength. Women can add menstrual blood for added potency. Close the jar and seal it tight.

Traditional Witches claim that it is best for you to bury the jar beneath the front steps of your home. However, in actual practice, it is just as effective for you to bury the Witch's jar anywhere in the vicinity of your dwelling.

As long as the bottle is buried, evil sent to you will be deflected.

Vibrational House-Clearing

When you want to clear your dwelling of unwanted energies and you don't have time to cast the circle, try this technique. It only involves censing the home with one of two excellent aura-cleansing herbs.

What You'll Need:

- Dried white sage or
- Dragon's blood resin

- A self-igniting charcoal
- A censer or a simple ceramic dish filled with sand

Light the charcoal and set it in the censer. Crumble the dried sage (or the dragon's Blood resin) onto the charcoal. Take the smoldering incense to the front door of your house. Walk clockwise around the inner perimeter of the house, renewing the dried sage (or resin) when you need more smoke. Return to the front door and use the censure to draw a banishing-earth pentagram in smoke.

Days 271-300

Magical Items to Gather:

Here are the magical items you will need during the next month of your training.

Day 271

- A lemon
- A dip pen (such as a feather quill)
- A 5–6 inch red taper candle

Day 272

- A 5–6 inch white taper candle

Day 282

- 2 tablespoons dried woodruff
- 1 bottle of wine
- Lemon juice
- Honey

Day 284

- A *Universal Tarot* deck

Day 300

- A 5–6 inch white taper candle.

Day 271

Practice: A Thought-Clearing Spell

Often at the root of strange and unwanted energies that linger around the home is our own indulgence in thoughts of anger, resentment, sadness, fear, or jealousy. All human emotions are natural, and we should honor and respect each one. However, engaging with these feelings, developing them and expanding upon them can cause you to inadvertently direct or even attract unwanted energies. You need neither to resist nor to gratify these energies and thoughts within you. Simply observe them and allow them to be, naturally—without any help from you.

Here is a spell to help magically dispel harmful patterns of thinking.

What You'll Need:

- Circle-casting tools
- A lemon
- A dip pen (such as a feather quill)
- A blank white piece of paper
- A 5–6 inch red taper candle
- A thurible (or a deep pot in which you can burn an item safely)

This is an all-day spell. From the moment you awaken, focus your attention so that you have an awareness of what thought patterns arise. Whenever you notice a harmful thought, write it down on a piece of paper. Continue this practice until sundown. Then, when the sun has set, squeeze the juice of a lemon into a small bowl. Dip the tip of your pen into the lemon juice and use this to rewrite each of your harmful thoughts on a clean white sheet of paper. At the top and the bottom of each page draw a banishing-earth pentagram with the lemon juice ink. Remain silent while completing this rewriting task and allow no interruptions. Please note that the lemon juice will transfer to the page invisibly, so take care not to write over anything you have previously transferred on to the page.

Wait for the lemon juice to dry. Cast your circle as usual. Light a red taper candle. Hold the paper with the lemon juice writing on it close to the flame, but not so close that the page ignites. The writing should appear now.

During this ritual action, chant continuously:

> ***From the void you have emerged,***
> ***And to the void you shall return!***

Once you see all of your writing, fold the page in half, then in half again. Light it on fire with the red candle and drop it into the thurible. Continue chanting until there is nothing left but ash. Close your circle as usual. Bury the ash far from your dwelling.

Day 272

Contemplative Day: Original Essence

Meditative Question: What is the original essence of all things?

Symbolic Color: White

Symbolic Direction: Center

At first glance, this month's question might appear simply answered with a platitude such as, "Spirit is the essence of all." However, to say this is to simply overlay learned ideas and sentiments, and to not experience your own reality. You may be surprised by the conclusions at which you arrive while exploring this mystery.

A Word to the Wise: This question begins the final series of four inner mysteries. For each of these inner mysteries contemplations, begin by blessing yourself with each of the elements, as you would in a circle-casting ceremony.

Find a comfortable meditative sitting position. Light a white candle and sit approximately two feet away from the flame. Cast your gaze upon the flickering candle and hold the question firmly at the level of the abdomen for 20 to 30 minutes.

As you have learned with the other meditative questions, it is not spiritually productive to explore this mystery through logic and deduction. Instead, become one with it in each of your tasks. Allow your body, mind, and spirit to become this question as you eat, sleep, work, and play. Over time, a shift in your perception will take place and you will realize your own answer.

Day 273

Devotional Day: Honoring Janicot

Table of Correspondences: Janicot

Symbols: Spoked wheel, the phallus, black and yellow birds

Tools: The wand, the priapus, the athame

Magical Essences/Herbs: Musk, patchouli

Direction: South and east

He Rules: The ability to see the big picture, understanding the true nature of things, understanding the rhythm of life

Animal Symbols: Goat, black birds

Sacred Foods: Phallic- or rod-shaped foods (such as asparagus, carrots, sausage, etc.)

Magical Stones: Ruby, turquoise

The French pronounce his name *schan-i-co*. He is the Basque god of the oak, of doorways, and of the wheel of the year. Not much is written of him. However, he was referred to by Pierre de Lancre during an early seventeenth-century campaign against Witches. He may be related to an old Basque sprite called *Basa-Juan*, whose name means "goat man." His name may also be related to the Basque word for god, *Jaincoa*. Old woodcuts portray Janicot as a satyr-like being with the torso of a human male and legs and feet of a goat. He is a god of dancing and merriment, since he represents the turning of the wheel and the celebration of the sabbats.

When you tap into the ancient archetypal energies of Janicot, you also evoke your ability to see the big picture, to understand the true nature of things, to understand the rhythm of life and that all things have seasons. He also evokes your ability to see the true nature of your spirit. Janicot reminds you to stay focused on the season at hand, to release the past and to see each moment in time as a doorway to renewal. His sacred symbols are the eight-spoked wheel, which represents the eight sabbats of the Witches' calendar, the phallus, and black birds. His magical essence is musk and his sacred colors are black and dark blue. His sacred stones are rubies and turquoise. Phallic-shaped foods such as asparagus and sausage are Janicot's sacred foods.

Janicot Practice

In honoring Janicot today, make an altar that includes his sacred symbols. Cast a magic circle and then slowly intone this old Basque rhyme:

> ***In nomine patrica,***
> ***Aragueaco petrica***
> ***Gastellaco Janicot,***
> ***Equidae ipordian pot.***

Imagine the image of Janicot entering your sacred space until you feel or sense his presence with you. Once he has arrived, spend some time contemplating what it might mean to serve this aspect of deity. Take time to ask Janicot what it would mean to live life through his energy. Contemplate the sacred dimensions and principles of the lingam: action, movement, passion, drive. When you are finished, close the circle as usual.

Spend the day honoring this god by taking action while keeping in mind the big picture (meaning your overall goals, or perhaps even your community or the world).

DAY 274

Day of Silence and Review

Today, as you observe silence, focus your attention on your sense of taste. As you eat focus your attention on flavors and textures. Of course, between your meals, remain silent. When the day is complete, answer these questions:

- What was it like to focus my attention on my sense of taste?
- Am I a person who reacts strongly to the taste of things?
- How do I react to tastes that I don't particularly enjoy?
- In what way did my sense of taste impact my thoughts, emotions, or spirit?
- How does what I taste affect my physical energy?

Review

For today's practice, take time to ask yourself the following:

- Of the information I have learned up to now, what stands out most as vital?
- What information seems least relevant to my spiritual development?
- Which of the practices seemed to move me spiritually, and which had little impact?
- Of the information I have learned so far, what would be best to review? (Take time to review it now.)

DAY 275

Herbs: Magical Helpers

The history of herbs and our relationship to the plant world undoubtedly stretches back to prehistory. Herbs must have been highly revered in ancient societies. After all, these mysterious plants had practical uses—they could both cure or kill; they could ease pain or poison the body. Some herbs were known for their religious purposes; they could open the spiritual senses, heighten awareness, and yield teaching.

The history of herbs and their uses (both medicinal and magical) is far too complex to cover in its entirety here. However, the following brief summary highlights the influential moments within herbal history. It wasn't until roughly 3000 BCE that the first references to herbs and their powers were mentioned in writing. It was then that China's "Red-Emperor" Shen Nung documented his accounts of experiments to study the physical effects of various herbs.[84] Later Egyptian records, from as early as 1500 BCE, describe the medicinal and magical use of herbs. The Greeks were the first to codify herbal lore in the centuries spanning 500 and 400 BCE, and in 50 BCE the Roman physician Pedanius Dioscorides penned his celebrated *De Materia Medica*, which forever influenced herbals in both the Eastern and Western cultures.[85] Centuries later, in 1653, Nicholas Culpepper wrote his *Complete Herbal*, documenting the astrological associations between herbs and planetary forces. Much of contemporary herbal lore and magical practice is founded on this influential work.

The power of herbs continues to influence us today in both medical and magical ways. Approximately 50 percent of all drugs listed in the *U.S. Pharmacopia* are herb derived.[86] In magical practice, Witches actively use herbs as part of their craft for both their healing and magical influences. In contemporary magical practice, Wiccans often draw upon the old tables of correspondence drafted in the Middles Ages and Renaissance, yet they honor the roots of this practice that reach back to the ancient world.

Herbs to Know

Spend time today acquainting yourself with the following list of herbs and their magical purposes. In order to gain some mastery of magical herbalism, commit to your memory at least four of these magical herbs. To help you gain practical knowledge, devise a spell that incorporates one of these herbs in combination with color, planetary glyph, day of the week, magical hour, and magical stone.

Over the next several days, you will be introduced to a selection of magical herbs. The list is incomplete, as there are literally hundreds of herbs that Witches use in magical operations. Each herb can be used fresh, dried, or in an essential oil form. Most Witches use fresh and dried herbs in healing practices, in making brews and ointments, and in spellwork. Herbal essential oils distill the vibratory and occult qualities of fresh herbs. In some instances they function in magical work much more efficiently than fresh or dried herbs. Essential oils can be worn either on the body or on clothing. You can also incorporate them into ritual by anointing people, animals, or ritual objects.

Poisonous Herbs 101

Some of the herbs in this magical list are poisonous. You should not, *under any circumstances*, consume poisonous herbs. Never use your bare hands to handle poisonous herbs. Instead, use surgical gloves (obtainable at any pharmacy) or plastic food-handling gloves (obtainable at most grocery stores) when working with these plants. Remember never to touch your eyes or mouth while handling poisonous items, and wash your hands thoroughly with soap and warm water immediately after contact. Do not store toxic herbs in closed or unventilated spaces.

Caution

Exercise caution when consuming herbs internally or when applying them to your skin. Many herbs can create allergic reactions. Some herbs cannot be taken internally at all—and some you cannot use externally—because they are known poisons or toxins. Herbal manuals such as the *Grieve's Manual*, *The Master Book of Herbalism* by Paul Beryl, or *Mastering Herbalism* by Paul Huson can give you in-depth information regarding which herbs contain toxins and which do not.

Herbs and Brews

Brews are an infusion of a single herb (or an herb blend) that Witches use for magical purposes. A Witch typically consumes a potion to attain specific magical attributes. For example, a Witch might brew together sage and anise, and then drink it to obtain wisdom or harmony. Witches also use infusions topically as an herbal wash or as a bath. In both instances the Witch can obtain the magical virtues of herbs without consuming them.

Practice: Making a Brew or Wash

Choose one of the herbs in the list below and prepare a brew or wash.

Brew/Wash Basic Recipe

Use 1 teaspoon of dried herb (or 3 teaspoons of fresh) to 1 cup boiling water. Place herbs in a tea bag or use a tea-straining device. Stir the herbs into the cup of hot water and allow it to steep for at least five minutes. For herbal baths, allow the herbs to steep in the tub for 15 minutes. Alternatively, you can make a brew and pour this into your bathwater.

To use an herb as a wash, simply create the brew as directed above, allow it to cool and then rub it into your seven chakra points. A Witch takes an herbal bath by submerging her body into a tub of very hot water that has been infused with herbs.

Herbs to Know – Day 275

Key: F=Use herb *D=Use herb* *O=Essential oil* *☠=Warning: Poisonous/toxic herb*

Herb	*Planet*	*Part Used*	*Form*	*Magical Purpose*
Acorn ☠	Earth	acorn (seed)	F, ☠	Fertility magic, male virility, fruition, creative potential
Angelica	Sun	leaf	F, D, O	Protection, counter-magic, good fortune
Anise	Moon	seed, leaves	F, D, O	Friendship, love; protects against bad dreams, harmonizes spiritual and physical dimensions
Apple	Venus, Moon	fruit, wood, seed	F, D, O	Love spells, pleasure, luck, wisdom
Ash	Sun & Moon	wood	F, D	Tree magic; summons the old gods, controls unwanted spirits
Balm of Gilead	Venus, Jupiter	leaf	D, O	Healing
Basil	Mars	leaf	F, D, O	Fire energies, salamander magic; invokes the archetype of the dragon and its magical power; temple-blessing herb
Bay Laurel	Sun	leaf	F, D, O	Psychic vision, prophecy; protection from thunderstorms
Benzoin	Pluto	resin	D, O	Harmony, enhances spiritual qualities, astral journeys, meditation, spiritual mastery
Blessed Thistle	Mars	leaf, flower/ seed pod	D	Sharpening of the mind, protection from unwanted energies, reversal of hexes

Day 276

Herbs to Know

Spend time today acquainting yourself with the following list of herbs and their magical purposes. In order to gain some mastery of magical herbalism, commit to your memory at least four of these magical herbs. To help you gain practical knowledge of these herbs, try using one or more of them in a magical brew or potion. Devise a spell in which you would use one of the herbs in the list in combination with: color, planetary glyph, day of the week, magical hour, and magical stone.

Herb Gathering Lore

The texts of Pliny, Magnus, and Tusser, (as well as other ancient herbals) outline several ritual rules for the proper gathering of herbs. These rules were alleged to preserve the plant's many virtues.

- Pluck herbs associated with the Moon, Venus and Neptune with your left hand; pluck herbs associated with the Sun, Jupiter, Mars, and Pluto with your right hand; herbs associated with Saturn and Mercury can be picked with either hand
- Herbs must be picked secretly, in solitary circumstances
- Never face into the wind when plucking an herb
- No matter what occurs, never look behind you
- Never cut herbs with iron tools
- Cut herbs during the twenty-third through the twenty-eighth day of the lunar cycle
- After harvesting herbs, lay them out on wheat or barley
- Leave a small offering to the earth (spirits) whenever you pluck an herb; some herbals suggest offerings of small silver coins, wine, mead, honey, bread, or corn

Herbs to Know – Day 276

Key: F=Use fresh D=Use dried O=Essential oil ☠=Warning: Poisonous/toxic herb

Herb	*Planet*	*Part Used*	*Form*	*Magical Purpose*
Borage	Jupiter	leaves	F, D	Spiritual strength, happiness, changes one's mood
Broom N	Mars, Moon	flowers, leaves	F, D, O, ☠	Luck, deep sleep, magical enhancement
Catnip	Venus	leaves	F, D	Transfiguration, shape-shifting, brings the power of the cat into your life
Cedar ☠	Mercury	wood	D, O, ☠	Consecration, money drawing, archetypal energies of the unicorn, attainment of ideals
Chamomile	Sun	flower	F, D, O	Communication with fairies, increases power of spellwork, success, victory, health
Cinnamon	Sun	bark	D, O	Concentration, purification, fire magic, mental focus
Cinquefoil	Jupiter, Mercury	leaves	D, F	Contacts Mother goddess, love dreams, safe journeys
Cornflower	Venus	flower	F, D	Psychic visions, prophecy
Damiana	Pluto	leaves	F, D	Sexuality, secrets revealed, psychic prowess, quartz crystal protection
Dittany of Crete ☠	Venus, Moon	leaves	F, D, ☠	Communication with the dead, brings knowledge of the afterlife

Day 277

Drying Herbs

Drying herbs preserves their magical properties over time. To begin drying herbs, make sure you have a well-ventilated, cool, dry, dark storage/drying area. You might consider using a closet in your home. Or if you live where the weather is temperate, the rafters of a garage make a nice herb-drying space. It is important that you make sure that your drying herbs are not exposed to heat above 90 degrees (Fahrenheit), or else they'll begin to lose their potency.

Herbs vary in the length of their drying time. The amount of time it takes for an herb to dry depends on the woodiness, the density of the herb, and the part of the herb you are trying to dry. Leaves tend to dry much more quickly than roots, for example.

The traditional Wiccan way of herb drying begins with the gathering process. Witches use a specific tool called the boline when they gather herbs. The boline is a white handled knife that has a curved, sickle-shaped blade. Wiccan lore suggests that the boline is a relative of the mythic golden sickle used by Druid priests in herb-gathering rituals. If you cannot procure a boline, you can simply use a white-handled knife—or some other knife that you have set aside for mundane work.

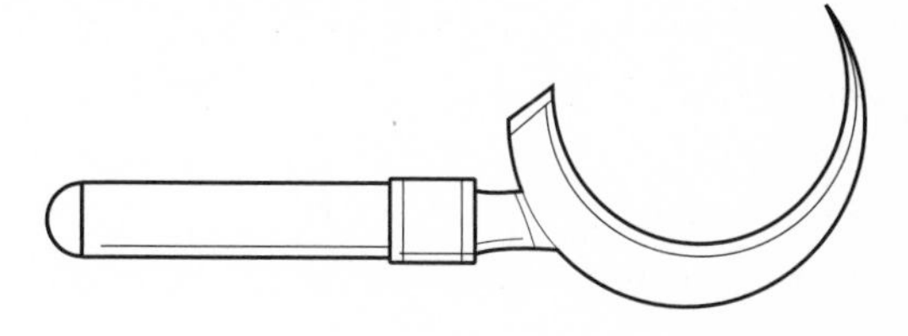

A Witch's boline, and the inscription to be set on its handle.

Herbs to Know – Day 277

Key: F=Use fresh *D=Use dried* *O=Essential oil* *☠=Warning: Poisonous/toxic herb*

Herb	*Planet*	*Part Used*	*Form*	*Magical Purpose*
Dragon's Blood	Mercury,	resin	D, O	Magical strength and vitality, commanding, protection
Elm	Saturn	leaf	F, D	Crush fresh leaves, inhale the vapors for psychic dreams or prior to divination
Eyebright	Sun	leaf	F, D	Joy, optimism, brings clarity to any situation
Fennel	Mercury	seed, leaf	F, D, O	Fertility, blessing, consecration of magic circle.
Ferns	Mercury, Moon	spore, leaf	F	Invisibility, to act and go unobserved
Foxgloves ☠	Venus, Pluto	flower	F, ☠	Communication with elemental beings, used in flying ointments
Frankincense	Sun	resin	D, O	Solar magic, compassion, protection, concentration
Garlic	Mars	root/Bulb	F	Protection, purification, invokes the Crone aspect of the triple goddess
Ginger	Moon	root	F, D	Improves health
Holly ☠	Saturn	leaf	F, ☠	Immortality, magical aid from elemental beings

Herbs are best harvested at either dawn or dusk, as the natural essential oils and magical properties of the plant are strongest at these times. Stand before the herb that you plan to harvest and touch it with the appropriate hand (see Herb-Gathering Lore, Day 276). Close your eyes and breathe deeply. Imagine that your feet become roots and your body becomes the herb you are about to harvest. As you imagine this, try to sense whether or not the herb is willing to be harvested. If the plant has an unwilling energy at this time, try to harvest the herb again at a later date. If you sense agreement from the herb, a cooperative energy, use your boline in the appropriate hand to cut through the herb in a single stroke. Be sure to silently thank the plant for offering itself to your magical aid.

Tie the stalks of the harvested herb with twine and hang it up to dry inverted. This inversion, with stalks on top and leaves on the bottom, allows the essential oils to hold in the leaves. After the herb is hung, hold your hands near the cuttings and say:

Leaf and bud, root and seed,
Aid me in my sacred need!

Herbs to Know

Spend time today acquainting yourself with the list of herbs and their magical purposes that appears on the following page. In order to gain some mastery of magical herbalism, commit to your memory at least four of these magical herbs. To help you gain knowledge of these herbs, try using one or more of them in a magical brew or potion. Devise a spell in which you would use one of the herbs in the list in combination with: color, planetary glyph, day of the week, magical hour, and magical stone.

Day 278

Herbs to Know

Spend time today acquainting yourself with the list of herbs and their magical purposes, as shown in the table for Day 278 on page 291. In order to gain some mastery of magical herbalism, commit to your memory at least four of these magical herbs. To help you gain knowledge of these herbs, try using one or more of them in a magical brew or potion. Devise a spell in which you would use one of the herbs in the list in combination with: color, planetary glyph, day of the week, magical hour, and magical stone.

Day 279

"Cutting" Essential Oils

Witches like to wear herbal essential oils, especially since it helps connect them to the earth, to nature, and to the occult vibrations of their specific magical workings. Even when there is no formal magical working at hand, Witches still enjoy anointing themselves to alter their aura and their energies. However, before using any essential oil, it is important to know that some can be skin irritants and they need diluting before application. For this purpose, many practitioners cut the full strength of an essential oil with a *carrier oil.* The basic cutting ratio is two to four drops of an essential oil to one teaspoon (or even a tablespoon, depending on the strength of the essential oil) of carrier oil. Below is a list of the carrier oils that Witches most commonly use.

Almond Oil: This oil has a slight scent. Slow to become rancid, almond oil helps maintain your magical blends for long periods of time. Almond oil can also have a magical effect of its own. Almond imparts fertility, fecundity, and growth. It is closely linked with the power of magic and the planet Mercury.

Apricot Oil: This oil is odorless and is good for dry skin. It penetrates deeply. Apricot's magical effect is calming. Apricot soothes and opens the mind. Apricot oil is aligned with the planetary energies of Venus.

Avocado Oil: This odorless oil mixes well with other carrier oils. Avocado's magical power is its ability to link the wearer with the mother aspect of the triple goddess. Avocado oil aligns with the planetary influences of Earth and the Moon.

Grape Seed Oil: This is a light, clear carrier oil. It does not imbalance oily skin conditions. Grape seed oil brings renewal, insight, and rebirth. This oil is linked with the mysteries of Dionysus, of death to the old (an old pattern, relationship, way of living, etc.) and birth to something new. Grape seed oil aligns with the planetary influences of Mercury.

Jojoba Oil: This oil is well known because it nourishes skin and has a softening effect. Good for

---

Herbs to Know – Day 278

Key: F=Use fresh *D=Use dried* *O=Essential oil* ☠=*Warning: Poisonous/toxic herb*

Herb	*Planet*	*Part Used*	*Form*	*Magical Purpose*
Hops	Pluto	leaf	F, D, O	Dreams, sleep, visions, prophecy
Hyssop	Moon, Jupiter	leaf	F, D, O	Cleansing, psychic protection, clears the aura
Iris (Orris Root)	Moon, Venus	root	D	Love, romance, attracts a mate
Juniper	Sun, Mars	leaf	F, D	Health, physical energy
Mandrake	Mercury	root	F, D	Aphrodisiac, magical potency, powerful protection
Mistletoe ☠	Sun, Jupiter	leaf	F, D, ☠	Sex, immortal life, protects the home.
Myrrh	Jupiter	resin	D	Protection, blessing, safety
Oak	Sun	wood	D	Luck, magical knowledge, secrets revealed
Patchouli	Pluto	leaf	D, F, O	Sex, physical pleasure
Pine	Mars	leaf	D, F, O	Brings wealth, riches

love, peace, and meditation oils/blends. Jojoba aligns with the planetary influences of Jupiter.

Vegetable Glycerine: This is not an oil at all. It is a colorless, odorless substance that can be cut with water. It is an excellent carrier for essential oils and will not become rancid. Vegetable glycerin has no magical association; it is able to take on the qualities of the essential oils that it carries.

Herbs to Know

Spend time today acquainting yourself with the following list of herbs and their magical purposes. In order to gain some mastery of magical herbalism, commit to your memory at least four of these magical herbs. To help you gain knowledge of these herbs, try using one or more of them in a magical brew or potion. Devise a spell in which you would use one of the herbs in the list in combination with color, planetary glyph, day of the week, magical hour, and magical stone.

Day 280

The "Baleful" Herbs

According to the *Merriam-Webster Dictionary*, the term *baleful* means "harmful or malignant in intent or effect." By the same source, it also reputedly means "ominous" or "portending evil." When thinking about this word, baleful, it is important to keep in mind that the ongoing work of Witches is to see beyond the limitations of words and concepts upheld by the mainstream of one's society. It is important to question why our culture labels some things harmful or ominous, and some things not. Bunnies and happy faces are not baleful. Witches and magic are. Why is that? This question penetrates layer upon layer of history and politics. It roots out ugly secrets that involve the church's suppression of

Herbs to Know – Day 279

Key: F=Use fresh D=Use dried O=Essential oil ☠=Warning: Poisonous/toxic herb

Herb	*Planet*	*Part Used*	*Form*	*Magical Purpose*
Rosemary	Sun	leaf	F, D, O	Protection, memory, healing
Sage ☠ (White Sage, Desert Sage)	Saturn	leaf	D, O, ☠	Wisdom, aura clearing, protection, elevates one's mind, body, and spirit
Sandalwood	Jupiter	wood	D, O	Meditation, trance work, sacred visions
Solomon's Seal	Saturn	flower, root	F, D	Consecration, seals spells
Toadflax	Venus	leaf	F, D	For working with familiars
Woodruff	Mars, Venus	leaf	F, D	Steeped in May wine for ritual, cakes and wine links one to the gods

women's power and their body of knowledge, which in the days of Old Europe consisted (in one aspect) of the ways of healing herbs and remedies. In the Middle Ages, the church had a powerful ally in the battle for the religious heart of Europe's peasant class, namely the emerging male-dominated medical profession. In order for this profession to succeed, they needed to stamp out the old pagan herbal practices and their healers. Thereafter, simple country healers and their practices were outlawed and branded as enemies of the Church. Many of the women who had devoted their lives to healing were later tortured and burned for their arts. Healing methods once deemed holy were now profane. Herbs that could halt an unwanted pregnancy or that could cause someone to see unseen realities were suddenly demonic and baleful.

In contemporary magical practice, Witches consider the so-called baleful herbs to be associated with advanced magical work. Astral travel, shape-shifting (or magical transfiguration) and psychic development are some of the uses that Witches find for the balefuls. Witches also link these herbs to counter magic and to bindings.

On page 294 is a listing of many of the baleful herbs, and a list of some of their potential uses in magical practice.

Spend time today acquainting yourself with the following list of herbs and their magical purposes. Commit at least four of these magical herbs to your memory. Devise a spell in which you would use one of the herbs in the list in combination with: color, planetary glyph, day of the week, magical hour and magical stone.

Caution

Baleful herbs are poisonous. They should *not* be ingested, inhaled or *even held in close contact with the skin.* Please use caution if you attempt to use these herbs for any reason. If you accidentally ingest any of these herbs, immediately contact your local poison control.

I have listed some of the traditional ways Witches and magical folk would use these herbs for historical purposes only and I do not recommend that the reader use these highly toxic herbs. Using them can be dangerous, both physically and magically.

Flying Ointment

Flying ointment is the name of an herbal salve that Witches rub on their bodies in order to induce altered states of awareness. In historical accounts, Witches who used the ointments would hallucinate that they had changed into animals, had attended the Witches' Sabbat, that they had sexual encounters with demons, spoke with birds and other animals, or that they had flown across the countryside on rakes, hoes, or brooms.

Baleful Herbs to Know – Day 280

Key: F=Use fresh D=Use dried O=Essential oil ☠=Warning: Poisonous/toxic herb

Herb	*Planet*	*Part Used*	*Form*	*Magical Purpose*
Aconite ☠	Saturn	leaf	F, D, ☠	Invokes dark aspects of deity and of the mind (for purification), psychic work, magical flight, this baleful herb can be used in curses and bindings
Fly Agaric ☠	Moon, Pluto	mushroom	F,D, ☠	Found in many ancient "flying ointment" recipes; psychic work; astral travel, a teaching herb
Jimson Weed ☠	Moon, Uranus	leaf	D, ☠	Astral travel; psychic work; opens vision to other worlds
Henbane ☠	Saturn	leaf	F,D, ☠	Bindings, counter-magic; deflects dark forces, invokes hidden knowledge
Hemlock ☠	Saturn, Moon	leaf	F, D, ☠	Bindings, counter-magic; summons Hecate and all dark moon goddesses; brings knowledge of one's own death
Wolfbane ☠	Mars, Saturn	leaf	F, D, ☠	Stops enemies; employs familiars in counter-magic; magical death and strong curses

Uses of Baleful Herbs – Day 280

Herb	*Zodiacal Influence*	*Day of the Week*	*Magical Color*	*Ways to Use this Herb*
Aconite	Capricorn	Saturday	Purple	Left at a crossroads as an offering to Hecate, to invoke her favor in counter-magic, protective magic, or in divination; used as an ingredient in a flying ointment; the athame was wrapped in fresh leaves as a traditional form of consecration; carried in small cloth bags as a protection against potential negative magical energies
Fly Agaric	Pisces	Monday	Red	An ingredient in traditional flying ointment; wrapped in oak leaves and worn as an amulet on a string to invoke visions and psychic power
Jimson Weed	Aquarius	Wednesday	Orange	Used to bring hallucinogenic visions of other worlds; used to invoke visions of the elementals
Henbane	Scorpio	Saturday	Black	Steeped in hot water and sprinkled outside the magic circle to invoke spirits of the departed; root was dried, engraved with someone's name and then buried to send negative energies back to the sender
Hemlock	Scorpio	Monday	Black	Dried and powdered leaves were strewn on one's front doorstep and across all windowsills to protect from harm
Wolfbane	Aries	Tuesday	Brown	A jar filled with this herb was said to bring protection from animal spirits (familiars); carried as a protection against enemies

Day 281

Making Magical Inks

When Witches create spells, they often do so, as the magical saying goes, "in their own hand of writ." As you have learned over the past days, creating a spell often involves inscribing magical words, names and symbols. Typically, magical folk use a variety of specialized inks—each with its own spiritual properties—to boost the power of their spells. You make your own magical ink from natural herbal sources, and then you use a "dip" pen or a sharpened feather quill in order to inscribe with the ink. Below is a listing of various herbal inks, what they do, and how to make them.

For today's practice, make one of the inks below and use to create a magical inscription.

Tree Ink

Burn a stick or twig from a magical tree and use this burned end to inscribe magical writings. The power from the tree imbues your spells. Here is a listing of some magical trees and their spiritual energies.

Ash: Protection, repels negativity, divination

Hazel: Knowledge, wisdom, truth

Oak: Wisdom, magical power, good fortune, health

Willow: New beginnings, rebirth, ends old cycles

Dragon's Blood Ink

Dragon's blood ink is a "compelling and commanding" type of ink. It manifests your desires with force and swiftness. Steep a teaspoon of powdered dragon's blood resin in ⅛ cup of alcohol and ⅛ cup of gum arabic. The result should be a red ink. Strain any remaining pieces out before you use it.

Dove's Blood Ink

This ink has the same power as dragon's blood, but to a lesser degree. It has a friendlier, less urgent quality to it. Use for love and friendship charms. Make it the same way as the dragon's blood ink, but when completed, add three drops of rose essential oil.

Black Frankincense and Myrrh Ink

This ink gives the power of success and influence to any of your spells. Burn frankincense and myrrh resins over hot coals. Collect the smoke from this on an inverted spoon. On the spoon add a few drops of hot, distilled water. Do this slowly to allow time for the black from the resin smoke to blend with the water. Add a minute amount of gum arabic to this mixture to thicken.

A Word to the Wise: Gum arabic is a substance derived from the acacia tree. Herbalists use gum arabic for its soothing qualities. You can use this substance as a general thickener of your magical preparations.

Day 282

Herbed Ritual Wine

One Wiccan tradition involves enhancing the flavor of wine used in the ritual of cakes and wine. Wiccans most commonly use woodruff to flavor their ritual wine. Woodruff has a traditional planetary association with Mars. Witches associate the herb with magical empowerment, the energies of the south of your circle, and the southern quarter's power to will. Witches drink wine infused with woodruff to reenergize the mind and reinvigorate the spirit, since typically the celebration of cakes and wine takes place at the end of a ritual when you might begin to grow weary.

Today, gather the ingredients and begin the process of herbing your own sacred wine.

What You'll Need:

- 2 tablespoons dried woodruff
- 1 bottle of wine
- 1 teaspoon lemon juice
- Honey to taste

Simply mix the ingredients together and allow them to sit for six hours or more. Pour the wine through cheesecloth to sift out the solid ingredients. Serve during the cakes and wine portion of your circle.

A Word to the Wise: Woodruff is a blood thinner, which heightens the effects of alcohol. It should not be ingested by anyone using blood-thinning medications.

Day 283

Divination

Perhaps you've heard of them: the tarot, magic mirrors, numerology, the runes—these are all various forms of *divination*. The word divination is derived from the word divine. In ancient times, individuals who possessed the ability to see into the future were considered to be linked to the gods, the divine force.

The methods of divination are partially art and partially craft. Well, let's face it. Some of us "got it" and some of us don't. The "it" I'm referring to is psychic ability. There are a number of methods, some of which rely on art (pure psychic ability) and some rely on craft (mostly mechanical methods that rely on recognizable symbolic patterns). Whether you are a "have" or a "have-not," you can be effective in divination. Most of us are in the have-not category. Those of us who are psychically challenged rely on techniques such as astrology, numerology, geomancy, and some tarot methods that do not require any special innate abilities for a successful divinatory reading.

Then there are those *other* methods. You know, the ones set aside for the gifted readers of this book who would likely cash in at the roulette wheel in a Las Vegas casino. These techniques rely on an individual's pure psychic ability. This category of nonmechanical or *scrying* techniques includes the crystal ball, pendulums, and the magic mirror.

If you don't know the category to which you belong, not to worry. During the next days, you will have a brief introduction to several divination techniques and you will gain a clear understanding of how to use the various methods involved in each. You will also learn more about your own psychic aptitude.

Before you get started with learning about divination, take time today to consider the following questions.

Practice: Questions about Divination

- What are my current beliefs and attitudes about divination?
- Is it right or wrong to glimpse the future?
- What are some possible results of knowing the future?
- Do I believe that human beings are guided by a predetermined plan or is choice involved in our destinies?
- Can knowing something about the future alter my current behavior or life patterns in some way?

Day 284

Learning the Tarot

The word tarot has an unusual origin. Scholars believe that the deck of seventy-eight cards began as the fifteenth-century Italian card game called *tarocchi.* Occult traditions claim that the tarot is an ancient system of divination that can be traced back to either eleventh-century Morocco or even as far back as ancient Egypt. The traditional tarot deck has fifty-six *minor arcana* (or lesser mysteries) cards, made up of suits such as wands, cups, swords, and pentacles. The remaining twenty-two cards, the *major arcana* (greater mysteries), depict *archetypal* or universal themes common to all humanity.

The subjects of the major arcana are a distillation of the themes you find throughout the minor arcana and they cover a broad range of our human experiences. Because of this, many tarot readers dispense with using the minor suit cards in divinatory readings altogether. While it is worthwhile to fully investigate all seventy-eight of the tarot cards, we will focus in on the twenty-two major arcana over the next weeks.

You will also learn how to use these cards for divinatory, meditative, and personal empowerment purposes. Throughout these lessons, I will refer to the imagery of the *Universal Tarot* deck (publisher: Lo Scarabeo). Most everyone new to the tarot gains initial training with a similar deck. You can find these decks at any well-stocked metaphysical shop or through an online service.

Our First Card: The Fool

The fool walks toward the edge of a cliff, while looking up into the sky. He is about to leap into the unknown. This too is how we enter the world. We are born not knowing. There is no conditioning of the mind, nor is there orientation to culture, language, time, place, person, family, etc. We simply *are.* This is our natural state of being. It is the magical state of empowerment inherent in all that exists: flowers, cars, planets, atoms, dogs and cats. We all have an existence that is independent of thought, free from the state of conditioned knowing.

Divinatory Meaning

The Fool represents a state of innocence, a state of unconditioned action; it is pure action that is not predicated on thought. It can represent a person who is acting from a state of innocence and not knowing, or simply a situation that calls for the questioner to enter this state of awareness.

Meditation

Sit comfortably in front of a white wall. Open your eyes and gaze as though you are focusing on a spot at least three feet through the wall. Breathe normally. Follow the breath with your mind and do not allow thoughts to interrupt your ability to follow the breath. You can count each breath from one to ten. Return to the number one each time you notice a thought arising.

Daily Practice

Keep the Fool card with you at all times today, or, if this is not practical, place it on your altar. Keep a "foolish" mind with you all day. Don't assume the reasons for the things that happen. Avoid internal dialogue and running commentary about the events of your day. Keep a simple mind that reflects everything and clings to nothing. Evoke the Fool state of mind whenever you need simplicity and truth in your life.

Day 285

The Magician

The Magician is card number one in the tarot. One is a number that carries a masculine energy. In its essence, the Magician and the number one represent forward-moving, directed willpower. The Magician stands before his altar with four of the magical tools spread before him. He holds a phallic wand in his upraised right hand. The lamnescate, the symbol for eternity, floats above the magician's head. The energy of the magician is that of fire; it is the primal energy that sustains creative action.

Divinatory Meaning

In a reading, the Magician represents the power to create change. When this card appears in the reading, remind the questioner that he or she holds all of the tools necessary for success. Once you are able to change your consciousness, you are able to change your circumstance. It also means that it is time to become active, to take some necessary practical action.

Meditation

Close your eyes and take several deep breaths. Imagine that you travel through time and space until you stand before the most primal of energies—the force behind all creation. How does this energy appear to you? As you stand there, begin to inhale and exhale slowly. As you inhale, imagine that you draw this force into your being. Fill your body entirely until there is no "you" left—only this creative force. After that, open your eyes. How does it feel to be one with the power of the Magician?

Daily Practice

Keep the Magician card with you at all times today, or place it on your altar. Stay focused on action today. What is it that you need to accomplish? Do you have goals? If not, why not? Set some goals today. Write down the steps to achieve your daily goals and complete each step. The power behind magic is that of movement—so stay active until you achieve your plans.

Day 286

The High Priestess

The High Priestess is the symbol for intuition and self-guidance. Just as the number one symbolizes masculine energy, the number two symbolizes the universal feminine. The High Priestess sits between two pillars, one black and one white. The pillars represent the polar energies (life and death, night and day, being and non-being, etc.) that pervade all of existence. Since the High Priestess is the divine feminine principle, the entirety of the universe, she contains these contrasting qualities. The crown on her head represents the full moon. The elemental energy of the High Priestess is that of water. The image of the High Priestess card teaches us that the primal waters (which symbolize the unformed, fluid unconscious mind) give birth to and guide all of life.

Divinatory Meaning

In a reading, the High Priestess represents your own intuitive power. The questioner must look into her own deep mind for the key answers in the reading. Intuition guides the questioner at this time; if only she were to acknowledge this, she would know the most empowering course of action.

Meditation

When you have a situation that requires your intuition, try this meditation. Before you begin, contemplate your situation thoroughly. Then close your eyes and take several deep breaths. Imagine that you stand before a great clear pool. This is the pool of your own internal wisdom. Beside the pool is a magical chalice. Fill the cup and drink deeply of the waters. Ask what it is you should do in the situation. Listen for an answer—and then follow it.

Daily Practice

Keep the High Priestess card with you, or alternatively, place it on your altar. For the duration of the day, maintain awareness of your hunches and intuitive perceptions. Follow your intuition today and see where it leads you. Release yourself into the vast supportive net of the universe, and know in your bones that nature always supports you. You are always connected to the people, places, and things of this world in ways that you can never full, consciously know.

Day 287

The Empress

The Empress is the symbol for birth and the universal mother principle. The Empress sits in a lush garden and at her feet sits the symbol for Venus, the goddess of love and beauty. As she sits on her plush throne, she holds up a pearl scepter. The empress represents the mother instinct, the desire to provide, to give birth to new things, to nurture, and to love.

Divinatory Meaning

In a reading, the Empress signifies that love, nurturing, and beauty are the necessary qualities that the questioner must bring forward in a given situation. Have the questioner think about how she has applied (or not) a fully accepting, nonjudgmental, loving attitude in the situation. Where this principle is applied, the questioner can be assured of the desirable outcome.

Meditation

Close your eyes and imagine that you travel down inside your body to the region of your heart. Once you are there, this region opens to a lush, green landscape. Beneath your feet is a path that you instinctively follow. At the end of the path is a robed woman with a full figure and a kindly face. This figure is the ideal archetypal mother. She opens her arms and holds you, deeply filling you with inner peace and a sense of harmony. Return to this place whenever you have need of this mother goddess' love or wisdom.

Daily Practice

Keep the Empress card with you at all times today, or place it on your altar. For the duration of the day, maintain focus on your interactions with other people. Are you able to speak with a voice of love? Are you able to listen with ears of loving acceptance? Are you able to be present to someone else's joy or pain? Try to develop your ability to open up to other people in these ways today.

Day 288

The Emperor

The Emperor is the symbol for the universal principle of activity. Occultists associate this card with the Germanic rune *Ansuz*, which represents the stag. The Emperor represents the Witch's horned god in all of his might. The Emperor sits on a throne adorned with ram's heads. The Emperor represents the power of Aries, the ram: force, pioneering, movement, command, and leadership. The bearded Emperor sits on his throne before a background of rugged, bare mountains, which evoke the feeling of sterility, a warning of the dangers that can come with unilateral and unchallenged power.

Divinatory Meaning

In a reading, the Emperor signifies leadership. The questioners should assess her leadership abilities, or perhaps should see how she id leading herself or others in the situation at hand. Remember that temperance moderates effective leadership and that a monarchical approach to matters can lead to oppression. Have the questioner think about how she might lead the situation in a new direction.

Meditation

Close your eyes and imagine that you sit on the Emperor's throne. Imagine yourself cloaked in his robes and feel the power that they impart. On the ground before you lies the Emperor's golden staff, which is formed in the shape of an Egyptian ankh. This is the symbol of immortal life and eternal power. Take the scepter in your hand, and immediately you will feel the power of the Emperor flooding through you. Ask yourself what action to take in your life. When you are done, open your eyes and take that leadership role.

Daily Practice

Keep the Emperor card with you at all times today, or place it on your altar. For the duration of the day, consider how you lead other people (or how you don't). How effective are you as a leader? Do you assume leadership duties or do you shrink away from them? During the course of the day, take the lead in some positive, inclusive way.

Day 289

The Heirophant

The Heirophant symbolizes conventionality, meaning the outer forms and structures of spirituality and ritual. The Heirophant sits with the triple crown of the pope upon his head. Close to his feet are keys that unlock sacred mysteries, and his feet rest on hidden doctrines. The Heirophant is built on the initiatory mysteries found in the previous High Priestess card, but he has no interest in the mysteries. His way is that of doctrine, words, interpretation, and culture. Traditional religious experiences often reflect the archetype of the Heirophant, as they rarely engage the mystical senses that can free and illuminate an individual.

Divinatory Meaning

In a reading, the Heirophant signifies a conventional approach to life's matters. The questioner may be stuck in the traditional modes of society and needs to break free—or at least question these structures. Questioners should ask themselves why they feel the need to conform in the situation. What exactly are they seeking by choosing a conforming approach to their lives? Questioners should accept themselves in all their strengths and imperfections. On the other hand, it could be that the questioner is somehow unconventional to the point of inaccessibility and this stance should likewise be thoroughly questioned.

Meditation

Close your eyes and breathe deeply. Imagine that you walk down a wide path that runs through the woods. It is midnight and the full moon lights your path. As you walk, think about a difficult situation in your life about which you have trouble deciding what to do. As you think and walk, you soon notice that the path comes to a fork. On the left-hand side is a narrow path that seems dark because it is shaded by trees. The small path is curved, so you cannot see what lies ahead. On the right is a wide, easily accessible path, brightly lit by the moon. Which path will you take?

From out of the woods emerges the Heirophant. Tell him about your life situation and allow him to guide you to the right path. Ask him which path you should take and why.

Daily Practice

Keep the Heirophant card with you at all times today, or place it on your altar. Spend time noticing how you might act from routine. Anything can become routine—even acting unconventionally can become habit, and all habitual patterns should come under the microscope. Question the origins of your routines. Is routine based in fear of the unknown? Is following a routine an easier way to live day to day? Does it help organize your existence? Why does your life need to be organized in any particular way? Try something that breaks your normal pattern or routine today.

Day 290

The Lovers

The Lovers is the symbol for universal love—the joining of two separate parts into one complete whole. The Lovers stand before two trees. The male figure stands before a tree with flames upon it. The female stands before the mythical Tree of the Knowledge of Good and Evil. An angel hovers above them, representing the divine quality of union. In Wicca, the lovers also stands for the divine union celebrated in the initiatory Great Rite, wherein two consenting Witches engage in ritualized (and sometimes purely symbolic) sexual union. The act represents the joining of disparate forces that come together as pieces of the grand whole. It is the joining of the conscious to the unconscious, sun to moon, action to nonaction, and being to non-being. The principle of the Lovers is best represented by the Chinese yin-yang symbol.

Divinatory Meaning

In a reading, the Lovers can indicate love or romance in the questioner's life. In any case it refers to relationship. The relationship does not have to be between human beings. It asks the questioner to consider how things interrelate. What is cause and what is effect? The Lovers might also ask the questioner to contemplate how sexuality plays a role in the current situation.

Meditation

Close your eyes and imagine that you stand before a great mirror that can show what it is you believe you lack. As you stand before the mirror, you initially behold your usual reflection, but then the image transforms and you see the part of you that you believe is missing. What does the mirror show you? Ask the mirror what steps to take to find wholeness and unity.

Daily Practice

Keep the Lovers card with you at all times today, or place it on your altar. Contemplate your relationships to people, to objects, to the environment, and to the world of spirit. Focus on building respectful, sacred, whole relationships today. Instead of viewing the objects of your environment as inanimate and lacking awareness, regard them as beings of consciousness and feeling. Change your approach to the world from an *it* consciousness to a *thou* consciousness. When everyone and everything is sacred, how will you behave toward them?

Day 291

The Chariot

The Chariot is the symbol for causation, movement, and the triumph of the human will over fear and adversity. The Chariot depicts the torso of a man showing from inside a chariot. Above him is a canopy of stars and beneath him are two sphinxes (one black and one white) that pull the chariot. The image evokes the archetype of human control over base instincts. The canopy of stars represents the heavens ultimately influencing earthly activity. The card suggests that through divine inspiration, we create movement and action in the world.

Divinatory Meaning

In a reading, the Chariot draws attention to the questioner's willpower. Have the questioner explore the influence of her will on the subject at hand. Examine all motivations. Are they strong or weak? What is *pulling* this questioner's chariot? If there is little motivation behind action, it will result in minimal results and vice-versa.

Meditation

Close your eyes and imagine a situation in which you would like movement or action to take place. Vividly bring to mind all of the characters and situations that come together to form the situation. Once you have this in your mind's eye, begin to breathe deeply. On each exhalation, imagine that you imbue the situation with a brilliant light. Fill each person involved with your motivating energy until all that you see before you is a brilliant light. Now allow the light to fade. As it does, envision the situation changing to reflect the preferred outcome.

Daily Practice

Keep the Chariot card with you at all times today, or place it on your altar. As you act throughout your day, take mental note of what motivates you. Are you moved by fear? Anxiety? Greed? Anger? Hope? At the day's end, journal about the experience and note what it was that motivated you the most. What do your motivating factors say about you? How would you like to change this?

Day 292

Strength

The Strength card symbolizes internal strength, spiritual strength, and the triumph of love over all. The Strength card depicts a woman controlling the gaping mouth of a lion. Her face is meditative, not strained. The power that she uses comes from sources beyond physical strength. Around her waist is a garland of roses, which represents love. Above her head is the lamniscate, a symbol for eternity. The card suggests that we derive true strength from the divine. In pagan practice, the greatest strength of all emerges from love for the natural world. This is not the sexual love of the Lovers, but *agape*—a universal love.

Divinatory Meaning

In a reading, Strength encourages the questioner to literally summon her strength. Remind the questioner that she must remain calm in the situation at hand and she should allow the strength of the universe to fill her and guide her through to the resolution. There is no outward, straining effort required of the situation, so the questioner should stop struggling. The strength needed in the situation is a serene, inner strength. Have the questioner assess her level of inner strength. Is she up to the task? Why or why not? Ask what steps she must take to summon strength.

Meditation

Close your eyes and imagine that you stand near a cliff pounded by the ocean's waves. Observe the serene strength of the cliff. Observe how it requires no effort. It stands by its own natural strength. In a flash, you become the cliff. Feel your sturdiness, your mass. Feel how the ocean swirls and crashes against you, yet does not move you in the slightest. Breathe deeply. With each inhalation you draw into your being this sturdy inner strength of the cliff. When you feel as though you have assumed the full virtues of the sea cliff, open your eyes.

Daily Practice

Keep the Strength card with you at all times today, or place it on your altar. As you go throughout your day try taking action with a sense of calm courage. Try the meditation above and then go about your day doing your normal activities as though you were this great, poised, unmovable cliff. How might this internalized image affect your daily life?

Day 293

The Hermit

The Hermit card symbolizes universal wisdom. The Hermit stands alone upon a snow-capped peak. He holds up a lantern containing a hexagon—a six-pointed star. This symbol represents the joining of two alchemical symbols/principles that you have already learned. It is the merging of earth and air. From the center point of this cosmic elemental meeting comes wisdom. He represents the human being who has relinquished his name, his titles, and honors to become nothing less than life itself. Once you open up and release the personal ego in favor of the impersonal (the natural energy that is your essence), wisdom begins to flow.

Divinatory Meaning

In a reading, the Hermit asks the questioner how she might be personalizing. The Hermit suggests that the questioner step back to recognize her life situation as an impersonal interplay of energy. It is one more manifestation of the yin and the yang, the light and the dark. The Hermit asks the questioner to take stock of what really matters here. The bigger picture, which includes questions of life and death, of existence itself, of life's meaning lie at the core of the issue in the questioner's mind. If the questioner were to summon her inner wisdom she could use the situation at hand to propel her into discovering her life's purpose. The card may also suggest that the questioner may meet someone who will guide her with the Hermit's impersonal wisdom.

Meditation

Close your eyes and imagine that you walk upward along a mountain path. Continue walking and notice that the further you climb the mountain, the more silent you become internally. When you reach the peak, you find a robed old man. Ask him what question you would like. Do not waste his time by ignoring his counsel. Do as the Hermit instructs you. Once you receive your message, open your eyes and take action.

Daily Practice

Keep the Hermit card with you or place it on your altar today. Go someplace in nature where you can be alone. Sit in silence, taking in the sights and sounds of your environment. If you have a situation that needs attention in your life, watch the natural world around you to see if it can offer you any wisdom. For example, a bird in flight may suggest that you get an overview of the situation. The sound of crickets may tell you to count your blessings. Who knows what it all may mean to you? You do. What is important is that you open up and let the wisdom of your own nature come forward.

Day 294

The Wheel of Fortune

The Wheel of Fortune symbolizes fate, destiny, and the true nature of reality. The Wheel of Fortune is an eight-spoked disk. Girding the disk are four archetypal images that correspond to zodiacal end elemental energies: The bull is Taurus (earth), the lion Leo (fire), the eagle is Scorpio (water), and the angel is Aquarius (air). Anubis, the jackal-headed god of the Egyptian underworld myths, supports the wheel. Here Anubis represents knowledge of one's own death as a fact of life. Opposite of Anubis is a snake descending from the sky. This represents form emerging from pure energy. The Wheel of Fortune reminds us that life is chancy. There are no rules except those we ourselves impose. Right, wrong, good, evil—all descriptions we can assign to the world are merely products of our own projections and life conditioning.

Divinatory Meaning

In a reading, the Wheel of Fortune points out the unpredictability of life. Remind the questioner that the outcome of her situation has little to do with human effort. Things simply happen as they happen. It is how we interpret the events and outcomes of our lives that cause us joy or suffering. Expect the unexpected. The questioner should explore her expectations and learn to come to a place of neutrality. She should release her insistence on some particular outcome.

Meditation

Close your eyes and bring into your imagination your current life situation. Now change the image to show your desired outcome. Take note of how this causes you to feel. Now change the image to show an undesirable outcome. Take note of how this causes you to feel. When you are finished, ask yourself this question: Why is it that one outcome versus another causes you peace of mind or emotional turmoil? Is it the outcome that propels your emotions? Or is it your interpretation of how things ought to be? Contemplate any habitual grasping on to personal desires and how this might contribute to a deluded, disempowered life.

Daily Practice

Keep the Wheel of Fortune card with you or place it on your altar. Whatever actions you take today, make your best efforts and accept the outcomes—no matter what they may be. Stay focused on the quality of your efforts as opposed to the outcome or effect. As Vietnamese author Thich Nhat Hanh says, "There is washing the dishes to get them clean, and then there is washing the dishes to wash the dishes."[87]

Day 295

Justice

The Justice card is the archetype of balance and it stands for spiritual justice. The Justice card depicts a figure seated between two pillars that represent a state of equilibrium. In one hand, the figure holds an upright sword, while the other hand holds the scales of justice. Our usual depiction in Western cultures is justice as the blindfolded figure. However, this card represents spiritual justice, which moves beyond our concepts of fairness and equality. Nature does not manifest itself in a state of fairness or equality as we understand these terms in the usual way. All human beings are *not* created equally; some of us are tall, our levels of intellect vary, and we all have unique interests and skills. It is true that all things are ultimately expressions of one great cosmic energy, but the justice of nature is simply how the world unfolds for us right here. Spiritual justice, then, moves beyond our usual notions of fairness and equality to reflect a natural state of balance.

Divinatory Meaning

In a reading, the Justice card asks the questioner to consider where she might be making judgments. In the ways of the Wise, it is well known that a person who discriminates and pulls the world apart through conceptualization is someone who ultimately loses power. Spiritual power emerges from aligning with the natural flow of the given situation. Have the questioner explore how she might achieve her own state of balance in the situation.

Meditation

Close your eyes and visualize a situation that you believe is causing difficulty in your life. Allow the image of this scene to become a blur of many colors. The colors blend and become a single hue. Simultaneously, imagine that you become hollow. Then imagine this empty space within you becoming the entire universe of planets, stars, and vast empty space. Once you see this, inhale deeply, taking in the color that represented your situation. See the color pass through you and dissipate in the vast neutrality of empty space.

Daily Practice

Keep the Justice card with you or place it on your altar. Focus your attention on your judgments and discriminations throughout the day. You do not have to change your actions or your thoughts. However, at the end of the day, take time to consider how often you deferred to the judging, discriminating mind. How did your thoughts influence your actions and decisions? How might daily judgment-influenced action add up to change the course of your life? What might a judging mind keep you from achieving or attaining? How does it affect your relationships with other people? How does it affect how you relate to the world?

Day 296

The Hanged Man

The Hanged Man represents the wisdom the one gains through effort or through enduring difficulties. The card depicts a man hanging upside down from a branch. His arms are folded behind his back (much like the arm position one encounters in traditional Wiccan initiatory rites). The figure does not appear to suffer; he appears calm despite his circumstance. An aura glows around his head. The figure represents the wisdom one gains through shocking initiatory insights or difficult life circumstances. The Hanged Man reminds us to wisely choose the circumstances into which we will direct our energies and which ones require us to surrender to life's flow.

Divinatory Meaning

In a reading, the Hanged Man suggests that the questioner's current situation will result in important life lessons. Shocks, surprises, or unpleasant circumstances may be involved in the learning process. There is a quality about the questioner's life that has gone yet unexamined, and now is the time to unflinchingly face the stark truth. The Hanged Man is suggesting that the questioner should not struggle against that which cannot be fought.

Meditation

This meditation is designed to help you learn to release to life and to embrace the power of surrendering. Close your eyes and begin to take deep breaths. Imagine that you stand before the ocean. Waves are crashing powerfully against the shore. Walk into the ocean and feel that it is warm and soothing. Allow the waves to sweep over your body. With each wave that caresses you, imagine that you become increasingly transparent. Slowly you become one with the tide itself. See yourself as nothing but ocean—a tide that moves in and out, free and boundless.

Daily Practice

Keep the Hanged Man card with you or place it on your altar. Difficulties do not cease of their own accord. When left unattended, they become worse, uglier, and meaner. Do not run any further from a difficult life situation. Face it today. Get to the bottom of it. Determine what it is you can and cannot do.

DAY 297

Death

Death symbolizes transformation. The card depicts a skeletal figure riding on horseback. The death figure carries the banner of the mystic rose, an occult symbol for the life principle. These two polar symbols (the skeleton and the rose) represent the emergence of life from death.

In contemplating death thoroughly, one always arrives at the conclusion that there can be no life without death. The universe is, metaphorically, an "on" and "off" system; it is a system of alternating light and dark, life and death. However, in the background of our minds broods a fear that this alternation of forces may not be true, and that the death principle will ultimately triumph. Many of us live with the fear that nonexistence will overcome existence and that death really means *extinction.* Since the "existence" part of life is the only component that we can physically experience, we mistakenly assume that all is lost at death. However, the life force continues on beyond our physical senses. The life force, the energy that makes up your essence, is an eternal element. It is always ready to take new forms.

Divinatory Meaning

In a reading, the Death card represents transformation. The questioner is facing a situation that either requires a transformation of consciousness, or can mean a pivotal, life-changing event. Ask the questioner what it is she must do to change her approach to her current situation. How is the questioner not living fully? The card may mean that the questioner needs to psychologically let go of something—and allow its death. The card may also signify that death is currently a significant issue in the questioner's life.

Meditation

Close your eyes and imagine that you stand before the skeletal death figure from the tarot card. He will point to an open grave, freshly dug in the earth. Peer into the grave and you will see a scene from your life that requires change. Ask this skeletal figure what must be done in the situation. After you hear the words of death, open your eyes. Heed death's advice and move into action.

Daily Practice

Keep the Death card with you or place it on your altar. Imagine that this is the last day of your life. Go about your usual day with this "final day" attitude. How will you approach this day knowing it is your last?

Day 298

Temperance

Temperance represents the psychological state of mind called detachment. This card depicts a winged figure—probably an angel—with a solar disk emblazoned on his forehead. The solar disk at the center of the brow represents a state of mind that is immortal. The sun has no shadow (unlike the moon); symbolically the sun goes untouched by time, by aging and death. The winged figure carefully pours water from one vessel to another, signifying the strict attention one should pay to the details of life.

Divinatory Meaning

In a reading, Temperance represents detachment. The questioner is asked to find out how she is too close to the situation to make rational decisions. How is over-involvement clouding her judgment? The questioner would benefit from stepping back from her situation in order to gain perspective. It is time to take action based on cool-headed, rational thinking. The questioner should examine the situation rationally before committing to further involvement.

Meditation

Close your eyes and imagine that you stand in a great, grassy field on a clear, sunny day. Hold in your mind a question about your life that stirs your emotions. Take several deep breaths and then look to the sky. From above comes a spiral of colored light. The complexities of light are too great to define, but this spiral swirls down around your body. As it does, it transforms you. It also transforms the question you hold in your mind. This swirl of light sweeps away all of your emotional ties to the situation at hand and leaves you with a clear mind. The spiral of light recedes to the heavens again. Now that your mind is clear, what is the best action for you to take in the situation—if any?

Daily Practice

Keep the Temperance card with you or place it on your altar. For the duration of the day, attend to the small details of your life. The gods are in the details, so go find them there!

Day 299

The Devil

The Devil represents illusion. Pagans understand that the devil was a creation of a hierarchical monotheistic spiritual system and it was used to frighten and coerce the native Europeans into practicing Christianity. In light of this, it is fair to say that there is no such thing as the devil. It represents any illusory principle, idea, or fiction that holds individuals in bond-age. The Devil card depicts a bat-winged, horned devil with an inverted pentagram above his head. Attached to the cube upon which the devil sits are a male and female figure. Both are chained loosely enough to slip away. This imagery suggests the illusory nature of our bondage to things.

Divinatory Meaning:

In a reading, the Devil represents an unhealthy attachment. The questioner may feel as though she is trapped. However, she might consider her attachments to ideas, feelings, or perhaps the situation itself. No one is trapped here. Why is this questioner clinging? What is important to grasp so tightly? Have the questioner explore her illusory chains.

Meditation

Before you begin, take a moment to consider a difficult situation you face. Then close your eyes and imagine that you stand at the base of the Devil's cube (as depicted in the tarot card). You are chained to the cube. Notice that the chain is made up of words. These words tell you what it is that binds you in an unhealthy way to the situation. You will notice that the chains are loose around your neck. As you begin to slip them off, the devil figure will tell you all of the reasons why you must stay in the situation. Simply listen and take note of how the beliefs you hold keep you bound. Once you slip the chains off, the devil figure disappears. Open your eyes and note how much freer you feel.

Daily Practice

Keep the Devil card with you or place it on your altar. Take note today of your attachments. Keep a written record of the ideas, concepts, beliefs, and attitudes on which you insist. Are there friends or even enemies that remain tied to you based only on your conceptualizations (and not the presenting reality)? How has the "devil" of grasping controlled you?

Day 300

Contemplative Day: The Innermost Name

Meditative Question: What is the innermost secret name of deity?

Symbolic Color: White

Symbolic Direction: Nowhere and everywhere

Don't let the seeming impossibility of the question stump you. This contemplative question aims at completely cutting through concepts. The question gives nothing to think about, therefore it gives nothing to latch onto as you meditate on its meaning. With time, you will arrive at a powerful and consciousness-changing conclusion.

This question is the second in the final series of four inner mysteries. Remember that it is advisable to work with each of these inner-mysteries contemplations while sitting within the center of your magic circle.

Find a comfortable meditative sitting position in the center of your circle. Light a white candle and sit approximately two feet away from the flame. Cast your gaze upon the flickering candle and hold the question firmly for 20 to 30 minutes. Close the circle after this, but keep the question with you. Allow yourself to embody the question, and over time you will arrive at your own insight.

Days 310-366

Magical Items to Gather

Here are the items you will need for the last two months of your training.

Day 315

- An empty picture frame (with glass inset)
- High-gloss black paint (spray paint works best)
- As many of the following herbs as you can gather: dried mugwort, star anise, poppy seed, yarrow, cinquefoil, and hemp.

Day 316

- A 5–6 inch purple taper candle
- Dried white sage, frankincense, or dragon's blood resin

Day 318

- A 5–6 inch purple taper candle
- A piece of red, black or purple silk, large enough to cover the entire mirror

Days 323-352

During these days you will explore the runes and you will need the following:

- Four 5–6 inch white taper candles
- Three 5–6 inch purple taper candles
- Three 5–6 inch blue taper candles
- Three 5–6 inch green taper candles
- Three 5–6 inch yellow taper candles
- Three 5–6 inch orange taper candles
- Three 5–6 inch red taper candles

Recommended, but not required essential oils include:

- Lotus
- Anise
- Frankincense

- Lavender
- Carnation
- Gardenia
- Cedar

Day 361

- patchouli essential oil
- cinnamon essential oil
- eucalyptus essential oil
- musk essential oil
- Handful of dried powdered sandalwood
- 2 tablespoons dried patchouli leaf
- 2 tablespoons cinnamon bark (or powder)

Day 301

Devotional Day: Honoring Aradia

Table of Correspondences: Aradia

Symbols: Forests, the crescent moon, cypress trees

Tools: The pentacle, the moon crown, amber and jet necklace

Magical Essences/herbs: Cypress, John the Conqueror, lemon, jasmine, and anise

Direction: North

She Rules: Nature, magic, sexuality, opposites, justice, secrets, wisdom, teaching, learning, karma, protection, counter-magic, politics, social awareness

Animal Symbols: Cat, fish, wolf

Sacred Foods: Crescent moon cakes and *grapa*

Magical Stones: Moonstone

Aradia is a moon goddess from Tuscany. She is the most popular goddess form that Witches invoke in their ceremonies. Wiccans consider Aradia to be the patroness of the *stregoni* (Italian for Witches). The *Vangelo*, the so-called "Gospel of the Witches," names Aradia as the daughter of the hunter-goddess, Diana, and the god of light, Lucifer (his name literally means "light-bearer"). As in all mythic structures that stress polarity and opposites, the Vangelo depicts Diana as a goddess of night and of darkness (to complement Lucifer, the god of light). As the Vangelo states, "In her were all things; out of herself, the first darkness, she divided herself . . ." From the darkness she created light—Lucifer—and from their union came Aradia. Aradia, therefore, represents the blending of light and dark principles.

She is the keeper of secrets, both light and dark. She is the spirit of nature, and as such she is the complementary divine-feminine figure to the gods Cernunnos, Herne, or Pan.[88] She is the goddess who hangs between the balancing points of maiden and mother—perhaps we can call her the archetype of the temptress. She is fertile and she expresses sexuality openly, not for the sake of pleasure, but because it is a magical act. For Aradia, sexual union represents the blending of two into one, the blending of light, dark, up, down, positive, negative, yin and yang. She is the patroness of the woods, since that is where her devotees erected her sacred groves. She is also a goddess of justice, equality, wisdom, and magical policy.

Rely on Aradia when you need strength in your magic. Call on her whenever you need change, or whenever you want to see justice prevail. If you need to keep a secret, ask Aradia for her help. Her sacred symbols are cypress trees and the crescent moon. Her magical essences and herbs are cypress, John the Conqueror, lemon, jasmine, and anise. Aradia is aligned with the north, with earth and midnight. Her sacred colors are white and black. Her animal spirit is the cat, but she also takes the form of fish and the wolf. Aradia's sacred foods are crescent moon cakes, poppyseed cakes, and *grap*a (an Italian wine).

Aradia Practice

In honoring Aradia today, build a sacred altar to her divine presence. Take time to face the altar and intone her name, one syllable at a time (pronounced: *Ah-RAH-dee-ah*) until you feel her presence surrounding you. Once she has arrived, spend some time contemplating what it might mean to serve this aspect of deity. Take time to ask Aradia what it would mean to live life through her energy, and listen for her answer.

Spend the day honoring this goddess by working magic of any kind and by seeking to bring justice and social awareness to yourself and others.

Day 302

Day of Silence and Review

Today, as you observe silence, focus your attention on your spirit, the energy that pervades and sustains your existence. Spend time considering where this energy form may reside. Is this an internal or external aspect of yourself? What makes up your spirit? Consider how it moves you throughout your day. At the day's end, answer these questions:

- What was it like to focus my attention on my spirit?
- Is spirit something that I could find? How? Where is it?
- How does spirit move me throughout my day?
- Is there anything that seems to affect my spirit?
- How does my spirit seem to interact with my senses, my thoughts, and emotions?

Review

For today's practice, take time to ask yourself the following:

- Of the information I have learned up to now, what stands out most as vital?
- What information seems least relevant to my spiritual development?
- Which of the practices seemed to move me spiritually, and which had little impact?
- Of the information I have learned so far, what would be best to review? (Take time to review it now.)

DAY 303

The Tarot Continued: The Tower

The Tower is the universal symbol for the "wake up call." This card depicts a spire struck by lightning. Figures fall from the flaming tower through a field of mana, the pure energy of the universe. The crown of the tower also falls to the ground. The symbolism suggests the overthrow of an existing (and perhaps idealized or unquestioned) mode of life. In the Devil, you explored those things to which you cling, and in The Tower, any closely held principle, person, or situation is finally inadvertently taken away. The Tower represents a sudden awakening to the reality, the depth, and meaning of your current situation. It is not a symbol of regret, because there is still time to take appropriate action. This time, however, you are bade to act according to the presenting reality, and not on your concepts, hopes, or beliefs about the situation.

Divinatory Meaning

In a reading, The Tower is telling the questioner to awaken to the full unedited reality of her life. The questioner may be shocked by the complexity or gravity of the situation, but she should also bring awareness to the part she played. Sudden changes are in the air. Perhaps there is some good where she once saw only evil—or vice versa. The Tower suggests that the questioner's world has turned upside down; perhaps she loses her grip on ideas, people, and things that she once held dear. However, this overturning of her life will ultimately set things in their proper order. This is a necessary period of purification.

Meditation

Close your eyes and take several deep breaths. Imagine that your body radiates a color that represents your ideals. Imagine this color forms a bubble that surrounds you. Imagine now that you are able to step out of the bubble. Once you do this, the color collapses to the ground beside you. Now look at your spirit body and note how it appears without this color. How does it feel to be without it? This aura cannot survive without being attached to you, so imagine now that the aura dissipates into the ground, where it is neutralized.

Daily Practice

Keep The Tower card with you today or place it on your altar. In front of the altar, set a candle of a color that represents one of your closely held ideals. Take a pin and inscribe a word that represents this ideal on your candle. Light the candle, and while it burns, take out some paper. Write down how this ideal affects your life. Does it create rules? Impossibilities? Does it stifle or direct your behavior in some particular way? How does this ideal defend you from the reality of life? Where do these ideals come from? Who created them? Know that as the candle burns away, so will your ideal. Act throughout the day without sustaining any ideals.

Day 304

The Star

The Star is the universal symbol for optimism and hope. This card depicts a large eight-pointed star suspended above a female figure. Around this star are seven smaller stars. The female figure pours the waters of life into the pool of universal consciousness and upon the earth. The imagery represents the great goddess' gifts bestowed upon the world. Her gifts are those of nature. In The Tower card, you learned to let go of ideals. In the process you become more natural and spontaneous. This natural spontaneity is the gift of the star goddess.

Divinatory Meaning

In a reading, the Star signifies hope and optimism. It is time for the questioner to stop focusing on any held negativity and "what ifs" that lead to projected tragedy. The star shows the questioner that optimism is recommended at this time. It suggests that the questioner put forth her best effort without holding back, and without giving in to unrealistic fears. The card reminds us that optimism (not used as a defense against reality) is a state of mind that has little to do with one's circumstances.

Meditation

Is there some situation about which you have nurtured negative thoughts? Try this exercise to lift your spirits and to restore your goddess-given optimism. Close your eyes and imagine that you are standing beneath dark, rain-swollen clouds. The skies are threatening and the landscape before you appears gray and lifeless. Begin breathing deeply, and on each exhalation, imagine that the dark clouds begin to lighten. Gradually, with each exhaled breath, the clouds dissipate altogether and the bright, golden sun appears. Bask in the rays of the sun for several minutes. Open your eyes and resume your day with an attitude that represents this solar energy.

Daily Practice

Keep the Star card with you today or place it on your altar. Keep a positive frame of mind. No matter the situation, try to enter it with a sense of play, knowing that there is no harm that can ultimately affect you. Count your blessings today. For what do you have to be grateful? Acknowledge your gratitude and allow that to guide your optimistic spirit. Do something that makes you laugh today!

Day 305

The Moon

The Moon is the symbol for the unconscious mind as it manifests through the imagination. In the card, dogs howl at a glowing moon. A shellfish emerges from the waters to pay homage to the moon as well. The shellfish links directly with the moon's own astrological sign, Cancer, the crab. The baying canines represent natural instinct and common unconscious drives. The moon appears to be encased in a glowing sphere—perhaps the sun. The moon is, as Joseph Campbell suggests, the "first spiritual light." Our ancestors based many of their ancient customs on the moon and its cycles. Many of these rites these became lost or were driven underground by the emergence of Christianity as the dominant faith across the globe. When moon rites became outlawed, they drifted into memory and became the stuff of frightening folklore. But the truth of the moon, as Witches know it, is that it is a harbinger of wisdom. The ancients mostly associated it with women's wisdom—which also became a feared commodity in the ancient European world. The Moon card signifies that the truth of a situation is never quite as we had imagined.

Divinatory Meaning

In a reading, the Moon asks the questioner to examine how her imagination is influencing the situation at hand. The Moon card suggests that the truth may be unknowable for the moment, but that it is best to remain in a state of not-knowing in order to act appropriately in the situation. Life has so many variables, how can we ever truly know what will come next? The future is always in flux. Don't make up stories about your life.

Meditation

Sit and watch the moon tonight without any expectation in mind. Allow its energy to silently fill you. How does the energy of the moon feel inside of you? What wisdom does it seem to impart?

Daily Practice

Keep the Moon card with you today or place it on your altar. As you go through your day, remain in a state of readiness for anything that may come your way. Do not resist the situations that come up. Instead, flow with them effortlessly. Keep your imagination and any story about your life at bay.

Day 306

The Sun

The Sun is the symbol for the conscious mind, awareness, and simplicity. In this card, a sun blazes down upon a landscape. In the foreground, a child rides a horse bareback. He is perfectly balanced and aware. He represents the perfection of innocence. Behind him are four sunflowers that bask in the sun's blazing energy.

Divinatory Meaning

In a reading, the Sun represents clarity of mind and a return to innocence. Ask the questioner about the complexities of her life. It is time to simplify things. What does she hope to gain from a complex life? What is gained by excessive activity or things? Remind the questioner that through simplicity, she can begin to clarify her life situation, regaining strength and spiritual power.

Meditation

At dawn today, sit facing toward the east and watch the sun rise. As you do, begin to breathe deeply, consciously. On each inhalation, draw the power of the sun into your spirit. Allow it to fill your body and your mind. At sunset, sit and face the west. Watch the sunset. As it sinks into the horizon, begin to breathe deeply again. On each exhalation, breathe out your fears, anxieties, and illnesses. Allow the sun to absorb these. It will take them to the underworld, where it will burn them to ash.

Daily Practice

Keep the Sun card with you today or place it on your altar. Today is a day to simplify. Assess the activities of your day to determine if they are essential for existence, for basic happiness and health. If not, disregard them for the day. As one Eastern mystic said of life, "If it does not involve eating, sleeping, or shitting, it is none of your business."

DAY 307

Judgement

Judgement is the symbol for change and renewal. In this card an angel blows his trumpet, awakening human beings from death. In the fore and background, human beings stand in their opened graves, raising their arms in joy to the skies. The symbolism represents a transformation of consciousness. It is a card of alchemy—of magical change. However, this change of consciousness does not occur alone; our highest level of awareness comes when we yoke our normal efforts to the divine force that continually operates in our lives.

Divinatory Meaning

In a reading, Judgement is awakening the questioner to change. Remind the questioner that her circumstances cannot be changed from external efforts alone. The external world always remains the same, but when we change our position to the world, to the external forces, everything appears to change. The questioner is called to modify her approach to the situation at hand. How has she judged or labeled her situation? When she changes her judgement, the situation will inevitably change.

Meditation

Begin this exercise by thinking about a situation that is weighing heavily in your mind. Now take out a piece of paper and write down all of your thoughts and feelings about the situation. Try to keep the pen (and your thoughts) flowing for at least five nonstop minutes. Crumple the paper and cast it into a fire. As it burns, close your eyes and imagine the situation changing. Imagine that it loses its weight and power over you.

Daily Practice

Keep the Judgement card with you today or place it on your altar. Keep track of your judgments today. Are you labeling people and situations as "good," "bad," "desirable," or "undesirable?" Every time you catch yourself in a judging frame of mind, mentally say, "Stop!" Then continue your activity with a clear mind.

Day 308

The World

The World is the universal symbol for totality and wholeness. In this card, a wreath of leaves surrounds a woman who holds a wand in each of her hands. The figures in each of the card's corners (as in the Wheel of Fortune) represent the four elements, the four directions, and all of their magical associations. The card is somewhat of a mandala that connects the earthly and the spiritual realms of existence. The Hebrew letter that has magical influence through this card is Tav, the final letter of the alphabet. It is a letter linked to the Greek Tau and the Egyptian tau cross, which is a symbol for eternity. The card represents this energy of eternity, totality, beginning and end drawn together.

Divinatory Meaning

In a reading, the World traditionally represents success, but the card goes beyond this simple abstract concept. The World card represents actual attainment. It represents unison with the divine force, which is inherent in all manifestations. The questioner is asked to look for inspiration from her daily life and from nature. Ask the questioner how she understands wholeness in this situation. Can she put all the pieces together cohesively? If not, then perhaps there are pieces of the situation that are not yet resolved or have not come to her attention. Soon the whole picture will become clear and she will be able to make sound decisions. The World card calls for practicality. Ask the questioner what practical steps she can take to restore balance to her situation

Meditation

Close your eyes and breathe deeply. Concentrate your mind on your solar-plexus chakra. Follow your breathing; observe each inhalation and exhalation. In this way you unify the workings of your mind and your body. Now imagine an energy at the center of your solar plexus. With each exhalation, the energy enlarges. Watch it expand to fill your body. Then the energy moves past your body and fills the space in which you sit. Then the energy enlarges to fill your neighborhood. The energy continues to expand, flooding over cities, over vast areas of land. It moves across seas. It envelops the earth. When your energy reaches this stage, open your eyes. How do you feel?

Daily Practice

Keep the World card with you today or place it on your altar. Many of us appreciate the concept of nature, but we don't spend the time getting it *on us* and in us. Go into a natural setting today and spend time experiencing this place through the senses.

Day 309

Reading the Cards

It takes time to learn each of the tarot's symbols and to feel competent in integrating them into a cohesive whole when presenting a reading to someone. Set aside time for plenty of practice before reading the cards for anyone other than yourself.

There are many different tarot reading methods. Some of these methods involve the intuitive process. Other methods rely on a structure that assists the reader in interpretation. The structured methods also provide a predetermined context for each card.

For the next few days, you will learn and practice the structured methods. This practice will allow you time to become acquainted with the Tarot as a system. It will also give you an opportunity to practice integrating cards into a contextual whole. For our practices, you will only use the major arcana cards that we have studied.

The Inversion Rule

Tarot readers often ascribe unique meanings to inverted cards (a card with its imagery turned or reversed in its orientation to the reader). However, not all card readers observe this rule. While this reversal rule might have some merit, determining a reading based on reversals can distract the reader from the process of attuning the questioner to the Tarot's archetypal truths. Reliance on an image's directional orientation in a reading is akin to "fortune telling," as opposed to tapping into universal wisdom and guidance. A tarot reading involves interpretation of the archetypes, which are ancient, cross-cultural symbols. There are no reversed archetypes. I recommend if a reversed or inverted card appears in the reading, that you simply turn it so that the image is oriented in a manner that is convenient for your viewing. No special interpretation is necessary.

If you would like to investigate the special meanings of inverted cards, you can learn more about these by further reading in *The Tarot Revealed*, by Eden Gray or *Tarot Reversals* by Mary Greer.

One-Card Method

Witches refer to the method described below as the one-card draw. Practitioners use the one-card draw for several purposes:

- To gain specific guidance in a situation
- To gain general guidance for the day
- To understand the current energy or circumstances surrounding a situation or a person

To begin, hold in your mind's eye the question, "What influence governs my day?" Shuffle the major arcana cards together face down. (Don't go face down on the floor! I mean shuffle the cards so that you cannot view their imagery.) Shuffle them as long as you would care to do so. Lay the cards in a stack before you. Using your left hand, spread the cards with a single sweep from right to left. This move takes some practice. If you don't get it right, simply work the cards into an overlapping row from right to left.

While continuing to hold the question in your mind, draw a single card from the row and turn it over. This card represents a spiritual symbol important for you to keep in mind for the day. Refer to the previous pages if you have forgotten the interpretation of the card you have drawn.

When the day is completed, take time to journal about how the card did or did not provide meaningful guidance for your day.

Day 310

Problem-Solving Technique

Today you will learn a tarot method that can provide you with solutions to any difficulties or challenges in your life. To begin this method, shuffle the cards and spread them as you learned in yesterday's lesson. Then close your eyes and imagine your situation. As you view the situation with your inner eye, you should feel some emotion. There is a place in your body where you feel the emotion of this situation. Where is it? Once you locate the place where you hold the emotional energy of the situation, close your eyes and imagine that you travel down inside your body to that area. Once you are at the location in your body, view the energy and assign it a color and a shape. Imagine that you project yourself into this color/shape and then immediately open your eyes and draw one of the major arcana cards from the cards spread out before you.

The card you have chosen represents the approach you should best take to resolve the problem situation.

Day 311

Three-Card Spread

Use this tarot method whenever you have an open-ended question. (That means a question that is not answered with a simple "yes" or "no.") To begin this method, shuffle the cards face down so that you cannot see their symbols. As you shuffle, keep in mind the situation about which you would like clarity or information. When you are finished shuffling, spread the cards as you have learned.

Now close your eyes. Bring into your mind's eye the situation you have been thinking about. See all of the people involved, and most importantly, feel the feelings that arise because of the situation. Once you identify the feelings involved, notice where in your body you feel this first. It can be anywhere: stomach, chest, legs, hands, face.

Wherever that may be, imagine that you now travel through your body and you arrive at that place that holds the emotion. Give the emotional energy a color and a shape. Once you see it clearly, enter that color and shape. As soon as you do this, open your eyes and draw three cards from the spread.

Place the cards face up, one at a time, from your left to your right. Here is the meaning of each placement:

Card 1 Past	Card 2 Present	Card 3 Future

Card 1 (First card on your left): This card represents the past of the situation. It is the energy that is locked up by the passage of time. It represents the foundation of what is happening right now.

Card 2 (Center card): This represents the current situation. The card also presents you with the method, the approach to the situation that will result in action that is beneficial for all parties.

Card 3 (Last card on your right): This represents the future of the situation. This does not mean the future of the situation has already been decided. It indicates what can result if you do not intervene in the energy pattern, the cycle that is already underway.

Try this method today by yourself at first, then try it with a friend.

Day 312

The Inquirer's Wisdom

Your role in this intuitive reading method is to draw the wisdom out of the inquirer through questioning thoroughly the interpretations that spontaneously occur to her. Here is how it works. After spreading the cards face down, have the questioner think of her situation and draw a single card. Whatever card is drawn, guide the questioner in making verbal associations to the image as it relates to the situation she brings to the reading.

Start by asking the questioner about imagery from the card that appears to stand out for her. Ask about colors that seem to strike her as important or relevant. Ask about features of the imagery that seem particularly interesting. Whatever stands out, have the questioner make free *associations* with the imagery to her own past, to dreams, to family, friends, memories, and experiences.

Listen to the themes that come up for the questioner and help her to relate her associations to the presenting situation. Your final task in this method is to draw together the dominant (or repeated) imagery and the associations that the questioner has offered.

Of all the Tarot techniques, this one sharpens your skills as a guide. It also helps you to see deeper levels of meaning in the cards. Experiment with this method today and continue to attempt this method as a discipline for sharpening your own abilities in drawing pieces together into a cohesive whole.

Day 313

Yes and No

If you simply want a quick "yes" or "no" answer to a question, this is the method for you. You might use the entire deck, since this method relies on the orientation of cards rather than their imagery. To begin, think about your question and shuffle the cards very well. The shuffling process is important here because you want some card images to be upright and some to be reversed in the deck. Spread the whole deck before you and draw three cards out—one at a time. Turn each one over.

If all three cards are upright, with the picture oriented to you so that the image is not inverted, the answer to your question is "yes." If all three cards are reversed, meaning with the picture turned upside down from your view, the answer is "no."

So what about two cards upright, or two cards reversed? When two out of three cards are upright, this means a "qualified yes." This means, most likely the answer is yes. The issue that may disrupt the "yes" answer depends on the remaining inverted card and where it is placed. If the inverted card is the first to your left, the interruption comes from the past. If the inverted card is in the center, the interrupted energy comes from the present situation. If the inverted card is the last on your right, the "yes" energy might get blocked in the future.

The same process is true for a "no" answer. The reading yields a "qualified no" if two out of three cards are reversed and only one is upright in its presentation. This layout means that most likely the answer is "no." The issue that may disrupt the "no" answer depends on the upright card and where it is placed. If the upright card is the first to your left, the interruption comes from the past. If the upright card is in the center, the interrupted energy comes from the present situation. If the upright card is the last on your right, the "no" answer might get blocked in the future.

Day 314

Are We Dealing with a Full Deck?

This final method with the tarot is one that relies completely on your intuition. Use the full tarot deck (including both the major and the minor arcana cards) for this method. You do not need knowledge of the traditional divinatory meanings of each card. All you need is your imagination and a bit of creativity.

Before you begin, it is important to learn the basic ten-card spread called the Celtic Cross. First choose a card that is the *significator*. This card represents the questioner. The significator can be any card in the deck. Tarot specialists suggest using one of the *court cards* such as a king, queen, knight, or page as the significator. As you select your significator, you might also keep in mind that each of the four suits represents one of the four elements.

- Wands: Air
- Cups: Water
- Swords: Fire
- Pentacles: Earth

Which of these archetypes and elements best represents you? You alone can decide.

Place this significator card on the table at least 12 inches away from you. Shuffle the remaining cards, spread them, and draw cards out of that spread one at a time. Place the first one you draw directly on top of the significator, covering the significator card. Place the second card on top of the first but turn it 90 degrees so that it lies on its side. It should form somewhat of a "cross" with the first card. Next, place the third card in the space directly below the crossed cards. Roll up your sleeves and give yourself some room here! Place this third card at least two to three inches below the crossed cards. Place the fourth card to the left of the cross and place the fifth card above the cross. Place the sixth card directly to the right of the crossed cards.

After you draw out the next four cards, place them in an ascending line to the right of the configuration you have already created. Place the seventh card so that it is parallel to the third card of the spread. Place the eighth card in the space directly above the seventh. Place the ninth in the space directly above the eighth. Place the tenth card in the space directly above the ninth.

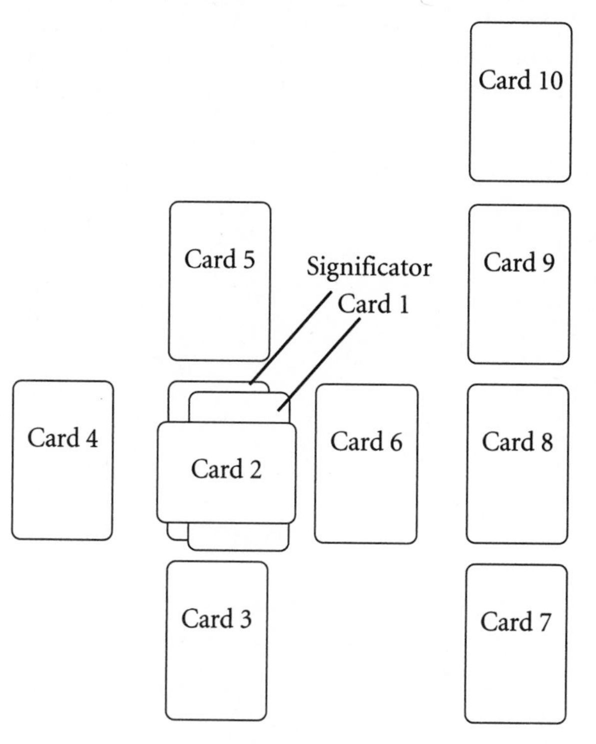

Meaning of the Placements

Here are the meanings of the card placements:

- Card 1: The general atmosphere surrounding the question
- Card 2: The challenge within the situation at ; t. The problem, the oppositional energies
- Card 3: The foundation of the matter at hand; this is how the situation evolved
- Card 4: The influence that is just passing or has recently passed away in the situation
- Card 5: The influence that may come into being
- Card 6: The influence that will come into being in the near future
- Card 7: The questioner's doubts and fears in the situation
- Card 8: How people who are close to the questioner feel about the situation
- Card 9: The questioner's hopes for the situation or for the people involved
- Card 10: The final outcome or the future pattern that can evolve based on current patterns

Now let us learn how to read the cards. Look at each one and see what imagery stands out for you. Ask yourself what the imagery suggests. Whatever it is that first comes into your imagination—that is what the card represents. Keep the significance of the card placements as I have outlined above, but allow the values of the cards to emerge from your own intuition and personal associations.

This method is not only fun to do, but it is surprisingly accurate and often it leads to profound change for both the reader and the questioner.

Day 315

The Magic Mirror

Mirror, mirror on the wall! Anyone familiar with Grimm's tales knows by heart the incantation that invokes the power of a magic mirror. Anyone familiar with Witchcraft knows that the tales are true. The magic mirror is real and it happens to be a powerful and versatile tool that Witches use for many purposes. The mirror is a shiny black surface set into a frame. Contemporary Wiccans use the mirror to divine the future, as a point of departure for astral travel and as a focal point through which they can cast their spells.

Making a Magic Mirror

What You'll Need:

- An empty picture frame (with glass inset)
- High-gloss black paint (spray paint works best)
- Gather together as many of the so-called "psychic condenser" herbs as possible; these herbs include a mixture of dried mugwort, star anise, poppyseed, yarrow, cinquefoil, and hemp.

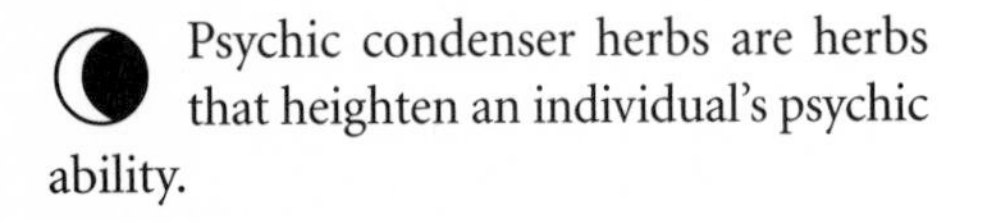

Psychic condenser herbs are herbs that heighten an individual's psychic ability.

Before you begin, take some time to consider the picture frame you would like to encase your "mirror." Choose a frame that is both aesthetically pleasing and large enough to allow for comfortable viewing. I have an antique cherrywood frame that provides about a 15-inch diameter viewing surface.

Once you choose your frame, open it up and take the backing off. Paint one side of the glass with the glossy black paint. Set the glass down with the paint side up so that it can dry. While the paint is still wet, sprinkle it with a mixture of the crushed dried herbs. As the paint dries, these herbs will adhere to the glass. Once the paint is dry, set the glass back inside the picture frame so that all you can see is a shiny black surface.

Voilà! You have created your first magic mirror. Before you go to bed tonight, set the magic mirror on a windowsill so that it can reflect the light of the moon, and the nighttime sky.

Day 316

Blessing the Mirror

What You'll Need:

- Circle-casting tools
- Magic mirror
- A 5–6 inch purple taper candle
- Dried white sage, frankincense, or dragon's blood resin

Cast a circle as you have learned to do. Sprinkle the mirror with your salt and water mixture, saying:

> ***I consecrate thee, O creature of the Art, with the elements of water and of earth.***

Carry the mirror to the west and then to the north of your circle. At each quarter show the mirror to the elementals, saying:

> ***(Undines/Gnomes), hear me now; reflect the truth of thy knowing!***

Return to the altar. Sprinkle the hot coals in your brazier with your chosen incense (sage, frankincense or dragon's blood) and allow it to smolder. Cense the entire mirror with this magical smoke, saying:

> ***I consecrate thee, O creature of the Art, with the element of air.***

Carry the mirror to the eastern quarter and show it to the elementals, saying:

> ***Fairies, hear me now; reflect the truth of thy knowing!***

Return to the altar. Pass the mirror surface quickly through your fire candle's flame (the red candle on your altar). As you do so, say:

> ***I consecrate thee, O creature of the Art, with the element of fire.***

Carry the mirror to the south of the circle and show it to the elemental spirits there, saying:

> ***Salamanders, hear me now; reflect the truth of thy knowing!***

Bring the mirror to the center of the circle and set it flat on the altar, with the dark mirror side facing up. Using your white-handled knife (or a pin, if you do not have a white-handled knife), inscribe the word "vision" onto the purple candle, using Theban script. Light the candle and place it in a holder. Set the holder on top of the mirror's surface.

Close your circle, but allow the candle to burn completely out. Once the candle has extinguished, set the mirror again on your windowsill so that the moon can reflect its light upon the mirror's surface throughout the night.

Day 317

Magic Mirror: Learning the Secret Name

In traditional magical lore, when you know the name of a thing, you have power over it. There is truth in this old axiom, and therefore it is very important in magical practice to know the names of things. I am not referring to the ordinary names of objects and of people that we all know. I am talking about secret, spiritual, or *subtle* names. Today you will learn how to discern secret names and you will learn how to apply this practice to your magic mirror. You can also apply this practice to all areas of your spellwork, but most importantly, you will learn how to use this technique to have complete magical effect with your mirror.

Everything in existence has its own spiritual name. Spiritual names represent a person or object's energy and subtle spiritual vibrations. Magical names are not words as we normally understand them. They are utterances, sounds, or sometimes simple vocalizations that represent spiritual energy as you sense it.

What you will discover is that spiritual names are distinctive for each person. Each of us connects energetically to the world in unique ways. Because of this, I may utter the spiritual, energetic name of an object differently than you do.

This technique may sound tricky, but you will find that this is simply an extension of your creativity. To begin, place the mirror in front of you. Hold out your hands and touch the mirror's surface. Close your eyes and begin to take several deep, slow breaths. Imagine that you travel down your arms, out through your hands and you project your spiritual body into the magic mirror. Sense yourself becoming united with the object. Expand your spirit so that you fill every crevice and nook of the mirror. When you are ready, a word, a sound, or a vibration will begin to form in your throat. Allow whatever this sound may be to emerge unedited.

Once you have connected with the sound, say it aloud. Open your eyes and write it down. This is the spiritual name of your magic mirror. You might try this exercise with people, animals, plants, and other objects today. How does it feel once you utter the spiritual names of things? What is *your* spiritual name?

On this third night, set the mirror once again on your windowsill so that the moon can reflect its light upon the mirror's surface throughout the night.

Day 318

Charging Your Magic Mirror

You have created and blessed your mirror with the four elements. You have discovered its secret name and you have charged it with the moon for three nights running. Today's practice centers on charging the mirror with the subtle, spiritual energies of the four elements as well as with your secret name. After this, your mirror will be ready for all forms of magical use.

What You'll Need:

- Your circle-casting tools/equipment
- A 5–6 inch purple taper candle
- A piece of red, black, or purple silk, large enough to cover the entire mirror

Cast your circle as usual. Using Theban script, scribe with a pin (or with your white-handled knife) the mirror's spiritual name on the purple candle. Go to the east of your circle and place the magic mirror in front of you so that you can see its dark reflective surface. Hold your hands palms facing outward (toward the east) just above the mirror. Close your eyes and imagine that you gather the spiritual energy of the element of air in your hands. Imagine a bright yellow mist that forms in the palms of your hands. Once you see this clearly, bring your palms together, forming the yellow mist into a single ball of energy. Now thrust the ball of energy toward the mirror's surface. Imagine the yellow energy entering and infusing the mirror with the spiritual energies of air.

Now take the mirror to the south of the circle, set it before you, and repeat the process with the element of fire. Hold your hands palms facing outward (toward the south) just above the mirror. Close your eyes and imagine that you gather the spiritual energy of the element of fire in your hands. Imagine a bright red mist that forms in the palms of your hands. Once you see this clearly, bring your palms together, forming the red mist into a single ball of energy. Direct the ball of energy toward the mirror's surface. Imagine the red energy entering and infusing the mirror with the spiritual energies of fire.

Repeat this process in the west, forming a blue ball of energy that you will thrust into the mirror. Finally, repeat this process in the north, forming a green ball of energy that you set into the mirror.

Now return the mirror to the altar in the center of your circle. Hold your hands on the mirror's surface and intone its secret name. As you do this, bring your cupped hands to your mouth. Continue to intone the word in your cupped hands. Feel the vibration of sound. Close your eyes and imagine that as you intone the secret name, a white ball of energy forms inside of your cupped hands. When you see the energy clearly, stop intoning the name and propel the white ball of energy into the mirror's dark surface.

Light the purple candle with the inscribed secret name. Turn the inscription so that it faces the mirror's black reflective surface. Allow the candle to burn out completely. While the candle burns, close your circle.

In magical lore, silk has a retentive property to it, so when the candle has burned out, cover the mirror's surface completely with a length of red, black, or purple silk. From now on, whenever you finish magical work with your mirror, cover it with this silk cloth.

Day 319

Using Your Magic Mirror

Now that you have your magic mirror, how do you use it? The mirror is a scrying tool. The old occult term "scry" means "to divine" or "to see the future." Scrying tools such as the magic mirror are typically those in which the diviner focuses his or her gaze upon an object and, through this activity, he or she is able to see into the astral realm where the future begins to take shape.

In magical theory, the astral realm is one of seven dimensions of existence. It is a realm invisible to the ordinary eye because its frequency or vibratory rate is higher than that of our material world. In this astral realm, our mental images, our hopes and dreams (as well as our fears) begin to form into patterns that, in turn, take shape in the physical realm.

When you scry, you glimpse future patterns forming in the astral realm. Once you know what these are, you are better able to take action, change your consciousness, your attitude, and beliefs, so that new realities form in the astral realm (and therefore new realities can form within the physical plane).

To use the mirror, go to a darkened room and light a candle. Set the candle behind the mirror. Place the mirror so that you can sit and comfortably gaze into its reflective surface. After everything is set in place, hold your hands to the mirror's surface and whisper three times the mirror's secret, subtle name. This activates the energies you have set into the mirror.

As you gaze into the mirror, allow your mind to become a blank page. Let your critical thinking take a well-deserved break for the next twenty minutes or so. If you notice thoughts coming up, simply notice them. Don't try to stop your thoughts, just observe them.

With the aide of this psychic tool, your vision will eventually break through to the astral plane. You will know that you are there because you will begin to see random imagery. For today's practice, do not concern yourself with the meaning of the imagery. Simply jot down what it is you see in the mirror. When you are finished, cover the mirror with your silk and extinguish the candle.

Day 320

Asking a Question

Today you will consult the mirror for an answer to a specific question. As you did before, go to a darkened room and light a candle. Set the candle behind the mirror, hold your hands to the mirror's surface, and whisper your secret word three times.

Gaze into the mirror while holding the question that you have in your mind. You will begin to see random imagery. Jot down any imagery you see. Try not to make any mental associations between what it is you see and your question at this time. Simply note the images without editing. When you are finished scrying, cover the mirror with your silk and extinguish the candle.

Finally, sit down and make associations to the imagery you saw. Let's say, for example, I asked about my relationship and the image I saw was a maple tree. What do I associate with maple trees? Maple syrup, the East Coast of North America, and the changing of the seasons. From here I can perhaps read the symbols in this way:

1. Perhaps my relationship will be going through a change, but this change, like that the maple tree goes through, will be natural; it would therefore be important for me to keep in mind that all things have their rhythms.
2. My relationship is solid as a maple tree. At its center is a certain sweetness that I find satisfying
3. Perhaps there will be renewal in my relationship (East Coast—the direction east and its associations with newness, beginnings, etc.) and I can look forward to things starting in a fresh new way

Day 321

The Runes

So far, you have learned about the tarot and the magic mirror, both of which are fine examples of structured (mechanical) and nonstructured (intuitive) divination methods. Our next method of divination—reading the runes—contains elements of both the structured and nonstructured methods. The runes are a set of ancient Germanic inscriptions consisting of straight lines that come together at various angles to form what historians believe to be an alphabet. There is no consensus among scholars as to when the runes first made their appearance; However, it is safe to say that they were present throughout northern and western Europe prior to the Christianization of the European world. Archaeologists have unearthed some one hundred runic inscriptions that they found throughout Europe. These inscriptions date from roughly the third to the eighth centuries BCE.

The word rune seems to come from either the Germanic *ru* or the Gothic *runa*, both of which mean "secret" and "mystery." As with most forms of early writing found in ancient cultures across the globe, the Germanic people associated the runes with magic. They held a ritual function among the tribal cultures as a means of casting lots, of divination, and as a tool to evoke the powers of the gods.

As you learn more about the runes, you may first believe that each rune carries its own meaning and magical association, but these inscriptions are not meant to symbolize or represent anything. They are meant to actually *be* specific energies. Reading the runes is a process of tapping into the energies that surround the situation and the questioner's life.

From where do these mystic inscriptions originate? There is both a technical and a poetic answer to this question. Before the runes appeared in the form you will learn, the Germanic people of Bronze-Age Europe scratched pictographs into rocks to communicate basic ideas. From these pictographs, simple straight-line carvings evolved. Scholars believe that the runes evolved into their present form because their straight-line designs allowed people to easily notch them into wood—thus allowing written knowledge and communication to become something portable.

As for the poetic side of the story, the ancient Nordic people told a myth of Odin who hung himself upside down from the Yggdrasil, or *world tree.* He hung there for nine days until he finally saw a vision of the runes in either the depths of the tree, its roots, or in the earth below the tree. Below is a poem from the Poetic Edda (circa. CE 1200) that describes Odin's mystical experience.

Practice: Invoking Odin

Cast a circle or go to a secret place in nature. Face the west and read this magical poem aloud. After you read it, sit and meditate on its meaning and its symbolism. What stands out for you in these magical words? How does the portion that stands out in the poem relate to your own life, your current circumstances, or your growth and magical development?

I know I hung on that windswept tree,
Swung there for nine long nights,
Wounded by my own blade,
Bloodied for Odin,
Myself an offering to myself:
Bound to the tree
That no man knows
Whither the roots of it run.

None gave me bread,
None gave me drink.
Down to the deepest depths I peered
Until I spied the runes.
With a roaring cry I seized them up,
Then dizzy and fainting, I fell.

Well-being I won
And wisdom too.
I grew and took joy in my growth:
From a word to a word
I was led to a word,
From a deed to another deed.

DAY 322

Making Runes

There are very specific traditional methods that ancient rune masters would use to create their runes. The runes were most likely a descendant of oracle bones that shamans would throw and read. It comes as no surprise that one of the traditional rune-making materials was bone, usually of the human variety. The rune master might also make runes from wood. Trees that were local to the ancients served them best, as they believed that the spirits of the trees were contained in the wood. But rune makers most favored the wood from fruit-bearing trees. The rune master would look for a branch that was as big around as his thumb and would harvest it. Then he would slice the branch into twenty-four equal segments. While carving the runic symbols into the wood, he would prick his thumb and mark the rune with his own blood in order to create a magical link to the inscriptions.

For your own practice, you need not go to such lengths. The runes can be an easy project since they are made of simple interconnected straight-line markings. There are several ways to make your own runes. Many modern-day rune readers paint the runes using gold or silver metallic paints on small (2-inch diameter) flat river stones or small crystals of their liking. However, you can inscribe the runes on just about anything that awakens your divinatory imagination: small tiles, cut sections of deer antler, seashells, large nutshells, woody seedpods, tree bark, glass beads, or sea glass. If you don't have any of these materials, you can inscribe the runes with a beautiful ink on small (2 x 2 inch) squares of sturdy posterboard or cardboard.

If you want to try making your runes the ancient Germanic way, be sure to use your white-handled knife to carve the runes onto each of the branch pieces, using single knife strokes.

Below are the runes which are divided into their traditional three deity-name groupings: Freya's eight, Hagal's eight, and Tiu's eight.

Freya's eight:

Fehu	Uruz	Ansuz	Thurisaz
Raido	Gebo	Kano	Wunjo

Hagal's eight:

Sowelu	Eihwaz	Hagalaz	Algiz
Jera	Perth	Nauthiz	Isa

Tiu's eight:

Dagaz	Inguz	Laguz	Mannaz
Teiwaz	Ehwaz	Berkana	Othila

Inscribe your own set of runes today. You will learn more about their meaning and magic in the days to come.

Day 323

Freya's Eight: Fehu

Literal Meaning: Possessions, nourishment, cattle

Interpretive Meaning: Fehu is the rune of satisfaction. It signifies a fulfilled desire. Fehu asks the questioner to look deeply at the meaning of profit and gain in her or his life. Does the questioner have what he or she wants? Does he or she want what they have? Is he or she ruled by their desires? It is possible that the questioner's desires are leading him or her astray and causing powerlessness.

Aligning with Fehu

What You'll Need:

- Your usual circle-casting tools
- Recommended essential oil: Lotus
- A 5–6 inch white taper candle

For this simple ritual, it would be best to use lotus essential oil, which aligns with the 7th chakra, at the top of your head, and with Fehu. If you do not have access to this essential oil, simply practice this alignment without it.

Cast your circle as usual. Using your white-handled knife, carve the symbol for Fehu into a white candle. Anoint it with the lotus oil, light it, and silently contemplate the meaning of the rune. Dip your right middle finger into the lotus oil and then draw the symbol for Fehu on your crown chakra (at the top of your head).

Close your eyes and imagine that a brilliant white light etches the symbol Fehu into your crown chakra. The spiritual essence of this rune then permeates your entire being. Feel the vibration of this rune throughout your body.

When you are finished, close the circle and extinguish the candle.

Living Fehu

For the day, live by the principle of Fehu by allowing yourself to feel satisfaction with whatever is in your life.

Day 324

Freya's Eight: Uruz

Literal Meaning: Strength, man/womanhood, wild ox

Interpretive Meaning: Uruz represents endings and new beginnings. This rune aligns with the pagan celebration of Samhain, which attunes Witches to the cycles of death and rebirth. Uruz asks the questioner to remain open to new beginnings even in the face of what appears to be an ending. Ask the questioner to redefine endings. Is there really an end to things? How might the questioner be struggling against a transition to something new, not necessarily preferred or known? Have the questioner talk about what doors may be opening in her or his life—either wanted or not. Transition appears to be necessary at this time.

Aligning with Uruz

What You'll Need:

- Your usual circle-casting tools
- Recommended essential oil: Anise
- A 5–6 inch purple taper candle

For this simple ritual, it would be best to use *anise* essential oil, which aligns with the 6th chakra, at the level of your third eye, and with Uruz. If you do not have access to this essential oil, simply practice this alignment without it.

Cast your circle as usual. Then, using your white-handled knife, carve the symbol for Uruz into the purple candle. Anoint it with the essential oil, light it, and silently contemplate the meaning of the rune. Dip your right middle finger into the anise oil and then draw the symbol for Uruz on your third-eye chakra (at the center of your brow).

Close your eyes and imagine that a brilliant purple light etches the symbol Uruz into your third-eye chakra. The spiritual essence of this rune then permeates your entire being. Feel the vibration of this rune throughout your body.

When you are finished, close the circle and extinguish the candle.

Living Uruz

For the day, live by the principle of Uruz by determining the parts of your life that appear to be ending. Spend time today making peace with and putting to rest your old affairs so that newness can emerge.

Day 325

Freya's Eight: Ansuz

Literal Meaning: Signals, Messenger, Loki (deity)

Interpretive Meaning: Ansuz is the rune of receiving. Now is the time for the questioner to pay attention to intuition. The gods are sending messages and now is the time for the questioner to pay attention and receive them. Messages from the divine are all around the questioner, if only he were to look and listen.

Aligning with Ansuz

What You'll Need:

- Your usual circle-casting tools
- Recommended essential oil: Frankincense
- A 5–6 inch blue taper candle

For this simple ritual, it would be best to use frankincense essential oil, which aligns with the 5th chakra, (at the base of your throat) and with Ansuz. If you do not have access to this essential oil, simply practice this alignment without it.

Cast your circle as usual. Then, using your white-handled knife, carve the symbol for Ansuz into the blue candle. Anoint it with the essential oil, light it, and silently contemplate the meaning of the rune. Dip your right middle finger into the frankincense oil and then draw the symbol for Ansuz on your throat chakra.

Close your eyes and imagine that a brilliant blue light etches the symbol Ansuz into your throat chakra. The spiritual essence of this rune then permeates your entire being. Feel the vibration of this rune throughout your body.

When you are finished, close the circle and extinguish the candle.

Living Ansuz

For the day, live by the principle of Ansuz by following your intuition and the hints left for you by birds, clouds, flowers, and everything in nature.

Day 326

Freya's Eight: Thurisaz

Literal Meaning: Gateway, non-action, Thor (deity)

Interpretive Meaning: Thurisaz is the rune of non-action; it is also called the "gateway." In Eastern traditions the concept of the "gateless gateway" refers to the process of passing through the barriers of your own mind. Usually this means your conditioning, your background, your cultural influences. To pass through this gate, the questioner must take a position that appears to be "non-action." In magical work, nonaction means action turned inward. The questioner's eye of attention must turn toward him- or herself to discover the gates that keep them locked into the current situation. The questioner may feel compelled to take physical action in the current situation, but now is the time for the questioner to move inward.

Aligning with Thurisaz

What You'll Need:

- Your usual circle-casting tools
- Recommended essential oil: Lavender
- A 5–6 inch green taper candle

For this simple ritual, it would be best to use lavender essential oil, which aligns with the 4th chakra (at the center of your chest) and with Thurisaz. If you do not have access to this essential oil, simply practice this alignment without it.

Cast your circle as usual. Using your white-handled knife, carve the symbol for Thurisaz into the green candle. Anoint it with the essential oil, light it, and silently contemplate the meaning of the rune. Dip your right middle finger into the lavender oil and then draw the symbol for Thurisaz on your heart chakra. You may wish to remove your shirt, blouse, or robe for this magical inscription.

Close your eyes and imagine that a brilliant green light etches the symbol Thurisaz into your heart chakra. The spiritual essence of this rune then permeates your entire being. Feel the vibration of this rune throughout your body.

When you are finished, close the circle and extinguish the candle.

Living Thurisaz

For the day, live by the principle of Thurisaz by moving into your inward life. Explore what gates you have set up for yourself and attempt to intentionally break through these barriers today.

Day 327

Freya's Eight: Raido

Literal Meaning: Journey, communication, union/reunion

Interpretive Meaning: Raido is the rune of "powerful action." It reminds the questioner that the old magical axiom of "As above, so below" is at work now. What is the powerful action to take in the current situation? This is a matter that only the questioner will know. The questioner is reminded to put effort into whatever will become fruitful—making change where it is possible. Do not waste effort on that which cannot be changed. Do not waste good seed on unfertile land.

Aligning with Raido

What You'll Need:

- Your usual circle-casting tools
- Recommended essential oil: Carnation
- A 5–6 inch yellow taper candle

For this simple ritual, it would be best to use carnation essential oil, which aligns with the 3rd chakra, at the solar-plexus, and with Raido. If you do not have access to this essential oil, simply practice this alignment without it.

Cast your circle as usual. Using your white-handled knife, carve the symbol for Raido into the yellow candle. Anoint it with the essential oil, light it, and silently contemplate the meaning of the rune. Dip your right middle finger into the carnation oil and then draw the symbol for Raido on your solar-plexus chakra. You may wish to remove your shirt, blouse, or robe for this magical inscription.

Close your eyes and imagine that a brilliant yellow light etches the symbol Raido into your solar plexus chakra. The spiritual essence of this rune then permeates your entire being. Feel the vibration of this rune throughout your body.

When you are finished, close the circle and extinguish the candle.

Living Raido

For the day, live by the principle of Raido by focusing awareness on when you are needlessly expending effort by attempting to change what cannot be changed. Likewise, be aware when you put effort into that which can be changed.

Day 328

Freya's Eight: Gebo

Literal Meaning: Partnership, gift

Interpretive Meaning: Gebo is the rune of true partnership. The rune asks the questioner to recognize where partnership would be of value in his current situation. Partnership does not mean reliance or dependence on another person. The questioner finds empowerment through cooperative, united action.

Aligning with Gebo

What You'll Need:

- Your usual circle-casting tools
- Recommended essential oil: Gardenia
- A 6-inch orange taper candle

For this simple ritual, it would be best to use gardenia essential oil, which aligns with the 2nd chakra just above the genitals, and with Gebo. If you do not have access to this essential oil, simply practice this alignment without it.

Cast your circle as usual. Then, using your white-handled knife, carve the symbol for Gebo into the orange candle. Anoint it with the essential oil, light it, and silently contemplate the meaning of the rune. Dip your right middle finger into the gardenia oil and then draw the symbol for Gebo on your pelvic chakra. You may wish to remove your clothing for this magical inscription.

Close your eyes and imagine that a brilliant orange light etches the symbol Gebo into your pelvic chakra. The spiritual essence of this rune then permeates your entire being. Feel the vibration of this rune throughout your body.

When you are finished, close the circle and extinguish the candle.

Living Gebo

For the day, live by the principle of Gebo through cooperative action. Don't do things alone; find someone with whom you can share a portion of your life, your work, your laughter or love. Build community today.

Day 329

Freya's Eight: Kano

Literal Meaning: Opening, fire, torch

Interpretive Meaning: Kano is the rune of seriousness and of clear-minded intention. Kano is intention fueled by the energy of fire—the fire of conscious attention. The questioner is asked to detach emotionally from the issue at hand in order to become clear-minded. He should pay close attention to his surroundings and to every detail of his life. From attentive analysis of the situation, the questioner can determine the most practical solution.

Aligning with Kano

What You'll Need:

- Your usual circle-casting tools
- Recommended essential oil: Cedar
- A 5–6 inch red taper candle

For this simple ritual, it would be best to use cedar essential oil, which aligns with the 1st chakra, at the base of your spine, and with Kano. If you do not have access to this essential oil, simply practice this alignment without it.

Cast your circle as usual. Then, using your white-handled knife, carve the symbol for Kano into the red candle. Anoint it with the essential oil, light it, and silently contemplate the meaning of the rune. Dip your right middle finger into the cedar oil and then draw the symbol for Kano on your root chakra. You may wish to remove your clothing for this magical inscription.

Close your eyes and imagine that a brilliant red light etches the symbol Kano into your root chakra. The spiritual essence of this rune then permeates your entire being. Feel the vibration of this rune throughout your body.

When you are finished, close the circle and extinguish the candle.

Living Kano

For the day, live by the principle of Kano by leading your life from attentive awareness of your environment. This process facilitates an emergence of the facts of your life and avoids any emotional overlays or interpretations. Analyze information rationally and then take action based on the facts alone.

Day 330

Freya's Eight: Wunjo

Literal Meaning: Joy, light

Interpretive Meaning: Wunjo represents joy. The questioner is asked to probe deeply into the roots of joy. From where does it come? Where does it go? What seems to control the comings and goings of joy? If he or she looks deeply enough, they can see that joy is not predicated on any external circumstance. Joy is a state of mind. It is mind that has found contentment with the things of everyday living. Joy is at hand for the questioner, if only she or he opens their eyes to see it before them! Nothing is blocking joy at this time.

Aligning with Wunjo

What You'll Need:

- Your usual circle-casting tools
- Recommended essential oil: None
- A 5–6 inch taper candle (choose any color that represents "joy" to you)

There is no chakra alignment for Wunjo. This is because joy is one of the divine mysteries. It belongs to all chakras and to none. Joy is sometimes a mystery; it appears to come and go of some unseen accord. So, for this simple ritual, you will use an essential oil or some other fragrant oil that represents joy to you. Similarly you will use a small taper candle that has a color that you associate with a feeling of joy.

Cast your circle as usual. Then, using your white-handled knife, carve the symbol for Wunjo into the candle. Anoint it with the essential oil, light it, and silently contemplate the meaning of the rune. Dip your right middle finger into the essential oil. With your eyes closed, allow your hand to move of its own accord. Do not edit the movement of your hand. Eventually your finger will settle on a part of the body that for you aligns with Wunjo. It could be anywhere, so be ready for this. Now draw the symbol for Wunjo on your body.

Close your eyes and imagine that the energy of Wunjo permeates your entire being. Feel the vibration of this rune throughout your body.

When you are finished, close the circle and extinguish the candle.

Living Wunjo

For the day, live by the principle of Wunjo by living simply. Set aside tasks, conversations and stresses that are not essential for the day. In this simplicity, look for joy. Note how you might be holding back any joyous feelings. Show your happiness to everyone and elicit joy from the people around you.

Day 331

Casting Freya's Eight

Gather together all eight of Freya's eight runes. Turn them over so that you cannot see their inscriptions. Stir the runes with your *left* hand while you look skyward. Think of a question about which you would like some insight. Hold both hands over the runes, look skyward, and say:

> ***Guide my hand with the hand of fate,***
> ***Goddess drawn from Freya's eight!***

Draw a single rune for your answer. Make the connection between your question and the rune symbol. Now take action based on the insight you receive.

Day 332

Contemplative Day: Where Are the Gods?

Meditative Question: In what realm is deity found?

Symbolic Color: White

Symbolic Direction: center

Where on earth are the gods? That's a good question. Nobody knows; that's because knowing is not the same as feeling and experiencing. It may take you some time before you see what is hidden in plain view. It is through this question that seekers are able to access the realm of deity to awaken their spiritual and magical abilities.

Remember that it is advisable to work with each of these inner-mystery contemplations while sitting within the center of your magic circle. As usual, find a comfortable meditative sitting position in the center of your circle. Light a white candle and sit approximately two feet away from the flame. Cast your gaze upon the flickering candle and hold the question firmly for 20 to 30 minutes. Close the circle, but retain the question throughout the day. Soon you will find the gods' realm.

Day 333

Devotional Day: Honoring Odin

Table of Correspondences: Odin

Symbols: The World-Tree, the spear, and the runes

Tools: Living trees, the runes

Magical Essences/Herbs: Black pepper, clove, hops, aconite, fly agaric, jimson weed, henbane, hemlock, wolfbane

Direction: South

He Rules: Enlightenment, inner vision, and deep insight

Animal Symbols: Raven, wolf

Sacred Foods: All root vegetables, fruits that ripen on trees, and ale

Magical Stones: Bone

Odin is the Norse god of the universe, of magic and poetic vision. He is also lord of the dead and an archetypal underworld figure. In mythology, Odin was the father-god who set the sun and the moon in motion at the beginning of time. The early Norsemen believed that Odin lived in Valhalla—the afterworld. Nordic myths say that he hung upside down from the World Tree for nine days and nights, "myself sacrificed to myself," in order to bring up the runes from the well of Mimir. Causing the body physical distress is an ancient technique that shamans use to cause rapid changes of consciousness and altered states of awareness, and it comes as no surprise that the Norse knew of these types of trance-induction techniques. Odin is in many ways a patron of the shaman; he is their archetypal figure. Odin, therefore, represents sudden enlightenment, inner vision, and unexpected insight.

When you tap into the ancient archetypal energies of Odin, you also evoke self-knowledge, the ability to see the roots of all problems, and to evoke inner wisdom. Odin reminds each of us not to turn away from difficulties, because it is through them that we have opportunity to develop strength. His sacred symbols are the World Tree, the spear, ravens, wolves, and the runes. His magical essences and herbs are black pepper, clove, hops, aconite, fly agaric, jimson weed, henbane, hemlock, and wolfbane. Odin is aligned with the south and with noon. His sacred colors are red, black, and gold. Odin's sacred foods include all root vegetables, fruits that ripen on trees, and psychoactive foods such as hallucinogenic mushrooms and ale.

Odin Practice

In honoring Odin today, make an altar that includes his sacred symbols. Light appropriately colored candles and intone his name, one syllable at a time (pronounced: *OH-din*), until you feel his presence surrounding you. Once he has arrived, spend some time contemplating what it might mean to serve this aspect of deity. Take time to ask Odin what it would mean to live life through his energy, and listen for his answer.

Spend the day honoring this god by consulting the runes for yourself and for someone else.

Day 334

Day of Silence and Review

Today, as you observe silence, focus your attention on your intuitive process. Listen to the small voice that tells you to turn left instead of right. Listen to the messages of crows and floor-creaks. Pay attention to what the snow crunching beneath your feet is saying to you. Spend time tuning into the minds and hearts of other people. Spend time tuning into the energies of the planet. Take some time at various points throughout the day to write down whatever intuitive messages cross your mind. When the day is complete, answer these questions:

- What was it like to focus my attention on my intuition?
- Do I trust my intuitive mind? Why? Why not?
- Could I substantiate any of my intuitions today?
- How does intuition inform me throughout my usual day?
- Is there anything that seems to affect my intuition?
- How does my intuition seem to interact with my senses, my thoughts and emotions?

Review

- For today's practice, ask yourself the following:
- Of the information I have learned up to now, what stands out most as vital?
- What information seems least relevant to my spiritual development?
- Which of the practices seemed to move me spiritually, and which had little impact?
- Of the information I have learned so far, what would be best to review? (Take time to review it now.)

Day 335

Hagal's Eight: Sowelu

ᛋ

Literal Meaning: Wholeness, life, sun-energy

Interpretive Meaning: Sowelu is the rune of wholeness. In the traditional Wiccan lunar prayer called "The Charge of the Goddess," it states that "[the goddess] is from the beginning and she is that which is attained at the end of desire." In other words, she is all encompassing. The rune is telling you that what you seek is really a part of what you already are, in your essence. It is time to stop looking outside of yourself for fulfillment—it is right here, right now. The questioner should know that only he or she an create wholeness in their life. They know what parts are missing and how to fill in the gaps.

Aligning with Sowelu

What You'll Need:

- Your usual circle-casting tools
- Recommended essential oil: Lotus
- A 5–6 inch white taper candle

For this simple ritual, it would be best to use lotus essential oil, which aligns with the 7th chakra and Sowelu. If you do not have access to this essential oil, simply practice this alignment without it.

Cast your circle as usual. Then, using your white-handled knife, carve the symbol for Sowelu into the white candle. Anoint it with the essential oil, light it, and silently contemplate the meaning of the rune. Dip your right middle finger into the lotus oil and then draw the symbol for Sowelu on your crown chakra.

Close your eyes and imagine that a brilliant white light etches the symbol Sowelu into your crown chakra. The spiritual essence of this rune then permeates your entire being. Feel the vibration of this rune throughout your body.

When you are finished, close the circle and extinguish the candle.

Living Sowelu

For the day, live by the principle of Sowelu by doing things that evoke a sense of wholeness for you. Meditate. Walk along the edge of some body of water. Take a hot bath by candlelight. Read a detective novel. Listen to the wind chimes on your porch. Drink a cup of tea.

Day 336

Hagal's Eight: Eihwaz

Literal Meaning: Movement, progress, horse

Interpretive Meaning: Eihwaz reminds us to think before we act. Karma is more than a fancy word. It means that everything we do has repercussions. We are all linked together; as Chief Seattle said, "Man did not weave the web of life, but is merely a strand in it. Whatever he does to the web, he does to himself."[89] The questioner should keep in mind that whatever action he takes will come back to him eventually. Is action really necessary right now? It would be wise for him to examine his desire for action and contemplate the possible consequences.

Aligning with Eihwaz

What You'll Need:

- Your usual circle-casting tools
- Recommended essential oil: Anise
- A 5–6 purple taper candle

For this simple ritual, it would be best to use anise essential oil, as it aligns with the 6th chakra and Eihwaz. If you do not have access to this essential oil, simply practice this alignment without it.

Cast your circle as usual. Then, using your white-handled knife, carve the symbol for Eihwaz into the purple candle. Anoint it with the essential oil, light it, and silently contemplate the meaning of the rune. Dip your right middle finger into the anise oil and then draw the symbol for Eihwaz on your third-eye chakra (at the center of your brow).

Close your eyes and imagine that a brilliant purple light etches the symbol Eihwaz into your third-eye chakra. The spiritual essence of this rune then permeates your entire being. Feel the vibration of this rune throughout your body.

When you are finished, close the circle and extinguish the candle.

Living Eihwaz

For the day, live by the principle of Eihwaz by taking the time to think before you act. Contemplate the possible outcomes of your action and then decide if the action you might take is warranted.

Day 337

Hagal's Eight: Hagalaz

Literal Meaning: Disruptive natural forces, hail, sleet

Interpretive Meaning: Hagalaz is the rune of freedom. Hagalaz asks the questioner to break free from existing patterns, for this is exactly what keeps the situation at hand from growth. Instead of viewing his or her actions to make change as perfunctory, they might view them as necessary to break through to the world of spirit. Spirit needs to infuse the situation at hand and the questioner's actions will guide spirit into the right direction.

Aligning with Hagalaz

What You'll Need:

- Your usual circle-casting tools
- Recommended essential oil: Frankincense
- A 5–6 inch blue taper candle

For this simple ritual, it would be best to use frankincense essential oil, which aligns with the 5th chakra and Hagalaz. If you do not have access to this essential oil, simply practice this alignment without it.

Cast your circle as usual. Then, using your white-handled knife, carve the symbol for Hagalaz into the blue candle. Anoint it with the essential oil, light it, and silently contemplate the meaning of the rune. Dip your right middle finger into the frankincense oil and then draw the symbol for Hagalaz on your throat chakra.

Close your eyes and imagine that a brilliant blue light etches the symbol Hagalaz into your throat chakra. The spiritual essence of this rune then permeates your entire being. Feel the vibration of this rune throughout your body.

When you are finished, close the circle and extinguish the candle.

Living Hagalaz

For the day, live by the principle of Hagalaz by studying each situation of your life to determine if it is "stuck" or inhibited from growth. What are you doing to contribute to growth and movement or not? Take steps that do not impede the flow of life's action.

Day 338

Hagal's Eight: Algiz

Literal Meaning: Elk, protection, defense

Interpretive Meaning: Algiz asks the questioner to examine their emotional life thoroughly. Are emotions influencing the situation right now? Instead of trying to hide, it is best if they stand still and bravely face their internal turmoil. That is not to say that they should act on what it is they face within themselves. Instead of visiting their turmoil on others, they should simply view the internal drama without getting caught up in it. Remember that timing is everything. The questioner should try not to allow feelings to influence appropriate timing.

Aligning with Algiz

What You'll Need:

- Your usual circle-casting tools
- Recommended essential oil: Lavender
- A 5–6 inch green taper candle

For this simple ritual, use lavender essential oil, which aligns with the 4th chakra and Algiz. If you do not have access to this essential oil, simply practice this alignment without it.

Cast your circle as usual. Then, using your white-handled knife, carve the symbol for Algiz into the green candle. Anoint it with the essential oil, light it, and silently contemplate the meaning of the rune. Dip your right middle finger into the lavender oil and then draw the symbol for Algiz on your heart chakra. You may wish to remove your shirt, blouse, or robe for this magical inscription.

Close your eyes and imagine that a brilliant green light etches the symbol Algiz into your heart chakra.

The spiritual essence of this rune then permeates your entire being. Feel the vibration of this rune throughout your body.

When you are finished, close the circle and extinguish the candle.

Living Algiz

For the day, live by the principle of Algiz by considering your timing. Are you rushing to meet deadlines? Or are you allowing the natural timetable of things to emerge? Remember that no one is forcing you to rush around in your life. Make room for natural timing today.

Day 339

Hagal's Eight: Jera

Literal Meaning: Harvest, year

Interpretive Meaning: Jera has arrived on the scene as a harbinger of good news. Jera lets the questioner know that the fruits of his labor are at hand. However, it is important for the questioner to remain patient and to wait for the proper season in order to reap his harvest. Cultivate the situation carefully and watch for signs of full ripening.

Aligning with Jera

What You'll Need:

- Your usual circle-casting tools
- Recommended essential oil: Carnation
- A 5–6 inch yellow taper candle

For this ritual, use carnation essential oil, which aligns with the 3rd chakra and Jera. If you do not have access to this essential oil, simply practice this alignment without it.

Cast your circle as usual. Then, using your white-handled knife, carve the symbol for Jera into the yellow candle. Anoint it with the essential oil, light it, and silently contemplate the meaning of the rune. Dip your right middle finger into the carnation oil and then draw the symbol for Jera on your solar-plexus chakra. You may wish to remove your shirt, blouse, or robe for this magical inscription.

Close your eyes and imagine that a brilliant yellow light etches the symbol Jera into your solar plexus. The spiritual essence of this rune then permeates your entire being. Feel the vibration of this rune throughout your body.

When you are finished, close the circle and extinguish the candle.

Living Jera

For the day, live by the principle of Jera by taking an optimistic frame of mind. No matter the difficulty of your circumstances, try to see what else might be beneficial, joyful, humorous, sweet or light in your life. Try to make the best of any situation today—with a cheerful attitude. Hey, why not? Note if this optimistic approach to things makes any changes in your life circumstances.

Day 340

Hagal's Eight: Perth

Literal Meaning: Secret, initiation

Interpretive Meaning: Perth is the rune of secrets, hidden or spiritual forces at play in the circumstances of the questioner's life. It is best if guidance is sought from the realm of spirit. Now is the time to look for a sign. Also, the questioner's current situation is initiatory. Karma is at work here; perhaps there are influences from lifetimes unknown to the questioner. The outcome may shock or displease in some way, but it will inevitably bring about the greater good and highest learning.

Aligning with Perth

What You'll Need:

- Your usual circle-casting tools.
- Recommended essential oil: Gardenia
- A 5-6 inch orange taper candle

For this ritual, use gardenia essential oil, which aligns with the 2nd chakra and Perth. If you do not have access to this essential oil, simply practice this alignment without it.

Cast your circle as usual. Then, using your white-handled knife, carve the symbol for Perth into the orange candle. Anoint it with the essential oil, light it, and silently contemplate the meaning of the rune. Dip your right middle finger into the gardenia oil and then draw the symbol for Perth on your pelvic chakra. You may wish to remove your clothing for this magical inscription.

Close your eyes and imagine that a brilliant orange light etches the symbol Perth into your pelvic chakra. The spiritual essence of this rune then permeates your entire being. Feel the vibration of this rune throughout your body.

When you are finished, close the circle and extinguish the candle.

Living Perth

For the day, live by the principle of Perth by seeking signs of the divine manifesting in your daily activities. If you have a difficulty in your life, ask the gods for a guiding sign and then look for their answer in the world around you.

Day 341

Hagal's Eight: Nauthiz

Literal Meaning: Need, constraint

Interpretive Meaning: Nauthiz is the rune of constraint. The rune asks the questioner to examine his current restrictions. Are his limits actual, real? From where have these constraints come? What is his participation in the limitations he faces? The universe asks that the questioner deeply contemplate those aspects of the self that appear to bind him. He should not look outward to the situation at hand, but inward to his own limitations and shadows as he responds to life.

Aligning with Nauthiz

What You'll Need:

- Your usual circle-casting tools
- Recommended essential oil: Cedar
- A 5–6 inch red taper candle

For this ritual, use cedar essential oil, which aligns with the 1st chakra and Nauthiz. If you do not have access to this essential oil, simply practice this alignment without it.

Cast your circle as usual. Then, using your white-handled knife, carve the symbol for Nauthiz into the red candle. Anoint it with the essential oil, light it, and silently contemplate the meaning of the rune. Dip your right middle finger into the cedar oil and then draw the symbol for Nauthiz on your root chakra. You may wish to remove your clothing for this magical inscription.

Close your eyes and imagine that a brilliant red light etches the symbol Nauthiz into your root chakra. The spiritual essence of this rune then permeates your entire being. Feel the vibration of this rune throughout your body.

When you are finished, close the circle and extinguish the candle.

Living Nauthiz

For the day, live by the principle of Nauthiz by staying alert to your own participation in the limitations of your life. Are you really a victim? Have you no responsibility in your current situations? Try to break out of the patterns of behavior that you normally take to arrive at a new outcome in your life.

Day 342

Hagal's Eight: Isa

ᛁ

Literal Meaning: Ice, freezing, standstill

Interpretive Meaning: Isa is the rune of winter and of gestation. When Isa is selected, the energy of the questioner's life (or current situation) is frozen; action may not be likely or feasible now. Or, movement in the situation may simply not be visible at this time. The questioner should view the current time as a period of rest; he or she should take the example of the bear who hibernates in winter. The questioner should be patient; all seasons turn and winter melts to spring.

Aligning with Isa

What You'll Need:

- Your usual circle-casting tools
- Recommended essential oil: None
- A 5–6 inch taper candle (choose any color that represents "winter" to you)

There is no chakra alignment for Isa. This is because internal movement, such as that indicated by Isa, is one of the divine mysteries. It belongs to all chakras and to none. It seems to have its own timing. For this simple ritual you will use an essential oil or some other fragrant oil that represents this internal movement to you. Similarly you will use a small taper candle that has a color that you associate with internalized workings.

Cast your circle as usual. Then, using your white-handled knife, carve the symbol for Isa into the candle. Anoint it with the essential oil, light it, and silently contemplate the meaning of the rune. Dip your right middle finger into the essential oil. With your eyes closed, allow your hand to move of its own accord. Do not edit the movement of your hand. Eventually your finger will settle on a part of the body that for you aligns with Isa. It could be anywhere, so be ready for this. Now draw the symbol for Isa on your body.

Close your eyes and imagine that the energy of Isa permeates your entire being. Feel the vibration of this rune throughout your body.

When you are finished, close the circle and extinguish the candle.

Living Isa

For the day, live by the principle of Isa by examining your internal life. What's going on inside of you? What has gone dormant? What is frozen, at a standstill? Take time to honor those things that require dormancy by taking non-action at this time. Lie low and allow nature to take its own course.

Day 343

Casting Hagal's Eight

Gather together all eight of Hagal's eight runes. Turn them over so that you cannot see their inscriptions. Stir the runes with your left hand while you look skyward. Think of a question about which you would like some insight. Hold both hands over the runes, look skyward, and say:

> ***Guide my hand with the hand of fate,***
> ***Goddess drawn from Hagal's eight!***

Draw a single rune for your answer. Make the connection between your question and the rune symbol. Now take action based on the insight you receive.

Day 344

Tyr's Eight: Dagaz

Literal Meaning: Day, light, breakthrough

Interpretive Meaning: Dagaz is the rune that denotes both awakening and breakthrough. The rune signifies that the questioner has arrived at a life-altering realization about the situation at hand. Whether or notone chooses to act on this realization is another matter. Change is difficult. However, once light has been cast on the situation and he can clearly see what is before one, it is senseless to turn away from such knowledge. Therefore insight is not always pleasant, but it should inform action.

Aligning with Dagaz

What You'll Need:

- Your usual circle-casting tools
- Recommended essential oil: Lotus
- A 5–6 inch white taper candle

As with the other rune rituals of the 7th chakra, you will use lotus essential oil. If you do not have access to this essential oil, simply practice this alignment without it.

Cast your circle as usual. Then, using your white-handled knife, carve the symbol for Dagaz into the white candle. Anoint it with the essential oil, light it, and silently contemplate the meaning of the rune. Dip your right middle finger into the lotus oil and then draw the symbol for Dagaz on your crown chakra.

Close your eyes and imagine that a brilliant white light etches the symbol Dagaz into your crown chakra. The spiritual essence of this rune then permeates your entire being. Feel the vibration of this rune throughout your body.

When you are finished, close the circle and extinguish the candle.

Living Dagaz

For the day, live by the principle of Dagaz by considering what you are avoiding. Whatever it is you avoid is a spiritual shadow that holds great power. Explore that shadow and cast light into your darkened corners.

Day 345

Tyr's Eight: Inguz

Literal Meaning: Hero, fertility

Interpretive Meaning: Inguz is the symbol for new beginnings. It suggests that the questioner should allow the intuitive process to guide him. Through the intuitive process, he or she can align their personal will with the universal flow of nature. It may mark the beginning of some new path, a new way of thinking, of feeling or of approaching life. Once he or she clears away the old, restrictive patterns of his or her life, newness can more easily emerge.

Aligning with Inguz

What You'll Need:

- Your usual circle-casting tools
- Recommended essential oil: Anise
- A 5–6 inch purple taper candle

As with the other rune rituals of the 6th chakra, you will use anise essential oil. If you do not have access to this essential oil, simply practice this alignment without it.

Cast your circle as usual. Then, using your white-handled knife, carve the symbol for Inguz into the purple candle. Anoint it with the essential oil, light it, and silently contemplate the meaning of the rune. Dip your right middle finger into the anise oil and then draw the symbol for Inguz on your third-eye chakra (at the center of your brow).

Close your eyes and imagine that a brilliant purple light etches the symbol Inguz into your third eye chakra. The spiritual essence of this rune then permeates your entire being. Feel the vibration of this rune throughout your body.

When finished, close the circle and extinguish the candle.

Living Inguz

For the day, live by the principle of Inguz by sitting still and feeling the movement of your own body, the air that you breathe, and the movement of the world around you. Look through old photos and see how your life has transitioned over the years.

Day 346

Tyr's Eight: Laguz

Literal Meaning: Water, sea

Interpretive Meaning: Laguz is a rune that aligns with the element of water. Laguz appears in a reading to let the questioner know that there are powerful and unseen flows of energy at work in his current situation. He needs to learn not to personalize the usual movements of life, and the comings and goings of people. In the matter at hand, he is perhaps only playing a part in much bigger workings. This rune also signifies a time for cleansing the spirit through reevaluation and deep meditation.

Aligning with Laguz

What You'll Need:

- Your usual circle-casting tools
- Recommended essential oil: Frankincense
- A 5–6 inch blue taper candle

As with the other rune rituals of the 5th chakra, you will use frankincense essential oil. If you do not have access to this essential oil, simply practice this alignment without it.

Cast your circle as usual. Then, using your white-handled knife, carve the symbol for Laguz into the blue candle. Anoint it with the essential oil, light it, and silently contemplate the meaning of the rune. Dip your right middle finger into the frankincense oil and then draw the symbol for Laguz on your throat chakra.

Close your eyes and imagine that a brilliant blue light etches the symbol Laguz into your throat chakra. The spiritual essence of this rune then permeates your entire being. Feel the vibration of this rune throughout your body.

When finished, close the circle and extinguish the candle.

Living Laguz

For the day, live by the principle of Laguz by allowing other people's concerns to come before your own. Set your issues and interests aside and allow your partner, your children, your friends, and family to come first.

Day 347

Tyr's Eight: Mannaz

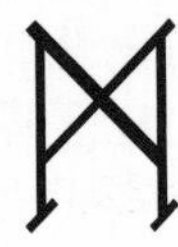

Literal Meaning: Man, human race, self

Interpretive Meaning: Mannaz represents the self. Interestingly, the element of Mannaz (as with Laguz) is water. The rune suggests that the questioner will function best by learning to be adaptive and fluid (like water) in his current situation. Mannaz proposes the question, "Who are you?" Are you what other people say you are? Are you what you say about yourself? What makes you a self in the first place? Probing these mysteries will deepen the questioner's wisdom and ability to face her or his life circumstances.

Aligning with Mannaz

What You'll Need:

- Your usual circle-casting tools
- Recommended essential oil: Lavender
- A 5–6 inch green taper candle

As with the other rune rituals of the 4th chakra, you will use lavender essential oil. If you do not have access to this essential oil, simply practice this alignment without it.

Cast your circle as usual. Then, using your white-handled knife, carve the symbol for Mannaz into the green candle. Anoint it with the essential oil, light it, and silently contemplate the meaning of the rune. Dip your right middle finger into the lavender oil and then draw the symbol for Mannaz on your heart chakra. You may wish to remove your shirt, blouse, or robe for this magical inscription.

Close your eyes and imagine that a brilliant green light etches the symbol Mannaz into your heart chakra. The spiritual essence of this rune then permeates your entire being. Feel the vibration of this rune throughout your body.

When finished, close the circle and extinguish the candle.

Living Mannaz

For the day, live by the principle of Mannaz by questioning your existence. What or who are you? Explore this deeply through writing, meditation, and discussion with magical friends. Act as water does by flowing naturally, impersonally, in each circumstance.

Day 348

Tyr's Eight: Teiwaz

Literal Meaning: Harvest, year

Interpretive Meaning: Teiwaz is the rune of the spiritual warrior, or perhaps it is like certain aspects of the crone or sage. This rune represents someone who is able to cut away the dross, the excess, in their life without regard for any sentimental attachment. Teiwaz suggests that the questioner cut loose in two ways. First it asks himor her to cut loose from whatever may be holding them back at this time. It also asks them to cut loose from anything to which they may be clinging. Now is the time to release their grip on the situation and allow the natural outcome to emerge. The questioner is asked to bear in mind the principles of cause and effect. Natural consequences follow actions—that may either benefit them or not.

Aligning with Teiwaz

What You'll Need:

- Your usual circle-casting tools
- Recommended essential oil: Carnation
- A 5-6 inch yellow taper candle

As with the other rune rituals of the 3rd chakra, you will use carnation essential oil. If you do not have access to this essential oil, simply practice this alignment without it.

Cast your circle as usual. Then, using your white-handled knife, carve the symbol for Teiwaz into the yellow candle. Anoint it with the essential oil, light it, and silently contemplate the meaning of the rune. Dip your right middle finger into the carnation oil and then draw the symbol for Teiwaz on your solar-plexus chakra. You may wish to remove your shirt, blouse, or robe for this magical inscription.

Close your eyes and imagine that a brilliant yellow light etches the symbol Teiwaz into your solar-plexus chakra. The spiritual essence of this rune then permeates your entire being. Feel the vibration of this rune throughout your body.

When finished, close the circle and extinguish the candle.

Living Teiwaz

For the day, live by the principle of Teiwaz by releasing your hold on your life situation. Contemplate how you might be investing time, energy, and effort into specific outcomes for your life. Are your particular outcomes really necessary? Explore what would happen if none of your life turned out as you had planned.

Day 349

Tyr's Eight: Ehwaz

Literal Meaning: Horse, course of the sun, movement

Interpretive Meaning: The rune Ehwaz symbolizes a horse, and it is the rune of movement and transition. If this rune trots your way, it suggests that the questioner should prepare for transition or change in the current situation. All things change and develop over time; nothing remains static. The questioner may mistakenly grasp at a moment, but as soon as he or she believes the moment is caught, it has gone. No matter the current status of her or his life, the questioner should know that "this too shall pass."

Aligning with Ehwaz

What You'll Need:

- Your usual circle-casting tools.
- Recommended essential oil: Gardenia
- A 5–6 inch orange taper candle

As with the other rune rituals of the 2nd chakra, you will use gardenia essential oil. If you do not have access to this essential oil, simply practice this alignment without it.

Cast your circle as usual. Then, using your white-handled knife, carve the symbol for Ehwaz into the orange candle. Anoint it with the essential oil, light it, and silently contemplate the meaning of the rune. Dip your right middle finger into the gardenia oil and then draw the symbol for Ehwaz on your pelvic chakra. You may wish to remove your clothing for this magical inscription.

Close your eyes and imagine that a brilliant orange light etches the symbol Ehwaz into your pelvic chakra. The spiritual essence of this rune then permeates your entire being. Feel the vibration of this rune throughout your body.

When finished, close the circle and extinguish the candle.

Living Ehwaz

For the day, live by the principle of Ehwaz by spending time feeling the movements of your own body. Begin with body parts in isolation, such as the hand or the fingers. Feel how they move and transition from one position to another. Begin to combine the isolated parts and see how the body moves fluidly as it transitions from one posture to another. Notice that the body never maintains one posture for long. Neither does life. Ehwaz is teaching you about the activity inherent in each moment—no matter how quiet that moment may be.

Day 350

Tyr's Eight: Berkana

Literal Meaning: Birch tree, growth

Interpretive Meaning: Berkana is the symbol of the birch tree, of growth and ripening. The questioner should focus attention on what it is he or she has in life. He or she should try not to focus in on what is missing or what has been lost. This is a rune of hope; the seeds that were planted are already beginning to root.

Aligning with Berkana

What You'll Need:

- Your usual circle-casting tools
- Recommended essential oil: Cedar
- A 5–6 inch red taper candle

As with the other rune rituals of the 1st chakra, you will use cedar essential oil. If you do not have access to this essential oil, simply practice this alignment without it.

Cast your circle as usual. Then, using your white-handled knife, carve the symbol for Berkana into the red candle. Anoint it with the essential oil, light it, and silently contemplate the meaning of the rune. Dip your right middle finger into the cedar oil and then draw the symbol for Berkana on your root chakra. You may wish to remove your clothing for this magical inscription.

Close your eyes and imagine that a brilliant red light etches the symbol Berkana into your root chakra. The spiritual essence of this rune then permeates your entire being. Feel the vibration of this rune throughout your body.

When finished, close the circle and extinguish the candle.

Living Berkana

For the day, live by the principle of Berkana by assessing what it is you have in your life. Count your blessings and hold a small ceremony that gives thanks for them. Thank people who have contributed to your life—even in small ways.

Day 351

Tyr's Eight: Othila

Literal Meaning: Home, possessions, retreat

Interpretive Meaning: This is the rune of separation. When Othila appears in the reading, it does so to remind the questioner to recognize the appropriateness of endings. All things must end, so says Othila. And when this rune appears, the questioner should expect an end to the current situation. It may also mean that you he learning how to grapple with closure in the situation. It asks the questioner to step aside so that the natural processes already set in motion can come to completion.

Aligning with Othila

What You'll Need:

- Your usual circle-casting tools
- Recommended essential oil: none
- A 5–6 inch taper candle (choose any color that represents "closure" or "endings" to you)

There is no chakra alignment for Othila. This is because the archetypal energy expressed in the concept of endings is universal. It belongs to all chakras and to none. So, for this simple ritual, you will use an essential oil or some other fragrant oil that represents or expresses the concept of endings to you. Similarly you will use a small taper candle that has a color that you associate with endings. Use your imagination!

Cast your circle as usual. Then, using your white-handled knife, carve the symbol for Othila into the candle. Anoint it with the essential oil, light it, and silently contemplate the meaning of the rune. Dip your right middle finger into the essential oil. With your eyes closed, allow your hand to move of its own accord. Do not edit the movement of your hand. Eventually your finger will settle on a part of the body that for you aligns with Othila. It could be anywhere, so be ready for this. Now draw the symbol for Othila on your body.

Close your eyes and imagine that the energy of Othila permeates your entire being. Feel the vibration of this rune throughout your body.

When finished, close the circle and extinguish the candle.

Living Othila

For the day, live by the principle of Othila by living your day with the knowledge that each moment is an ending. You will not get back the time that you have already spent. How will you best live your day with this knowledge? Stop procrastinating! Finish tasks that are incomplete.

Day 352

Casting Tyr's Eight

Gather together all of Tyr's eight runes. Turn them over so that you cannot see their inscriptions. Stir the runes with your left hand while you look skyward. Think of a question about which you would like some insight. Hold both hands over the runes, look skyward, and say:

> *Guide my hand with the hand of fate,*
> *Goddess drawn from Tyr's eight!*

Draw a single rune for your answer. Make the connection between your question and the rune symbol. Now take action based on the insight you receive.

Day 353

Casting All the Runes

Casting the runes is a creative process that involves both the mechanical means of divination as well as the intuitive process. There is a wide range of methods available to rune readers. Below I have shown a spread that rune readers most commonly use.

The Action Rune Spread

Turn all of the runes over so that you cannot see any markings. Lay them in front of you in a large grouping. Have the questioner think of a situation—not a question—that needs clarity and a new understanding. Have the questioner draw three rune-stones, one at a time. The first one she picks represents the current situation. This rune does not offer a solution, but it sheds light on the deeper workings beneath the visible situation. The second rune represents the action that the situation requires. The third rune represents the outcome if the questioner takes the action suggested by the runes.

The Elemental Rune Spread

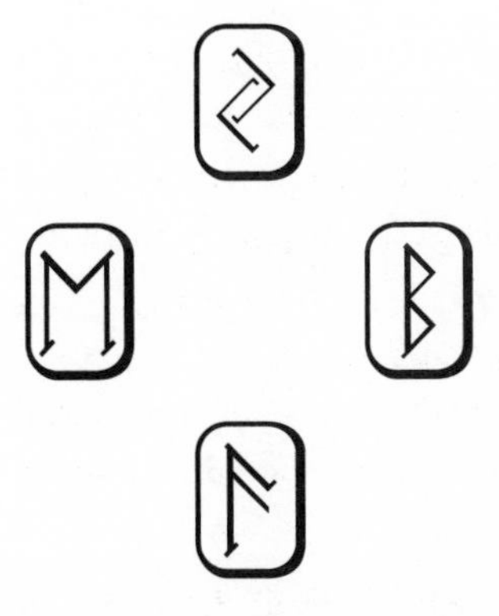

As you did with the action rune spread, lay all of the runes with their designs face down. Have the questioner think of a situation and then draw four runes, one at a time. Place the first rune at the top.

This represents the element of earth. The earth rune represents the way the situation presents itself in the here and now. It is the current manifestation of the situation.

Place the second rune below and to the right of the first rune. This rune is the rune of air. The air rune represents the questioner's thoughts and ideas about the situation. It could also represent any first actions that have already taken place in the situation. Place the third rune below and to the left of the first rune. This represents the element of water. The water rune shows the questioner's feelings surrounding the situation. It may also represent the questioner's dreams or intuitions up to this point. Place the final rune directly below the other three, in a straight line with the first rune. This is the fire rune, which represents the action that the questioner needs to take in order to successfully approach/resolve the situation.

Try one complete rune reading today for yourself. When you feel confident with one of the methods, try casting the runes for a magical partner or for a friend.

DAY 354

Using the Runes in Magic

As you learned over the past several days, the runes carry their own magic, their own energies. You can put these energies to use by incorporating the runes in your spellwork. (See list of magical associations and powers on page 365.) There are several ways to do this.

- Draw runes on candles, or on parchment paper that you bless; you can even carry or wear your runes in order to draw specific circumstances into your life
- Use your athame to ritually draw runes in the air to invoke their powers
- Inscribe runes above doorways to summon their energies
- Do "instant magic" by visualizing glowing in front of you a rune that you choose for a specific purpose
- Try one of these techniques today in order to help you experience the power of the runes

Magical Associations & Powers of the Runes

Here are some of the magical associations and powers of the runes.

Rune Name	*Sigil*	*Magical Power*	*Astrological Symbol*
Fehu	ᚠ	Wealth, comfort	Aries
Uruz	ᚢ	Strength, healing	Taurus
Thurisaz	ᚦ	Opens locked doors, stops enemies	Gemini
Ansuz	ᚨ	Wisdom, communication	Cancer
Raido	ᚱ	Protection in travel	Leo
Kano	ᚲ	Heals wounds	Virgo
Gebo	ᚷ	For relationships	Libra
Wunjo	ᚹ	Joy, happiness	Scorpio
Hagalaz	ᚺ	Reverses spells	Sagittarius
Nauthiz	ᚠ	Transforms troubles, lightens the heart	Capricorn
Isa	ᛁ	Changes the tides, reverses the current situation	Aquarius
Jera	ᛃ	Brings desires through a natural cycle	Pisces
Eihwaz	ᛇ	Love, lust	Pisces
Perth	ᛈ	Reveals secrets, keeps secrets	Aquarius
Algiz	ᛉ	Charms animal spirits	Capricorn
Sowelu	ᛋ	Solar magic, draws on the power of the sun	Sagittarius
Teiwaz	ᛏ	Brings courage to the heart	Scorpio
Berkana	ᛒ	New beginnings	Libra
Ehwaz	ᛖ	Creates movement in your current circumstances	Virgo
Mannaz	ᛞ	Adaptation	Leo
Laguz	ᚹ	Commands the seas	Cancer
Inguz	ᛟ	Fertility	Gemini
Dagaz	ᛞ	Breakthroughs, insight	Taurus
Othila	ᛟ	Peace of mind	Aries

DAY 355

Numerology

Numerology is the study of mystical relationships between numbers and the spiritual properties of objects and living things. The great megalithic stone rings, which appear to indicate early man's mathematical knowledge of solar activity, pay tribute to the fact that numbers and their symbolic meaning must have been important to humans long before history or even numbers were ever written.

Pythagoras, the ancient Greek mathematician, was the first in our Western history to speculate freely in his writings about the mystical qualities of numbers. Pythagoras held to literal beliefs that the universe was composed of numbers. He also felt that the number 1 was the ancestor from which all other numbers were derived. It was also Pythagoras who proposed that odd numbers were male in their energy, while even numbers were essentially female.

Over the course of history, western occultists elaborated on Pythagoras' mystical arithmetical ideas. The Hebrew esoteric traditions of the Qabalah also played their part in the evolution of the numerology most commonly practiced in Western cultures today. Our system maintains that the nine primary numbers are each imbued with occult powers. The numbers are all associated with English language letters. Each of the numbers (and, therefore, the letters) symbolically links to planets, natural elements, and divinatory meanings. When it comes to the English alphabet, occultists over the centuries have tried to devise universal methods for number-letter association. Although there has never been full agreement across all magical disciplines, most modern occultists rely on the simplest and most readily understandable method called the *Serial English-Qabalah.*

Here are the number/letter combinations of this system:

A = 1	J = 10 = 1	S = 19 = 1
B = 2	K = 11 = 2	T = 20 = 2
C = 3	L = 12 = 3	U = 21 = 3
D = 4	M = 13 = 4	V = 22 = 4
E = 5	N = 14 = 5	W = 23 = 5
F = 6	O = 15 = 6	X = 24 = 6
G = 7	P = 16 = 7	Y = 25 = 7
H = 8	Q = 17 = 8	Z = 26 = 8
I = 9	R = 18 = 9	

To arrive at these numbers, each letter was first placed in its usual sequence and then numbered. Double-digit numbers assigned to letters (which is every letter above the ninth) are added up to arrive at a final single digit. For example, the letter R is the eighteenth letter of the alphabet. Add together the numbers 1 and 8 and you arrive at the single digit of 9.

The entire system of numerology is based on these same numeral-reducing principles. Each word in the English language has numerical associations. When you add the single digits together, you can reduce multiple-digit numbers into a single value. The only exception to this is if your name or word total adds up to a master number. The master numbers are never reduced. The master numbers are: 11, 22, and 33.

Numerology Example

Let's use the name Mary as an example of how to set up a basic numerology chart.

Step 1: Associate each letter of a word with its numeric value.

M A R Y
4 1 9 7

Step 2: Add all of the digits together.

4+1+9+7=21

Step 3: Add together each digit of a multiple-digit number until you arrive at a single digit.

2+1=3

Therefore, the name Mary adds up to the number 3.

Now let's try with the name Timothy.

Step 1: Associate each letter of a word with its numeric value.

T I M O T H Y
2 9 4 6 2 8 7

Step 2: Add all of the digits together.

2+9+4+6+2+8+7= 38

Step 3: Add together each digit of a multiple-digit number until you arrive at a single digit.

3+8=11

Although you might initially suspect that the name Timothy should further reduce to the number 2 (by adding 1+1), it does not. That is because the name total arrived at a "master number," which was 11.

Practice: I've Got Your Number

Try this technique with your own name and keep track of the numeric value of your first, middle, and last names. Then add them all together to create a single-digit number that represents your whole name.

Keep all of your notes and numbers for tomorrow's practice.

Day 356

The General Meaning of Numbers

Now that you have tried setting up your own numerology chart, let us look at what the numbers signify.

Number 1 Traits

Independent, original, pioneering, bossy, fiery, driven, goal-oriented, self-centered, masculine energy, courageous, determined, freedom-loving.

Number 2 Traits

Feminine energy, balanced, intuitive, cooperative, receptive, diplomatic, loving, moody, ambivalent, indecisive, intelligent, process-oriented, circular in thinking and expression, relationship-oriented.

Number 3 Traits

Creative, expressive, good with written and spoken expression, enthusiastic, sociable, quick-minded and quick to speak, flirtatious, impractical, lighthearted, analytical, judgmental, scattered.

Number 4 Traits

Stable, solid, reliable, slow-minded but practical in thought, rational, grounded, clear-headed, strong work ethic, model citizen, disciplinarian, harsh, stubborn.

Number 5 Traits

Loves travel, resourceful, versatile, unpredictable, sometimes irresponsible, desires freedom and expansion, insatiable curiosity, impulsive, adventurous, loves speculation and gambling, risk-taking.

Number 6 Traits

Need for companionship, kind, tolerant, strives for peace and harmony, family-oriented, smothering, good sense of timing, can be argumentative.

Number 7 Traits

Thoughtful, considerate, analytical, spiritual, deep thinker, knowledge-seeking, dislike of manual labor, perfectionistic, down to earth, can easily recognize deception, attracted to animals.

Number 8 Traits

Just, self-disciplined, cautious, successful, lives by the Golden Rule, organized, interested in finances and monetary gain, executive material, power-hungry.

Number 9 Traits

Governed by love, humanistic, compassionate, selfless, a giver (sometimes unwisely), flexible, broad-minded, forgiving, emotional or possibly indifferent, escapist tendencies.

Number 11 Traits

Spiritual revelation, idealism, emotionalism, visionary, feelings of futility, imperiousness, depression.

Number 22 Traits

Extroverted, financially stable, complete control, mastery, can be destructive and exploitative.

Number 33 Traits

Master teacher, worldly success, skillful, famous, perfect in relationships, can be oppressive, poor or misuse of power.

Check out the numbers for your first, middle, and last names. Then look at the names in combination. You are a unique blend of these numbers.

DAY 357

The Birthpath

The birthpath is the numerological name for your destiny, or what it is you are here to do in this lifetime. The birthpath is easily calculated. Add together the month, day, and year of your birth. I have listed the numeric value of each month below.

January=1	May=5	September=9
February=2	June=6	October=10=1
March=3	July=7	November=11=2
April=4	August=8	December=12=3

Birthpath Example

Let us use December 21, 1985 as our example while you learn the steps for calculating the birthpath.

1) Lay out your birthdate on paper:

December	21	1985 is the same as:
12	21	1985

2) Add all of these digits together now:
   1+2+2+1+1+9+8+5=29

3) Reduce the double digits (except master numbers) to a single digit: 2+9=11

You shouldn't reduce this 11 further, unless the description of 11 does not seem to fit your life path or interests. If it does not, then reduce one more time: 1+1=2.

Try this with your own birth date to determine your birthpath number. Once you have your birthpath number, look up the meaning as described below.

Number 1 Birthpath

You are here to be a leader. Strike out boldly. It is the lifetime for you to do things independently. Express your originality. Teach people the "right way" to get things done.

Number 2 Birthpath

You are here to express and channel the goddess' energy. Express kindness and nurturing to other people and to the planet. Teach others about getting in touch with their divine feminine and their gentility. Work as a relationship counselor, diplomat, or psychic. You'll be a good parent.

Number 3 Birthpath

You are here to express yourself creatively. Don't settle for any way of life that may hold back your creative juices. Write, act, create artistic masterpieces. Whatever you do, find some format to express your vision.

Number 4 Birthpath

You are here to explore a life of stability. Teach other people how to be as practical as you are. You will mostly teach others by your example. You are also here to show others how to use the mind rationally.

Number 5 Birthpath

You are here to explore life as an adventure. You feel best when you dig into life with no formal plans. Travel and unpredictability are in store for you, but this won't worry you as you are freedom-loving and versatile.

Number 6 Birthpath

You are here to explore life through partnership and family. You will work best in partnership and your life is best realized when you have formed a solid relationship with a suitable life-partner. You will be drawn to having children and will most likely be a good parent.

Number 7 Birthpath

You are here to explore the spiritual side of things. You should look deeply into the nature of life and explore the spiritual mysteries of many different paths. Or you might be drawn to a life of asceticism or of monastic living. Since this may not be a viable choice for you, be sure to spend time each day exploring your spiritual nature.

Number 8 Birthpath

You are here to explore the world of material gain. Don't fight it. Your interest in finances, monetary gain, and the power these things can bring is valid. Through this path you will learn how to be reasonable, fair-minded, and how to balance physical with spiritual needs.

Number 9 Birthpath

You are here to express your humanistic tendencies. You will be drawn to work and activities that allow you to give all that you can and to care for the needs of others. Be careful of giving beyond your means.

Number 11 Birthpath

You are here to express your ideals. You will be motivational to other people and some might say you are a visionary. You may not be very practical, but you will inspire those around you who will have the practical know-how. You are also here to learn to trust your psychic senses.

Number 22 Birthpath

You are here to work on behalf of the world community. You may think in terms of global concerns and you will most likely have the practical ability to express or even carry out large-scale plans. You are here to put the larger community ahead of your own concerns.

Number 33 Birthpath

You are here as a master teacher or guru. In this lifetime you can easily teach spiritual principles and your truth will change the lives of everyone who hears it. You are a force to be reckoned with. You are here to serve spiritually in a public life.

Day 358

Numerology and Magic

Numerology can also boost your magical work. Each number has a correspondence in color, magical stone, and planet. Here is how you can use numerology to boost your spells.

- Write down the purpose of your spell in one word—for example, "love," "success," "understanding," etc.
- Analyze the numeric value of the spell's essence—for example, "love" would be the number 9, since it is a combination of 3+6+4+5)
- Choose a candle color and a gemstone, and use the appropriate planetary seal in the creation of your spell—for example, if you use the color gold, you could use an opal, and you would inscribe the sigil for the sun, either on your candle or anywhere else in your spell materials

Practice: Your Personal Correspondences

On the following page is a table of correspondences for each of the numbers. Practice analyzing your own name and determine the correspondences to your own energies. What are your stones, colors, and planetary energies? Also practice analyzing various words that you might use in your spellwork to determine their correspondences.

Basic Number Correspondences

Here is a basic table of correspondence for the numbers:

Number	*Color*	*Gemstone*	*Planet*	*Metal*
1	red	diamond	Mars	iron
	white, silver	pearl, moonstone	Moon	silver
3	yellow	agate	Mercury	mercury
4	black	turquoise	Saturn	lead
5	maroon	opal	Pluto	steel
6	pale green, pink, or blue	sapphire	Venus	copper
7	sea green	bloodstone	Neptune	tin
8	brown, green	quartz crystals	Earth	copper
9	bright blue	amethyst	Uranus	platinum
11	gold	ruby	Sun	gold
22	red-gold	coral	(none)	none
33	sky blue	lapis lazuli	(none)	none

Additional Number Correspondences

Number	*Herbs*	*God Aspect*	*Goddess Aspect*	*Element*
1	basil, woodruff	Mars	Kali	fire
2	anise, orris root	Pan	Diana	water
3	fennel, lavender	Hermes	Athena	air
4	comfrey, mullein	Cernunnos	Demeter	earth
5	damiana, dragon's blood	Shiva	Ereshkegal	fire
6	boneset, catnip	Cupid	Venus	water
7	mugwort, poppy	Osiris	Hecate	water
8	lovage, hyssop	Faunus	Gaia	earth
9	cinnamon, clove	Dionysus	Isis	air
11	chamomile, rosemary	Helios, Zeus	Kwan-Yin	fire
22	(fly agaric)	See 4		all four
33	(hemp)	See 6		all four

Day 359

More Numerology Correspondences

Below are some additional correspondences to the numbers. After reviewing these, take time to analyze words that you might use in a spell and determine how you might incorporate the appropriate correspondences into your spellwork.

Practice: More Personal Correspondences

Practice analyzing your own name and determine the correspondences to your own energies. What are your herbs, gods, goddesses, and elemental energies? Try the technique for your birthpath as well. Find out the correspondences of friends and family members. Once you know their elemental energies, you can see how and why various people have harmonious relationships (or don't). Here is a brief list of the energies that complement one another:

- Each element balances best with its own element (e.g., air with air, water with water).
- Male energies harmonize (e.g., air and fire) because both are active principles. The drawback is that air tends to fuel fire, so air might make fire angry. On the positive side, fire might feel stimulated by air. Air might feel depleted by fire, or air might feel as though it is the center of attention.
- The female elements of water and earth make another good pairing, because they are both receptive principles. However, water and earth make mud and these two can potentially lose their relational boundaries easily.
- Air is least harmonious with earth and water. Earth believes air is too flighty and insubstantial. Water wants to feel and air wants to think and analyze, so water will feel as though air is lacking in emotional depth.
- Fire harmonizes least with water and earth. Fire feels extinguished or grounded by both of these energies. Earth believes that fire is too energetic.

Day 360

Animal Powers

When most people think of a Witch, they can't help but imagine her sidekick, the black cat. It is a fanciful image that actually digs up Witchcraft's most ancient roots. The popular image of the black cat is one of the few direct remnants of the ancient shamanic practices that linked the animal and human worlds.

The oldest pagan rites are those reflected in the Paleolithic cave paintings that sprawl across the vast caverns of Lascaux and Trois Freres, France. There, within the depths of the earth, you will find enormous renderings of half-man, half-animal figures dancing and hunting. These images—among the oldest of religious iconography known to date—suggest that the earliest notions of the divine were tethered to the animal world. It is no accident that one of the first human instinct was to represent the divine in zoomorphic form. To the ready imagination animals appear to have powers beyond human limits. The task of the shaman was to tap into the spirit of the animal and harness its power for good. Each animal spirit was believed to bestow powers on human beings. For example, the bison brought the powers of endurance. Deer brought swiftness of foot. Hares could elude predators. Owls brought messages from the gods.

Buffalo, bison, elk, deer, and owls were among the most popular animal representations of the divine in ancient European cave art. In later periods of Old Europe, as we learned from anthropologist Marija Gimbutas, skilled artists symbolized the forces of the divine in such varied animal forms as frog, bee, snake, and bird—just to name a few.

It seems that the practice of linking the animal world to that of the divine was not limited to Europe. The most well-known and perhaps some of the most vivid, animal representations of the divine emerged from ancient Egypt. Their sacred beasts included hawks, cats, jackals, leopards, dogs, and many other creatures. Other places in the world where archeologists find evidence of animal deities include Australia, Mexico, throughout the continents of Asia, South America, and North America. There is evidence of animal-god symbolism in virtually every corner of the world inhabited by human beings.

How does this relate to Witches? What we know of the Witch's familiar—the black cat, and other documented animal spirits—can be traced to extant tribal cultures across the globe that still venerate animal gods and spirits. Within these primal cultures, shamans maintain that each of us has an animal spirit dwelling within us. They sometimes refer to these animal spirits as "powers," "dwellers," or even "familiar spirits." The Witch's familiar is a direct link to these primal practices.

The records of the old European Witch trials show us perhaps not what real Witches believed, but what folk customs and beliefs had survived from ancient times. Accused Witches often made reference to the familiar spirits that would come to aid them in magic. Most often these familiars appeared to the accused in animal form, although some testimonies refer to unseen spirits. Clearly, it is more than coincidence that there are similarities between the Witch's familiar spirit and those of tribal cultures.

In fact, psychoanalyst Carl Jung stated in *Man and His Symbols* that the animal spirit is an archetype. It is a cross-cultural symbol that represents the unconscious mind, which is wild, unfettered, and unlimited in its abilities. This, perhaps, is one explanation for the animal spirit as a reoccurring motif across cultures and history.

Animal Spirit Practices

Over the next several days we will explore two main types of familiars that are part of Wiccan practice. I have based the two types of familiars on the research of Margaret Murray, author of *The Witch Cult in Western Europe*. Through her in-depth studies of Witch trial transcripts, Murray explored the folk practices and beliefs of the pre-Christian Europeans. The two main types of familiars she found as constant themes were "domestic" and "divining" familiars.

The domestic familiar was the physical animal that magical workers kept in their presence as a tool of powerful magic. This was the black cat, ferret, owl, or other physical animal. The divining familiar was a spirit helper that could apparently change over time and directly linked to the animal spirit beliefs, customs, and practices of tribal people globally. This spiritual aspect of the familiar is what I call the *familiar self.*

Practice: Personal Animal Traits

Before you understand more about the familiar self, try today's magical practice. Make a list of your personal traits, characteristics, and habits. Try not to edit the list. Once you are finished, try to look at the traits objectively to determine what kind of animal might closely resemble your traits. Make a short list of animals that you think might fit your profile. One mistake to avoid in this exercise is altering your traits so that you fit the profile of an animal you admire. Not everyone is a wolf, tiger, lion, or bear. Some of us might more closely resemble pigs, skunks, porcupines, or black widow spiders! Allow your reality to shine through fully, unedited.

Practice: Tracking the Familiar-Self

The familiar self is the animal spirit that resides within each of us. Your animal spirit lends you specific strengths, traits, and certain magical abilities. It also shapes the personality. Now that you have created a list of your personality traits, compare this list with the traits of various animals. If you don't know much about the traits of animals in the wild, take a trip to the library and do some old-fashioned research, go to the zoo, or find an online resource that will help you to compare your personal traits to those of animals.

Through this comparison process, you can develop a list of potential animal candidates that might represent your familiar-self. Try not to consider the list of animals you've compiled as definitive. Although you may have certain traits similar to a specific animal, you may ultimately find a surprising animal spirit residing within. It happens, so stay open to the possibilities.

Day 361

Animal Spirit Oil and Incense

Now that you have developed a list of possible candidates for the familiar self, you will prepare for the final phase of discovery. In today's practice, you will create an essential oil and incense blend that will help facilitate your discovery of the animal spirit in tomorrow's ritual. Here is the formulary for your magical incense and oil.

Animal Spirit Oil

Blend the following oils and herbs into 1 ounce of safflower oil, grape seed oil, or vegetable glycerin:

- 3 drops patchouli essential oil
- 1 drop cinnamon essential oil
- 1 drop eucalyptus essential oil
- 5 drops vetiver or iris essential oil
- A pinch of dried patchouli

Animal Spirit Incense

- Handful of dried, powdered sandalwood
- 2 tablespoons dried patchouli leaf
- 2 tablespoons cinnamon bark (or powder)

To these dry ingredients, mix in 5 drops of vetiver or iris essential oil and 2 drops of eucalyptus essential oil.

Day 362

Discovering the Animal Power

What You'll Need:

- Your usual circle-casting tools
- Animal spirit incense
- Animal Spirit Oil
- Blank paper and a pen or pencil

Cast your circle as usual. Sprinkle the animal power incense on a hot coal and allow it to smolder. Offer the incense at each of the four compass points of your circle: east, south, west, and north. As you offer the incense around the circle, say the following:

> ***Bull-beggars, spirits, Witches,***
> ***Hags, Satyrs, Pans, Sylens,***
> ***Changelings, Dragons, Men of the Oak,***
> ***Open the way to the sacred hunt,***
> ***From thy thunder echo the voices of***
> ***Feather and fur, claw and talon.***

Return the incense to the altar and then use your left hand to fan the smoke across your body. Carry your animal spirit essential oil blend to the east of your circle. Once there, face the perimeter of the circle. Anoint yourself with the oil at the base of the throat, saying:

> ***I open to the voices of the animal world.***

Repeat the oil anointing in the south of your circle. This time, dab the oil to your solar-plexus area, saying:

> ***I open to the power of the animal world.***

Repeat the oil anointing in the west of your circle. This time, dab the oil between your eyes at the center of the brow, saying:

> ***I open to the wisdom of the animal world.***

Repeat the oil anointing in the north of your circle. Dab the oil to your root chakra, saying:

> ***I find my root in the animal world.***

Now lie down on your back in the south of your circle with your feet pointed north and your head south. Anoint yourself with the essential oil on the insides of your elbows and the backs of your knees. Have a magical partner read the guided imagery provided below, or tape record it before your ritual and play it back now.

Reader:
Close your eyes and imagine that you stand before a great oak tree. Take several deep breaths, and, with each breath, imagine that your body becomes increasingly transparent. Now move close to the tree and walk into the trunk. You are now one with the tree.

Imagine that you travel down through the heavy roots of the tree as they descend through layers of sediment, rock, and soil. You follow the roots even more deeply into the dark, cold earth. Follow the roots until you come to their end, which places you inside a large cave. You cannot see anything before you, but you can sense the enormity of the cavern. Listen in silence and soon you will hear the noise of your animal spirit. What is this noise?

> ***(Reader: pause for a moment.)***

Follow the sound of the animal in the cave and know that you will not be harmed. The floor of the cave is smooth and soft. There are no obstructions in your way. Simply follow the sound in the dark. Soon you will feel something brush up against you. This is the feel of your animal spirit. How did it feel?

> ***(Reader: pause for a moment.)***

The animal spirit continues to summon you with its sound. Follow the sound and eventually you will catch the scent of your animal spirit. What is that scent?

> ***(Reader: pause for a moment.)***

Finally, you notice a speck of glowing light on the floor of the cave. As you approach the soft glow, you can see it is not a speck at all, but a large luminous symbol. This is the mark of the animal spirit. What is this symbol? Remember it for future reference. Reach down and touch the glowing symbol and the cave crumbles around you to reveal a landscape. Where are you? Is this the beach? Is this the desert? A forest? A mountain top?

Wherever you are, begin to explore the terrain. Soon you will encounter a single animal. This is your animal power, your familiar self. Greet the animal power and ask its name.

(Reader: pause for a moment.)

It is now time to return to the upper world. Thank the animal spirit for revealing itself and bid it farewell. Soon the vision of the landscape and the animal fades and you find yourself back inside the cave holding on to the oak tree root. The root seems to quickly draw you back to the upper trunk. Step out of the trunk and then watch your body as it becomes visible and solid again.

Once you are ready, open your eyes and write down what it was you saw. Write down the animal power you found, write its name, and draw its symbol.

Close your circle as usual.

DAY 363

The Animal Spirit's Magic

What You'll Need:

- Animal spirit incense
- Animal spirit oil
- Blank paper and a pen or pencil

Now that you have found your way to the shamanic *lowerworld*, you can return any time you like by following the roots of the oak tree. That is where you will find the animal spirit whenever you seek contact. You do not need to cast a circle for future trips to the lower world. Now that you have found your way, you do not need the safety of the magic circle. However, I do recommend that you anoint yourself at the backs of the knees and the insides of the elbows with animal power oil. For added boost to your lowerworld journeys, you can also burn animal power incense.

Today, you will return to the lower world to learn about your familiar-self's magic. Have a magical partner read the following guided imagery or tape record it and play it back when you are ready.

Reader:

Close your eyes and imagine that you stand before a great oak tree. Take several deep breaths and, with each breath imagine that your body becomes increasingly transparent. Now, move close to the tree and walk into the trunk. You are now one with the tree.

Follow the heavy roots of the tree as they descend through layers of sediment, rock, and soil. You follow the roots even more deeply into the dark, cold earth. Follow the roots until you come to their end, which sets you inside a large cave. You cannot see anything before you, but you can sense the enormity of the cavern.

Eventually, as you stand in the darkness of the cave, you spot the glowing mark or symbol of the animal spirit. Walk toward it, reach down, and touch the glowing symbol, and watch the cave as it crumbles around you to reveal the animal spirit's landscape. Your animal power is waiting there for you.

Ask the animal spirit what magical power it lends to you.

(Reader: pause for a moment.)

Now ask the animal spirit what drawbacks it brings to your life.

(Reader: pause for a moment.)

Finally, ask the familiar spirit for a chant or a word of power that you might use to summon your animal's power.

Once you are ready to leave the lowerworld, bid the animal power farewell. When you do this, the cave will surround you once more. Reach up and you will find the root of the oak tree. Follow it back to the upper realm. Step out of the tree trunk. Open your eyes and write down what you were told.

Whenever you need the animal spirit's power, use your chant or word of power. Do not share this word or chant with anyone else.

Practice: Animal Instinct

In tribal cultures throughout the world, the animal spirit—the familiar self—is a source of wisdom. Here is a method to use whenever you want to seek the advice of the familiar spirit on any matter.

To begin, take time to formulate your question. Try to ask open-ended questions, so that the wisdom of the familiar-self will not end with a simple yes or no. The familiar spirit may become frustrated if you do not allow it to express fully. Likewise it may become frustrated if you do not follow the advice it gives, so be prepared to follow whatever it is you hear. The familiar spirit has a good overview of life and gives answers that apply to the best resolution of your query over the long range. Even if the answer you receive does not seem to coincide with what is needed, follow the advice you receive. Over time, you will see how the familiar self has guided you toward your greater good.

What You'll Need:

- Animal power incense
- Animal power oil
- Blank paper and a pen or pencil

Light the animal power incense and anoint yourself with the animal power oil. Close your eyes and return to the lower realm, as you have done before, by following the roots of the oak tree that you visualize. Follow the roots until you come to their end, which sets you inside a large cave.

As you stand in the darkness of the cave, you spot the glowing mark or symbol of the animal spirit. Walk toward it, reach down, and touch the glowing symbol, and watch the cave as it crumbles around you to reveal the animal spirit's landscape. Your animal power is waiting there for you.

Ask the animal spirit for its guidance in your situation. Wait for your answer. Once you receive it, bid the animal power farewell. When you do this, the cave will surround you once more. Reach up and you will find the root of the oak tree. Follow it back to the upper realm. Step out of the tree trunk. Open your eyes and write down what you were told.

Follow the advice of the familiar self.

DAY 364

Contemplative Day: Nothingness

Meditative Question: What lies at the center of nothing?

Symbolic Color: None

Symbolic Direction: Nowhere

This is the final meditative question of your year and a day study. Freud once stated that life is a circular journey; it emerges from nothingness and then it submerges once again into the void. It is a brief reverberation between two silences.

Mythologist Joseph Campbell says that the chant word "Aum" is really a four-syllable word. The first three syllables are the sounds of the word (*ah-uu-mm*). The fourth syllable is the silence from which the sound came and to which it returns. This sound, represents the complete round of our human life.

Since we have come full circle in our year, today's question is apropos. However, the question poses a paradox for us. How can there be a center of nothing? The ultimate realization of the divine, of life, and of your own self resides within the answer to this contemplative question.

Remember that it is advisable to work with these inner-mystery contemplations while sitting within the center of your magic circle. Find a comfortable meditative sitting position. Use no candle, no incense or oil. Simply rely on your own abilities to go within and search for the truth. Cast your gaze downward toward the ground and blur your vision so that you do not focus on any one point on the floor. Look *through* the ground in front of you instead of *at* the ground. Hold today's question firmly for 20 to 30 minutes. If you notice extraneous thoughts intruding as you concentrate on your contemplative question, simply take note of the thoughts and shift your focus back to the question.

Now that a year has gone by, what lies at the center of nothing? You tell me.

DAY 365

Devotional Day: Honoring Yourself

By now you should realize that you are an aspect of the divine. This is what you are in your essence. That's right, the divine is flawed, goes to the bathroom, takes kids to school, buys groceries, eats meals, and lives life. Your life, just as it is, is the life of the gods. Take time to honor yourself, to take your own place among the pantheon of honored mythological beings.

Begin by reviewing your numerological correspondences. From that, review other magical correspondences so that you can create symbolism to decorate your own shrine. Build the shrine around a photograph of yourself. Add candles, colors, planetary sigils, and other objects that are important to you.

Now add an object to the altar that represents each of the gods and goddesses you have studied and honored throughout the year. When you have finished this altar, sit before it and contemplate each of the gods and goddesses as an aspect of yourself.

Make Your Own

Make your own tables of correspondences that include:

Symbols: Design your own magical symbol, perhaps based on runes, and astrological signs, or do some meditative work to discover a symbol that represents your energies

Tools: With which of the Witch's tools do you most connect?

Magical Essences/Herbs: Which herbs align with you numerologically? Which essential oils seem to draw your attention and feel representative of your energies?

Direction: With which direction do you feel the most affinity?

You Rule: What is your greatest skill or asset? What do you have to offer to the world? What are your greatest spiritual gifts?

Animal Symbols: What is your animal power?

Sacred Foods: What foods do you find sacred, or at least delicious?

Stones: Which stones align with you numerologically?

Day 366

Day of Silence

Congratulations on completing your year and a day of study, magic, ritual, and contemplation! Your final day is symbolic of life's journey, and it relates to this month's contemplative question. Your final magical act is a day of silence. Be mindful of your actions, your breath, and your thoughts throughout the day. When the day is complete, answer these questions:

- How do I feel now that my year and a day is complete?
- Am I considering taking the next step and becoming initiated as a Witch? Why?
- What stands out as the most important aspect of my training this year?
- How have I changed or grown during the year?
- What areas of magical study do I intend to study in depth?
- How do I plan to maintain a spiritual practice beyond this 366th day?

Appendix A

Esbat Ritual Format

The following is a ritual format suitable for full moon esbat celebrations. During your year and a day of initial study, it is advisable to celebrate only the eight sabbats and the thirteen full moons. Later you can adapt this format for other workings, such as new moon and waning moon esbat celebrations.

Format

- Gather all your ritual tools
- Gather ritual objects for any magic you might plan to do during celebration
- Clear or cleanse chakras with an infusion of hyssop in water
- Cast your circle as usual
- After the invocations of the god and goddess, read the "Charge of the Goddess" (below)
- Practice any magic you have planned
- Cakes and wine
- Close the circle

The Charge of the Goddess

To begin, stand at the north of your circle. Turn your back to the northern perimeter so that you face the center of the circle. Hold the wand in your left hand and the athame in the right. Using the left hand (holding the wand) draw an upright triangle of manifestation in the air before you. To start, point the wand above your head and draw the left slant of the triangle. Draw the bottom and then the right side of the triangle. With your right hand (holding the athame) draw an upside-down triangle in the air before you. Start by pointing the athame at the floor, then form the right slant of the triangle. Form the level top and then finish with the left slant.

Fold your arms across your chest (in the sage/crone piosition) and recite the charge:

Whenever you have need of anything, once in the month and better it be when the moon is full, then shall you assemble in some secret place and adore the spirit of me, who am Queen of all the witches. There shall ye assemble, ye who are feign to learn all sorcery, yet have not won its deepest secrets; to these will I teach all things that are as yet unknown. And ye shall be free from slavery; and as a sign that ye be truly free, you shall be naked in your rites; and ye shall dance, sing, feast, make music and love all in my praise. For mine is the ecstasy of the spirit, and mine is also joy on earth; for my law is love unto all beings. Keep pure your highest ideals; strive ever toward them, let nothing stop you or turn you aside. For mine is the secret door which opens upon the Land of Youth, and mine is the cup of the wine of life, and the Cauldron of Ceridwen, which is the Holy Vessel of Immortality. I am the gracious Goddess, who gives the gift of joy unto the heart of man. Upon the earth, I give knowledge of the spirit eternal; and beyond death, I give peace and freedom, and reunion with those who have gone before.

Nor do I demand sacrifice; for behold, I am the Mother of all living, and my love is poured out upon the earth. I am the beauty of the green earth, and the white moon among the stars, and the mystery of the waters, and the desire of the heart of man. Call unto thy soul, arise, and come unto me. For I am the soul of Nature who gives life to the Universe. From me all things proceed, and unto me all things must return; and before my face, beloved of Gods and of men, let thine innermost self be enfolded in the rapture of the infinite. Let my worship be in the heart that rejoicest, for behold, all acts of love *and pleasure are my rituals.*

Therefore let there be beauty and strength, power and compassion, honor and humility, mirth and reverence within you. And thou who thinketh to seek for me, know thy seeking and yearning shall avail thee not unless thou knoweth the mystery; that if that which thou seekest thou findest not within thee, thou wilt never find it without thee, for behold, I have been with thee from the beginning; and I am that which is attained at the end of desire.•

* Based on the "Charge of the Goddess," as described by Stewart Farrar in *What Witches Do*, 1971. Versions of this traditional ritual charge also appear in the writings of Doreen Valiente, Charles Leland, and others.

Appendix B

Magical Resources Guide

StarWest Botanicals
11253 Trade Center Drive
Rancho Cordova, CA 95742

What they sell: Botanicals, dried herbs, essential oils, vegetable glycerin

Ordering: (916) 631-9755, Fax: (916) 853-9673, Toll Free: (888) 3694372

Online: starwest-botanicals.com

Glenbrook Farms Herbs & Such
7817 193rd Road
Live Oak, FL 32060

What they sell: Bulk herbs, botanicals, dried herbs, essential oils

Ordering: Toll Free: (888) 716-7627, Fax (386) 362-6481

Online: glenbrookfarm.com

Stony Mountain Botanicals
155 N Water Street
Loudonville, OH 44842

What they sell: Botanicals, dried herbs, essential oils

Ordering: (888) 994-4857, Phone: (419) 994-4857

Online: wildroots.com

Xeonix Inc.
1906 Moser Avenue
Dallas, TX 75206

What they sell: Magic mirrors, pendulums, glass pentacles

Ordering: (800) 800-7971

Online: Xenoxinc.com

The Moving Center
P.O. Box 271
Cooper Station
New York, NY 10276

What they sell: Books, music, and videos related to shamanic/ecstatic dance and Gabrielle Roth

Ordering: (212) 760-1381, Fax: (212) 760-1387

Online: Ravenrecording.com

White Light Pentacles/Sacred Spirit Products
88 Wharf Street
Pickering Wharf
Salem, MA 01970

What they sell: Magical tools of all kinds

Ordering: (978) 745-8668

Online: wlpssp.com

Flora Pathics
P.O. Box 66723
Houston, TX 7726

What they sell: Essential oils, candles, herbs

Online: florapathics.com

Nature's Gift
314 Old Hickory Boulevard.
East Madison, TN 37115

What they sell: Herbs, essential oils

Online: naturesgift.com

Nag Champa
c/o Nandi Imports
P. O. Box 751269
Petaluma, CA 94975

What they sell: Hard to find essential oils and incense

Online: nagchampa.com

Crystal Cauldron
360 South Thomas Street
Pomona, CA 91766

What they sell: Robes, tools, incense, oils, books, jewelry, Pagan/Wiccan supplies

Ordering: (909) 620-9565

Online: willowscrystalcauldron.com

Raven's Flight
5042 Vineland Avenue
North Hollywood, CA 91601

What they sell: Robes, tools, incense, oils, books, jewelry, Pagan/Wiccan supplies

Ordering: (818) 985-2944

Online: avensflight.net

Dragon Marsh
3744 Main Street
Riverside, CA 92501

What they sell: Robes, tools, incense, oils, books, jewelry, Pagan/Wiccan supplies

Ordering: (909) 276-1116

Online: dragonmarsh.com

NOTES

1 See, e.g., Christopher Penczak, *The Inner Temple of Witchcraft* (St. Paul: Llewellyn Publications, 2003), 37–40.

2 See, e.g.: Barbara Ardinger, *A Woman's Book of Rituals and Celebrations* (Albany, CA: New World Library, 1992).

3 Stewart Piggott, *The Druids* (New York: Thames and Hudson, 1989), 184–185.

4 Carl Jung, *Collected Works*, Vol.11, *Psychology and Religion: West and East*, Trans.: R. F. C. Hull (New York: Pantheon Books, 1958), 440.

5 As heard in a lecture presented by Joseph Campbell in "Transformations of Myth Through Time, Program 5: The Perennial Philosophy of the East," Highbridge Productions, 1990.

6 It was later that the fathers of psychology, Freud and Jung, apprehended Bastian's concept and began calling the elementary ideas archetypes.

7 Robert E. Ryan, Ph.D., *The Strong Eye of Shamanism* (Vermont: Inner Traditions, 1999), 17.

8 Joseph Campbell, *Transformations of Myth Through Time* (New York, Harper & Row, 1990), 94.

9 See, e.g., Cassandra Eason, *The Complete Guide to Labyrinths (*Freedom: The Crossing Press, 2004).

10 e.g., Christianity, Judaism, and Islam.

11 Elizabeth Moran and Val Biktashev, *The Complete Idiot's Guide to Feng Shui* (Alpha Books, 1999), 49–53.

12 See, e.g.: Anodea Judith, *Wheels of Life,* (St. Paul: Llewellyn Publications, 1987).

13 The name Baphomet seems to be a composition of abbreviations: "Temp. ohp. Ab." which originates from the Latin *Templi omnium hominum pacis abhas*, meaning "the father of universal peace among men."

14 See, e.g., Starhawk, *Truth or Dare* (San Francisco: Harper & Row, 1987).

15 Robert Graves, *The White Goddess* (New York: Farrar, Straus and Giroux, 1948; 14th printing, 1981), 27–28.

16 See, e.g., Janet and Stewart Farrar, *The Witches' Goddess* (Washington: Phoenix Publishing, 1987).

17 For a more detailed explanation of shadow work, ritual, and magic, see, e.g., Timothy Roderick, *Dark Moon Mysteries,* 10th Anniversary—Expanded and Revised Edition (Aptos, CA: New Brighton Books, 2003).

18 This verse is based on a British Traditional Midwinter chant. The chant does not appear in its entirety or in its original form to preserve what is oathbound material.

19 For more information about Yule log customs, see, e.g., Robert Graves, *The White Goddess* (New York: Farrar, Straus and Giroux, 1948; 14th printing, 1981).

20 Joseph Campbell, *Transformations of Myth Through Time* (New York: Perennial Library, 1990), see, e.g. 1–2.

21 I prefer kosher salt because of its look and texture. You can use any form of table salt or sea salt for this procedure.

22 Janet & Stewart Farrar, *A Witches Bible*, Vol. 1: *The Sabbats* (New York: Magical Childe, 1984), 72.

23 See, e.g., Raven Grimassi, *The Encyclopedia of Wicca and Witchcraft* (St. Paul: Llewellyn Publications, 2000), 281.

24 Barbara G. Walker, *The Woman's Encyclopedia of Myths and Secrets* (New York: Harper SanFrancisco, 1983), 266.

25 Claudia de Lys, *The Giant Book of Superstitions* (New Jersey: Citadel Press, 1979), 117.

26 Theodore Gaster, *Myth, Legend and Custom of the Old Testament* (New York: Harper and Row, 1969), 603.

27 Paraphrased from a lecture conducted by Roshi Wendy Egyoku Nakao at the Zen Center of Los Angeles, August, 2003.

28 See, e.g., Barbara G. Walker, *The Woman's Dictionary of Symbols and Sacred Objects* (New York: HarperCollins, 1988), 168.

29 Janet & Stewart Farrar, *A Witches Bible,* Vol. 1: *The Sabbats* (New York: Magical Childe, 1984), 80.

30 James G. Frazer, *The Golden Bough* (New York: Avenel Books, 1981; from the original work published in 1890), 74.

31 Ibid, 72.

32 Ibid, 73.

33 Walker, *The Woman's Dictionary of Symbols and Sacred Objects*, 25.

34 Guy Ragland Phillips, *Brigantia* (London: Routledge & Kegan Paul, 1976), 169.

35 This chant has been noted to be an adaptation from the original Rudyard Kipling. See, e.g., Janet & Stewart Farrar, *A Witches Bible, Vol. 1: The Sabbats* (New York: Magical Childe, 1984).

36 Joseph Campbell, *The Hero with A Thousand Faces* (New Jersey: Bollingen Press, 1972), 109.

37 The Fire of Azrael recipe first surfaced in Dion Fortune's novel *The Sea Priestess* in 1938. The recipe also is said to begin with driftwood from the ocean. See, e.g., Dion Fortune, *The Sea Priestess* (Red Wheel/ Weiser, 1972).

38 These are Enochian names that evoke the element of water. See, e.g., David Allen Hulse, *The Western Mysteries* (St. Paul: Llewellyn, 2000).

39 In the most ancient accounts, Romans would make the priaptic wand from a stalk of fennel.

40 Frazer, 75.

41 A new chant with adapted lines from "Consecration of Work" in *Book of Shadows*, Gardnerian Rite Church.

42 Robert Crooks, Karla Baur, *Our Sexuality* (Redwood City, CA: The Benjamin/Cummings Publishing Company, 1993), see, e.g., 4–17

43 J. Elia, "History, Etymology, and Fallacy: Attitudes toward male masturbation in the ancient Western world" (*Journal of Homosexuality*, 1987), v. 14, 1–19.

44 Barrie Thorne, Zella Luria, *Sexuality and Gender in Children's Daily Words, Down to Earth Sociology* (New York: The Free Press, 1988), 133–135.

45 This pattern is the invoking-earth pentagram.

46 This rite is a highly modified version of the initiatory Great Rite as described in Janet and Stewart Farrar, *The Witches' Way*, London: Robert Hale, 1985. The Farrars suggest that the rite be performed only within the confines of a magic circle. However, here in this modified form, you may practice it either within a formal magic circle or outside of it in a simple "sacred space" that you create for the rite. Further along in your year's practice, you will gain the skills of casting a true magic circle. After that time, if you practice the Great Rite again, do so inside the formal circle.

47 This pattern is the invoking-earth pentagram.

48 See, e.g., Raven Grimassi, *Encyclopedia.*

49 Margaret Murray, *The God of the Witches* (New York: Oxford University Press, 1931), 111.

50 Ibid, 107–108.

51 Frazer, 75–76.

52 Ibid, 258.

53 Ibid, 260–263.

54 Timothy Roderick, *Apprentice to Power* (Freedom: The Crossing Press, 2000), 286.

55 Francis King and Stephen Skinner, *Techniques of High Magic* (New York: Destiny Books, 1976), 0–86.

56 See, e.g. Margie McArthur, *Faery Healing* (Aptos: New Brighton Books, 2003).

57 Walker, *The Woman's Encyclopedia of Myths and Secrets*, 300.

58 Mary Beith, *Healing Threads: Traditional Medicines of the Highlands and Islands of Scotland* (Edinburgh: Polygon, 1989), 154.

59 Robert Graves, *The White Goddess* (New York: Farrar, Straus and Giroux, 1966), 178.

60 Frazer, 373.

61. Grimassi (Encyclopedia), 227.

62 Farrar, *A Witches Bible*, Vol. 1: *The Sabbats*, 105.

63 Graves, *The White Goddess*, 178.

64 Ellen Everett Hopman, *A Druid's Herbal* (Vermont: Destiny Books, 1995), 76.

65 Joseph Campbell, Betty Sue Flowers, ed., *The Power of Myth* (New York: Doubleday, 1987), 72–73.

66 Farrar, *A Witches Bible*, Vol. 1: *The Sabbats*, 117.

67 Frazer, 172.

68 See, e.g., Frazer, vol. i, 332–337.

69 Hopman, 148.

70 See, e.g., Joseph Campbell, *Transformations of Myth Through Time.*

71 See, e.g., Mircea Eliade, *Rites and Symbols of Initiation*, Trans. Willard R. Trask (New York: Harper Touchbooks, 1965).

72 This is a highly specialized shamanic ceremonial rite and it is offered as an example only. Attempts at sucking or blowing techniques without proper training can result in spiritual "illness." Michael Harner, *The Way of the Shaman* (New York: Bantam, 1982), 148–157.

73 See, e.g., Marija Gimbutas, *The Language of the Goddess* (New York: HarperCollins, 1991).

74 See, e.g., Barbara C. Sproul, *Primal Myths* (New York: HarperCollins, 1991).

75 See, e.g., Francesco Maria Guazzo, *Compendium Maleficarum* (New York: Dover Publications, 1988).

76 Grimassi, *Encyclopedia*, 115.

77 Paul Huson, *Mastering Witchcraft*, New York: Perigee Books, 1970, 73–75.

78 See, e.g. Francis Barrett, *The Magus, A Complete System of Occult Philosophy* (New Jersey: Citadel Press, 1967; originally published 1801).

79 Each day and hour is ruled by a planet. Mars rules Tuesday. On Tuesdays, Mars rules the first hour after sunrise and every seventh hour thereafter.

80 See, e.g., Franz Bardon, *Initiation Into Hermetics*, Trans. Graz A. Radspieler (West Germany: Wuppertal, 1987).

81 See, e.g., Barrett, *The Magus* (New Jersey: Citadel Press, 1967, from the original manuscript published in 1801).

82 Raymond Buckland, *Buckland's Complete Book of Witchcraft* (St. Paul: Llewellyn Publications, 1986), 149–150.

83 As quoted from Lady Sheba, *The Grimoire of Lady Sheba* (St. Paul: Llewellyn Publications, 2001), 235.

84 Paul Huson, *Mastering Herbalism* (New York: Stein and Day, 1974), 13–24.

85 Lesley Bremness, *The Complete Book of Herbs* (New York: Viking Studio, 1988), 8–9.

86 For example, Digitalis is derived from foxgloves, Aspirin comes from white willow bark, ephedrine comes from the ephedra plant, and the cinchona tree gives us quinine. See, e.g., Earl Mindell, *Earl Mindell's Herb Bible* (New York: Fireside Books, 1992).

87 See, e.g., Sean Murphy, *One Bird, One Stone: American Zen Stories* (New York: St. Martin's Press, 2002).

88 Janet and Stewart Farrar, *The Witches' Goddess* (Custer: Phoenix Books, 1987), 167.

99 This is not the authentic text of Chief Seattle's treaty agreement, spoken in 1854. There is no verbatim translation available of his speech. The text provided, which is possibly the most popular version of Seattle's speech, is actually an adaptation written by Texas professor Ted Perry.

Bibliography

Ardinger, Barbara. *A Woman's Book of Rituals and Celebrations.* Albany, CA: New World Library, 1992.

Bardon, Franz. *Initiation Into Hermetics*, Trans. Graz A. Radspieler. West Germany: Wuppertal, 1987.

Barrett, Francis. *The Magus, A Complete System of Occult Philosophy.* New Jersey: Citadel Press, 1967; originally published in 1801.

Beith,Mary. *Healing Threads: Traditional Medicines of the Highlands and Islands of Scotland.* Edinburgh: Polygon, 1989.

Bremness, Lesley. *The Complete Book of Herbs*. New York: Viking Studio, 1988.

Buckland, Raymond. *Buckland's Complete Book of Witchcraft.* St. Paul: Llewellyn Publications, 1986.

Campbell, Joseph. *The Hero with A Thousand Faces.* New Jersey: Bollingen Press, 1972.

———. *The Power of Myth.* Edited by Betty Sue Flowers. New York: Doubleday, 1987.

———. *Transformations of Myth Through Time.* New York, Harper & Row, 1990.

Campbell, Joseph. Edited by Betty Sue Flowers. *The Power of Myth* (New York: Doubleday, 1987), 72–73.

Crooks, Robert, and Karla Baur, *Our Sexuality.* Redwood City, CA: The Benjamin/Cummings Publishing Company, 1993.

de Lys, Claudia. *The Giant Book of Superstitions.* New Jersey: Citadel Press, 1979.

Eason, Cassandra. *The Complete Guide to Labyrinths.* Freedom: The Crossing Press, 2004.

Elia, J. "History, Etymology, and Fallacy: Attitudes toward male masturbation in the ancient Western world," *Journal of Homosexuality*, 1987, v. 14.

Eliade, Mircea. *Rites and Symbols of Initiation,* Trans. Willard R. Trask. New York: Harper Touchbooks, 1965.

Farrar, Stewart , and Janet. *A Witches Bible*, Vol. 1: *The Sabbats.* New York: Magical Childe, 1984.

———. *The Witches' Goddess.* Washington: Phoenix Publishing, 1987.

Fortune, Dion. *The Sea Priestess.* Red Wheel/Weiser, 1972)

Frazer, James G. *The Golden Bough.* New York: Avenel Books, 1981; from the originally published work in 1890.

Gaster,Theodore. *Myth, Legend and Custom of the Old Testament.* New York: Harper and Row.

Gimbutas, Marija. *The Language of the Goddess.* New York: HarperCollins, 1991.

Graves, Robert. *The White Goddess.* New York: Farrar, Straus and Giroux, 1948; 14th printing, 1981.

Grimassi, Raven. *The Encyclopedia of Wicca and Witchcraft.* St. Paul: Llewellyn Publications, 2000.

Guazzo, Francesco Maria. *Compendium Maleficarum.* New York: Dover Publications, 1988.

Harner, Michael. *The Way of the Shaman.* New York: Bantam, 1982.

Hopman, Ellen Everett. *A Druid's Herba*l. Vermont: Destiny Books, 1995.

Hulse, David Allen. *The Western Mysteries.* St. Paul: Llewellyn, 2000.

Huson, Paul. *Mastering Herbalism.* New York: Stein and Day, 1974.

———. *Mastering Witchcraft,* New York: Perigee Books, 1970.

Judith, Anodea, *Wheels of Life.* St. Paul: Llewellyn Publications, 1987.

Jung, Carl. *Collected Works,* Vol.11, *Psychology and Religion: West and East,* Trans.: R. F. C. Hull (New York: Pantheon Books, 1958.

King, Francis , and Stephen Skinner. *Techniques of High Magic.* New York: Destiny Books, 1976.

McArthur, Margie. *Faery Healing.* Aptos, CA: New Brighton Books, 2000.

Moran, Elizabeth, and Val Biktashev, *The Complete Idiot's Guide to Feng Shui.* Alpha Books, 1999.

Mindell, Earl. *Earl Mindell's Herb Bible.* New York: Fireside Books, 1992.

Murphy, Sean. *One Bird, One Stone: American Zen Stories.* New York: St. Martin's Press, 2002.

Murray, Margaret. *The God of the Witches.* New York: Oxford University Press, 1931.

Penczak, Christopher. *The Inner Temple of Witchcraft.* St. Paul: Llewellyn Publications, 2003.

Piggott, Stewart. *The Druids.* New York: Thames and Hudson, 1989.

Phillips, Guy Ragland. *Brigantia.* London: Routledge & Kegan Paul, 1976.

Roderick, Timothy. *Apprentice to Power.* Freedom: The Crossing Press, 2000.

———. *Dark Moon Mysteries,* Aptos, CA: New Brighton Books, 10th Anniversary, Expanded and Revised Edition, 2003.

Ryan, Robert E., Ph.D. *The Strong Eye of Shamanism.* Vermont: Inner Traditions, 1999.

Sheba, Lady. *The Grimoire of Lady Sheba.* St. Paul: Llewellyn Publications, 2001.

Sproul, Barbara C. *Primal Myths.* New York: Harper-Collins, 1991.

Starhawk. *Truth or Dare.* San Francisco: Harper & Row, 1987.

Thorne, Barrie, and Zella Luria. *Sexuality and Gender in Children's Daily Words, Down to Earth Sociology.* New York: The Free Press, 1988.

Walker, Barbara G. *The Woman's Dictionary of Symbols and Sacred Objects.* New York: HarperCollins, 1988.

———. *The Woman's Encyclopedia of Myths and Secrets.* New York: Harper SanFrancisco, 1983.

INDEX